TV INSIDE-OUT
Flukes, Flakes, Feuds and Felonies

TV INSIDE-OUT
Flukes, Flakes, Feuds and Felonies

The backstage blunders, bloopers and blasphemy of celebrities in search of success

By

Randy West

BearManor Media
2022

TV Inside-Out © 2022 Randy West

All rights reserved.

No portion of this publication may be reproduced, stored, and/or copied electronically (except for academic use as a source), nor transmitted in any form or by any means without the prior written permission of the publisher and/or author.

This is a work of non-fiction. Every effort has been made to ensure that all information was correct at press time. That includes accurate representations of the events and narratives described, as well as factual portrayals of the author's interactions with all persons named. Neither the author nor publisher assume and hereby disclaim any liability to any party for any loss, damage, devaluation or disruption caused by errors or omissions, whether or not such errors or omissions resulted from negligence, accident, faulty recollection, or any other cause. Readers wishing to correct a possible error or omission in content, add a missing credit or acknowledgement, or offer a suggestion for future editions are encouraged to contact the author.

All quotes are sourced from the author's contemporaneous written accounts of interviews and conversations, as well as from printed, recorded and broadcast sources.

Photos are in the public domain except where credited. Cover photos credit: Merv Griffin by Linda Bisset; Betty White and Ellen Degeneres by Alan Light; Steve Harvey by Angela George; Oprah Winfrey by Milwaukee Independent; Chris Rock and Joan Rivers by David Shankbone; Jay Leno by slgckge; Kevin Spacey by Pinguino k; Bill Cosby by The World Affairs Council of Philadelphia.

Published in the United States of America by:

BearManor Media

4700 Millenia Blvd.
Suite 175 PMB 90497
Orlando, FL 32839

bearmanormedia.com

Printed in the United States.

Typesetting and layout by BearManor Media

ISBN—978-1-62933-931-3

Dedicated to all of us for whom the television has always been far more than an appliance or a piece of furniture.

With heartfelt appreciation to the loved ones and friends who took part of the journey with me. And with thanks to the audiences for the special hugs only they can give.

About the author

Randy West was inspired and mentored into a career in broadcasting by legendary television announcer Johnny Olson. Armed with Johnny's classic sensibilities and professionalism, Randy was first behind radio microphones while still in his teens in suburban New York City. Once he earned his B.A. degree, Randy cast his fates to the airwaves on a coast-to-coast journey that eventually led to KMGG - "Magic 106" in Los Angeles. It was his stepping stone to television announcing.

TV work began with Group W's *Hour Magazine* in 1988, followed by a long list of programs that paired Randy with Ryan Seacrest, Dick Clark, Wink Martindale, Chuck Woolery, Bob Eubanks, Howie Mandel, Ray Combs, Marc Summers, Ben Stein and other iconic television personalities. Randy's resume includes an exhaustive list of game, talk and awards shows including *Supermarket Sweep, Deal or No Deal, Weakest Link, The Daytime Emmy Awards* and ten annual live broadcasts of Nick's *Kids Choice Awards*. His television voice work continues, most recently on CBS' *Big Brother*.

Randy cites his work with Bob Barker announcing CBS' *The Price is Right* during the 2003-2004 season as both a career pinnacle and an especially poignant honor, as it was his mentor's signature program. Randy continues his association with America's longest-running game show, performing during the past 19 years in FremantleMedia's *The Price is Right – Live* stage show which now tours the country following successful residences in Bally's Las Vegas and Harrah's Atlantic City showrooms. Starting in 2019, Randy expanded his casino showroom work freelancing as a host of stage presentations for Game Show America.

Randy presently serves on the Board of Directors of Pacific Pioneer Broadcasters and the Hollywood Media Professionals. He's actively involved as a voting member of the Television Academy, was an organizer and speaker for several years' annual Game Show Congress events, and periodically serves on committees at SAG-AFTRA.

Most recently, Randy was honored by the request to aid in establishing the new *National Archives of Game Show History* at The Strong National Museum of Play. The new gallery will feature interactive exhibits, while the archives will serve as a research resource and repository for scripts, props, production materials, set designs, technical schematics, production bibles, marketing materials and other artifacts from 75 years of television game shows.

Randy is also a published author specializing in television history. The success of his *Johnny Olson: A Voice in Time* led to opportunities to pen articles and features, as well as invitations to speak on television and radio at a number of colleges and universities. His 2022 release *TV Inside-Out* is a backstage pass to the truest form of reality TV, as it reveals the most outrageous behind-the-scenes flukes, flakes, feuds and a few conveniently-forgotten felonies. It's a compelling read that guarantees you'll never watch TV the same way again!

Randy is represented by Susan A. Simons at David Shapira & Associates of Beverly Hills.

Introduction

Marc Summers: Show biz ain't for everybody!

Bill Kirchenbauer: Stepping in front of the cameras as a comedian is wildly unpredictable.

Bob Eubanks: When I was hired to be the youngest host to ever front a network TV game show, I only wish that I'd had a clue of what kind of a world I'd be spending the rest of my career in.

Roger Dobkowitz: I was overwhelmed at the beginning of my career by the politics, egomania, self-importance, and secrets that go on behind the scenes of TV shows.

Wink Martindale: I realized long ago that sometimes the most amazing show is the one that is playing out in the studio, behind the scenes.

Bob: Then and now, it seems the television business must be like no other in the world.

Wink: It seems everybody has had a nightmare incident they'd sooner forget. I've been in broadcasting since the early days of television and have had my tally of unpredictable moments sharing the stage with Elvis Presley as well as performing live before all of America on *The Ed Sullivan Show*.

Roger: … witnessing Bob Barker starting to walk off our show over a dispute about a game line-up.

Marc: Those of us who have been in the TV biz for years have a boatload of these stories.

Bob: Audiences have seen so little of the true craziness that has played out just out of their view.

Stone Wallace

Through his long and impressive career in broadcasting Randy West has explored the intriguing world behind the curtain where the TV stars, actors, hosts and crewmembers have kept their secrets hidden. Through *TV INSIDE-OUT* viewers now have a rare chance to learn about that surprising world that's just out of frame.

Randy candidly and affectionately shares heartwarming breakthrough stories of fan-favorite personalities who have become legends, while revealing the heartbreaking truth of others who have failed to survive the inevitable blunders and bloopers in the unpredictable and whimsical realm of show business. Some of these fascinating behind-the-scenes stories of familiar names from our living room televisions are humorous, some are poignant, and some are tragic. But all are touching and sure to evoke memories.

Most of these tales of stars' misadventures have never been whispered about before now, while others that have been gist for the gossip mill and fan "ragazines" have never been presented with the well-researched background insight that bring them to life. With Randy's unique conversational style of writing he takes each *TV INSIDE-OUT* reader on a private guided tour of backstage mishaps that are guaranteed to open their eyes to an entire world that has remained unseen by television viewers.

Wink Martindale

While hosting, producing and creating over 20 nationally broadcast television programs I realized long ago that sometimes the most amazing show is the one that is playing out in the studio, behind the scenes. At times I've even thought that turning the cameras around to show the backstage action would be infinitely entertaining, but it would capture action so outrageous that the audience would never believe it - not to mention that it might not get past the censors! In *TV INSIDE-OUT* Randy has captured the TV business as it really is, warts and all.

This book has also confirmed for me that the insanity behind the curtain at other shows has been equally unpredictable and even occasionally scandalous. Everybody is in the studio to do their best work, but the time constraints and pressure to turn out top product during long days of marathon tapings is enough to cause emotional meltdowns among the less experienced, exacerbate personality conflicts and ego clashes. as well as bring out the worst in some people who may already be a few sandwiches short of a picnic.

I've been in broadcasting since the early days of television and have had my tally of unpredictable moments sharing the stage with Elvis Presley as well as performing live before all of America on *The Ed Sullivan Show*. I'm happy that things have never gotten so fully out of control as to warrant a few pages in this book, although I do remember when I was only 18, at WTJS, Jackson, Tennessee.

It was my first job in radio, and I did a terrible job reading the 10 p.m. news one night. Then I played a Pabst Beer commercial transcription at 78 RPM instead of 33 1/3 RPM. With the mic open I yelled, "God dammit! What the shit's gonna' happen next ?!" I thought that I had just ended my dream of a career in radio. Surprisingly, there was just one complaint. A lady called and said, "Tell that announcer he's swearing on the air". My response: "Yes, ma'am. I'll tell him right now!"

It seems everybody has had a nightmare incident they'd sooner forget, as Randy has done a most amazing deep dive to reveal what must be the most shocking behind the scenes moments from among our favorite TV shows and our most beloved TV stars. Little did the home audience know that sometimes the kind of mayhem that was just out of camera range required the broadcasting equivalent of a hazmat team to do the mop up. Enjoy the *TV INSIDE-OUT* journey. I'm enjoying the ride with you!

Marc Summers

Show biz ain't for everybody! Passion, desire and talent are important, but overcoming obstacles (meaning the suits who generally don't have a clue) is another story. Case in point:

Iconic television game show producing veteran Bob Noah called me about a year or two after my Nickelodeon series *Double Dare* launched. NBC was doing a week of favorite game show hosts playing *Scrabble* and he asked if I would like to be included. Exploding with enthusiasm, I said "Yes!" He said he had a meeting with the network and would call me back.

Four hours later my phone rang and Bob said, "I have good news and bad news, which would you like to hear first?" I said "You decide." He said, "They turned you down as a favorite host. They said you had not been on TV long enough to be a favorite anything!" But, Bob said he wanted *Scrabble* host, Chuck Woolery, to play the game himself a few days and he asked the network if Marc Summers could host it when Chuck plays. The geniuses said, "of course," which is how I made my network debut!!

Those of us who have been in the TV biz for years have a boatload of these stories. Somehow, Randy West knows a ton of them - in fact, he was around when many of them happened! Intrigued? You should be. Put on your seat belt for *TV INSIDE-OUT*. You are about to hear all true stories about what a bumpy ride many of us have experienced. Have fun!

Bob Eubanks

When I was hired to be the youngest host to ever front a network TV game show, I only wish that I'd had a clue of what kind of a world I'd be spending the rest of my career in. Randy West's *TV INSIDE-OUT* would have been the perfect introduction to the unpredictable strangeness that lay ahead when I started working on *The Newlywed Game*.

I was still working as a disc jockey when I was hired by Chuck Barris. Moments before I was to step onto the stage to tape my very first appearance as a television host there was a knock on my dressing room door. I assumed it was the ABC brass coming to wish me success on the new show. Instead, it was two very serious FBI agents who flashed their badges and served me with an order to appear to give testimony in the federal payola investigation. They left as quickly as they came with the intimidating message, "If you know what's good for you, you'd better show up!" I did the first episode of The Newlywed Game with the subpoena in my suit jacket.

Then and now it seems the television business must be like no other in the world. When I asked a woman what's the number one thing your husband wouldn't want you to talk about on national TV, she spilled the beans that her husband and cousin were going to kill their uncle for the insurance money. I almost fell to the floor. Then, when the husbands joined their wives on stage, he told the same story! They matched and got the points.

During over 50 years in television I've seen a lot of strangeness, and I've lived through some of the stories Randy tells. Audiences have seen so little of the true craziness that has played out just out of their view. That's no longer the case, as *TV INSIDE-OUT* documents some of the most unpredictable and shocking moments that played out in front of and behind live television cameras.

Roger Dobkowitz

Being a child of television and finally realizing my dream job of working on a game show—which turned into a 36 year stint on *The Price Is Right*—I was overwhelmed at the beginning of my career by the politics, egomania, self-importance, and secrets that go on behind the scenes of TV shows. Randy's book *TV INSIDE-OUT* is a treasure chest of many of these stories.

As producer of *The Price is Right* I witnessed over my career similar incidents to those that Randy relates. They included hearing a CBS television executive sternly warn us "You can't eat the prizes" (Kentucky Fried Chicken), witnessing Bob Barker starting to walk off our show over a dispute about a game line-up, or hearing that an entire episode of our show had to be thrown out because of a scoring error made by a young man (that was me!).

There is no doubt that Randy's book *TV INSIDE-OUT* is a great read. Thanks to the lack of social media years ago, many of the stories were kept quiet... until now!

Bill Kirchenbauer

Stepping in front of the cameras as a comedian is wildly unpredictable. Who could guess John Davidson would decide to heckle me by reading my personal cue cards to the audience?

How about *Tonight Show* guest host Bill Cosby repeatedly telling the audience that I was mispronouncing my own name? I got the last laugh calling him Mr. cos-BEE! If you have a weak heart, don't read Randy's *TV INSIDE-OUT!*

George Gray

I've known Randy West for long enough that I would make me sound really old, and I've even had the pleasure of working with him on multiple occasions over the years. Now he's written a behind-the-scenes book about the industry, *TV INSIDE-OUT*.

Just remember, if you read anything about me in it, he probably made it up—unless it makes me look good, then he's totally telling the truth!

Jim MacKrell

I love TV. I love everything about it, I am a fan of TV. I love my time in TV. The memories, the people, the stories, the experiences; hell, I even love the TV sets.

My life is chock full of TV. My dear friends who have passed on were from TV. I loved the stars I worked with and the crews that made it all possible. Now I have something more to love about TV. One of the most gifted writers about TV has a new book.

I had the privilege of reading an advance copy of Randy West's *TV INSIDE-OUT*. I laughed, I cried, I loved the stories about those I admired and those that didn't ring up my all-time list of faves. Randy is a talented author who understands and appreciates the love affair America has with TV. I can't recommend this book enough. "And now, Here's Randy."

Preface

Broadcasting is an industry with a relatively short history, and an even shorter memory. That's unfortunate, as television's tapestry is woven from precious, often little-known but captivating stories of career heights, personal slights, tough breaks, and breakthrough moments that are all too soon forgotten. Beyond simply feeding readers' fascination with the inner workings of show business, this book shines a penetrating and discerning light on the people who contribute to TV and its hidden history. That illumination provides unique insight into the true nature of the entertainment industry, and helps elucidate the human condition through the stories of some of America's favorite television personalities. After all, it's the choices people make when the stakes are highest that reveal their true character, and TV's stakes are indeed high.

Actors on hit series are routinely paid over $1 million per episode with additional sweetening that frequently includes profit participation and studio development deals. In some cases the value placed on the fruits of their labor defy comprehension as NBCUniversal paid over $500 million for their Peacock streaming service's exclusive right to rerun *The Office*. It just slightly eclipsed the over $425 million shelled out for *Friends* to stream on HBO Max. Nobody has dared publicly whisper exactly how much higher than a half billion dollars Netflix ponied-up for a five-year lock on the already well-exposed repeats of *Seinfeld*.

Then came the big deal that would stupefy even TV's top traders, *Let's Make a Deal* power-pitchmen Monty Hall or Wayne Brady. In 2019 WarnerMedia agreed to pay what *The Hollywood Reporter* estimated was over a billion dollars for five years of exclusive rights to reruns of *The Big Bang Theory* for TBS and its streaming HBO Max. It's a massive return on investment even for a show with a production budget that spiraled to a reported $9 million per half-hour episode in its final season.

Emmy-winning producer Nick Weidenfeld revealed to the New York Times that the costs to produce dramas such as *Game of Thrones* have approached $10 million per episode. Disney/ABC alone spent $30 billion on content in 2021. Scores of programs come and go each season in the studios' search for something that will deliver viewers' eyes to the advertisers who spend over $70 billion each year on TV commercial time.

As for revealing character, Lord knows the broadcasting business is populated with extraordinary characters. Some are drawn to the spotlights like moths to a flame, while others are simply well-paid craftspeople working in a factory that churns out entertainment. It's an industry that manufactures content using an unusual business model. Everything is deficit financed—mass-produced at a loss. Only a small percentage of the content that comes off the assembly line will eventually turn a profit, but those unpredictable hits such as *Seinfeld* or *The Simpsons* with their seemingly endless shelf life each generate the hundreds of millions of dollars that more than keep the business in the black.

In this unusual milieu as in every industry people work towards the goals that they believe will bring them security, admiration, creative fulfillment, and their own nebulous visions of success. The fact is while we spend much of our lives pursuing success most people haven't bothered to define it, few have mapped a route, and even fewer have the autonomy needed to steer their careers to that goal. That's why some of the most popular and prosperous celebrities, the lucky few who seemingly should have not a care in the world, are miserable. Those lucky enough to have grabbed a nugget of TV gold carry the added burden of knowing they run the risk of squeezing it so tightly that it slips out of their hand.

This book is packed with confirmed and well-vetted surprising true stories that provide insights into some of the strangeness that seems unique to the world of entertainment. Few industries tolerate the kind of misbehavior, lapses of judgment, and troubled personalities as the studios, distribution networks, and production companies do. At the same time many self-respecting people would never put up with the unpredictability, insecurity, and daily job evaluations that come every 24 hours with the release of new overnight ratings.

Both parties do their best to make the marriage work because when times are good, they're spectacular. In the realm of the tangible there are few business pursuits that can boast a return on investment like a hit TV show. On the other side of the bed are the intangibles. You'd think little can feel sweeter or serve as a better marker of success than having throngs of adoring strangers ready to riot for a clear view of you waving as you are whisked away in decadent luxury to some remote villa where you can review the financial statements that place your ever-growing personal fortune in excess of the gross domestic product of half the world's countries. If that's all it will take to sustain you long after the adulation stops and the cash flow is barely a trickle, you truly do have the world by the balls. Many who thought those kinds of riches would suffice have since come to feel very differently about it all. It must be hard to wake up some morning thinking that the success you chased and finally caught was an empty box of Cracker Jack, without the promised prize.

True success, real fulfillment requires first illuminating the fragile and elusive elements that combine to determine our own unique personal sense of satisfaction, joy, contentment, and serenity. It's a process of discovery, evaluating our triumphs, reflecting on our accomplishments, and identifying the sources of our self-worth. Without taking that inventory we invariably revert to someone else's measure of success. We then use it to guide our pursuits, whether or not it serves us.

Living that life can never satisfy because it's based on somebody else's script. The resulting discontent leads many to ever-escalating their search for ways to fill the void, accumulating more and more things—luxuries, toys, friends, drugs, sexual conquests, extraordinary experiences, power, fame, control. These things are all doomed to disappoint because they fail to satisfy our basic unique needs. Simply put, you stand little chance of finding joy until you know what makes you happy.

A fruitful chase for a sense of achievement can be empowering, soul-nurturing, and motivating, but that journey only becomes truly meaningful, and its joy lasting, after first abandoning whatever default criteria for success we simply inherited or unthinkingly adopted. For example, a celebrated artist may not recognize the gift he has given to the many who find inspiration, joy, and meaning in viewing his work, and consider his life an abject failure because he's yet to accumulate wealth. Money seems to be in everyone's default definition of success even though it so often fails to bring happiness.

That gifted yet unfulfilled artist's personal sense of failure can loom so large that it's akin to a solar eclipse. That despair can obscure the light and warmth of the sun, as well as the light and warmth in a person's psyche, overshadowing the capacity for joy. Leonardo da Vinci was lauded in his time as a great artist, yet considered himself a disappointment as a painter. It's even sadder to think that the feeling of failure is purely self-imposed. It's all about perception. In fact, the majority of psychology professionals agree that all unhappiness comes from our thoughts. Excluding people with mental illnesses, chemical or hormonal imbalances, or other medical conditions, our happiness or unhappiness is entirely determined by our thought process. It's totally an inside job. That's a sad revelation for any performer hoping to wring lasting pleasure from audiences' applause.

There's new research to support one of the oldest theories about our emotions. Joy, fear, or psychic pain are among the choices we make in our interpretation of events, circumstances, and the changes in our body chemistry. The sudden showers of hormones such as epinephrine, cortisol, dopamine and serotonin carry with them no emotion. Only after the rush has begun does our brain combine what we see, hear, smell, and taste in order to deduce a cause for the change in chemistry. Only then do we interpret it, label it, judge it as good or bad, and determine what to do.

Most coaching for acting and public speaking teaches the biological similarity between fear and excitement. That feeling before stepping out in front of a crowd can be interpreted as positive exhilaration that spurs us on to greater creativity, increased energy, and heightened awareness. It can also be perceived as mind-numbing fear and paralyzing anxiety. Our interpretations create our mood, our view of the world and our self-image, including our spot along the continuum between success and failure.

Modern cognitive behavioral therapy has re-embraced an ancient belief that can be traced back a couple of thousand years to the time of Greek Stoicism. Epictetus and other philosophers of the time claimed men are not disturbed by things, but by the view they take of them. This fundamental truth was revisited in more recent times in the writings of Alfred Ellis, Aaron Beck, David Burns, and Ken Keyes. Read any of their works or simply revert to Google and see the over 300,000,000 results that return from a search of cognitive therapy.

Three hundred million search results yet, amazing, so little is spoken about any of this. Strange, considering it's been over 100 years since James Allen helped propel the modern understanding of the relationships between thoughts, feelings, and reality. In his *As a Man Thinketh* (1903) Allen concisely explained how we become the content of our thoughts. Because "we are what we think," he advocated for directing our thinking. At its most basic it means ignore what you don't want and embrace what you prefer.

It's a practice that requires recognizing the difference between instinctive thought and analytical thought. Instinctive thought is the natural and spontaneous hard-wired understanding we have for things without any learning, previous experience, accumulated knowledge, or conscious thought. Animals live solely by instinctive thought. A mother instinctively protects her baby, while we instinctively run from danger.

Analytical thought is, in a sense, the opposite. When you aren't trusting your instincts, you're contemplating and computing. The more time you spend in analytical thought the more joy you miss by not living life in the moment. Beyond the relatively brief few minutes during a day rightfully spent actively analyzing situations in constructive deliberation—solving problems and making plans—the more time spent calculating and devising scenarios, the greater the anxiety. More time spent evaluating past events or preparing for the future rarely results in anything positive. Instead of greater insight we create greater angst. For chronic worriers it's hard to accept the proven truth: There's nothing to be gained from living in your head, constructing and deconstructing past experiences or deliberating anticipated situations—nothing to be gained except unhappiness. There's no joy in living life as if it were a chess game.

Beyond the way we think about events and circumstances the most basic truth seems to be that success comes from following a passion. The self-satisfaction found in pursuing a dream seems to be less about how far we come towards reaching the ultimate goal, and more about how we interpret our achievements along the way. We've all heard the old adage, and there's truth in it: "It's not the destination, it's the journey." In his short 24 years of life actor James Dean arrived at the realization, "The gratification comes in the doing, not in the results." There's more to that philosophy that's rarely mentioned. That is that not reaching the goal can actually be the more rewarding scenario. Living a life with specific still-to-be-achieved quests provides a foundation for direction, hope, and purpose.

From her long tenure as *Billboard* magazine's radio editor and her hours in the warm glow from a hot microphone, Rollye Bornstein James has sufficient wisdom and wit to fill a few million fortune cookies. She speaks the truth: "Once a long term goal is achieved, and once the thrill of victory fades, it's virtually guaranteed that an emptiness will fill all the places where the dream used to be—and the bigger the dream was, the bigger the emptiness." In her book, *What Am I Doing Here?* (2010) Rollye cites examples that prove her point convincingly. It's also a tremendously fun read about adventures in the wacky world of radio. Confucius never had a fraction of the audience that Rollye has enjoyed as a broadcaster, but they both agree: "If you want to change the world, first change your heart."

To a great degree you really do create your own success from the way you think, feel, and behave. Actor and ventriloquist Jay Johnson, best known from the TV hit *Soap* believes that's the way to play the Hollywood game. He thinks success can be little more than just an illusion, it's all in the optics. Jay says, "In America you are not judged by the qualities of your character or the depth of your talents, you are simply judged by your income and credit score. I don't know much about other businesses but for show business … it is better to look successful than to be successful. The truth is, only a few creative types in Hollywood really know what they are doing… the rule is, 'Get me that successful writer, actor, producer, director.' So success in show business will always be a matter of what [it appears] you've done lately."

Even when what you've done lately is close to nothing there really is a bounty of positive energy to be tapped. As Auntie Mame said, "Life is a banquet and most damn fools are starving to death!" Enlightened people all share the same hopes and are all on parallel paths with yours, pursuing their own personal brand of success.

Finding encouragement along the way is usually not hard. Approached with the right spirit most people making the journey will share their time, knowledge, experience, and advice with someone who has a seemingly sincere desire to gain insight.

The worst question to ask anyone is anything like, "What should I do?" You want to gather information that helps you to define your own goals, and then devise your own plan towards their achievement. Never relinquish the power or the responsibility for making your own decisions. If you do, you'll never own the outcome. Besides, anyone who thinks they can predict the future path for another person with any specificity is beyond arrogant. If anyone deigns to tell you what to do, they're not someone you want to take much advice from.

Show business is a well-illuminated high-stakes world where most everything plays out in public, and then gets macro-magnified by the insatiable public interest. The immutable magnetic pull of Tinseltown is likely the only force that has overridden people's logic in every far flung corner of the Earth for the approximately 100 years during which Hollywood has exported entertainment. That drawing power doesn't discriminate by age, gender, race, or economic status. That lure even reached the little girl who hid from the Nazis during their ravaging of Europe and courageously wrote of her epic struggle, Anne Frank.

Young Anne's chronicling of hatred and hope was published in 1947 after her death in a concentration camp. *The Diary of a Young Girl* became a bestseller that has since been translated and released in over 70 languages. The 13 year-old's writings were subsequently staged as a play and *The Diary of Anne Frank* was later adapted into an Academy Award-winning motion picture.

Well-known actor Robert Stack explained that Audrey Hepburn turned down the leading role because it resonated far too deeply with her own hellish existence during the war. Hepburn said, "I was reading what was inside me and still there. This child who was locked up…had written a full report of everything I'd experienced and felt." Stack went on to reveal how pervasive the myth, magic, and magnetic draw of Hollywood had spread around the globe.

Even during her all-consuming struggle to survive another day through the unimaginable horrors of war, Anne Frank wasn't immune from the great dream that has drawn millions. Stack told me that found among the pages of that famous diary was a photograph of young Anne. Her handwritten caption says it all: "This is a photo as I wish myself to look all of the time. Then maybe I would have a chance to come to Hollywood."

So what about the millions whose grandiose yearnings for stardom make them fresh meat for the dishonest talent scouts who have always exploited newcomers to the showbiz capitol? In 2017 there was another round-up of scammers with charges filed against 25 would-be agents in violation of L.A.'s Krekorian Talent Scam Prevention Act. These bloodthirsty piranhas were accepting cash for all kinds of services and events that would supposedly help get gullible wannabes cast. You know, photos, workshops, showcases, etc. Nobody deserves to be ripped off for daring to dream big, only for letting their dreams blind them from reality. Empower your passion with common sense, skepticism, wisdom, and courage.

Consider swimmer Diana Nyad who trained for decades but was unsuccessful in four different attempts to achieve her impossible dream. Starting at age 28 Diana repeatedly tried to swim, non-stop, the nearly 110 miles between Key West, Florida and Cuba. Who would suggest that she try it a fifth time, especially now that she was 64 years old? Amazingly, it was that fifth attempt that was successful, at an age when most people are resigning themselves to the belief that their unachieved goals will remain so. Nyad is the first person of any age ever to make that swim without a shark cage, and she did it in a grueling nonstop 53 hours. I did say age 64, 110 miles, 53 hours, non-stop.

If you're not impressed by our senior swimmer, consider 105-year-old Robert Marchand. In 2017 Marchand set a world record in cycling. In a timed one-hour event he covered 14.01 miles on a circular indoor track. Barely breathing heavily the centenarian declared, "I could have done better, if I had seen the 10-minute warning… I would have pedaled slightly faster." A former record holder for both the 100-meter and 50-meter dash events laced up again in 2021 to establish a new record for a new age category. Louisiana's Julia "Hurricane" Hawkins finished the 100-meter with a time of 1:02.95. "Hurricane" was 105 years old. On the other end of the age spectrum there's 11-year-old Laurent Simons who in

2021 became the second youngest college graduate in history, earning a bachelor's degree in the no-mercy major, physics.

The liberating truth is that it's impossible to rule out anyone's chances for achieving any goal that they passionately aspire to, clearly envision, fully embrace, and doggedly pursue. In the realm of improbable stardom who on Earth would look at Danny DeVito and suggest he quit his hairdressing gig to become a movie star?

In 1965 the man who started FedEx, Frederick W. Smith was a student at Yale. He wrote a term paper in which he outlined his dream for a new world of overnight deliveries. At the time airfreight shippers relied on commercial airlines' passenger route systems. Smith understood it was an inefficient process that didn't make sense for urgent shipments. His term paper laid out the entire business plan for what became FedEx but the paper earned only a "C." He'd have been fully justified in overnighting a supply of humble pie to his professor.

Harland Sanders' life was a meandering mishmash of career misadventures. He worked as a farmhand, a streetcar conductor, and a railroad worker. Sanders also served in the U.S. Army, stationed in Cuba. Upon his return he studied law, passed the bar exam, and became an attorney. After a courtroom brawl with a client Sanders left the profession. He then captained a steamboat ferry that crossed the Ohio River. Next he went into sales, hawking everything from life insurance to automobile tires. Although not a doctor, during his time in rural Kentucky Sanders even made house calls delivering babies. He also ran a gas station where he began cooking and selling meals to truckers.

Sanders then came upon a recipe for pressure cooking chicken that had been written-up in a travel guide. You may think his life then instantly fell into place, but his big dream remained vexingly unattainable. The honorary Kentucky colonel wrote that he made 1,008 sales calls before he could get one single restaurant to agree to buy his recipe and cooking process for fried chicken. If he's to be believed, it was only by persisting through over 1,000 rejections that Sanders was able to begin to build the franchising behemoth now called KFC.

Then, brilliantly resourceful networking and marketing helped Sanders land some of the first of those franchises. The colonel had a friend who knew the legendary New York saloon host Toots Shor. As a favor, the friend forwarded Sanders' bio, photos, and press clippings to be handed to one particular customer. Toots had boasted that *What's My Line?* host John Daly was a frequent patron and, that's right, when Daly dropped Sanders' package on a casting producer's desk the colonel's compelling story and telegenic appearance charmed the staff to where they invited him onto the program. Before his segment was over Sanders managed to steal enough airtime to intrigue a few potential investors with his story of 11 secret herbs and spices.

The show's director, Franklin Heller, later saw a *Wall Street Journal* article that traced the origins of the KFC empire. He remembers reading one early franchisee's boast, "The colonel had a pretty good recipe, but the whole shebang would never have gotten off the ground if Toots Shor up in New York hadn't managed to arrange to get Colonel Sanders onto *What's My Line?*" Apparently it indeed was the clever kick-start that helped to grow a half-billion dollar a year, finger-lickin' good, pressure-cooked chicken wingding.

We dissuade ourselves from trying to make realities of these kinds of lofty goals. It's a form of self-protection to avoid experiencing defeat. It's a rare friend who will encourage your attempts to be a rock star, supermodel, or astronaut because the chances of success are so slim. Ben Nemtin of *The Buried Life* (2010) and *What Do You Want to Do Before You Die?* (2012) believes in challenging those self-imposed restraints. He says, "The level of competition is highest for realistic goals because most people don't set high enough goals for themselves." Nemtin advocates taking the leap of faith in shooting for your wildest dream. It may take more effort, but if you are truly focused on the journey there are opportunities for smaller successes along the way. Besides, what's so terrible about experiencing a defeat? It doesn't brand you as a loser. If anything it defines you as someone unwilling to settle for a life of mediocrity.

Those of us who are fervently reality-based and who sometimes struggle with concepts like faith and trust, are reticent to invest in our super-sized extreme dreams. Rational thinkers also struggle more with trying to accept life as it plays. They have a harder time focusing solely on the current moment, unencumbered by thoughts of yesterdays and tomorrows. The antidote is what Eckhart Tolle calls "The Power of Now." There's only this moment and there's no rewind button. Miss it and there's no going back. Rational thinkers are also the last to cast their fates to the wind—the last people to be found at sunset wishing upon the night's first star.

Realists generally agree that everything is possible but fail to accept that, with an open mind as well as a measure of faith and trust, more things can be probable. On the way to breathing the rarified air of celebrity there's more satisfaction to be found from making and achieving intermediate career goals. If fame, glory, and renown are part of your dream, there's success to be celebrated in finding steady work that's challenging and creative in the field of endeavor you desire to dominate. The climb towards prominence may get you close enough to see that the fame and celebrity come with tons of unforeseen baggage.

Another truth suggests that if you live long enough you'll see everything. The gift of reaching an advanced age with good health carries with it chances to amass greater experience, knowledge, and self-acceptance as well as more opportunities to reach more goals. Diane Nyad's continuing success as a senior-citizen swimmer and health advocate is proof. Yet, some of the most celebrated have left profound marks within the short time afforded them. Amazingly, musicians Kurt Cobain, Janis Joplin, Jim Morrison, Jimmie Hendrix, Amy Winehouse and Rolling Stones guitarist Brian Jones all made their exits at exactly the same age. Likewise for actors Jonathan Brandis from *One Life to Live*, and Anton Yelchim, whose big-screen *Star Trek* portrayal of Chekov was well received. All eight were precisely 27 years old when they died.

Poet and dramatist Percy Shelley and Author Stephen Crane were in their 20s. Composer Franz Schubert was 31, Eva Peron was 33, Wolfgang Mozart was 35, and Vincent Van Gogh was 37. Both George Gershwin and Martin Luther King were only 39 when their lives ended. Joan of Arc, canonized 500 years later, was burned at the stake as a teenager. John Lennon only made it to age 40, but his contributions had already assured his place in history by age 25. There's also much to be said for being among those who blossom much later. Late bloomers are saved from suffering the syndrome explored by the great songwriting team Jerry Leiber and Mike Stoller, and immortalized by Peggy Lee, *Is That All There Is?*

So, success correlates with being unwilling to give up on a dream in the face of long odds, unanimous discouragement, and even abject disappointments. Our swimming sensation says it's all about "the drive to summon your spirit for something that moves you. Don't let anybody else's limitations define you. Envision your dream and don't give up until you get there, or at least get so close that your own effort inspires you." Others who have realized their wildest fantasies say you should never abandon your greatest hopes. Arsenio Hall, who achieved his goal of breaking the color barrier in late night TV talk expounds, "If there's anything you want to do, don't let them take your dream away."

You can make that a guiding principle, but the harsh reality is that many dreams simply will never come true. No matter how many hours you spend in the gym, without a minimum of the appropriate inherited genes you will never win a world-class body-building competition. To that reality Diane Nyad says, "What if you never touch that dream star of yours? I had come to peace with the feeling that the journey itself was noble and worth taking, even if I never reached the destination."

Bingo! There's that mantra again: success is not about the end result, it's all in the pursuit. With that insight, a paradigm shift from most people's thinking, it's now truly our own perception, and only our perception that determines our success. With that, we've come full circle back to the thinking behind cognitive therapy. The goal you pursue, how you work towards it, and how you feel about your progress are the determinant factors in the making of success. The outcome is not a necessary part of the equation. When some actors read the trade papers it's less about keeping up with the news and more about measuring their own careers against others. With the exception of the obituary page there's a whole lot of "That could have and should have been me."

Contentment can cripple ambition, but in limited quantities it's also a major ingredient in the recipes for success and joy. The balance lies partly in embracing satisfaction in your present accomplishments, and recognizing that your efforts to date are all part of a larger journey towards your goals. Each of the disappointments along the way presents far greater opportunity to learn and grow than any of the so-called successes. As such, those defeats can't rightfully be defined as failures because they illuminate where to best focus our attention. Set high goals and enjoy the pursuit of those lofty dreams, both the wins and the losses. Without dreams, our lives are so ordinary. With dreams, they can be extraordinary.

There's one more important component at play when it comes to making huge dreams come true. Many authors, life coaches, and motivational speakers talk about creating your own luck; it's a major touchstone in the huge self-actualization movement. Creating your own luck implies you can somehow increase the odds of buying a winning lottery ticket or decrease the chances of a losing come-out roll of two, three, or twelve at a casino craps table. I'm here, many thousands of dollars poorer, to assure you that I don't believe you can create that kind of luck. The kind of good fortune that you're able to create is better called serendipity.

There are few stories of Hollywood stardom that don't include a healthy helping of serendipity. It's been the secret ingredient in many career breakthroughs in business as well as the arts. Serendipity is neither destiny on one extreme, nor pure chance luck on the other end of the continuum. It's the ability to turn an event or a random discovery into something pleasant, valuable, or useful. There's no shortage of opportunities for serendipity to play a role in our success if we are open, observant, resourceful, and creative with the people and things we encounter all day, every day. The raw materials are everywhere. The trick is being aware and being imaginative.

For example, in 1980 Wolfman Jack's manager, Don Kelly, told me that an easily overlooked tiny two-sentence item in *Billboard* magazine about the start-up of a new company ultimately led him to a highly profitable business partnership. Simply standing in line at the bank or waiting for an elevator we encounter other people at an approachable moment. By offering a smile and a simple greeting, testing the opportunity for a quick connection and taking advantage of its possibility, we may find we're already face-to-face with a potential friend or business contact. It could be someone who ultimately brings a huge benefit to our lives.

In this case the good luck, the serendipity is created by making the overture that might spark a conversation and then being open and imaginative with the response. Is there some commonality, harmony, congruence, or chemistry? The only investment you risk is a smile. The more associations we attempt, the more creative our thinking becomes. In this same paradigm the connections that ultimately don't spark aren't viewed as failures. They were seeds that simply didn't germinate. There's no value judgment to be made.

Labeling something a failure is a sweeping and dismissive interpretation. The stench from a perceived embarrassing fiasco can linger and poison the psychic energy needed to move forward. If necessary, analyze, redefine, and de-stigmatize the event. There are no failures, just attempts that didn't yield an exploitable opportunity. Why? Because a defeat is… well, defeating. Feelings of failure beget failure. The antidote: heal quickly and let go of disappointments.

Here's the ultimate liberating thought. Simon Helberg, who played Howard Wolowitz in the sitcom *The Big Bang Theory*, questions the idea that there is even such a thing as failure. The successful 30-something actor says, "Failing passionately is success in its own right." Wow! Most people I know, sadly, are resistant to that kind of reinterpretation. Some people use their past failures as an excuse to remain in a seemingly safe zone of mediocrity. Others carry failures with them, appearing to enjoy endlessly marinating in them. Still others are chronically self-defeating by subconsciously creating, one by one, their own string of failures. Unaware, they wonder who is behind all of their bad luck, never considering that they're acting as their own worst enemy.

Steven Bochco was among Hollywood's most successful creators with bragging rights for *Hill Street Blues*, *L.A. Law*, *NYPD Blue*, and other celebrated ratings winners. He drew his own conclusions about personal failure, some quite profound. Bochco came to these realizations during the course of working in the trenches, earning some 300 Emmy nominations along the way. Of the people with great talent who go careening off the rails, Bochco believed they are doomed to repeatedly create that reality in order to bring harmony to their existence. In other words, over and over again they unknowingly screw-up their external life so that their outsides can match their insides.

He says, "These self-inflicted wounds are the direct result of a deeply ingrained sense of unworthiness that success threatens to upend. It's ultimately easier for these people to blow up their own sandbox than to live with the responsibilities and compromises that sustained success requires. There's a certain personality type… that, unlike the majority of us, flourishes in a dysfunctional environment and is therefore masterful at creating it."

Bochco described a pretty disheartening reality for some creative people who, despite an abundance of talent, are doomed to a fruitless struggle. If his comments ring true they could be striking a bell of self-discovery that can lead to a cognitive healing. By the way, Bochco referenced actor David Caruso as an example of this self-destructive pattern. The long-unhealed wound between the two began when the actor bailed from *NYPD Blue* after only 26 shows of the hit that eventually tallied 261. Caruso was dissatisfied with the $42,500 he received per episode and wanted a bump to over $100,000 along with a larger trailer and various other perks. The showrunner remembers the actor as appearing terminally unhappy on the set, adding that when "[I'd] call Caruso into my office for a conversation about his problems, he'd shut down like a sullen teenager."

In the campaigning for Hollywood's many accolades and statuettes January seems to be the start of what is actually referred to as "awards season." Despite not having significant variations in weather, a year in L.A. still has its four seasons: fire, flood, pilot season and awards season. In the studios' quest for every possible vote from members of the Television Academy for Emmys and the Screen Actors Guild for SAG Awards, I'm included in the screenings, meetings, dinners, discussions, cocktail affairs, and interviews that are rampant during awards season. Much of it is mindless, but occasionally there's a speck of sand that can become a pearl of wisdom.

At a 2015 unspooling of *Birdman*, the writer-director who ultimately took home Oscar gold for that year's Best Picture as well as Best Director discussed his film. In doing so Alejandro G. Inarritu expanded on Bochco's analysis while precisely nailing the intentional subtext of this book. He spoke of "the difference between what we really need, which is affection and love, and what we are normally seeking, which is admiration. In the end, no matter how successful you are, nothing will fulfill you. It's impossible. An Oscar will fulfill you? To have that statue, you will be happy? Life will be easy?" While heavy stuff to ponder, it's the same seed from which this book grew.

Alejandro was gifted with incredible clarity and insight, or he has spent more than his share of hours on therapists' couches. He's got a firm grasp on his reality which I suspect resonates with a lot of other people. Listen to his continuing observations about life and the inspirations behind his original *Birdman* screenplay. "The film is about mediocrity, how we deal with our limitations. What our parents told us we are capable of doing and who we are—we are great, we are unique, all that—but we are not. It's brutal, but it's true. Honestly, that's why there's a lot of psychology and a lot of antidepressants, because we arc not."

Here's a bottom line. For many creative people the essence of success—the greatest moments of joy—are found through what has been described as "peak experience." I suspect we've all been there it at times. At its most basic, peak experience has its roots in those moments when we're so consumed by an activity that we lose track of time and space. Peak experience is the unique, all-encompassing sensation found at the intersection of mastery and flow. It's a state of profound creativity or productivity during which we surrender to the fullest experience of living. Credit Abraham Maslow's 1964 work *Religions, Values, and Peak Experiences* for this insight.

Think of peak experience as coming while studying to play the piano. The early exercises are tedious. There's little joy in learning to read music, striving to become proficient at recognizing which notes on the musical staff represent which piano keys. It may take many months but, eventually you're able to recognize chords on the page. With further concentration you're able to bring that information to your fingers. As you continue to practice you reach a point where your fingers easily find the proper notes without having to consciously analyze and translate each marking on the sheet music. It eventually becomes automatic and you begin to feel the music you are making even before your fingers hit the keys. This is the beginning of mastery.

With talent, heart, and passion you may find yourself swept up in the experience of playing. The music flows effortlessly. You become unaware of your surroundings, oblivious to your body movements and facial expressions. You may not even be fully aware that you're sitting at a big wooden instrument with strings. You're creating music, not with your mind or fingers but with your heart and perhaps your soul. The music is a direct expression of your emotions, flowing without a single thought about the process. You get swept up in feeling, instead of thinking. It's living in the moment, free of inhibition, fear, doubt, self-criticism, and inner conflict. It's a divine and Zen-like altered state of consciousness; it's blissful and soul nurturing. In short, it's peak experience.

Michelle Williams, the award-winning actress from 2017's *Manchester by The Sea* is acutely aware of how she relies on peak experience every time the cameras roll. She explains, "The moment between 'action' and 'cut' is like a deep state of forgetfulness and remembering at the same time. You sort of let go. I let myself, for a brief period of time, suspend all my self-judgment and self-criticism and insecurity." Comic actor Jim Carrey works much the same way. Borrowing the term for a rare dissociative psychiatric condition he calls the experience "Fugue State." Peak experience is described by others as being at the epicenter of pleasure, in harmony with the world, in a state of grace approaching bliss.

The recent buzzword, "mindfulness," refers to being aware of your existence in the moment, aware of your breathing, your movements, and the random thoughts that cross your mind. I see peak experience as the opposite, which is about being unaware. It's about being extraordinarily engrossed and productive in some pursuit while totally oblivious to your surroundings, movements, and all extraneous thought. It's about being fully possessed by the activity. Like a basketball player who is instinctively aware of when, where, and how he can steal possession, sidestep opposing team players, then shoot and score. There's almost no time-consuming conscious deliberation.

For the athletes and performers who have visited this sacred state of being, it's transcendent. That is, they say they seem to exceed the limits of their skill and experience and reach new levels of proficiency. At its most extreme it could be thought of existing outside of the material universe and, as such, not limited by it. Some artists, writers especially who achieve that state say they are simply a conduit. They feel they are delivering a level of quality, productivity, or performance that they believe to be beyond their own capability, attributable to some higher source.

Many people have experienced those breakthroughs many times in their creative lives, while others seem to reach this altered state less frequently. It may sound like, but it clearly isn't a diagnosable manic phase of some bipolar condition. Those episodes last a minimum of several days and often months at a time and they include destructive thoughts and behaviors.

You can't force the feeling but you can recognize, reinforce, and nurture peak experience when it occurs naturally. For some it feels like tapping into part of the 90 percent of our brain power that scientists say we rarely use. It's a measurable state of altered consciousness related to hypnosis where the critical mind is at rest. It can be encouraged, but not coerced. Surrendering to peak experience just may be as good a reason as any to treasure and appreciate being alive.

As the television business divulges its secrets and exposes what makes people tick, this lesson comes into focus: Life is short. Live it. Don't squander the time lusting after some definition of success. Instead, find joy. Try new things and explore new interests to discover your passions. Once you find them, run with them. Pursuing our passions enhances our lives and our sense of purpose. Beyond increasing our own joy it makes us of greater value to our loved ones and friends. Contribute something to the world. That generosity of spirit generates its own internal joyfulness. For some, the elusive idea of living a successful life is pretty much that simple. For others, it's an unsolvable puzzle.

It's the choices people make when the stakes are highest that reveal their true character, and how many pieces of that puzzle they've been able to put together. The intensely competitive nature of the entertainment industry brings out the most resourceful in some, and the ugliest side of others. As a venue in which the super-sized risks and rewards are often daunting, the television business exposes infinitely more than the camera sees.

Through these pages you're invited to share lessons learned from witnessing some of the medium's best known personalities on their journeys. Some are joyful, some miserably sad. Some are delightfully generous and caring people, and some are self-consumed narcissistic jerks. All are on their own journeys in search of personal fulfillment and career success, but far too few seem to have recognized the simple truth: Above and beyond basic survival, success is about the intangibles—the inner peace and the joy that we create for ourselves and those we care about.

As my departed friend Alan O'Day wrote, "If you believe in forever, then life is just a one-night stand."

Chapter 1

It's a tight-knit community populated by pros. Skilled specialists of all stripes who are relied upon to contribute their unique expertise on cue, first try, in tight collaboration with other talented professionals, sometimes under stressful and challenging circumstances. The citizens of the mythical Tinseltown are the front-line workers who create America's most enduring pop culture—our beloved television programs.

However, Hollywood is also a world full of troubled souls, double-dealing, broken promises, broken hearts, bold-faced lies, alcohol, drugs, sex, debauchery, misdemeanors, felonies, and biblical sin. There's an un-mined mother lode of mishaps, a legacy rich with gaffes and goofs, flukes and flakes, celebrity embarrassments, classic moments of dysfunction, and squandered good intentions. I'd been naïve, oblivious to this secret truth until this hidden reality began to reveal itself. With the passage of time a few transition from cringe-worthy, occasionally to become the impetus for unstifleable laughter. All remain fascinating.

There's the convicted murdering rapist who won a date on *The Dating Game*, the comedy club owner who swears *Sanford and Son* star Redd Foxx whipped out his penis and appeared to be masturbating in front of his audience, the backstage backbiting between Barker's Beauties at *The Price is Right*, *American Idol* disqualifying its contestant Frenchie Davis for having posed topless, Alana "Honey Boo Boo" Thompson's drug use and cancellation after reports that Mama June was dating a convicted child molester, *Mary Hartman, Mary Hartman* star Louise Lasser's arrest after a freak-out in a Beverly Hills boutique, the *Barney Miller* dysfunctional marathon tapings that continued past 3:00 a.m., sportscaster Marv Albert being kicked off team NBC for biting a partner during cross-dressing three-way sex.

Beloved actor James Gandolfini's failure to show up on the set of *The Sopranos* for days on end while the cast and crew stood idle, Milton Berle's pathetic fall from TV super-stardom, Arthur Godfrey's stunning plummet from grace after his on-air firing of beloved crooner Julius LaRosa, grief on the *Moonlighting* set caused by the mutual disdain between co-stars Bruce Willis and Cybil Shepherd, the *M*A*S*H* episode that was cut short by a Malibu wildfire that destroyed the Korea-substitute filming location, the 1950s game show rigging with its impudent denials, *Seinfeld* co-star Michael Richards's "n-word"-laced racist meltdown at the Laugh Factory, how Johnny Carson's white hot feud with a former manager kept client Peter Marshall off *The Tonight Show*.

Jack Paar's walking off of *The Tonight Show* over an edited joke, 15-year-old Disney star Miley *Hanna Montana* Cyrus posing for nude photos, "Mama" Cass Elliot's 1974 collapse on the set of *The Tonight Show* from extreme dieting, Actor Phillip Loeb's suicide following his blacklisting as a Communist, TBS cancelling *The Good Life* after host Cee Lo Green's rape scandal, Sid Caesar's battle with booze and pills, how appearing completely nude on stage led to both Bill Macy's and Adrienne Barbeau's auditions for the sitcom *Maude*, the cover-up and mystery surrounding George *Superman* Reeves's death, Charlie Sheen's drug-fueled rants from the *Two and a Half Men* studio.

Vivian Vance and William Frawley's endless bickering on the set of *I Love Lucy*, the NAACP's boycott of the hit sitcom *Amos and Andy*, the $20 million lawsuit that broke up *Laverne and Shirley*, Johnny Carson's raging anger the day he permanently banned producer Freddie DeCordova from *The Tonight Show* studio, Bill Maher's *Politically Incorrect* rant crediting the 9/11 hijackers' courage for remaining in the airplanes they flew into the World Trade towers, Paula Deen being jettisoned from the Food Network after acknowledging her repeated use of the "n-word," killing off Columbus Short's character from ABC's *Scandal* after the actor was busted for spousal battery and a restaurant fistfight.

Tea Time Movie Matinee Lady Carol Wayne's mysterious drowning and Art Linkletter's daughter Diane's supposed suicide—both in the company of the same car salesman, Mark Goodson and the Secret Service nabbing a forger at the *Password* offices, sponsors' concern about Mary Tyler Moore's butt-tight "under-cupping" Capri pants, the seething animosity between co-hosts Arthur Godfrey and

Candid Camera creator Allen Funt, all the dark drama backstage at the primetime soaps *Dynasty, The Colbys,* and *Dallas,* and the worst shooting in a theater since Abraham Lincoln: Paul *Pee Wee Herman* Reubens arrest for masturbating to the XXX flick *Nurse Nancy* in Florida's Sarasota South Trail Cinema.

Other embarrassingly ignorant and imprudent ejaculations came from the mouths of otherwise intelligent people. They include Howard Cosell's *Monday Night Football* comment about Washington Redskin wide receiver Alvin Garret. After the African-American player's sixth reception of the evening Howard adlibbed that coach Joe Gibbs "wanted that kid… [because] that little monkey gets loose doesn't he?" Howard was eventually uninvited from the *Monday Night Football* press booth.

Three years after that boner from ABC's sports maven came an even more outlandish racial slur from CBS football commentator, "Jimmy the Greek" Snyder. He explained, "The black is a better athlete to begin with, because he's been bred to be that way. Because of his high thighs and big thighs that goes up into his back. And they can jump higher and run faster because of their bigger thighs. And he's bred to be the better athlete because this goes back all the way to the Civil War, when, during the slave trading, the big, the owner, the slave owner would, would, would, would breed his big black to his big woman so that he could have a, uh big, uh big, uh big black kid, see. That's where it all started!"

In this massive hall of shame, Andy Rooney just may have won the award for self-destructing with a combination of both racist and anti-LGBTQ remarks. It was an astounding one-two punch as he shared closing comments about the year 1989. It started with "…too much food, drugs, homosexual unions, cigarettes. They're all known to lead quite often to premature death." He then included this invective while on-the-record with a magazine reporter, "Most people are born with equal intelligence, but blacks have watered down their genes because the less intelligent ones are the ones that have the most children. They drop out of school early, do drugs and get pregnant." Rooney's prize was merely a temporary suspension from *60 Minutes* for spouting that startlingly toxic talk. His last word on the suspension was, "They should have paid me the two weeks salary anyway."

Andy Rooney also expounded on the evils of drug use during the years of first lady Nancy Reagan's trite "just say no" mantra. They were both late to that party considering one of Andy's broadcasting brethren had already been an addict as far back as 1952 when NBC signed-on television's very first morning show, *Today*. From day one, dealing with the host's drug habit became increasingly difficult. After nine years of waking up America Dave Garroway short-circuited one morning on live television. Legend holds that he lay down on the studio floor, refusing to get up until the network met his contract demands. There was no contract forthcoming as the network strongly encouraged their first morning star's resignation.

Garroway's long-term blatant drug use was part of a downward spiral of deepening dependency and depression, compounded by a variety of stressors. They included his second wife ending her life with an apparent overdose of barbiturates. As the writer he hired, celebrated news personality Barbara Walters, told *The New York Times* of Garroway's demise, "Things were never quite the same after her suicide." The talented communicator took to self-medicating with more and more frequent on-set sipping of his own concoction, a green-colored liquid cocktail of codeine, tranquilizers, amphetamines, and vitamin B-12 that he called "The Doctor."

TV's beloved Florence Henderson was a "*Today* Girl," a member of Garroway's wake-up team early in her career. She regaled me with stories of all manner of live-TV surprises, including more on the brilliant broadcaster's drug use. In an extreme example of the difference between some performers' on-camera and off-camera existences, viewers who enjoyed their morning coffee watching Garroway's erudite, authoritative, and witty presence would be shocked to know the depth of his depression that eventually led to his shotgun-blast suicide. Florence's memories of her *Today* co-host are among other eyewitness accounts of small-screen stars' indulgences recounted in these pages. Garroway's was just one case of addictions accommodated, covered up, catered to, and enabled in order to keep the entertainment factory humming at peak efficiency.

Where the inept, incompetent, and untalented are quickly weeded out, the emotionally off-kilter are given a pass. They always have. It's only during the last handful of years that acting out in any of various inappropriate ways can get you run out of town. If they keep their hands to themselves and watch what they say, even the most idiosyncratic misfit can be celebrated. Why tolerate the lunatic fringe? Because show business is the BUSINESS of show, and creativity often means thinking outside the box. Some of the more creative also live outside the box. There's no knowing whose idea will be the next multi-million dollar hit, or billion dollar franchise.

Phil Rosenthal became an overnight success as the architect who created Ray Romano's TV world that we came to know as *Everybody Loves Raymond*, but before that breakthrough he was peddling sitcom scripts. Phil was just another writer, a population that Jack Warner dismissed as "schmucks with Underwoods." For accuracy's sake I believe Phil had an IBM Selectric, but the idea is the same.

CBS recognized *Everybody Loves Raymond* as a potential hit and was fully prepared to write him weekly checks, but Phil says the network was dead set on taking his baby for their own. They wanted to assign their own showrunner, and was already usurping his vision for casting by advocating for Ray's wife to be played by an actress who Phil says was "hotter." He remembers their pick was "10 times worse for the part than I thought she would be." Phil did what few of us would have the integrity to do, he resigned. He remembers, "I was actually shitting my pants because I quit the thing I loved." Three days later he was named the one and only showrunner and got to cast his creation.

Chuck Lorre is the mega-producer with credit for creating hits including *Grace Under Fire, Dharma & Greg, Two and a Half Men, The Big Bang Theory, Mike & Molly, Young Sheldon* and *The Kominsky Method*. He let word slip about some of his fights with network casting departments over hiring actors. Looking to book Jon Cryer for *Two and a Half Men* Lorre remembers CBS branding Cryer a "show killer" based on previous failed pilots. The network initially refused to even consider him. In the same conference room the spectacular Christine Baranski was labeled "death of comedy." Likewise, Lorre reports that it was a tough fight to get network approval for Melissa McCarthy before *Bridesmaids* made her bankable.

Having survived battles with Charlie Sheen, Brett Butler, and Roseanne Barr, Lorre long ago learned that the world of television is no place for the weak of heart. Those first two stars brought the challenges that often accompany drug users and abusers. As to the third, Lorre claims that before she had him fired, Roseanne repeatedly walked off the set threatening to quit if scripts didn't tackle issues of social relevance. It resonated with his memories of also being canned from Cybil Shepherd's eponymous sitcom *Cybil* when he disagreed with the star about the quality of the second act of one week's script. All of the agita sharpened his sense of humor: "One of the benefits of working 70 hours a week in hell is that the mind covers itself so you can't remember it."

TV is the arena where egos have clashed since the very beginning, even back when Philo Farnsworth invented what Ed Murrow called "wires and lights in a box." The hostility and slandering started instantly with a seemingly endless legal battle over who actually invented television, Farnsworth or RCA's Vladimir Zworkin. The medium has since matured, but the immaturity of fragile egos and the vanity of textbook narcissism have guaranteed no shortage of subsequent vendettas.

CBS's Sunday night mainstay Ed Sullivan was ruthless in seeking revenge after mistakenly believing comedian Jackie Mason shot him the bird—gave him the middle finger, the cabdrivers' salute—on live TV. He canceled a $37,500 five-show contract and sullied Mason's reputation. By then, Ed was a pro PR pugilist. He'd already battled publicly with rival newspaperman Walter Winchell. The Sunday night stone-faced host also had a run-in with no lesser star than Frank Sinatra. That feud boiled over when the singer bought an ad in a trade paper to publicly proclaim that Ed is "sick, sick, sick."

Both Jack Paar and Arthur Godfrey each had their own public tiffs with Ed, the latter calling Ed "a dope." Those were nothing compared to the battle between Ed and Steve Allen when they went to war for the same Sunday night audience. Ed called Steve a "Johnny-come-lately" to primetime network air after Steve accused his rival of pirating his guests and stealing planned program elements. After Ed turned down an offer from Elvis Presley's manager, Steve booked the future king of rock and roll and bested Ed's rating for the night. Ed sent this telegram the next morning:

>TO: STEVEN PRESLEY ALLEN, NBC-TV, NEW YORK CITY
>   STINKER.
>LOVE AND KISSES,
>ED SULLIVAN.

Unlike the contempt that was behind some grudges, Ed Sullivan actually enjoyed the light-hearted ribbing that came with being the brunt of comedians' and impressionists' joshing. Fred Allen quipped, "Ed will be successful as long as other people have talent." Ed also laughed along with another classic line that was carbon-dated back to Joe E. Lewis, "Ed is the only man who can brighten a room by leaving it."

It would have been no laughing matter when actress Jane Kean claimed that Ed had attempted to rape her, except that she waited decades to drop that bombshell. It wasn't until 2004, when she was in her 80s and Ed had been dead for 30 long years. For such a very public person as Ed Sullivan, who worked with hundreds of female performers over decades, to have only one person make such a startling accusation wouldn't warrant a mention except for the detailed account in her autobiography:

> "When we entered the apartment…Sullivan wasted no time. He pushed me down on the couch and got on top of me. He exposed himself and ripped off my underwear. I tried to fight him off but he was strong as an ox… I was terrified and ashamed. He kissed me on the cheek and said 'goodnight.' For the next two weeks, I walked around in a fog."

Kean may be best known these days for playing Trixie Norton in the 1970s color reboot of "The Honeymooners." Before that, she was half of what Broadway columnist Earl Wilson called, "the most successful women in nightclub comedy."

Sisters Betty and Jane Kean, he gushed were, "sometimes referred to as 'the female Martin and Lewis.'"

Oprah Winfrey and David Letterman didn't speak for 20 years until the two talkers buried the hatchet on CBS's *Late Show*. That night she proclaimed "I have never for a moment had a feud with you," but years later confessed that the arc of their acrimony began with her first appearance on his show which she recalled as "a terrible experience for me." Oprah claimed that members of the audience were drunk and unruly, and she told Dave, "You were sort of baiting the audience." Dave, however, thought it all stemmed from a chance meeting at a restaurant when he joked with his girlfriend, "I'm gonna make Oprah buy us lunch." Dave says he told the waiter, "Oh, this woman right over there has been kind enough to take care of our check." They smiled, waved, and left the restaurant, sticking her with the bill. "We got a free lunch and that's where it started," he recalled.

Delta Burke managed to get herself fired off of *Designing Women* after alienating herself from the cast and staff by publicly bad-mouthing producers Linda Bloodworth-Thomason and Harry Thomason in an *Orlando Sentinel* interview. Jackie Gleason and Milton Berle clashed after a couple of The Great One's writers were lured away by Berle. Red Skelton accused Sid Caesar of pantomime pilfering. You could see both their mouths moving when ventriloquists Paul Winchell and Jimmy Nelson exchanged words about who was stealing whose material.

After she fired the first shot in her newspaper column, Jack Paar lambasted Dorothy Kilgallen's sloppy speech saying "she must use Novocain lipstick." Carroll O'Connor battled with Norman Lear over the portrayal of the Archie Bunker character. Lear's revenge was vetoing O'Connor's chance to do lucrative beer commercials. David Letterman and Bryant Gumbel spent four years incommunicado. Not only did Dave leak the *Today Show* anchor's memo in which he criticized his co-workers, he also interrupted Gumbel during a 1985 outdoor remote interview from Rockefeller Plaza by shouting through a bullhorn from his 14th floor office window above. The fact that Gumbel's producer, Steve Friedman, had invited Dave to "interact" with the live show did nothing to redirect any of the anchor's anger.

Few feuds were as fierce as the heavyweight bout of egos for which I had a front-row seat. It was a battle royale between the king of late night, Johnny Carson, and the midnight idol, Mr. Las Vegas, Wayne Newton. From a petty rivalry the spat advanced to on-air ridicule. The clash then escalated to include Wayne paying a surprise visit to the *Tonight Show* offices for a terse face-to-face altercation with Johnny. In the midst of that hostility an unflattering NBC news story about Wayne led to the singer filing what became a successful $19-million lawsuit against Carson's network.

With animosity that rivaled a WWE death-cage match those two titans were next at war for a $100 million monument to their ego, one of their names in lights atop a massive resort and casino at the center of the famous Las Vegas Strip. During their battle for ownership of the Aladdin Hotel the drama really exploded when the FBI revealed that a Mafia hit had been ordered on Wayne's life. He took to wearing a bulletproof vest after NBC reported that he was the government's star witness in the trial of two mobsters. I didn't know whether or not Wayne was actually going to sing in a courtroom, and if the hit was somehow related to the competition for the prime real estate. What I did know was that working for Mr. Las Vegas unwittingly brought me uncomfortably close to some big-time madness.

Depending upon who you ask, the saga ended with either Wayne outfoxing Carson, or Carson having withdrawn his offer for the Aladdin. Either way, Wayne won. But like a kid with a new toy, the thrill of owning a hotel and casino quickly evaporated. Wayne soon sold the property remarking, "I didn't want people coming to me because the toilets are backed up."

The most serious death threats don't come as they did for Wayne, with an FBI warning. They come unexpectedly with a gun suddenly pointed at your heart. By virtue of just a few lucky hours I escaped a moment of terror that caused a lockdown at the NBC lot in Burbank. The last time I saw KNBC reporter David Horowitz he recounted his personal tale of TV trepidation that played out just a few yards from where I'd been standing earlier that day.

It was a typical Wednesday afternoon in 1987 when some nutcase with a gun found his way into Studio 10 at the network headquarters during a local newscast.

David was on the air, live, when the armed intruder took him hostage on-camera, demanding he read a statement. David remembered, "The guy came up and put a gun in my back. My first reaction was 'I can't believe this is happening.' His first words to me were, 'Read this or I'll shoot you!' I put on my glasses and said, 'Ladies and gentlemen, there's a man here who wants me to read a statement.' People later told me how calm I looked, but believe me, I wasn't!"

David began reading the rambling manifesto about aliens from outer space and the CIA. Unknown to David or the gunman, after 28 seconds the screen went black while a slide with an NBC logo was being found. It was then paired with a voiceover asking viewers to stand by "due to technical difficulties." Still thinking they were on the air, David continued to placate the armed mystery guest, during which time announcer Don Stanley began to adlib for the viewers. Fully aware of the crisis in the neighboring studio, the veteran voicer slowly ran through the various shows on the night's scheduled programming and offered quick mentions of the credits of Johnny Carson's guests until the newscast could resume.

When David finished reading the crazy rant, the stranger put the gun down and was escorted out of the studio. Only then did David learn that he was being threatened by a child's pellet gun, and that the would-be assassin was the son of a recently-fired KNBC news reporter. The 34-year-old interloper had also talked his way onto the lot during the previous week to scope out the logistics for his most unorthodox television debut.

The networks are always in rabid competition. In this case however, CBS would have gladly let NBC have the exclusive on armed intruders. Ah, but insanity is an equal opportunity offender. On an afternoon in the spring of 2002 a random wacko crashed his pickup truck through a security gate at Television City. He made his way into the building, pointed a gun at his own head and said, "I need help, now!" CBS employee Michael Grandinetti said the crazed intruder then pointed the gun at the mailroom supervisor and pulled the trigger. Twice. "I heard a clicking sound, but the gun didn't fire," he told the *Los Angeles Times*.

Police were called and Television City was evacuated. A four hour stand-off ended when the 29-year-old gatecrasher ultimately shot himself in the chest. He was taken to Cedars-Sinai hospital in critical condition. Actor David Tom, who played the character Billy Abbott on *The Young and the Restless* was taping a scene in which he was required to appear anxious. He said, "When the director told us there was a gunman on the lot and we would have to leave, I thought he was just trying to rile us up a little. Then I realized he was serious!" So much for method acting.

There's a 2016 movie about a Florida TV personality who packed a pistol, only to turn it on herself and pull the trigger, live, on the air. Sadly, it's true. Although 29-year-old Sarasota news reporter Christine Chubbuck apparently wanted her public suicide to be seen, don't search for it on YouTube. The station owner immediately locked away the only known copy of the tape and for nearly 50 years every request to view it, copy it or study it has been refused. While not certain of his motivation, Bob Nelson's widow continued to respect his wishes after his death, entrusting the tape to a law firm for safekeeping where it remains unviewed through all these decades. It's said to be that gory.

Personal problems were exacerbated by her boss's edict that Chubbock further sensationalize her reporting for supersized ratings. On July 14, 1974 the reporter became her own big story. Eight minutes into her Saturday morning WXLT-TV news and public affairs program, when there was a delay rolling a videotape, the host nonchalantly turned to the camera and said, "In keeping with Channel 40's policy of bringing you the latest in blood and guts, and in living color, you are going to see another first: attempted suicide." She pulled out a revolver and shot herself behind the right ear. Her head and much of its contents were blown forward, onto the lens of the camera which eventually cut to black.

The point: anything can happen in television, and pretty much everything has over the years. Much of the drama that plays out behind the TV screen is obscured by the manic 24-hour non-stop circus that's viewable on countless channels and streaming services that are all competing for a fragment of our attention. Some display a level of showmanship worthy of P.T. Barnum. For example, Jerry Springer's ratings surged in 1996 when he "rescued" a morbidly obese 37-year-old Ohio man.

Denny Welch weighed over 800 pounds and hadn't been out of his home in years. Jerry sat bedside while Welch cried, asking for his help. Jerry then directed a demolition crew in dramatically ripping away a wall of the home in order to extricate the huge man for transportation to a medical facility. Over 20 years later a highly-placed member of Jerry's producing team disclosed a glorious truth to me about the episode. Mr. Welch could actually have been carried through the front door of his home, but it was decided that tearing away a wall of the house was infinitely better television.

Chapter 2

Say hello to the perfect party guest. His down-home charm is wonderfully endearing. He's strikingly handsome, yet not at all conceited. His delightful self-deprecating demeanor and impeccable manners combine to make him irresistible from the moment you meet him. He's an easy conversationalist who's quick to laugh, and it seems impossible that he could ever wear out his welcome. As a bonus he brought his guitar and is willing, at the drop of a hat, to favor us with as many tunes as might be needed to keep the good times rolling. That perfect guest is Chuck Woolery. It was exactly that reputation as a party-perfect personality among the Beverly Hills glitterati that was Chuck's entrée into the realm of Hollywood celebrity.

Like so many TV hosts Chuck also started in radio, only briefly at Ashland, Kentucky's WCMI. He enjoyed more radio success as a singer-songwriter who managed to get some airplay when he was working the bars and clubs in Nashville. While Chuck came to L.A. to pursue his budding career in music, it was his chance meeting with comic genius Jonathan Winters at a Marie Calendar's restaurant that proved to be his break. It led to the comedian arranging an appearance for Chuck on Johnny Carson's *Tonight Show*. Another talk show host, none other than one-time Carson nemesis Merv Griffin saw that appearance. Merv then invited Chuck to sing on his program, as well.

While Chuck thought his crooning career was finally kicking into high gear, Merv had other plans for the singer. He was a sucker for Chuck's handsome face, southern charm, and emotional accessibility. Among other things, he thought they would be perfect attributes for a game show host. Merv was right. . . and he was wrong. Chuck is great on a game show, but more so as a guest judging by his first appearances on *Celebrity Bowling* and *Tattletales* with his former wife, actress Joanne Pflug. As a host, Chuck has always had occasional problems keeping the format straight and remembering the rules while trying to maintain a program's quick-paced forward momentum.

You see, Chuck can often be caught generally screwing-up the very basis of the job, leading the game play. With sufficient gaffes to likely nix anyone else's career as a host, Chuck has a secret weapon. It's his light-hearted "laugh-along-with-me, I'm-not-sure-what-the-hell-I'm-doing" attitude that has always been so honest, disarming, self-humbling, unique, and endearing that it more than makes up for his momentary uncertainty. It's proven to be his most appealing quality and a big part of his success.

Merv cast Chuck to front his clumsy pilot for *Shoppers' Bazaar*, with some of the fault for the poorly executed game perhaps being erroneously attributed to Chuck. When the troubled format evolved to become *Wheel of Fortune* other emcees were considered. The network's Lin Bolen wanted to test the even more studly Edd "Kookie" Burns. The actor stumbled through two pilots as dizzy and ditsy as if his head was spinning as quickly as the wheel itself. The former teen heartthrob from *77 Sunset Strip* admitted he had attempted to drown the butterflies in his stomach with a drink or three, confessing he was "scared to death." Suddenly, Chuck Woolery didn't look so bad and was back in the running.

For the *Wheel* pilots it was TV's master set designer Ed Flesh who took the upright carnival wheel, exploded its size, laid it on its side, face up, and positioned a camera some 30 feet above the stage. The lucky operator was perched on a tiny platform up in nosebleed territory shooting, with the help of a mirror, straight down from the studio rafters. NBC's engineering veteran Bruce Bottone was one of those cameramen. He remembers both the height and another challenge, "It was also hot sitting on that platform. I feel asleep once."

Economized crafting of the new wheel was adequate to demonstrate the innovation on the pilot, but reportedly its weight made it almost un-spinable by the players. The impromptu fix was to place a stagehand under the wheel with a video monitor. When the players tugged on it, he'd help start it spinning. Art director and set designer Ed Flesh explained that Merv freed up the cash for the series that enabled him to fashion a nearly indestructible steel wheel that weighed in at more than 2,400 pounds. It's mounted and balanced to be more easily set in motion, although it does take a strong yank.

One of Chuck Woolery's favorite adlibs when interviewing guests famous for their work in motion pictures was, "I'm no actor, and I have a couple of films to prove it." Those movies were *The Treasure of Jamaica Reef* with Stephen Boyd, Rosey Grier and Cheryl Ladd (1974), and *Cold Feet* starring Keith Carradine and Rip Torn (1989).

Optimizing Chuck's performance proved tougher than improving the original wheel's. In 2016, host extraordinaire Peter Marshall told me the story about the time early in Chuck's run as an emcee when NBC asked the master of the *Hollywood Squares* to sit in at a *Wheel of Fortune* taping. The network's idea was to have Peter give Chuck some host-to-host help with his hapless and halting delivery. Peter said, "I told them to leave Chuck alone." Sure, he was hopelessly lost at times, "but it was all so adorable! In trying to fix it, we'd only screw up Chuck's incredible charm."

NBC's head of daytime, Lin Bolen, described Chuck as "charming and folksy," adding warmth to the format. It seemed everybody agreed that he was adorable on *Wheel*. Almost everybody. Chuck eventually managed to piss off Merv. The story of his departure as the wheelmeister has been misreported so many times that it deserves to be set straight. Although we'd worked together for several months in 1991, the subject of his leaving *Wheel* hadn't then come up. More than a dozen years passed and we once again shared the stage, once more as host and announcer. This time it was at a new Harrah's Casino property on an Indian reservation near San Diego when we were re-teamed for *The Price is Right – Live* in 2004.

I'd been steady with the *Price* live production pretty much from its inception, hired for the gig while still on-stage after taping a CBS episode in 2003. Chuck was new to all things *Price*, brought in to cover a week between two of the several regular hosts who rotated in and out. Those guys knew the format well. Chuck was Chuck, and the audience loved him. Having had only minimal rehearsal time before fronting this unfamiliar 90-minute beast, Chuck was uncertain about the rules for most of the individual games that seem to be well known by every American with a television. Hell, it's all been on the air every day for half a century. More understandably, as this was a live stage production without commercial breaks Chuck was at a total loss with what to do after each game was played. He laughed at himself with "savers" such as, "I knew I should have been watching Bob Barker all these years." He'd get his laugh then add his own chuckle and say, "What do we do next, Randy?" Chuck's making fun of his foibles is probably the single most engaging attribute of any of the hosts I know.

That casino on the Rincon Indian Reservation was so new that the hotel wasn't built yet. As a result, Chuck, the cast, the staff, and I were all staying at an Embassy Suites about a half-hour from the venue. Sharing the drive between the two locations each day, as well as a few post-show dinners gave Chuck and me the chance to talk about everything—life, love, work, women, our adolescent sex lives, money, family, relationships, the TV biz, religion and politics. Jeez, we couldn't have more divergent political views. Guns, abortion, LGBTQ rights, U.S. foreign policy—there was zero common ground. With our mutual respect as a buffer to the usual rancor, it was enlightening to hear him articulate a heartfelt viewpoint so far removed from mine on so many issues. Good lord, I just hope he forgets to vote.

Chuck was such an engaging conversationalist that I hoped an occasional traffic jam might slow our drives. He spoke freely about his marital problems as well as the sad accidental death of his son, Chad. It was impossible not to draw closer to this guy. He was equally forthcoming about his dismissal from *Wheel of Fortune*, and shared a few candid thoughts about its creator. We agreed that Merv Griffin was a larger-than life character, gifted with many diverse talents. He could be magnanimous with his friends, and equally harsh with those he felt deserved his wrath. Chuck had crossed that line.

With the top down on his convertible at 50 mph on the two-lane winding mountain roads that connected with California Route 76, Chuck had one hand on the wheel and his mind on Merv's *Wheel*. The latter had spun to be a monster hit on NBC's daytime lineup and Chuck felt his contract was no longer doing him justice. Considering the show's success, Chuck was indeed being grossly underpaid. His ignorance was Merv's bliss, until Chuck caught wind of Richard Dawson's compensation at *Family Feud*. It motivated a little fact-finding mission into the kind of cash some other hosts with hits were pulling down. As someone else who traveled that path, Alex Trebek wrote in his 2020 autobiography, "Merv was notably stingy with performers. He did not like paying the going rate for his hosts or on-camera people."

When Chuck approached Merv for a raise, the country bumpkin was outclassed by the long-time veteran of big-time showbiz and real estate wheeling and dealing. Chuck made several unsuccessful attempts at having his deal revised. Members of the crew recall that included staging a sit-in with fellow raise-seeking letter-turner Susan Stafford. The two reportedly locked themselves in a dressing room, refusing to perform. After about an hour the pair relented when Merv, through the closed door, threatened to fire them both on the spot. The former big band singer-actor-host-producer-hotelier and mega-successful business mogul eventually came forward with a substantial bump in pay, but it was still short of the going rate for hosting a hit with something along the lines of a 40 share of the audience. Merv wouldn't budge further.

Chuck told me that, without any intent to extort any more money he once informally expressed his frustration about his deal with Merv to one of the NBC suits. Wanting to keep their hit's host happy, Chuck says the network volunteered to throw in enough of the peacock's cash to bring him to parity with other emcees. Chuck naively explained, "I wasn't expecting anything to come from the conversation, but the network found the extra money for me."

When word got to Merv that Chuck had committed what he considered a disloyal breach of protocol—going to the network with his salary concerns—Merv blew a gasket. Not because Chuck got more money, the networks are thought to have an endless supply. Merv felt betrayed by the end-run around him, over his head, right under his nose. All of Chuck's assurances that he hadn't overtly requested any money from NBC failed to calm his boss' outrage. How dare Chuck break the chain of command and negotiate anything for himself based on the strength of Merv's show? If the network was so happy with *Wheel* that they wanted to lubricate it with more money, that cash should go to the production company as a bump in the license fee. Seen through the eyes of a long-time supplier of programming to the networks and a veteran of Hollywood deal-making, Merv was right. From the vantage point of a hillbilly guitar picker, there was no real harm in any of it.

Art director Ed Flesh created an exciting yet elegant look for the huge *Wheel of Fortune* set that included a large puzzle board on wheels, a display area for prizes, and a home base for the host and players that incorporated his innovative idea for turning the wheel on its side.

My best recollection of the figures Chuck shared along our drive had him earning in the neighborhood of $300,000 to $325,000 a year. It was a nice neighborhood, but having heard salary quotes for network-mate Peter Marshall, ABC's Richard Dawson, and CBS's Bob Barker, Chuck quickly came to believe his neighborhood was a ghetto. He felt that $500,000, reportedly Peter's salary, was more appropriate for service as Merv's wheelman. Chuck said that Merv popped for a raise to around $375,000, and recalled that the network coughed-up another $10,000 a month. How quaint the fight for a half-million-dollar salary sounds in light of today's $5 million, $10 million, and $15 million annual paydays for game show emcees.

How much Chuck extorted from NBC was not the issue for Merv, it truly was the principle. So, after six successful seasons Chuck had sold his last vowel. Merv fired him, but with unusual kindness he gave his host a chance to say his on-air goodbyes on Christmas Day, 1981. Many years later Chuck courageously went public with a self-disclosing version of the tale that he only minimally whitewashed. Chuck confessed that he overestimated his role in the runaway success that *Wheel of Fortune* was enjoying: "Looking back at it, I let my ego get in the way of my decision making and it was a terrible mistake. I'm happy for the success Merv has had with the show."

Belying that claim, Chuck made a point of telling *The Hollywood Reporter* in 2021 that "Merv was so upset with me, they started taping over all the old *Wheel of Fortune* [master tapes]." Painting Merv as a miser, Chuck made the highly questionable claims that the starting salary for his replacement, newcomer Pat Sajak, was a mere $65,000 a year. He added that Vanna White got a paltry $200 a show before the program was sold to Coca Cola. Then, "They bumped them all up to multi-million dollar contracts," said Chuck ruefully.

If life could be edited like a television program, I suspect there's much for which Chuck would like a chance at a "take two." His transition from struggling Nashville guitar picker to network star had its awkward and funny moments. Back when NBC's Burbank lot was churning out game shows, the peacock's hosts would often encounter each other. *Celebrity Sweepstakes* emcee Jim MacKrell remembers leaving the commissary with his lunch partner Peter Marshall, and their passing Chuck on the lot's midway. The *Wheel* host was wearing a red silk smoking jacket with an ascot tied around his neck. Jim says they stopped in their tracks long enough for Peter to ask Chuck, "Who the fuck do you think you are, John Barrymore?!"

The handsome host lived to fight again after his showdown with Merv, more than once. *Love Connection* was one of those rare times when the planets all aligned. It was the right show at the right moment with the right emcee. With over 2,000 episodes produced over the course of a dozen years the matchmaking series brought in the coveted young demographic which translated to millions for both Chuck and the showrunner Eric Lieber. Looking to extend his host's popularity during the successful dating show's run, Lieber had the other half of Stage 9 at Sunset-Bronson Studios outfitted with a trendy pastel-colored talk show set. He was hatching a grandiose plan after one of the times Johnny Carson was renegotiating his contract and teased that he might step down from his cushy throne.

The Chuck Woolery Show was a talk-variety hour formulated to prove that the affable game show host had what it takes to be the heir to *The Tonight Show*. Attempting an on-air audition of sorts, Lieber replicated many of the trappings—a live band, an opening monologue, and pre-interviewed guests who would engage in the *de rigueur* witty chatter and crass plugging. It was an attempt at a lower-budget clone of NBC's prized late night franchise. In execution, it didn't come close. It couldn't. Hell, there's only one Johnny. For nearly 30 years a parade of aspiring comics, singers, actors, and even sports stars have repeatedly proved that nobody has what Johnny had on-air.

I was invited aboard this ill-conceived voyage in what was pitched to me as a quasi off-camera Ed McMahon-type role. Long odds though they were, what if Lieber was somehow able to steer this boat into NBC's 11:30 p.m. berth? The guy had been in the business since the 1950s and worked with successful talkers Dick Cavett and Mike Douglas. He'd launched several popular creations into syndication before this one with Chuck and, who knows, he just might be able to navigate his ship of hopeful fools into boatloads of cash.

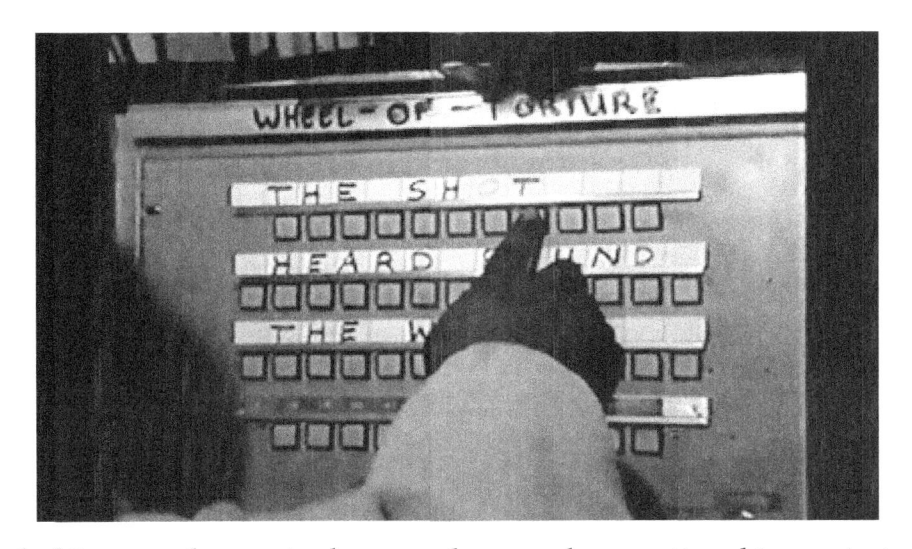

The *Wheel of Fortune* electronics have made several generational jumps in technology. In the early years at NBC the puzzle board needed to be rolled out of the studio to reload the large plexiglass letters for each new puzzle. Lighting the letters was very much an analog affair at first, with the label at the top of the control panel indicating that some tape dates were agony.

Well, it was the 13-week cruise from hell. I learned the hard way what dozens of his former employees came to know, which is that Lieber was among the most obnoxious people you could ever hope to avoid. Following on-air interviews with guests that were less than sparkling, I watched this ogre eviscerate segment producers. Lieber was too hot-headed to wait for the show to end. The drama of his screaming and the occasional crying by berated employees played out during commercial breaks in earshot of the live audience, and it was damned near impossible to distract the crowd from the shouted firings. There was an endless temptation to want to say, "Pay no attention to the asshole behind the curtain!" For the visiting tourists it was an infinitely more authentic look at show business than NBC's or Universal's ersatz behind-the-scenes tours.

I only wish I'd kept a count of the parade of staffers who were unceremoniously voted off of Lieber Island. A reunion of those whose snuffed careers, wounded emotional health, and even physical death might be attributed to Lieber could fill a very large Starbucks. Yes, I said death—a true medical flat line. You see, one beloved senior producer, the delightful pro Charlie Collaruso, suffered a heart attack soon after enduring one of Lieber's ridiculing rants. All of the angst through

Charlie's impressive 40-year career as a producer paled in comparison to a single soul-crushing dose of this boss' wrath.

Lieber's humiliating dressing down could injure even the hardiest veteran, and it was apparently overwhelming for a soft-hearted sweet guy like Charlie. I'm convinced it was a factor in precipitating the heart attack that suddenly ended Charlie's career and almost his life. Following several surgeries he rallied after receiving a heart transplant, but he was never the same again. Dear Charlie was one of the best of the good guys, mortally wounded on the job. For Lieber, it was just another day at the office.

Life was no better behind the curtain that separated us from *Love Connection*. There, other announcers were watching the same craziness that I was. Before he became the math whiz that game show developers turn to for computing odds, probabilities, and payouts David Hammett had a couple of conversations with my counterpart Gene Wood who summed it up pretty well: "It looked laid back, but the tension off camera was enormous. It was not a happy place."

I sensed the dysfunction in the air at Chuck's talk show on day one. I'm not clairvoyant; it hit like a two-by-four from Lumber City. Lieber was walking through the studio gathering employees in little groups to instruct us to avoid any dialogue with Chuck. It was fine to say "Hello" and "Goodbye," but we were to shun any and all conversation and inconsequential small talk with the host. The reason Lieber gave was that Chuck was very preoccupied with the details of this new assignment and that any distraction would break his concentration and hurt the show. It was like some mean elementary school teacher was ready to scold us for violating an arbitrary "no talking" rule.

Experienced crewmembers and staffers know to respect the talent, and know not to impose upon their time and divert their attention with idle chatter. Everybody already understands that it's a work environment. Pitching an occasional one-liner about the goings-on can lift the mood, reacting to emcee-initiated conversation can boost the energy, but it's not a social event. Talent has the obligation to be chatty and charming on cue, on camera. It's a huge imposition to put them in a position to deliver those same goods in uninitiated backstage small talk, or be obliged to react to the kind of fan fawning they get from the public. Even without Lieber's edict it was unlikely that anybody would have stepped past the line to break Chuck's concentration. The executive producer taking the time to warn everybody on set to keep their distance from the host was highly unusual and, I thought, downright asinine.

Now, in retrospect, understanding Eric Lieber's nature it was obviously just another manifestation of his control issues. He wanted to keep Chuck in a bubble and be the only influence. Lieber was an equal opportunity offender, sharing his gift for hostility among the entire staff and crew including me. Being the only other regular cast member didn't confer any immunity from my own small doses of ridicule. Whenever this putz producer walked across the stage during my pre-show warm-up he rarely missed the opportunity to brighten my day with a comment. Something like, "You told that joke yesterday and it wasn't funny then either." Lovely. I thought audience members were supposed to do the heckling.

Often warmer-uppers include someone from the audience in the act, giving outlet to the extroverts who seem insistent upon being noticed and somehow stand out from the crowd. Managed judiciously, giving them their moment to tell a joke or sing a verse can appease that showoff while also creating an opportunity for some laughs that can help the mob of strangers to bond. Eric's comment while an audience member was singing a quick ditty: "If I wanted that guy to do warm-up, I'd have hired him!" This many years later I think it's actually a funny line and something I might say, if I didn't care about anyone else's feelings.

The kicker to this whole affair came years later, after Eric Lieber's death, during the week that Chuck and I were re-teamed for *The Price is Right - Live*. You remember the "Don't talk to Chuck rule," right? Well, the meandering conversations he and I shared along the snaking back roads of San Diego County eventually turned to memories of his talk show. There was light-hearted nostalgia as it was now many years in the rear-view mirror of our respective careers. Recalling the experience with the benefit of that distance made for some interesting reflections on the whole affair. Suddenly, Chuck's mood changed. He became a bit somber as he mentioned that there was one uncomfortable memory about that series that remained bothersome all these years later.

Chuck confessed that he still had an unresolved feeling that he had somehow, unwittingly been a jerk to his co-workers. He was convinced that he must have committed some *faux pas* that had made the workplace feel sterile, if not bordering on hostile. He wondered what he had done to alienate the staff, stifle the crew's usual playful banter, and usurp the customary on-set spirit of camaraderie. As a sensitive guy, it had apparently bothered him for over a dozen years. What I said next blew Chuck away.

I told him the simple truth. On the very first day of taping Eric Lieber had instructed each and every person on the set, under penalty of being fired, not to engage him in conversation. Chuck had no idea there had been a gag order in effect, and couldn't believe that his partner had intentionally sucked the life out of that sound stage. With my explanation he sat silently, baffled, and dumbfounded. I could see him trying to process the absurdity. A moment later he shook his head and said, "I guess nothing Eric did should come as a surprise, but this does." After so many years and all their projects together Lieber was clearly still somewhat of a mystery to Chuck. Their strange relationship did much for Chuck's bank account, but did little for his sanity.

In some markets our *Chuck Woolery Show* was in head-to-head competition with Jenny Jones's chatfest. The former *Match Game* contestant, *Press Your Luck* champion, and *Star Search* winner managed to talk through a total of about 1,500 episodes, and survive the fallout from an unprecedented homophobic homicide. After her March 6, 1995 taping, one member of a gay secret crush surprise confrontation ended up murdering the other. The episode didn't air, but it got lots of play on Court TV's coverage of the trial. From the testimony we learned that the show had provided guests with a line of credit that was honored at the hotel bar. When the object of the affection called the producer to say he was nervous about meeting the man or woman—he wasn't told—who was infatuated with him, the advice he was given was to have a few drinks courtesy of the show before coming to the studio. Classy, huh?

The object of the secret crush, Jonathan Schmitz, was found guilty of second-degree murder for the shotgun blast that killed Scott Amedure after they returned home to Lake Orion, Michigan. A jury awarded $25 million in a finding that *The Jenny Jones Show* and Warner Bros. were irresponsible and negligent for intentionally creating an explosive situation without due concern for the possible consequences. The judgment was later overturned and, as recently as 2020 Jenny herself contacted me with a reminder that ultimately she, Warner Bros., and the show were all exonerated, held harmless. That was indeed the outcome. Nobody murdered anybody on Chuck's talk show. Too bad, maybe we would have lasted as long as Jenny.

Exploiting unrequited romances with surprise introductions of couples where the passion isn't reciprocal is like carnival fire eating in that there's so much that can go horribly wrong. You spray a mouthful of gasoline at an open flame and hope you don't set your hair ablaze. It's a dangerous hook on which to hang hopes for a single successful hour, much less an entire series. Just ask Bob Eubanks. He built his 1992 show *Infatuation* on secret crushes, luring unsuspecting objects of affection to meetings under false pretenses. It evaporated not too long after one contestant hired a lawyer, unhappy that the woman twice his age told America that her crush developed after they secretly had sex in the back seat of a car.

Bob got burned yet again when contestants on his *Family Secrets* had a bigger secret than anything they divulged to Bob or the producers. A father and his 10-year-old daughter appeared as a family on the 1993 NBC series, and they had an unexpected secret; dad's girlfriend was covertly posing as the wife and mother. They successfully played their con, but when word of their $6,000 prize reached the real mom, that lady and her lawyer were on the phone. The episode was pulled before its airdate. As Shakespeare might have said, the fault, dear Nielsen, is not in our stars, but in our pursuit of ratings.

Bob Eubanks as well as Chuck Woolery have both since passed the age where the current crop of television producers and programmers suffer apoplexy at the mere thought of putting them on camera. They're both still very much alive and well and, judging by the infomercials they've hosted in recent memory, still know what to do in front of a camera. Chuck is still witty when he's not talking politics. Bob still had his magic when he fronted a couple of stunt episodes of *Newlywed*

Game that I announced in 2009 and 2010. More recently he's returned to staging live shows that feature familiar games from television.

How old is too old? The number can be as low as 47. A smiling face that brightened mornings for ABC viewers for 21 years, Joan Lunden has had a few sharp words about being dumped from *Good Morning America.* Her audience appeal was rewarded with a promotion from feature reporter to co-host in 1980 where she worked opposite David Hartman and, later, Charlie Gibson. In September of 1997, just days from her 47th birthday, the new season debuted without Joan. Why? She already gives you credit for knowing: "When people see a person they've spent their mornings with for 20 years shown the door so a 30-year-old lookalike can come and take her place, they're not dumb."

The fact is that admiring audiences are receptive and even welcoming to a friendly familiar face they've enjoyed watching over the years, even if that face has a few more wrinkles. It's true regardless of their age, their Q-Score, or any focus-group mumbo-jumbo. For those just joining us, today's program is "Ageism; Discrimination or Wisdom of the Ages?"

Chapter 3

An acute case of advanced age was not the only reason that Gene Rayburn wasn't welcomed when his signature show, *Match Game,* was revived for ABC in 1990. Already in his 70s, Gene had heartfelt hopes about being asked to host, and was deeply disappointed to be passed over. The sting intensified when he learned that his longtime pal from the 1970s incarnation of the show, Charles Nelson Reilly, was returning to a seat on the panel. Gene was not delusional, however. He understood that Charles was about a dozen years younger and wasn't going to be the face of the show. It was a tough reality to accept that his days as the game show equivalent of a leading man were over.

The shocker that hit him like a sucker punch was the "no" that came loud and clear from an overture for him to return as another of the half-dozen jokesters on the panel. After serving as the host of every other version of this perennial over the span of 25 years, Gene felt inextricably linked to the program and couldn't understand how the TV gods didn't also see it that way. It broke his heart.

Gene's early TV years had included a marathon of game show appearances, starting with a panelist post on a list of long-forgotten 1950s parlor games from the industry's top game gurus Mark Goodson and Bill Todman. Then, after hosting *Make the Connection, Choose Up Sides,* and *Dough Re Mi* his long association with *The Match Game* started after senior staff producer Frank Wayne presented his idea for the show to Goodson. With the accepted theory that the simpler the game the better, Frank's pitch was as uncomplicated as his concept: With the goal of matching your teammates, "name something associated with an elephant."

A rehearsal of *The Match Game* in NBC's studio 8H with celebrity father and daughter Gordon and Meredith MacRae. Gene Rayburn added just enough sparkle to make the simple format afternoon appointment television through 1,760 episodes. Photo from the author's collection

With its debut during the final hours of December in 1962, *The Match Game* enjoyed seven years on NBC. Then, after resting for four, it returned in 1973 with a Los Angeles-based amped-up version for CBS. Producer Ira Skutch confirmed that tripling the number of celebrities was inspired by the success of NBC's star-studded *Hollywood Squares*. The freshened format ran for nine seasons both on network and in syndication during which time it regularly brought CBS the crown for daytime's top-rated program. While that would seemingly assure Gene's eternal affiliation, with the 1990 revival we learned otherwise.

Much credence has been placed on the theory that Gene's chances were dashed a few years earlier with a five-second mention of his 69th birthday on *Entertainment Tonight*. Promulgating that explanation was Gene himself saying that his phone stopped ringing after the world learned his age. What else is a guy going to say, "I was looking old and wasn't as sharp as I once was?" It's a rare performer who can take full ownership of the responsibility for their own fading marketability.

Friends and fans had been hopeful Gene could return to at least serve as an occasional panelist on the re-tooled version of the evergreen format. That included at least a couple of the dozen-plus old Goodson-Todman pals who had worked with Gene over the years and were now part of this revival. Certainly somebody in a decision-making position must have remembered that *Match Game* dominated the daytime ratings under his tutelage through much of the 1970s. Apparently not. When the idea was rejected, Gene's agent Fred Wostbrock pitched a mere cameo appearance—perhaps simply having Gene share a few words with the new host at the top of the premiere episode. Ross Shafer was that new host and I know he'd have been open to a moment of adlibbing with Gene. I'd bet a pallet of Lee Press-On Nails that the idea was never mentioned to him.

Gene attributed the rejection to the network, and it's possible his hosting was shot down by some ABC desk jockey with the memory and attention span of a gnat. Those nameless MBA-graduate stuffed suits who understand little about the cultural significance of television, much less any shows older than they are, get blamed for so many sins, only sometimes rightfully. At other times, pointing the finger at the network is a convenient ruse long perpetrated by producers who don't want to offend talent. Attribute it to some whiz kid who thinks something called *Match Game* must be a striking competition among pyromaniacs, but the fact is that after this property that had been a hit for both NBC and CBS, was now landing at the hat-trick network, nobody was going to tell Goodson how to cast his show.

Fred and friends argued that the veteran broadcaster was so identified with the hit that a quick appearance to perhaps pass the familiar long skinny Sony ECM-51 microphone to the new emcee might have actually helped to tie the new venture to the show's former glory. For viewers who didn't know nor care about any past it would have been over before there was a chance to ask, "Who's that old guy?" The sad truth is that Gene really wanted another opportunity to bask in the warm glow of a Mole Richardson 2K fresnel key light. There's an old adage that Billy Crystal referenced perfectly in his 1992 movie and 2022 Broadway musical, *Mr. Saturday Night*. For performers who long thrived on the love from audiences—

the metaphorical hug from strangers—when that lifeblood no longer flows, a little piece of them dies each day.

Over a couple of dinners with Gene and our mutual agent we reviewed the "no" that repeatedly came as the response to each idea that Fred pitched for getting Gene one last hurrah. The once-celebrated TV personality acted as if he wasn't miffed by the rejections, however as the conversations progressed Gene's attempt to appear dismissive of the insult was less and less convincing. TV had been Gene's home and the door had always been open to him during a lifelong career that started when TV first signed-on. He was crushed to learn that he was now considered to have zero value. It was cruel and harsh. In short, it was the unseen side of television.

What Gene didn't know was that this was also karma because Mark Goodson, himself 75 years old at the time, was still harboring animosity from his former trials and tribulations with Gene. They'd had their share of disagreements. Goodson's longtime colleague, former team member and prolific game creator Bob Stewart summed it up concisely saying, "Gene Rayburn was not a favorite of Mark Goodson's, just wasn't a favorite… a very talented guy, but… his humor was kind of cutting… a lot of us react personally."

Indeed the partnership hadn't been all smooth sailing, and there was a paper trail that documented the pair's disharmony. Among other things, there were the memos about Gene getting too many laughs. Despite the show's success Goodson eternally advocated for the traditional thinking to prevail, in which the contestants are always the most important people on a game show. TV's unwritten rulebook would also advise that on a show with six celebrity jokesters the host shouldn't be playing for laughs. The emcee's function would be more of a facilitator and catalyst for the celebrity guests' shtick. Peter Marshall was masterful in that straight man role at *Hollywood Squares*. However, to know Gene is to know that kind of performance would be all but impossible.

While it apparently offended some of Goodson's sensibilities that Gene's showmanship frequently upstaged the execution of the show's format, first and foremost Goodson was a practical man. He allowed himself to be mollified by the cash and cachet of another ratings hit. Along with the writing from Dick DeBartolo, Joe Neustein, Elliot Feldman, Joel Hecht, Jake Tauber, R. Patrick Neary, and Bobby Sherman it was Gene's antics that added the spice, elevating what was merely a simplistic program of "B" and "C" level celebrities playing fill-in-the-blank. Its rise to wear daytime's ratings crown a mere six weeks after its debut was an unprecedented achievement.

Goodson had sublimated similar misgivings in the past with other successful hosts, and would again in later years. He wasn't too proud to surrender a share of his battles to further his greater goals of respect, recognition, and acceptance, especially among the east coast cultural elite. Those rewards, seemingly in that order, appeared to be Goodson's motivators. By the mid-1970s and beyond, increased wealth no longer topped the list. While Goodson was critical of Gene's performance, Gene's chief complaint about Goodson concerned money.

Among the company's hosts he was indeed earning less than others responsible for lower Nielsen numbers. It's a lament that he apparently shared freely as a number of his past co-workers and friends, Burt Dubrow included, who remembers to this day Gene's venting his financial frustrations. Only in retrospect, decades after it was all history did Gene disclose to me that he had since come to realize how much of the responsibility he carried for his own salary inequity. He had made a poor choice in his selection of a business manager.

Looking to avoid high drama in contract negotiations, Gene mistakenly assumed that there would be some benefit for being, in a sense, a member of the boss's family. He explained that was his rationale for selecting the same financial guru as Mark Goodson. Instead of generating some sense of kinship with his employer, it backfired. Sharing the same business manager created a blatant conflict of interest during negotiations. In retrospect Gene came to the conclusion that being the lesser client, he got the short end of the deals. It was an "Aha moment" that came way too late.

So the 1990 *Match Game* reboot launched without its former captain and sank after a single season, earning the dubious distinction of being ABC's last daytime game. Had Gene been fronting the series it's unlikely its fate would have been any different. It would have merely given Gene a short reprieve. The fact was, the long run had ended for a man who simply loved the business.

I remember Gene's excitement sharing 60-year-old memories as he described NBC's gleaming and glamorous new 30 Rockefeller Plaza headquarters. His first dreams for a life in broadcasting came into focus there among the pioneering generation of network pages and tour guides shortly after the building first opened for business. He described how magnificently the new lobby black marble sparkled, and how the gold ornamentation shined as if it were 24 carat. He even remembered the carpeting. He said he'd never stepped on anything softer, more foot-caressing or more luxuriously accommodating.

Gene reminisced about his greatest pleasure during breaks as a page, standing outside of Studio 8H, holding the door open a few inches and watching the great maestro Arturo Toscanini rehearse the colossal NBC Symphony Orchestra. Gene claimed that the virtuoso could hear a single instrument's off-pitch note within the vast mass of music emitted by 100 players, and was not shy about openly denigrating that musician with a litany of crude Italian curses. Occasionally, after loudly chastising the players Toscanini would storm out of the immense studio into the elevator that was his exclusively, for a retreat to his private sanctuary deep within the building.

With talent, ambition, passion, and drive Gene bridged the chasm from minimum-wage page to respected broadcaster, and then to star by first plying his craft at a radio station 60 miles up the Hudson River, WGNY in Newburgh, New York. That was followed by brief stints at WITH in Baltimore and WFIL in Philadelphia, but Gene was happy to eventually find an opportunity back in the Big Apple. Although he ultimately became a cornerstone of NBC's national radio program *Monitor*, forgotten by most was Gene's tremendous success, and failure, years earlier on local New York City radio. He enjoyed a long run as half of WNEW's highly-rated morning team Rayburn and Finch, waking the lion's share of the metropolis' listeners. As Gene remembered his partner Dee Finch for a WNEW retrospective, "We enjoyed each other's companionship, we socialized and laughed a lot. But most of all, we loved our work."

A young Gene Rayburn remembered his earliest days in radio for WNEW's archivist, "I... eventually ended up at WNEW in New York where the base pay was very high by my standards: $45 a week. But we also got commercial fees: eight cents a spot. If you did 100 spots a week, you'd end up with $53!"

Gene Rayburn teamed with Dee Finch at WNEW. The duo's entertaining radio show brought them listeners, albeit not much more money. Gene remembered, "Over a period of years, we got up to $65 a week and 12-cents a spot!"

The lowest point in Gene's early career also played out behind a radio microphone. With plans for the successful team to move their show from WNEW, in 1952 Gene signed a five-year deal to return to 30 Rock for his old company's local flagship radio station, WNBC. His mic-mate, Dee Finch, was to do the same but opted last minute to stay at WNEW. Gene went solo into the WNBC studio and straight into the crapper. Without a partner to play off, react to, and counter-punch the punch lines, Gene himself said, "I fell on my ass."

That WNBC morning show was sinking like the Titanic, with Gene starring as the iceberg. While the station was prepared for him to walk the plank, his contract didn't allow for him to be jettisoned. NBC could consider him a flake, his show a flop, and his earlier success a fluke, but they couldn't simply take him off the air without continuing to write him weekly paychecks. His 1952 no-cut pay-or-play contract was negotiated when NBC badly wanted at least half of the city's favorite wake-up team. Rather than fire and pay him off, the network gave Gene a demotion all the way down to television. TV was the ne'er-do-well newborn division that had still not grown into profitability, and some of Gene's assignments were for the local NBC station WNBT, not even the network.

Gene announced WNBT's *Knickerbocker Beer Show* as well as hosted an aborted pilot that was, no doubt as exciting as its name, *Where Are You From?* There were random assignments to remotes and even a public affairs program or two. Some New Yorkers saw Gene on *The Sky's The Limit*, but tuned out in droves for his short-lived *Bright Ideas*. He became an all-around utility player, ready to cover any on-camera or radio assignment, local or network.

Forgotten by all, Gene included, until I asked about the experience of his being briefly pressed into service to fill-in for Buffalo Bob Smith as the facilitator of the magic in Doodyville. Yes, Gene guest-hosted television's first monster-sized hit kids show, *Howdy Doody*. Word is that as the ringleader in a world of silly characters Gene was brilliant. With others to counter-punch and react to—even puppets and a mute clown—Gene's imaginative playfulness and comedic gifts were obvious. Unfortunately, it's doubtful many of the network suits were watching.

By 1954 Gene's talent as an ensemble player was being fully recognized. He was on programming wizard Pat Weaver's radar during the development of the landmark series that's now old enough to be collecting Social Security. Gene was partnered with Steve Allen for the original *Tonight Show* where he was a reliable sidekick lobbing straight lines and pitching for advertisers, as well as clowning through little news summaries, weather breaks, and even ski reports that he remembered were part of the program's early format for a couple of weeks.

Not particularly enamored with the late night gig, Gene told me that he stayed longer than planned due to some medical issues, including a bout with hepatitis and weeks spent healing from skiing injuries. Excluding those hiatuses, even after his *Tonight Show* gig ended, not too many months passed during which Gene wasn't back on the tube. Those opportunities included everything, prestige and cockamamie, from hours on the respected *Today Show* to co-hosting an hour of a circus rehearsal in Florida, from Miss Universe pageants to forgettable time fillers such as *Helluva Town* on New York's local WNEW-TV. It also included 1958's *The Steve Lawrence-Eydie Gorme Show*, a summer replacement series that kept Steve Allen's timeslot warm. Funnyman Bill Dana remembers it was his first job as head writer, Nick Vanoff's first full-fledged producer gig, as well as both of theirs and Gene's first work from NBC's recently acquired Brooklyn studio facilities.

During his prime, Gene was appreciated for his boundary-bending wit which was tempered by an instinctive insight into what would play in American living rooms. Gene also carried a righteously-earned reputation as a troublemaking nonconformist among some of his co-workers. In addition to his country home in Connecticut, Gene had an apartment on Manhattan's East Side, sufficiently close to 30 Rock that he would often ride his bicycle to work. However, network management nearly ran through a ream of paper writing memos, warnings, and threats about his disruptive practice of riding the bike through the building's narrow hallways. They seemingly only served to encourage his rebellious spirit. Gene pedaled around the *Match Game* set in studio 8H, and even rode that bike into frame for his on-camera entrance at the top of an episode of the syndicated *What's My Line?* that was then taping in studio 8G. Years later and 3,000 miles away, Gene was still bucking authority.

Veteran producer Burt Dubrow is the genius behind Jerry Springer, Sally Jesse Raphael, Dr. Drew and other ratings-winners' TV successes. He remembers an occasion during which Gene was reciting a litany of his frustrations, something he did not infrequently for fellow professionals' sympathetic ears. Among them was how Mark Goodson and Ira Skutch were planning to lock him behind a podium for the 1973 *Match Game* reboot. It would have been an ill-conceived attempt to cram this walking and talking round peg into a very square hole at center stage. He won that battle. When taping began on June 25th, Gene prowled the set as a free-range emcee.

The author with Gene Rayburn holding the CBS *Match Game* clapperboard slate, a souvenir from the show that was his biggest success. For three years of its run *Match Game* was the highest rated of all daytime shows. Photo from the author's collection

While rating points are the most tangible yardstick, Gene's frustration with his salary also begs the question of what's fair compensation for exuding charm and wit while creating the illusion of intimacy with home viewers? On camera since TV's earliest years, Gene perfected the magic trick of reaching through the electronics to make an up close and personal connection, one-on-one with individual audience members. It was always the hallmark of the very best broadcasters. In the cases of Bill Cullen, Dennis James, and other ubiquitous guests in viewers' living rooms, it engendered the kind of loyalty that could help flip a flop into a hit as well as sell soap, soda, cereal, cigarettes, and cemetery plots.

What helped separate Gene from the pack was proving himself equally adept at playing large enough to reach the last row of a theater balcony. He had the singing, dancing, and acting chops to make his mark in summer stock and dinner theater, as well as touring with the national company of *Come Blow Your Horn* and other successful stage productions. Reflecting on his experiences in that world, Gene said the most exciting moments of his professional life were on a Broadway stage, breathing the rarified air that comes with treading the boards in the glorious theaters on New York's Great White Way.

Gene's triumphs as a broadcaster included more than sufficient highlights to make any performer proud, but he expressed a muted sadness over not having been able to create more opportunities in the realm that proved to be his truest passion. Then came the surprising admission that he would have traded all of his TV and radio victories for a career doing nightly battle in the theater. He considered his greatest professional achievement to have been standing center stage at the famed Schubert in 1961 playing the lead in *Bye, Bye Birdie*. Yes, the lead. He had the stage presence and he had the voice. In fact, among Gene's earliest dreams was to become an opera singer. The dancing posed the greatest challenge, in large part because of his skiing accidents.

Gene said he worked countless hours on developing the skill to hold his own when he inherited the role from a masterful hoofer, Dick Van Dyke. He explained for Long Beach, California's *Independent Press-Telegram* in 1972, "Weathering that dancing project was the hardest thing I've ever done, but it was worth it in every way. Particularly because it was the dancing itself—six solid months of it—that finally rehabilitated my left leg. Without it, I still might be a semi-cripple." Gene won the role in *Bye, Bye Birdie* when Hollywood beckoned Dick Van Dyke to replace Carl Reiner in his self-penned sitcom about a TV comedy writer.

The role on that television classic became Dick's after none other than Johnny Carson was briefly considered for the plum casting as Rob Petrie. *The Dick Van Dyke Show* was originally intended as a starring vehicle for its creator, Carl Reiner. Yes, when it came time to recast, Johnny turned down the sitcom which then opened the opportunity for Dick. There's one more random turn of fate in this story that makes the phrase "it's a small world" ring so true. Gene's understudy at one point during that run of *Bye, Bye Birdie* was future *Match Game* supporting player Charles Nelson Reilly. Even long before the game with Kevin Bacon the entertainment world's tiny degrees of separation were sometimes quite astonishing.

The Guinness World Records folks honored Regis Philbin on his syndicated morning show as the person who has appeared on television more than anyone else. As of 2011 they tallied a career total of 16,746.5 network, syndicated, and local hours. The computation behind that award is disputed by some who believe Hugh Downs continues to hold the true record that was earlier sanctified by Guinness, at least the record for network exposure. Gene Rayburn was not too far down that list, among the top five, after establishing an early beachhead on the television landscape and tallying hours on *The Tonight Show*.

During the years that Gene's star was ascending, the happiness in his home life was being eclipsed. His seemingly happy-go-lucky personality hid sadness from the past and present. His father died when he was an infant, followed by the passing of his only brother, the result of a traffic accident. That loss became especially traumatic as he suffered with the belief that his mother somehow blamed him for the death. As an adult, Gene spent years in therapy that his daughter felt were not especially productive. Lynne Rayburn was quite poetic in stating that her dad was far more adept at expressing what was in his head than he was at sharing what was in his heart. Poignantly, at our last dinner together Gene shared how sorry he was that he hadn't been the devoted supportive husband and father he would have liked to have been. I wonder if he ever expressed that to Lynne, or his wife, Helen.

At work, among Gene's last few series was his least favorite, co-hosting the short-run ill-conceived *Hollywood Squares - Match Game Hour* with John "Bowzer" Bauman that wrapped in 1984. The only slightly less odious *Break the Bank* followed in 1985. After a last muted roar fronting 1989's *The Movie Masters* on AMC cable the once celebrated emcee was reduced to only occasional appearances on the tube, usually as a talk show interviewee. By the early 1990s he'd been relegated to TV's low-rent district including *The Howard Stern Show*. Sorry, Howard fans. I also appreciate the talents of The King of All Media but his show is the last gig any pro underlines on their resume.

It was a sad reality that Gene had trouble accepting. After all, Betty White, roughly a contemporary, was as welcome as ever to walk onto the set and into a role on pretty much any show she chose. He'd heard his old friend wax philosophical about her advancing years: "You don't fall off the planet once you pass a given age. You don't lose any of your sense of humor. You don't lose any of your zest for life." Sure, easy for Betty to say.

As Gene Rayburn and the Earth rotated around the sun a few more times the once spry performer began to walk with a cane. His voice that had once filled Broadway theaters had lost much of its power, becoming thin and raspy. Gene had become forgetful, and was now a bit disoriented at times. He did have one last glorious moment just a few weeks before his death in 1999. It was a big one. Gene received a lifetime achievement award from the Academy of Television Arts and Sciences.

On stage to receive the honor it seemed Gene shared more tears than words in his acceptance. It was now noticeable to all that the veteran broadcaster was suffering in the early stages of dementia. He must have sensed, in Shakespearean terms, that he would soon be shuffled off this mortal coil as not long after that night at the Emmys he packed up his Sherman Oaks apartment and returned to New England. He spent his last days near his only child, Lynne. As we all will be,

Gene was canceled by the big network programmer in the sky. Lynne sprinkled Gene's ashes in her garden.

As knowledgeable and well-read as Gene was, and as articulate, quick-witted, and charismatic as he could be, no discussion of Gene could be considered complete without mention of his great attraction to members of the fairer sex. Despite a half-century marriage to Helen, Gene had a heightened interest in women that he was known to take past the flirting stage. Helen was attractive, witty, and charming, but I guess some people need more love than any one person can give. If you watch 1970s *Match Game* reruns with that insight in mind it's blatantly easy to spot him fawning over attractive women, both celebrity panelists and contestants alike. Beyond the occasional benign kissing, keep an eye out for him pulling pretty females close to him as he explains the "Super Match" rules.

I intend no disparagement of a man whom I respect and found to be positively delightful, open, friendly, and generous with his time and insight. If anything, I celebrate his honesty and I salute his prowess. I'll simply say that at one of our last long leisurely dinners Gene checked his watch a few times as we lingered over coffee at the now defunct Butterfields on the Sunset Strip. He explained that he was very much looking forward to returning to his hotel room and meeting with a new female friend. I assumed he was joking. After all, he was in his 70s.

Oh no. Gene insisted that he was not joking and that he had indeed arranged earlier in the day for the evening's female companionship. There was nothing that hinted the two would be playing a prototype Milton Bradley home version of *The Amateur's Guide to Love* in his hotel room. It appeared the talents that earned Gene his renowned reputation as a womanizer were still intact. If indeed he wasn't kidding, with his status as a widower at the time I could only cheer him on. Go, Gene, go!

Chapter 4

There are a great many truly wonderful people who have been in the business of producing and distributing television. Indisputably, TV's top trader from *Let's Make a Deal* and other series, Monty Hall, was as honest, warm, and charitable as just about anyone on the planet. Certainly Tyler Perry came into the world with virtually nothing and has since created an empire without any aspersions lodged against his character or criticism of his business acumen that has reached my ears. Is there anyone who ever worked with, met, or simply watched Betty White who didn't love her? Well there was one, and that very rare relationship is explored later in these pages.

Conversely, as there are in the general population there are also likely a proportionate number of reprobate, ne'er-do-well, morally bankrupt, purely evil people who have found their way into this industry. The less said about them the better.

Most everyone else lives somewhere in the middle as fallible humans who occasionally struggle to play by the rules, while striving toward their goals with their sights on success. Those are the people who arguably are the most interesting as their triumphs are the most glorious and their missteps the most fascinating. The stories of their errors in judgment also carry the greatest potential to benefit their fellows—us, and who among us has nothing to learn from others' trials and errors?

This book is focused primarily on illuminating stories of those imperfect people at their crossroads. It's not a collection of hateful exploitation but a study of the human condition and, overwhelmingly, a love letter to television. It's all purposely presented with a measure of humor and snark—well-meaning sarcasm, impertinence, and irreverence for its entertainment value because, after all, the television world is a world of entertainment.

It seems like no two people got into this TV world in exactly the same way. There are no licensing forms to fill out. There's no written test. No government agency stamps your passport, and climbing a fence or tunneling under a wall will only get you access for a day. I remember there was one man, one woman, and me all at one end of a long mahogany conference table in what felt like a massive, sterile room. It was devoid of personality, with beige walls and beige carpeting as far as the eye could see.

Pitching for my first big-time TV job there I confessed, "No, I've never announced a live-to-tape TV show, but I KNOW I can do it. As a disc jockey I've read thousands of live commercials. I've also emceed concerts, parades, car dealership grand openings, radiothons, fire musters, chili cook-offs, wet t-shirt competitions, even Cub Scout jamborees."

They may believe me, but do they believe IN me?

The abundance of joy that radiated from my family's old black-and-white 19-inch screen more than compensated for family dysfunction, school bullying, and childhood illnesses. Hitchhiking on the smiling effervescence of the singers, dancers, comics, and game show hosts, TV offered me an escape from trauma as well as every adolescent's frustrations and fears. Its power was transcending, otherworldly. I knew I HAD to live in that universe. The man about to determine my destiny is Ron Ziskin, executive producer of a successful syndicated show now starting its ninth year. He shifts in his chair and looks to the woman with him, talent executive Claudia Cagan.

"The live announce isn't any more challenging than the work I've done in post-production on other shows. I can nail it live, I promise!" I'm at the last step of the audition process, and my destiny lies in their hands. What can I say to close the deal without repelling them with the scent that Hollywood finds most repulsive? The stench of desperation—one whiff, and you're branded a loser.

They're listening, but they're not smiling.

"I do a great audience warm-up. I just worked on *The Mondo Variety Show* for HA!, the new comedy cable channel." Two beats of silence and I realize I'm sounding as naïve as a wanna-be outfielder hoping to join the roster of the Los Angeles Dodgers by recalling a ground ball he hit as a ten-year-old in Little League.

I'd bluffed my way into the outer orbit of this world many times. As a kid in New York I sat through a rehearsal of *The Tonight Show* as The Mighty Carson

Art Players camera-blocked a sketch for that night's taping. When director Bobby Quinn asked Johnny Carson for a second rehearsal NBC's top-earner started walking up the audience aisle straight towards me as he exited, saying "No Bobby, it's good." With that refusal the studio fell silent. The temperature instantly dropped ten degrees, but Johnny smiled and winked at me as he passed.

I don't know why my mind chose to rerun that memory while I'm in the middle of fighting for my fate. I continued, "Plus I've studied Johnny Olson and Don Pardo; I know every word of their warm-up acts. I CAN DO THIS, Mr. Ziskin!"

Forget Dale Carnegie, Zig Zigler, Tony Robbins, and Wayne Dyer, all of whom would have me think about BELIEVING I can do the job. Hell, I already KNOW with every fiber of my being that this is my calling. I feel like I've been preparing for a gig like this almost since birth. But how can I convince these people? Finally, there's an encouraging sign. He smiles and says, "Call me Ron. What do you mean 'you've studied these guys?'"

Ah, an opening! This just may be the chance to leap from the fringes of show-biz adjacency with my nose pressed against the glass, to being one of the sanctified in that sacrosanct inner circle. I explained, "All through junior high and high school, any day I could find a way to cut classes I would take the subway to 30 Rock and watch tapings, all day, one show after another. I was there so often that Johnny Olson even put me in his warm-up act."

It was all true, and I think he senses that honesty and sincerity. I remain silent and watch as he processes it all, afraid I've already talked too much. He leans forward towards me and breaks the momentary silence. "I started as a page at NBC in New York," he said. I instantly answer, "Then you probably threw me out of the building a bunch of times!"

She laughs. Then he laughs.

"If you were a page, then you know I'm telling the truth! *Match Game* taped in 8H on Tuesdays and Wednesdays. *Concentration* was usually in 8G; *Jeopardy!* was in 6A, and sometimes 8G. . ."

He's smiling—almost laughing—and nodding "Yes!"

"Of course *The Tonight Show* was in 6B. Wasn't that band great?" Carson was still on my mind, and I now realized why. I was only in California because I was hired by another superstar while in the middle of his white-hot personal blood feud with Carson. Being drafted into the war between these two showbiz titans was how I came to be sitting in this room on this former movie studio lot.

These two, Ziskin and Cagan, are standing between me and my manifest destiny. While I'm frantically ad-libbing, trying to keep their interest, they start giggling. I must have sounded like Dustin Hoffman in *Rain Man* as I rattled off more ancient history. "Joan Rivers was in 3K, the old *Howdy Doody* color studio. But most of the third floor was news. *The Today Show*, too, after they moved from the storefront. Did you know that they left their cameras hot all day? Once I discovered that, I played cameraman for hours. I got pretty good coordinating the zoom and focus."

I'm not sure exactly why, but they seem to be enjoying this. I have them. I keep going.

"Johnny Olson knew how much I loved watching him work. One time in the *What's My Line?* audience, when the show was running short he suddenly recommended me to writer Dick DeBartolo. Instantly, I was a contestant being used to fill the few extra minutes. That's where I got this ring." I twirl my hand to model the jewelry while putting on a stereotypically cheesy announcer voice to describe the "stunning 18-carat gold band highlighting the luminous round-cut Linde star sapphire, from the Sarah Coventry jewelry collection…"

This pair of earthly Saint Peters nod at each other. TV's pearly gates are about to open.

Ziskin cut to the chase. "We tape tomorrow, and I want to use you for the two shows that we'll do. No promises beyond that, understand? Claudia will get all your information and I'll have the office contact your agent with your call time and parking information. Have fun and do a great job. It'll be good having you on the team!" We shook hands and exchanged farewells. I tried to act calmly professional as he exited.

That's it! I'm in! Holy shit, I'm about to become a trusted member on these producers' A-team, responsible for helping to nurse their coast-to-coast baby. The far-fetched pie-in-the-sky childhood dream is starting to come true. I was effusive in expressing appreciation to Ms. Cagan, probably repeating "thank you" way too many times.

Numb and emotionless, I started walking to my car. As I drove off the lot I was suddenly flush with the rush—elated, nervous, excited, enthused, and more than a bit afraid. After watching from the living room and staring from studio audiences, looking for a crack in the impenetrable protective perimeter, there was no greater excitement than the thought of finally getting to work with the talent and technicians creating TV programs.

On one hand this is all deadly serious, but I'd also sat on a sufficient number of plywood game show sets as a contestant to already know that the whole business is mostly a silly illusion. Still, what the world of television lacks in delivering on that childhood promise of eternal joy, it more than makes up for with fascinating personalities, glitter and glamor, and hocus pocus in sharp focus. There's so much to learn and so much to enjoy working amid the highest per-capita population of beautiful people that can be found anywhere.

The syndicated daily talk show *Hour Magazine* hosted by Gary Collins added a combination announcer/audience warm-up personality for this season. After an apparently disappointing tryout with a female whose name I never heard spoken, the new guy was now me. I was to report to Stage 1 on the nearly 100-year-old studio facility on Sunset Boulevard where, a century earlier Rin Tin Tin was the highest paid actor on the lot. The top dog to boast that honor years later would be Judge Judy. In the tradition of Hollywood deceptions, for each their bark was worse than their bite.

This historic Hollywood property has an imposing façade with a long line of pillars that looks something like the Supreme Court or some ancient Greek monument, built decades ago for some long-forgotten Warner Bros. movie. It had been the studio's home from 1919 until soon after talkies replaced silent pictures. The pioneering film that ushered in that new era, *The Jazz Singer*, was partially shot here along with hundreds of other movies. All of the great Looney Tunes and Merry Melodies cartoons with Bugs, Daffy, Porky Pig and Yosemite Sam were also created on this hallowed real estate in a wooden building lovingly referred to as Termite Terrace.

The next morning, I arrived at the former home of *Gene Autry's Melody Ranch*. With the exception of the square footage devoted to the onetime cowboy star's Golden West Broadcasting and his KTLA-TV, the former Warner Bros acreage had become a rental lot for all manner of programs, from the ancient *Seven Keys* with host Jack Narz, to *Solid Gold* and *Name That Tune*. Even *Donny and Marie* and *Gunsmoke* had brief stays. I was a contestant on *Face the Music* about eight years earlier in Studio 3. *The Biggest Loser* staged weigh-ins here, where singles once told Chuck Woolery about their *Love Connection*, and grocery shoppers went wild in the *Supermarket Sweep* aisles. Tough guy Jimmy Cagney shoved a grapefruit into his co-star's face when his controversial *Public Enemy* filmed in these studios where Alex Trebek, Wink Martindale, and Ben Stein all queried game players. For a few seasons Wayne Brady zonked countless costumed contestants here, where Agent 86, Maxwell Smart first sought to foil archenemy K.A.O.S., and a favorite sitcom family set a record for kitsch with *The Brady Bunch Variety Hour*. Today, this facility is called Sunset-Bronson Studios. It's home to Netflix, and the rented sound stages buzz with the work of various content creators.

I adjusted my tie and headed for Studio 1 and *Hour Magazine*. The daily hour was the latest in a lineage spawned by the pioneering success of *The Mike Douglas Show*. It was a formula that Westinghouse Broadcasting, Group W, created to provide programming for its handful of owned stations, many of which lost network affiliation when the ancient DuMont network folded. The company had successfully exploited variations on the basic recipe for decades with hosts including Steve Allen, Merv Griffin, David Frost, and John Davidson. Later, Wil Shriner, Vicki Lawrence and Marilu Henner were similarly packaged for syndication.

Yes, this is the same Westinghouse that made your grandmother's refrigerator. The conglomerate that grew from the invention, patent, and manufacture of the rotary steam engine and railroad air brakes was now manufacturing entertainment. *Hour Magazine* host Gary Collins was a delightful and charming occasional actor and broadcast host who easily filled a couple of thousand hours with glib conversation. Entertaining in the moment, none of it was particularly memorable. It was the talk equivalent of an all-kale diet, pleasant but not the least bit filling, and you eventually stop eating out of sheer boredom. Gary could well be considered beefcake to the perimenopausal female viewers stereotypically believed to be the bulk of the daytime audience. He was as handsome and elegant on the set as he was on the screen. As the show's patriarch, Gary immediately made me feel welcome.

The funniest story I heard about Gary was from the 1965 filming of NBC's single-season comedy-adventure hybrid *Wackiest Ship in the Army*. As Lt. Rip Riddle, Gary was to jump into a small boat with a couple of other crew members and row like hell to the mother ship while supposedly dodging enemy fire. Halfway across the artificial lake on Columbia Studio's backlot the skiff starting taking on water, quickly sinking while the cast members tried their best not to ruin the take. In less than a minute they were up to their tits in water, laughing while the enraged director yelled "CUT!" He immediately walked off the set never to return. Indeed, then and there the director quit the 29-episode series as the actors stood in the shallow pool, laughing their wet asses off. Gary claims he wasn't the only one peeing his pants, but there was no way to be sure.

Gary Collins as George Adamson in NBC's short-lived series *Born Free* (1974).

I quickly learned how beloved Gary Collins was in the social circles populated by the elite among television talent, producers, and executives. He was a golf or tennis partner to many and, with his wife Mary Ann Mobley, the couple was seemingly in every other famous married pair's address book. Gary also helped launch a few friends' careers, Marc Summers' included. To me, he seemed almost too sane and well-adjusted to be in show business.

My faith in Hollywood's unfailing ability to attract, create or nurture a touch of irrationality in all who spend too much time breathing the recycled studio air was ultimately restored. Years later, I learned that Gary had not escaped that reality. Sadly for such a sweet guy, he had been arrested for at least three DUIs as well as a couple of other assorted misdemeanors. None of that diminishes his talent or his kindness. To me, it simply confirms that he belonged in the television milieu.

To my thinking, a few DUIs only proved that Gary Collins had respect for showbiz history, simply carrying-on a vestige of a deeply-rooted tradition. Boozing wasn't a ritual reserved only for the ranks of talent. In New York, Hurley's Bar was conveniently located on the ground floor of NBC's headquarters and was so well patronized by talent, staffs, and crews that it earned its own extension on the network's in-house phone system. Things weren't quite as convenient on the opposite coast. You had to cross the street from CBS Television City to join your show's imbibing brethren. One senior engineer who worked some of that facility's most prestigious programs recalls there was a similar direct line between CBS's phones and the closest bar. "Everybody went over to Kelbo's on the other side of Fairfax to get smashed before the show. The technical director would ring us just in time to get back before air." *The Young and the Restless* actress Melody Thomas Scott confesses, "Kelbo's is no more, but oh, if its walls could talk. They would've said, 'Pssst! The entire cast and crew of *Y and R* gets drunk here! And then they go back to work! Still drunk!'"

You have to go way back before TV or radio, and even before vaudeville to try to discern when panicky performers first partnered with potent potables. As the saying went, there was nothing better than booze to drown the butterflies. Seeking reinforcement for the unnatural act of stepping out on a stage in front of throngs of staring strangers, vaudevillians who relied on liquid fortification used to say, "I wouldn't think of going out there alone!"

One of the 20th century's most respected comedy writers, Hal Kanter, told me the story of how W.C. Fields wouldn't begin to get out of bed until Paramount sent a driver to the comedian's home with the day's salary, in cash, in advance, and his breakfast—that was ten $100 bills and a bottle of booze. Eventually Fields took the bottle down from his lips long enough to get dressed and into the studio's car for the trip to the set.

There are a sad number of entertainment professionals who liked distilled spirits more than the alcohol liked them. That includes one broadcaster whose drinking ended his career just as he was helping to start mine, dear Jay Stewart. The veteran broadcaster and TV sidekick from Monty Hall's *Let's Make a Deal* came to anesthetizing the stresses of his work and the emotional pain from a troubled home life. The production company of the final series he worked, *Sale of the Century*, was a co-conspirator in keeping Jay's secret hidden and keeping him employed for as long as possible before, ultimately, there was no way to avoid firing him. Months later I was with Jay in his office on a Friday evening saying goodbye and responding to his "I'll talk with you Monday." It was just hours before he used a gun to say goodbye to the world that Sunday afternoon.

Accommodating television performers' peculiarities and peccadillos started before TV sets were in most homes. A man I worked for in the 1970s had long ago been a respected radio director before rising to the presidency of the once mighty Mutual Radio Network. Some 25 years before our paths crossed he helmed several ancient hit series including the popular *The Romance of Helen Trent* and *Backstage Wife*. His name was Blair Walliser, and by the time I met him he was in the earliest stages of dementia. If not, then his hard drive of memories needed some serious defragmentation. Just the same, the recollection of his first television experience was intact. The story never varied the dozen or so times he told it to me, each time thinking it was the first.

In 1950 Blair was hired by the embryonic ABC television network to produce one of their very first attempts to match the prestigious live dramas for which CBS was becoming celebrated. For this early installment of their new *Pulitzer Prize Playhouse* ABC was presenting "Abe Lincoln in Illinois" starring the distinguished actor Raymond Massey who'd been celebrated for his portrayal of our honored 16th President both on Broadway and in movies. As a radio director looking to establish himself in this new world, Blair was fixated on proving his understanding that television was more than just radio with pictures. Extra effort was made to keep any microphones out of sight.

Actor Raymond Massey joked that he was "the only actor ever typecast as a president" after his celebrated performances in *Abe Lincoln in Illinois* on Broadway, film and television. (1940)

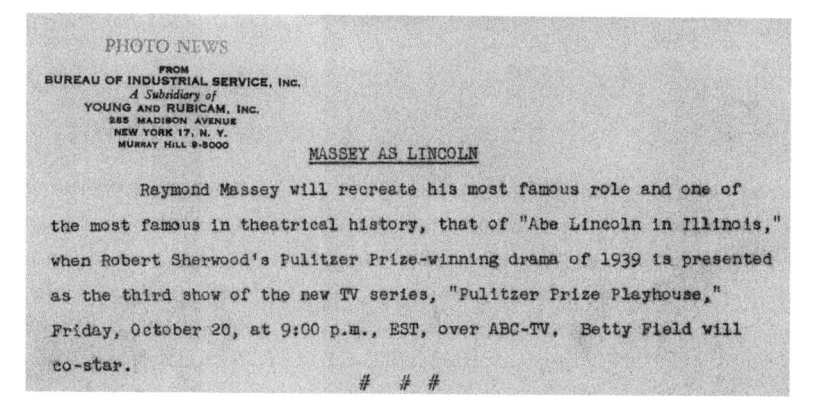

Radio director Blair Walliser's first television assignment was a baptism of fire bringing an award-winning drama to the small screen for ABC and advertising agency Young and Rubicam.

With audio of the entire drama to be captured by a pair of non-directional RCA-44BX microphones following the action on booms over the heads of the actors, on the night they were to go live Blair directed that all performers remove their shoes to keep the dialogue from being muddied by the sound of their footsteps. Understanding that the cameras would never go low enough to reveal that simple cheat, everybody complied. Everybody except for the great thespian in the lead role. Although apparently happy through hours of rehearsal to have donned an elaborate costume including a recreation of Lincoln's familiar and unwieldy eight-inch-high felt stovepipe hat, Raymond Massey steadfastly refused to simply remove his shoes. As time ticked down to the broadcast, Blair directed, asked, cajoled, and begged the star to cooperate. Still, Massey silently declined the request.

With mere minutes before the broadcast was to begin, with his own reputation at stake, Blair finally resorted to threatening the actor with physical violence, something along the lines of "By the time I'm through with you, no fucking Abe Lincoln beard will be able to hide the damage I'm going to do to your goddamned face!" With that, the stoic actor asked to speak to Blair in private. Massey finally explained with great humility that he had been too embarrassed to remove his shoes in front of the cast and crew because he had holes in his socks. This was no way for an award-winning thespian to be viewed by his fellow performers. With the star's dignity in serious jeopardy, Blair simply exchanged socks with Raymond Massey and the show began with few seconds to spare.

Sometimes obliging a performer is far less stressful. The day Dom DeLuise guested with Gary Collins on *Hour Magazine* was memorably funny. The comic actor's joking was a refreshing break from the two mainstays of daytime talk shows—shameless plugging and cooking demonstrations. Dom was one of the quickest-witted people ever to grace the tube, and had more than enough personality to fill an IMAX screen. As Mel Brooks has said, "Dom created so much joy and laughter on the set that you couldn't get your work done. So every time I made a movie with Dom, I would plan another two days on the schedule just for laughter."

Dom had the chops when it came to improvisation and adlibbing. Dean Martin's no-rehearsal contract stipulation and his single-take rule for the Sunday afternoon tapings of his old Thursday night NBC show made booking guest stars tricky. Dom, Bob Newhart, Charles Nelson Reilly, Nipsey Russell, and Jonathan Winters were in the small cadre that producer Greg Garrison felt confident would always be up to the task of freewheeling with the crooner.

Always a welcome guest, actor and comedian Dom DeLuise made over 100 talk and variety show appearances on television, in addition to on-camera and voice acting roles in over 100 motion pictures.

Dom was incredibly funny and endearing both on-air and off, and he was delighted when I told him I thought so. I had intended to ask about his little-known gig as one of the run-through contestants at *The Newlywed Game* presentation that helped Chuck Barris successfully sell the format to ABC. Dom and his wife Carol added to the laughter to such an extent that host Bob Eubanks credits the couple with helping to fast-track the series onto the network schedule without a pilot. I didn't pursue the conversation after seeing how sadly incapacitated Dom was in his unsuccessful battle with added avoirdupois.

Shortly after his arrival Dom faced an embarrassing challenge. While he seemed to be walking without difficulty, he was in no condition to climb the tall flight of stairs to the second floor make-up and dressing rooms. This was before the Americans with Disability Act required easy wheelchair access everywhere, before the ancient stages were brought into compliance by adding passenger elevators.

While Dom made it all one giant opportunity to mine the bottomless pit of fat jokes, I can't help but think how humiliated I would have felt in his position, forced to wait while a crewmember was summoned to operate the prehistoric, creaking dusty freight elevator in the far corner of the soundstage. That metal cage that resembled a medieval prison cell was his only way to get to the second floor, and back down.

As heavy as he was, Dom was energized, kinetic, and as lighthearted as ever on the set and especially when tape rolled. He had one of the more unusual demo segments, far better than yet another celebrity stinking-up the windowless stage by cooking some garlic-pasta concoction. He explained how he and his friend Burt Reynolds had lamented the relentless progress of their receding hair lines. This was no trivial matter. After all, among the $4.5 million of debts in Burt's bankruptcy filing was a giant unpaid $12,200 bill from Edward Katz Hair Design. Apparently the wigmaker was kind enough not to repossess Reynolds' rug.

Dom's demo revealed how he and Burt had one-upped medical science, finally discerning once and for all a major cause of male baldness. It is (cue: tympani drum roll) washing one's face! If these follicly-challenged friends were to be believed, the proper way to show respect for thinning hair is to not get it wet indiscriminately. Dom demonstrated the correct procedure he and Burt had adopted for face washing. It began with a plastic shower cap worn to cover the diminishing tresses, all the way forward to cover the hairline lest the repeated wetting and drying overtax the dermal papillae.

Gary and Dom in shower caps splashing each other would have been even funnier, except that Dom was serious. Apparently he and Burt had spent many hours lamenting, reflecting, and conjecturing about their lost strands. After the show, Dom volunteered that this hair issue was indeed serious business. He outed not only Burt, but also Elton John, Sean Connery, William Shatner, Mel Gibson, Ed Asner, Bruce Willis, and John Travolta. Dom also had the full list of senior classmen, naming Frank Sinatra, Bing Crosby, George Burns, Jack Benny, Steve Allen, Don Knotts, Tony Bennett, John Wayne, Charlton Heston, Humphrey Bogart, and Henry Fonda as all being among the afflicted toupee-topped talent.

No sooner than Dom's washbasin was struck, props for another demo segment were being prepped. Producing six of these *Hour Magazine* shows during a three-day taping week was a logistical challenge. My only responsibilities were to deliver the big scripted show openings that billboard the guests, introducing Gary, teasing into commercial breaks, and rattling-off sponsor plugs. Oh, and to keep the studio audience entertained and enthusiastically reacting to the show. That warm-up gig provided a small bump in pay as I was a performer already seen or heard on the show, but for charismatic and funny non-cast members who can carry an audience through a four or five hour sitcom taping the prize usually exceeds $5,000 a night.

The higher hierarchies of producers also get big bucks. Theirs are for staying calm while anticipating the myriad of potential problems, big and small. One day it was apparent a huge problem was on the mind of one segment producer. It was the day Shirley MacLaine was a guest.

Chapter 5

Few of the A-level celebrity guests who have circulated through the talk show circuit were as charming as Shirley MacLaine. With a mantle weighted down from Oscar, BAFTA, a Kennedy Center Honor, and lifetime achievement awards, this star has almost as many Golden Globes orbiting her living room as there are moons circling Jupiter. She's still active, most recently performing as the tart-tongued American Martha Levinson on the British series *Downton Abbey*. Ms. MacLaine is Hollywood royalty. You can see her in movies from the years during which she was an honorary member of the Frank-Dean-Sammy Rat Pack. As Sinatra might say about this former hoofer, she's a dame with ring-a-ding gams.

The otherwise mellow *Hour Magazine* staffer charged with producing the actress' appearance that day was in a tizzy. Ms. MacLaine hadn't caused any uproar, she hadn't even arrived yet. Merely anticipating her presence on the set was enough to trigger Defcon Two, prepare to deploy for a nuclear conflict. What could possibly be so scary about a lady who reportedly has "Welcome aliens and UFOs" on her front door mat? The high anxiety was rooted in the fear that somebody might offend the star by making mention of—or lord help us—making a joke about her being imbued with ESP, Extra Strange Philosophies.

Beyond her most impressive body of work as an actress, a mention of Ms. MacLaine's name often brings to mind her outspokenness about all manner of new-age spiritualism. MacLaine's career longevity has benefitted from her gift for continuing to look good through her many centuries on Earth. You see, nobody has lived longer or lived as many lifetimes. At the 2017 Academy Awards she acknowledged a standing ovation self-mockingly by saying "That's the nicest reception I've had in 250,000 years."

Through books, speaking engagements, magazine articles, interviews, and perhaps mental telepathy Ms. MacLaine has expounded about her beliefs at times with a vigor that one witness reported can approach the religious fervor usually reserved for revival meetings. It would all be boring except for her fantastic claims, such as her previous life in Atlantis as the brother of a 35,000-year-old spirit named Ramtha. That's just the beginning. *The Daily Mail* reports the star has also been "a Turkish harem girl, a Hebrew slave, a prostitute put to death by beheading, and an ancient Egyptian princess."

It's all good with me. However, as Ms. MacLaine has fielded a lifetime of questions on the subject, some laced with ridicule, our semi-neurotic segment producer had a look of terror in her eyes as she kid-proofed the stage. There was to be no fooling around. I was not to deviate from the script in any reference to the star. Perhaps she'd heard about the time in 1963 when Ms. MacLaine allegedly cold-cocked a *Hollywood Reporter* gossip columnist who dared to diss her. It was the punch heard around the world, as it reportedly even motivated President John F. Kennedy to send the star a congratulatory telegram.

Enrolled at age three in ballet school to correct her difficulty walking, Shirley MacLaine danced her way into a highly-celebrated 60-plus year acting career.

Segment producers and talent coordinators are expendable. If a celebrity complains about their treatment the only way to have them entertain an invitation for a future return booking is to assure the star and their agent that the offending producer has been jettisoned from the show, if not the entire industry. It would be the kiss of death if word circulated among publicists in celebrity-land that a visit to a particular program was anything less than a lovefest both on and off-camera. With that knowledge, our producer responsible for the star's visit added the instruction that, even in chatting with the audience during stopdowns—the breaks during taping—I was to steer clear of any seemingly clever repartee about new-age spirituality that could be misconstrued. I planned to follow that advice but, well, all plans are subject to change.

During their on-air chat Ms. MacLaine told Gary Collins about her life, the one she's living now. They discussed her dancing into show business, her first acting experiences and, predictably, her belief in reincarnation. Later, during a commercial break after we had all seen that the star was not an ogre and indeed had a sense of humor about herself, I dared take a dangerous detour into jokeland. It's my job to keep the audience entertained, so when inspired by a funny thought it's hard to fight the urge to make good use of it. Plus, with the self-destructive streak that's in all of us I guess I couldn't resist touching this hot stove.

There was appreciative laughter from our spectators, mixed with the simultaneous sound of producers' rectums puckering when I made a glancing reference to our guest's just-discussed belief in re-embodiment. It was the perfect set-up. I told the audience, "Ms. MacLaine is one actress who we are sure has never appeared on… *One Life to Live*." Bada-bing. Surprise. She heard it, and she laughed!

As Ms. MacLaine walked off the set a few minutes later she passed by my little podium, paused, and smiled. That's as much personal interaction as we ever had, until about 20 years later. It was stranger than strange. After so much time, so much water over our respective dams, so many people passing through both of our lives, and—for her—so many lives, this amazing lady blew my mind. We were suddenly and unexpectedly face-to-face in a grocery store in Malibu. Respecting her privacy I merely smiled and nodded to acknowledge her without saying a word. It was Ms. MacLaine who started a conversation with, "I have met you before."

What the hell? She said it quite emphatically as a simple statement of fact, not as a question. There's no way anybody could remember a silly joke, with a passing glance and a smile more than a dozen years earlier. I don't consider myself to be that memorable, but she's convinced that our paths had crossed and instantly rejected my suggestion that perhaps I resemble someone she knows. Maybe she thought she recognized me from Atlantis 35,000 years ago.

"No, it's you. I'm certain we met before." Ms. MacLaine was unwavering so I confirmed that we indeed had encountered each other once previously. Then the actress sent a little chill down my spine by nailing that moment from the past. "It was at that talk show…" I interrupted her with my amazed reaction, saying that I couldn't believe her powers of recall. She asserted that it was more than simple memory: "There are forces in the universe that most people fail to recognize…" Suddenly entering the Twilight Zone of unexplainable phenomenon she demonstrated her point by telling a story right there in the produce aisle as I admired her melons, and other produce selections.

The actress explained that a few years earlier while renting an oceanfront bungalow there in Malibu, she took a trip to New Mexico. On that visit she bought a house up on a mountain in Santa Fe. She said, "When I walked into that house for the very first time with the real estate agent, I immediately sensed that a dancer had lived there. Not only had a dancer lived there, but she also died there in that house. I told the agent exactly that. The agent immediately confirmed, 'Yes. Ballerina Vera Zorina was a previous owner and she died in the home in 2003.'"

With my eyes no doubt registering astonishment, Ms. MacLaine continued. She immediately bought the home right on the spot, without even seeing many of the rooms and has loved the place ever since. That's all she said. That's all she needed to say to make her point. She simply punctuated our encounter with a big smile and a wink. Although her lips weren't moving I got her message loud and clear: "Believe, trust, be open." I'd have talked longer with Ms. MacLaine but she probably already knew whatever I could possibly have said.

Ms. MacLaine's familiarity with the netherworld would have been welcome at the Walt Disney Studios' 2015 unveiling of the founder's restored offices. VIPs can now visit the plush suite complete with the piano and bar just as Walt left it. Executives of the company known for its creativity swore they hadn't "imagineered" any of the several strange occurrences during that dedication. When composer Richard Sherman approached the piano to play Walt's favorite song, *Feed the Birds*, "The piano started… beating time," Sherman said. "It was amazing. Something was clicking away."

Actress Karen Dotrice of *Mary Poppins* fame remembered, "The lights were flickering. All of the heads of the studio were there. The people who organized the [event] were mortified. We went, 'Don't worry. That's Walt. He's joining in.' Walt was completely present." By the way, this was a couple of years before California legalized recreational marijuana use.

So, Shirley MacLaine isn't the only believer in the unknown realm of the afterlife, or afterlives. She's certainly had enough unique earthbound adventures for several lifetimes. The star has appeared in over 65 films despite winning lawsuits against a major movie studio and against an influential producer, events that would have ended lesser careers. Beyond her UFO sightings and the personal encounters with aliens she's documented, who else can claim they danced with Soviet leader Nikita Khrushchev?

That one is irrefutable, as President Eisenhower was among the dozens who were present for that moment on the 20th Century-Fox set of her movie *Can-Can*. It was on September 19, 1959 during Premier Khrushchev's visit to Los Angeles. When a trip to Disneyland for the Soviet statesman was ruled out for security reasons, the U.S.A.'s full roster of entertainment ambassadors was present for a lunch at the studio commissary, invited to join the odd couple, Shirley and Nikita.

A strange moment at the height of the cold war on the set of 20th Century-Fox's *Can-Can*. Shirley MacLaine greeted Soviet Premier Nikita Khrushchev in broken Russian, and then attempted to engage him in an impromptu dance. Khrushchev jovially begged off, preferring to shake hands with Frank Sinatra. (September 19. 1959)

The meal was anything but an intimate interlude as the attendees included Bob Hope, Frank Sinatra, Marilyn Monroe, Kirk Douglas, Jack Benny, Dean Martin, Edward G. Robinson, Judy Garland, Elizabeth Taylor and Eddie Fisher, Tony Curtis and Janet Leigh, Shelley Winters, Kim Novak, Ginger Rogers, and Zsa Zsa Gabor. As spectacular an event as that lunch must have been on the movie's set, the Russian premier called *Can-Can* exploitive and pornographic. He complained that he'd rather have spent the afternoon with Mickey Mouse.

Dancing with Khrushchev and guesting on *Hour Magazine*, Shirley MacLaine proved on both occasions not to be the temperamental, hypersensitive, evil prima donna that our segment producer feared. However, there are contrasting opinions. For one, we needn't look any further than her daughter, Sachi Parker. While making the rounds on the interview circuit to promote her book, the star's only child lambasted her famous mom for making a decision that should, in Sachi's opinion, forever brand her an unfit mother.

While denying most of the rancor, Shirley MacLaine did acknowledge that motherhood was not among her priorities. I heard her explain that after watching her own mother, daughter Sachi's grandmother, suppress her creativity the actress vowed to never give her own career a back seat to any other pursuit. It also superseded being a faithful wife, as the MacLaine marriage was an open one with the couple sometimes seeing each other only a few times a year. Sachi believes the greater sin came when her famous mom renounced her motherly obligations, all but abandoning the infant.

As Sachi tells it, when she was just two years old her mother shipped her off alone on a flight to Japan to live with her father and his mistress, relying on the airline to assure the toddler's safe passage. She also balks that support ended for her early, forcing her to work as a flight attendant, a maid, and a waitress to make ends meet. Sachi reports that Shirley MacLaine was so absent from her life that the closest connection she felt with her mother was no more intimate than the relationship between the Oscar winner and her fans. Sachi claims to remember years during which she saw her mother very rarely and only while flying as a stewardess glancing over the heads of passengers in the bulkhead seats, on airplane movie screens.

More credibly than her daughter's crucifixion of the star, years later I came to understand that the nervous *Hour Magazine* producer might actually have been right in the handle-with-care attitude. At a 50th anniversary reunion of *The Dick Van Dyke Show* at Hollywood's Egyptian Theater I heard from the assembled writers and producers about the grief that Ms. MacLaine caused their executive producer, Sheldon Leonard.

That actor-turned-mogul had an amazing track record, but among Sheldon Leonard's hits was at least one miss. The huge strikeout that barely made it to TV screens was *Shirley's World*. Who knows who bears the brunt of the responsibility, but the experience was apparently a nightmare for both Leonard and MacLaine. ABC had agreed to the sitcom that followed the exploits of a photojournalist in Britain only to later wish they hadn't. It was off the air after only 17 episodes. At one point, both the star and the producer must have been on the same page. Apparently that moment came and went quickly. It's claimed that, before long, the actress changed the tone of the characterization to such an extent that Leonard insisted the show no longer resembled a comedy. Despite his flying back and forth to the filming location across the Atlantic to try to solve a litany of problems and delays, the show self-destructed.

Leonard kept at least one painful keepsake. It was a cassette tape from his U.K. showrunner, Ray Austin. Assumedly to squarely place the blame at the star's feet, Leonard transcribed some of Austin's comments in his autobiography: "Well, she did it again," Austin said of MacLaine. "She sent word down from her dressing room that she wasn't going to do the shot until the scene was re-written. Frank Tarloff went up to see what she wanted and made some changes, but we still didn't get a shot until after the lunch break."

Artists, actors included, are often emotionally fragile. Show business then exacerbates that temperamental nature by further indulging the artists' whims. Actor Henry Winkler believes the stakes are raised every time a director surrenders to a performer's wish, simply to get them out of their trailer so the production can remain on schedule and within budget. I've seen producers willing to do almost anything in efforts to coax difficult actors onto the set so they can get the performances they need. That includes placating moods, soothing bruised egos, feigning friendship, lavishing stars with all manner of gifts, and mollycoddling their capricious dispositions as if they were some priceless 24-carat antique Faberge egg.

One prominent warm-up entertainer-turned-host-turned announcer I worked with on a couple of series mentioned in passing that he loved the swinging and swaggering retro style of the 1960s Vegas Rat Pack. Seemingly overnight George Gray's dressing room wall was adorned with a massive blow-up of a photo of Sinatra and the gang on stage in the Sands' Copa showroom. Don't even begin to talk about gift baskets. While I occasionally found one in my dressing rooms on the first days of work on a few series, some of the baskets I saw waiting for these shows' stars must have been delivered by forklifts. Lord knows how many geese gave their lives for the vats of foie gras.

A big day on Stage 6 at Culver Studios when Fran Drescher and husband, producer Peter Marc Jacobson, welcomed Elizabeth Taylor as a guest star on CBS's The Nanny. *In the 1996 episode nanny Fran Fine lost Elizabeth Taylor's string of black pearls.*

Before Elizabeth Taylor guested on an episode of *The Nanny* there was, of course, the ability for her to suggest all manner of changes before granting script approval. That's to be expected. What wasn't expected for her three days on the set were the requirements to paint her dressing suite lavender and provide matching lavender towels, bedding and, I was told, bars of lavender soap. A specific brand of bottled water had to be stocked for the legend, and a different brand of designer water for her dog. I don't know how anyone could know, but apparently Ms. Taylor's dog didn't care for the taste of Ms. Taylor's favorite water. When *The Nanny* costars reflected back on that week for TV Land, Renee Taylor remembered admiring the diva's ostentatious ring but having her hand slapped away when she asked to try it on. Then castmember Ann Guilbert recalled, "She didn't let us look at her… we weren't supposed to eyeball her."

The escalating jealousies between Eric Estrada and Larry Wilcox on the Culver City set of the international television hit *CHiPS* had the future of the cash cow series circling the drain several times. Estrada was even replaced for several episodes while sulking. In order to keep the production from becoming a 10-55—a case for the coroner—each of the actors was given one of a pair of identical, fully tricked-out Rolls Royces. It calmed the hostility for about as long as the first tank of gas lasted.

Larry Wilcox was so obscured behind Estrada's shadow that we never knew he set speed records driving at Utah's Bonneville Salt Flats, was a professional rodeo cowboy, was a pilot who flew with the Blue Angels, and was sentenced to three years of probation for conspiracy to commit securities fraud in 2011. That last one is not a good way to get noticed.

Hell on wheels. Eric Estrada and Larry Wilcox on a bumpy ride as CHiPs officers. (1977)

We also didn't know Larry was a singer. I heard his record *Me and My Love* b/w *Part Time Love* dozens of times during the couple of months in 1980 when I was hired along with other radio-friendly promoters to try to get airplay for his single, and we're still not sure he's a singer. Some of the radio station music directors who took our calls may still be laughing, but kudos to Larry for taking the shot while he was hot. As he said in 2013, "During *CHiPs* I realized actors are like fashion; you have a shelf life." He thinks he quit the gig at the right moment, "I felt the managers and attorneys with Erik Estrada were doing everything they could to remove or injure me… I knew that shit was brewing, so I left in the nick of time."

From gift baskets to Rolls Royces, pampering and pacifying celebrities is a time-honored tradition despite further escalating the expectations and demands of some. There was an afternoon in 1993 when veteran talent agent Don Pitts' and my eyes met as another star was being treated with kid gloves. We were both watching Wink Martindale as he stepped out from under the hot lights during a break from a *Trivial Pursuit* rehearsal. He was immediately wrapped in a blanket to protect against the advent of a draft from the air conditioning. Don came over and whispered to me, "See? Just like a thoroughbred racehorse." It was funny, but neither of us laughed aloud. Thankfully, Wink has remained well grounded and unaffected throughout his amazing career.

To my knowledge only Ms. MacLaine presented any star-sized challenges to Sheldon Leonard. Once he paired with actor-comedian Danny Thomas, the producing duo gave birth to several hugely successful sitcoms and one truly groundbreaking drama. The team struck gold with *The Danny Thomas Show*. Its spinoffs included *The Andy Griffith Show, Mayberry R.F.D.* and its cousin *Gomer Pyle, USMC*. Sheldon was also responsible for saving the concept that became *The Dick Van Dyke Show* and championing the history-making *I Spy*. Of all the hits, *The Danny Thomas Show* aka *Make Room for Daddy* was closest to being stillborn.

As a humorist and raconteur Danny Thomas was a master monologist, but his early television work was not well received. After playing clubs for years his desire to get off the road and onto another television vehicle presented a challenge. Even with Leonard as its showrunner it wasn't an easy sell. Meeting Danny's expectation for getting another turn at bat took the work of no lesser powerbroker than Abe Lastfogel, the legendary talent representative who built the mighty William Morris Agency. He pressured third-place ABC into buying Thomas as part of a leveraged deal in which they also got to sign in-demand talent Ray Bolger.

Surprisingly for the naysayers, Danny Thomas enjoyed tremendous success with the resulting *Make Room for Daddy*. The series graduated from ABC to CBS in its fifth season before wrapping after an 11 year run. Much of the credit belonged to a star-studded supporting cast that included two of the era's breakthrough black actresses, Louise Beavers and Amanda Randolph. They were joined by comedy greats Hans Conried, Sid Melton, Pat Carroll, Ben Lessy, Mary Wickes, Pat Harrington, Jr., Jesse White and producer Sheldon Leonard.

Fresh from portraying Lina Lamont in *Singin' in the Rain* (1952) Jean Hagen came to the small screen as Danny Thomas' wife on ABC's *Make Room for Daddy* (1953)

Staring as a six-year-old, Rusty Hamer portrayed Danny's son, Rusty Williams. This talented youngster went on to have one of the more difficult lives among former kid stars, and I only recently learned the extent to which his TV dad generously attempted numerous rescues as his emotional health deteriorated. Most only heard about Rusty's problems around 1966 when he shot himself. The young actor claimed it was a freak accident in which a gun he was carrying in a shoulder holster slid out, fell to the ground, and discharged. He was 19 at the time and no longer the adorable precocious prepubescent who had enjoyed a successful start in show business. With the exception of *Make Room for Daddy* revivals, Rusty's acting career consisted of fewer than a handful of gigs over a half-dozen years.

The former child actor drifted through a series of odd jobs as he became increasingly angry, confused, unstable, unhealthfully obese, occasionally violent, and outwardly hostile even to his TV dad. His fall into a deep depression ended in 1990 when he pulled the trigger of a .357 Magnum pointed at his head. He was 42 years old. It was the moment that inspired fellow former kid star Paul Peterson, Jeff from *The Donna Reed Show*, to establish the entity that has done more good for generations of child actors than any other single resource, "A Minor Consideration."

Was it a sitcom or a soap? Danny was married to Margaret (Jean Hagen), with daughter Terry (Sherry Jackson) and son Rusty. Then, with Margaret written out, Danny spent a season as a widower.

Danny married Kathy (Marjorie Lord) and adopted her daughter Linda (Angela Cartright). Then Terry (Sherry) was written out for a season as being away at school. She returns, played by actress Penney Parker, marries Pat Hannigan (Pat Harrington, Jr.), and moves away leaving just Danny, Kathy, Rusty and Linda. The cast in 1958 (l-r) Rusty Hamer, Penney Parker, Danny Thomas, Angela Cartright, and Marjorie Lord.

Rusty's older brother, John Hamer reflected on the memory of discovering his brother's body. He revealed that Danny Thomas had made many overtures to help Rusty during his downward spiral, but all had been rebuffed. John explained to Paul how Danny "made sure the family had an income, he paid for [John's] flight lessons and remained close to the Hamer family. Danny was an unsung hero, a true father figure to me when Rusty wouldn't listen or even try to get rid of his demons."

Some of this history was the topic of discussion one evening with one of the former members of that show's extended cast who wishes to remain nameless on this subject. As the conversation flowed, this performer mentioned how "poor Jean Hagen" was so disgusted playing Danny Thomas' wife that she walked off the hit. I questioned what could have been so off-putting as to cause an actress to quit the successful run of a series, especially after three seasons that brought her three Emmy nominations. The answer was not forthcoming. What I heard instead was an angry diatribe about what an evil person Danny was—how he berated the kids on the series for their shortcomings in remembering their lines or failure to hit their marks, and how he traded on their cuteness to curry favor at meetings with advertisers and in other business dealings.

It took a few years, but I heard a couple of other stories from a former associate of one of the most in-demand directors of the era, John Rich. Considered a specialist in comedy, the director began at the dawn of television as stage manager for Dean Martin and Jerry Lewis's *Colgate Comedy Hour*. Rich's colleague conjectured that "poor Jean Hagen" was resentful that she was unable to leverage her Emmy nominations into profit participation or even a raise above the compensation called for in her original deal. He then relayed the director's story of a day he worked with the star on *Make Room for Daddy* and was disgusted himself by Thomas' behavior. I was told the problem started with the comic's penchant for chewing tobacco and the requisite spitting that accompanies it. Rich had recounted that Thomas used an empty coffee can as a cuspidor, but missed the target almost as often as he hit it. Just as I was reconciling that breach of good hygiene and how the rancid smell of well-chewed tobacco could have been the cause for Jean Hagen's quitting, the story got darker.

Apparently director John Rich asked Thomas to stop all the spitting, or at least move the coffee can closer. That was met by the actor pulling a gun! Rich said that Thomas suddenly produced a pistol from either his pocket or attaché case, and placed it on the table. At first, Rich thought it was a poor attempt at humor. He soon learned it wasn't when Thomas said something to the effect of, "I keep this with me so that I don't have to deal with stupid requests like that." When Rich asked if the gun was loaded, Thomas' response left no doubt this wasn't a joke, "Of course it's loaded. What good is an unloaded gun?"

Wow, there's a side of the singing storyteller that came as a shock. Several friends who worked with Thomas in various venues over the years have since confirmed that his gun was always close at hand, except when on stage. Two who worked with him in nightclubs each individually added that the Derringer rested in his dressing room, in one of his shoes while the comedian did his act. As far as pulling a handgun at a table read, if true, how can a successful performer's conduct stray so far from social norms? Seated at that table, no doubt young Rusty Hamer saw that incident. Did that play a role in the teenaged actor's decision to also carry a gun? Does celebrity exempt someone from conforming to expectations for acceptable behavior?

The answer to that mystery came at yet another time and place, in the enlightened words of warning from one long-time staffer on a massive hit show. On the morning of my first day working on the set she was kind enough to warn me about the publicly-adored host's mercurial nature. She said, "Bob Barker has been in this artificial terrarium so long that he thinks it's real."

Bingo. I'd never heard it said more succinctly. It turned out to be more prophetic than I could have imagined. The special indulgences afforded top talent, over time, distance those celebrities further and further from real life. They're indeed in a controlled environment, interacting with as many as 100 people who are all working from the same simple script: smile, don't create stress, no negative innuendo, keep things light and breezy. The answer to any of the star's questions or requests is always an emphatic "yes."

I had the opportunity to remind this wise lady of that encounter in 2018, a full 15 years after her shrewd observation about stardom. She confirmed that she indeed did share those words with a few select co-workers that she thought could benefit from the heads-up when they were hired onto *The Price is Right*. It was valuable insight that helped those treated to the admonition to understand that legend's changing moods and occasionally unexpected impertinences. Fans have held this emcee's public persona in such high regard that some would be ready to advocate for his sainthood. In reality, for some, simply staying in Bob Barker's good graces and keeping out of his way were high on the unwritten list of job survival skills. It wasn't true only after superstardom, as one writer and one production assistant on the host's old *Truth or Consequences* each report seeing that difficult side of their boss. Possibly because of a respect reserved for fellow performers I enjoyed only friendship and a sense of camaraderie from Barker.

Even after 3-D TV is perfected, viewers will still have only a two-dimensional view of their beloved television stars—limited to what they see and hear on the screen. How accurate is it?

Chapter 6

It's easy to unwittingly misjudge someone's temperament. There's a natural tendency for our perception of performers' off-screen demeanor to be colored by the characters they portray. A great example is actor William Talman who, week after week for almost a decade became inextricably associated with his portrayal of the sober, upstanding straight-shooting honorable District Attorney Hamilton Burger on *Perry Mason.*

That denizen of law and order was, in real life, busted at a West Hollywood pot party in 1960, arrested for drug possession and lewdness. The 45-year-old actor was stark naked and higher than Perry Mason's ratings. It resulted in Tallman's suspension from all CBS programming, *Perry Mason* included. Having underestimated the public's outcry as measured by the number of letters requesting his reinstatement, the network soon reversed itself. It proved to be only a brief TV disbarment for prime time's favorite DA.

Even Walt Disney could throw a party that belied his carefully crafted wholesome image. To celebrate the record-setting box office success of *Snow White,* in 1938 Walt treated his 1,400 employees to two days of reverie at the Lake Narconian Resort in Riverside, California. What was billed as "Walt's Field Day" became legendary for its weekend of mass drunkenness that, legend holds, led to at least one animator falling out of a second floor window and into a tree. Other unplanned activities reportedly included a nude swim and horse races through the hotel lobby. In the Disney tradition, you could say the party was animated. Thoroughly embarrassed by his employees' outrageous behavior, Walt refused to speak of the party ever again.

Talking about a dichotomy between public and private guises, consider the Grand Canyon-sized rift between the personas of one fan-favorite performer. It's perhaps the greatest "I can't believe it" scandal of all time. It was so long overdue in shocking the public that those who were in the know had long since become bored with the topic. Only many years later did the world finally come to believe the claims from a parade of dozens of women who reported being drugged victims of non-consensual sex. They were no match for audiences' adoration of the married family-friendly star. Such was the long-overdue free-fall from grace of the self-appointed paragon of social values, Bill Cosby.

Even more surprising than the vast number of accusers—something like 60 at last count—was the revelation that the debauchery had been so open and notorious that it became well known throughout much of the entertainment industry. By the time I was first in the loop of touring showroom performers in 2003, Cosby had already long been a subject of backstage gossip. When asked, crews at seemingly every Las Vegas, Atlantic City, Lake Tahoe and Reno showroom had their own very similar torrid tales. There were decades of eyewitness accounts involving both willing and unwilling Cosby conquests, sometimes consummated in flagrant and open escapades. The horror is that seemingly nobody spoke up for all those years. For those who did, I have to believe that the truth was no match for the legend.

Comedian W. Kamau Bell chronicled the descent from respected exemplar to accused sexual predator as director of the 2022 Showtime documentary series *We Need to Talk About Cosby*. He revealed the weekly ritual that appeared to present *The Cosby Show* star with a smorgasbord of carnal encounters as far back as 1984: "During rehearsal you would look out into the bleachers where people sat and there was clearly a section where there was just nothing but young model-looking women. . . they called it 'the parade.' There would be a line of them parading to Bill Cosby's dressing room. . . one at a time and the door would close." Bell named one of Cosby's assistants who allegedly coordinated with modeling agencies to stock fresh women for the parade, "the idea being that like, he's a big star, the big star gets what he wants. He's the biggest star at NBC."

It was incongruous to think of this self-anointed role model as a philanderer. After all, he was endlessly pontificating about the ills of society and pretending to be the prototype of proper personage for young black males to emulate. Cosby had apparently breezed through background checks to earn millions as a shill for image-conscious brands such as Coca Cola. His 25-year run as spokesman for

Jello was an unprecedented commitment to the power of his credibility. In 1981 Coke's Pooh-Bah of PR, Anthony Tortorici, told a reporter that the "three most believable personalities are God, Walter Cronkite, and Bill Cosby."

A former stage manager at *The Tonight Show*, Dan Ford, reports that he saw a random piece of the jigsaw puzzle decades ago when Bill Cosby subbed for Johnny Carson. It was custom for the show to provide a member of the staff to assist guest hosts with any secretarial and logistical support they might need—handling phone calls, typing letters, making reservations, arranging for flowers, etc. They're the kind of nitty-gritty mundane tasks that keep a small army of VIP personal assistants busy 24/7. At *The Tonight Show* it was just a few hours of support and pampering to go along with a job that offered an unspectacular salary and very modest accommodations. The secretary worked in a narrow room that connected with the substitute host's identically sized dressing room, the two separated by a sliding pocket door that could be closed for privacy.

Dan remembers the day that Johnny Carson's secretary, Drue-Ann Wilson, came to producer Fred De Cordova's office to complain that she couldn't continue to work with Cosby. She reported that he had been walking around their two rooms sometimes in tighty-whitie briefs and sometimes stark naked. Dan says Fred immediately called Cosby to say "Get your own secretary." The favor was never extended to him again during his many subsequent bookings as guest host. Yes, he was invited back over and over again with the withholding of an assistant apparently the only consequence for his past indiscretion.

Not always a sitcom sensation, Cosby had several hits and misses on the tube including a two-season run as a high school gym teacher on NBC. Following failed variety shows on CBS and ABC he re-teamed with the peacock for what became the mega-successful 1980s hit that rocked the industry. During its eight-year run *Cosby* scored honors as the number-one program in all of television during each of five consecutive seasons. Then, even at the height of his popularity with the most to lose, the star allegedly continued his nefarious exploits and carnal crusades at both the network's Brooklyn studio and the Kaufman Astoria stages. In addition to the parade of models, at least one actress booked for a role in a single episode has gone on record with an account of sex with The Cos against her will in one of those facilities' dressing rooms.

It's open for conjecture as to when this gifted raconteur may have first crossed the line into the uncharted Area 51 of outrageous behavior. It's been rumored to go all the way back to his first burst of fame. The producer who initially cast Cosby as a lead actor was Shirley MacLaine's nemesis, Sheldon Leonard. The former actor valiantly broke with tradition in 1968 by building a TV series around an African-American co-star who had minimal camera time under his belt.

Fresh from a budding career in stand-up, Bill Cosby's portrayal of Alexander Scott on NBC's *I Spy* broke the color barrier, with the comedian becoming the first African American to win a Primetime Emmy Award for Outstanding Lead Actor (1966).

Leonard recalled in his autobiography that Cosby was carefully directed through his *I Spy* scenes by on-screen partner Robert Culp. Who better? Culp was more than a co-star and part-time acting coach, he had a hand in creating the original concept, owned a percentage of the series, and wrote many of its best episodes. As a cheat for his difficulty with memorization, Cosby was also given the freedom to play fast and loose with each week's script, paraphrasing and injecting adlibs at will.

These concessions for the novice actor helped him become a breakthrough star. "As soon as *I Spy* went on the air Bill Cosby gained sensational acceptance," Leonard recounted. "He became the darling of the critics. Fan mail poured in. His fee as a nightclub performer skyrocketed." By then, the production company was allegedly hushing several international incidents of Cosby's indiscretions. A team was apparently mopping up behind him as the production of *I Spy* globe-hopped from one location to the next in the process of filming 82 episodes. If the instantaneous transition into the ranks of super-celebrity was a precipitating factor behind his transgressions, then The Cos wouldn't be the first to have been seduced by sudden fame.

Cosby's bed could be considered ground zero for the subsequent #MeToo wave on which a tsunami of TV personalities have surfed into oblivion for past offenses. Hollywood gasped while fortunes were lost each time another revelation surfaced. Claims against Tom Brokaw and Ryan Seacrest weren't adequately convincing, but news/talk giants Matt Lauer, Charlie Rose, Bill O'Reilly, and Tavis Smiley all disappeared faster than a David Copperfield illusion. Oh, and David Copperfield was accused, as well.

It was happy days for Scott Baio when no charges were filed following a claim of misbehavior. Chef Mario Batali, comedian Louis CK, and public radio host Garrison Keillor all but vanished while singer Seal sailed past a 2016 sexual battery complaint. Then came accusations against MTV host Nev Schulman, singers Nick Carter, and Def Jam's Russell Simmons. R&B heavyweight R. Kelly faced the music for decades of alleged outrageous behavior, much of it behind the gates of his Chicago-area estate called the "Chocolate Factory." His guilty verdict for an assortment of lesser sex crimes pales in comparison to the convictions for racketeering, kidnapping, bribery, sex trafficking, and sexual exploitation of a child.

Geraldo Rivera didn't deny Bette Midler's renewed claim that he groped her breasts over 40 years ago. As someone joked, "They were higher on her body back then." Accusations against Hollywood heavyweights Michael Douglas, James Franco, Dustin Hoffman, Ben Affleck, Steven Seagal, and Morgan Freeman each registered to varying degrees on the Richter scale. In the final days of 2021, rape accusations from 2004 and 2015 echoed to find *Law and Order* veteran Chris

Noth, Mr. Big himself from *Sex in the City*, dropped from both CBS's *The Equalizer* and his talent agency. The creative force behind *The Sopranos* and *The Romanoffs*, Matthew Weiner has one very mad woman from his *Mad Men* writing team. Emmy-winner Kater Gordon asserted, "My memory is intact," in response to his denials of alleged sexual harassment.

After being accused of making sexual advances towards several men and a 14-year-old boy, two-time Oscar winner Kevin Spacey was exiled from mainstream Hollywood. In addition to film roles, it cost him an estimated $500,000 per episode when Netflix folded *House of Cards*. Netflix lost another series lead in April, 2022 when 84-year-old Oscar-nominated Frank Langella was ushered from *The Fall of the House of Usher* following an investigation of sexual harassment and "unacceptable conduct on set." TV actor-comedian Aziz Ansari answered his accuser without apparent repercussions, but actors Danny Masterson and Andy Dick each disappeared from their respective Netflix shows. Similarly, Jeffrey Tambor was scratched from Amazon's critical success, *Transparent,* and the once-angelic Fred Savage has been ousted from producing and directing the reboot of his former series, *The Wonder Years* for inappropriate conduct.

With the exception of a body double and some CGI magic with past images, Jeff Garlin all but vanished from ABC's *The Goldbergs* at the end of 2021 following a human resources investigation into allegations of lewd language and unwarranted touching. *Gossip Girl* actor Ed Westwick was dropped from a BBC series and, likewise, CBS canceled Jeremy Piven's *Wisdom of the Crowd.* Then, no one less than CBS's chief Les Moonves was in the spotlight and out of his $50-plus million a year gig. Of course there's one man who may have actually outdone Cosby, the Lothario who birthed the backlash, defrocked movie mogul Harvey Weinstein.

As titillating as it might be to read, you'll have to look elsewhere for more. There aren't enough trees for paper nor gigabytes of storage for reviewing all of the offensive overtures, angry accusations, demeaning misdemeanors, and disgraceful felonies. Cosby earned his ink by virtue of his ability to maintain a charade of such breadth and depth for so many years despite eyewitness accounts from armies of backstage workers. In game show parlance Cosby stumped us, the panel, on a variation of another classic. It was his own too-hot-for-broadcast, personal, real-life immoral version of *I've Got a* (really big) *Secret*.

The trick to maximizing the number of backstage secrets to which you're privy is to borrow the precept of the real estate industry: location, location, location. Where you hang your hat can make a world of difference as a well-placed dressing room with thin walls is where you can hear the most recent ratings, the first word of anticipated hirings and firings, cancellations and renewals, as well as an occasional tryst. If knowledge is power, there's power in proximity. At the very least, being next door to a show's top talent helps establish a little rapport with the star and the suits who visit them.

When I stepped in to substitute for my longtime friend, announcer Rod Roddy at *The Price is Right* in 2003, Bob Barker praised Rod in recalling their first day together. Barker told me that Rod had been offered a larger, newer, and better appointed suite but had such respect for his predecessor that he wanted to stay in Johnny Olson's old, small, dressing room. If that's what Barker thought, it's certainly a quaint sentiment. I did nothing to disturb the fairy tale, but I knew Rod far better than that. Anyone who knew Rod would have known better.

Johnny Olson in his tiny utilitarian dressing room in Studio 33 at CBS Television City, prepping to warm-up another of the over 2,500 audiences he charmed at *The Price is Right*. Rod Roddy and the author subsequently used the same room years before the square footage was absorbed in an enlargement of the studio's adjacent green room.
Photo from the author's collection

I was tempted to tell Bob that Rod stayed in the small quarters (Room 33J) adjacent to his own star suite (Room 33K) as I now also opted to do, simply to remain directly in the flow of energy and vital information. You see, the two dressing room doors were only about four feet apart, across a narrow walkway. The louvered slats at the bottom of both doors were for ventilation, but they also transmitted sound. No mere mortal can resist the temptation to occasionally pay attention to the random, unguarded, believed-to-be-private conversations of the rich and famous as they waft across your threshold. It's especially true when the dialogue often includes insight into the inner workings of the production, and the unfortunate ever-present on-set politics that have the potential to affect your longevity. While the Johnny Olson I knew was above flagrant eavesdropping, nobody stays fully-employed and beloved in a career for 58 years, as he did, without at least some fluency in the language of politics and power.

By virtue of its location this oversized closet with attached bathroom imbued each of its occupants with valuable access. Indeed, one day, no one less than the network's gand high exalted mystic ruler at the time, Les Moonves, stopped in for a mutual ego-massaging session with Bob. When I introduced myself we shared only a very few purposely-brief words assuming that with Les, less is more. That was another nugget of advice from Johnny Olson's mentoring.

When it came to interaction with VIPs, both on-air luminaries and corporate big shots Johnny's mantra was, "friendly, but never familiar." It was sound counsel, seconded by many who make their living wrangling prominent personalities. While working with Johnny Carson, David Letterman, Tom Snyder, Jon Stewart, Craig Kilborn, and Craig Ferguson, producer Peter Lassally subscribed to the same philosophy. He learned it early while working with Arthur Godfrey. As Peter frames it, "familiarity breeds contempt, keep a respectful distance." Bob Mackie, who has costumed show biz royalty for decades, also learned it early apprenticing on Judy Garland's CBS show. As he remembers it, Mackie's boss had crossed the line and was regularly getting middle-of-the-night drunken calls from the occasionally suicidal star.

No backstage worker wants to be sucked into a vortex of dysfunction or sufficiently raise their profile to become potentially controversial, therefore vulnerable. Watch the old pros on the set. Their longevity is often the result of learning how to remain cheerfully non-partisan. They do the gig, smile, and generally stay in the background. Some even seem to have found a way to blend in with the wallpaper when things become contentious. Although it may never be spoken, some of the people they dress, buff, puff, and polish are looking to enjoy no more than a cordial professional relationship. If they encourage a deeper connection, it's at their own peril.

For the uninitiated it begs the question, what's so wrong about trying to add a celebrity or a network executive to your inner circle of friends? What could be the downside of ingratiating yourself, giving them opportunities to get to know you? Well… read on!

Chapter 7

When a member of the cast or crew breaches etiquette and is obvious in their cozying up to a star or top-line executive it's awkwardly unprofessional at best, and pathetic at its worst. Besides, it's a double-edged sword. Game show announcer Gene Wood's experience is a classic case in point.

Gene was among the elite coterie of announcers who auditioned to step in as Bob Barker's new second banana after Johnny Olson's death in 1985. It was a gig Gene wanted badly, but he misjudged the vibe. It was a surprising blunder for a pro with his decades of experience, and it illustrates the pitfalls of pandering. If Gene had been treated to Johnny's or Peter Lassally's admonition about not being intrusive he might have enjoyed a huge career boost, a significant pay hike, and have had a job for the rest of his useful life at TV's longest-running game show.

Gene was short on insight for someone so long on experience. He had written comedy, worked on a cartoon series that aired on CBS's *Captain Kangaroo*, and teamed for stand-up work with Bill Dana during that respected comedian-writer's earliest days. During lean times in the 1960s Gene was trying to keep food on the table by schlepping boxes with a job as a delivery man. Even with that gig he admitted he relied on the kindness of a Manhattan restaurant owner for an occasional free meal.

Although he had studied acting in college, the closest Gene had gotten to earning a living on a stage was as a stand-in. He gladly sat on-set for lighting and camera rehearsals at Goodson-Todman programs in New York, including *Snap Judgment*. In addition to being the site of my initial encounter with Gene, that show's set in NBC's Studio 8H was where I first chatted with the world's most celebrated audience member.

Miss Lillian Miller appeared to be a crazy old spinster, sporting an ever-present hat and eyeglasses with lenses thicker than the bulletproof glass at Bank of

America's premier game show host, Bill Cullen, on stage at CBS Television City's Studio 33, helping announcer Gene Wood keep an audience entertained between episodes. Photo courtesy of Fred Wostbrock.

America. Before her retirement she would make the round trip by train between her home in Philadelphia and midtown Manhattan every weekday for the dubious thrill of sitting in audiences. After years of faithful fanship Miss Miller began to be singled-out on camera by Steve Allen, and later by Jack Paar and Merv Griffin. She spoke with her marbles-in-her-mouth garble so frequently that she lost her amateur standing and was required to join the performers' union, AFTRA.

As programs moved to L.A., so did she. Once retired from her job as a clerk-typist for the U.S. Army Quartermaster Corps, Miller settled into a very modest apartment three blocks up Vine Street from Merv's theater. Gene Wood was among the warm-up performers who would continue to see her in audiences well into the 1980s. The old crow was tough to miss as she continually drew attention to herself in attempts to score a few of the dollar bills some audience babysitters gave away. It usually worked. Only on the rarest occasions in her later years did she enjoy the thrill and the union scale payment from being seen speaking on camera.

From stand-up to stand-in, with his acting chops and everyman looks Gene Wood began to book a string of lucrative commercials in New York. Once in the spotlight, it became his goal to stay there. He fronted a single season of a Canadian stunt show *Anything You Can Do* while simultaneously announcing a low budget incarnation of Goodson-Todman's *Beat the Clock* that also taped on the cheap north of the border. Host Jack Narz had quit the gig after realizing his piddling salary barely covered the cost of his commute between L.A. and Montreal, and Gene was all too happy to fill the opening for the remainder of the run.

Ultimately, Gene spent the bulk of his years announcing a vast array of the Goodson-Todman game show factory's series, a fine career even if he didn't find it sufficiently fulfilling. Gene was a proud man who'd already risen to the upper echelon of off-camera broadcasters enjoying a very-respectable, enviable, and lucrative career, but was clearly unfulfilled having aspirations to return to center stage. He was a showman through and through when delivering his legendary pre-show warm-up. It was unique, very creative, totally original, terrifically funny, and a treat for audiences, but that performance was limited to in-person crowds of 300 as opposed to his desire to be playing to 30 million viewers.

Gene took to buddying-up with the hosts of the programs on which he worked, primarily it seemed to expand his on-air role. The strategy worked especially well with Richard Dawson and Burt Convy who each periodically included Gene during adlib moments at *Family Feud* and *Super Password*, respectively. They welcomed an occasional unsolicited off-the-cuff comment, and even afforded Gene opportunities for moments on camera. Good lord, he relished each and every second on the screen. Beloved prototypical host Tom Kennedy once brought him on stage to briefly acknowledge his being responsibile for a particularly energetic audience during a *Password Plus* episode and you could see Gene beaming with pride.

In explaining why he didn't get the announcing gig at *The Price is Right,* Gene told me how he felt his concentration and confidence were broken in the moments just before tape rolled for his first fill-in test episode. He claimed that Bob Barker told him something along the lines of "I know how you try to pad your part on other shows. I want you to understand there's only one host here. So just stick to your scripted copy unless I ask you to say something else." Ouch! If it truly happened as Gene said, it could have indeed deflated his ego and shattered his out-sized expectations for the audition.

Gene is still loved by many of his former co-workers, so this observation may be unpopular. Knowing the players and the circumstances, I'm willing to bet that Gene himself invited Barker's harsh admonition. I can just see him backstage, stepping over the line in his eagerness to buddy-up with the host, violating rule number one of his predecessor: "keep it friendly but not familiar." I highly doubt Bob would have put Gene in his place so sternly without some impetus. Bob isn't unfeeling, but he's also no fool. Sensing he was being disingenuously manipulated and excessively ass-kissed would be exactly what it would take.

However it went down, there's no doubt the ego-deflated Gene must have had a long ride back home to Malibu that evening. If there was ever a home for retrenchment, regrouping, relaxation, and entertaining, Gene had it. It was nothing particularly elegant, but the Massachusetts native had a single-story old ranch-style retreat with painted wooden walls that gave it a distinctive New England feel. With its large open floor plan, the home was perched high up in the hills overlooking some of the northernmost waters off Malibu. The property's greatest attribute was the panorama that spread before you as you stepped out of the wide French doors that lined the rear of the house. It afforded an ocean view from the flat 75-foot wide and 30-foot deep patio.

Gene Wood's Malibu home included a horse stable and backyard overlooking the Pacific Ocean. Photo from the author's collection

Gene returned to Television City the next day to continue the try-out. Truth be told, Gene's failure to land the plum job was less about any perceived battle of egos with Bob Barker than it was simply his style. It's obvious to any sensitive ear and was explicitly confirmed for me by the triumvirate of executives who then headed CBS daytime, Gene's sound was just not right for the show. Indeed, producer Roger Dobkowitz called his voice "harsh." His delivery was a million miles from that of his predecessor's, Johnny Olson's, which Tom Kennedy long admired as "crisp, clear and clarion-sounding." Gene was also more foreground and intrusive than the conversational flowing prosodic approach that's best suited to accommodate the show's reams of advertising copy.

Ultimately, the coveted *Price* gig went to Rod Roddy via a most circuitous route. In fact, when it was first offered Rod actually turned it down. His attorney bargained for a compensation package the show was simply unwilling to pay; the deal was dead and the talent search resumed. CBS's Bob Boden confirmed that, after nobody else seemed a better fit than Rod the money was found. As I half-joked at the time, "Rod got the last seat on the last gravy train in town." It was true. His deal was uncharacteristically generous, especially as the industry soon began a slow and merciless belt tightening.

Rod had huge shoes to fill. If there was ever a perfect pairing of announcer and show it was in evidence for the thirteen years Johnny presided over the prizes on *Price*. Even Bob Barker's mother blessed that pairing in 1972. Coincidentally, she remembered being thoroughly entertained as a member of Johnny's audience at a remote broadcast of his radio hit *Ladies Be Seated* decades earlier. Bob told me that when he first mentioned Johnny's name during the weeks before the debut episodes taped, Tillie Barker enthusiastically endorsed their teaming. He came to fully appreciate Johnny himself soon after they began working together, eventually crediting him as one of the broadcasters he most respected.

A camera operator I worked with more recently at Sony Studios had spent much of his career at *Price*. His affront to Rod was simultaneously another glowing tribute to Johnny. He volunteered, "Johnny learned my name on the first day we worked together, and called me by name for the next dozen years. Rod was there a dozen years and he still has no idea who the hell I am." Six miles away at the set of *Family Feud*, ABC's senior video engineer claims that Gene Wood didn't care to return his greeting most days. In contrast to the studio employee's experience, those on the production company's staff saw an entirely different side of Gene.

Beyond the goodwill Johnny created in honoring crewmembers and staff alike by introducing them to the audiences, producers can't remember the old pro ever publicly using any coarse or off-color language. In fact, any sort of negative comment from the eternally up-beat Minnesota native was apparently rare. *The Price is Right* model Holly Hallstrom, who has had her own share of unflattering remarks about some of the goings-on at that beloved show, can only recall one utterance of exasperation from Johnny during their years together. That aside was remembered as, "Good Lord, this day feels like it will never end. Let's just keep our heads down, out of the line of fire." That benign comment was whispered to Holly during the camera blocking of one of the showcases in which Johnny and the models presented prizes in some fun and flighty under-rehearsed skit.

The two of them were stuck on-stage, waiting silently for a resolution to one of the screaming matches between a pair of senior creative team members over some minor staging issue. The argument was very likely more about wielding power, confirming the pecking order, and marking turf than about the matter seemingly in dispute. The regular combatants were producer Frank Wayne and director Marc Breslow. They were two supreme alpha males, each with the talent and track record deserving of greater respect than they likely felt they were receiving. Their era of cursing, verbal assaults, and slander was light years from the current measure of workplace appropriateness.

In recalling that incident during a phone call between Las Vegas and Colorado in the late 2000s, Holly volunteered that from among all of the models who sought legal redress over the years for alleged wrongful termination, libel, slander, defamation, emotional abuse, intimidation, and harassment, as well as discrimination based on race, age, weight, and pregnancy, she refused to sign a non-disclosure agreement as part of a settlement. She said it added years to her pursuit of justice, including months of homelessness, couch-surfing with friends, and actually living out of her car for a while. When the smoke cleared however, Holly claimed she got the lion's share of a $3 million judgment and the ability to tell her story. Understandably, for several years it was something she did with relish, a pinch of resentment, and a hearty helping of righteous vindication.

Despite some of the impropriety that the models claimed was playing out behind backstage doors, and the firings they attribute to their honest testimony in legal depositions, there was a tremendous esprit de corps, professionalism, and teamwork on the set. The same was true in the offices shared by the relatively small production staff that brought *The Price is Right* to viewers. That was especially the case in its early years. Despite that underlying harmony, even long after the Wayne-Breslow era *Price* was not completely immune from the kind of in-fighting and power plays that go on behind the scenes at many programs. As late as 2003 when I suggested that perhaps the producer should be appraised of the unusual performance instructions I was then being given by the director for presenting the showcases, that hothead responded loudly and clearly in my headset, "Fuck Roger!"

Throughout the business, what staffs and crews witnessed in decades past would be enough to give today's HR departments apoplexy. During TV's first half century it seems that nobody ever sued anybody for any on-set insensitivity, impropriety, or even unwelcome sexual advances. Back when larger-than-life egotists exerted unchecked power, outlandish behaviors were regularly tolerated, suffered in silence. Some were even excused as mere eccentricities. For one faithful contributor to television's longest running game show it seemed that little had changed between what was called "the golden age" and 2019. Allegedly, after a producer's pointed finger sternly and repeatedly poked that employee in the chest while angrily berating them, the response to the complaint lodged with the HR department was reportedly, "That's just his style of management."

At one time the only way to win money from a television show was by answering quiz questions. Now, those who choose to seek retribution find that the lovely couple of harassment and fee-contingent litigation met, fell in love, and married. Not until the death of perceived victimization shall the wedded couple part. "Sue the bastard" doesn't apply only to inappropriate behavior and sexual violation. Students of entertainment and copyright law have heard the details of one of the biggest winners ever on *Wheel of Fortune*, Vanna White herself.

The first lady of game show models won $403,000 in 1994 in her suit against Samsung. The electronics company ran a print ad for their VCRs with artwork of a robot version of Vanna, complete with a look-alike wig, evening gown, and jewelry standing next to a very familiar-looking letter board. The case set new precedent in California law with the court eventually ruling that the right of publicity can be violated without necessarily using a person's name, voice, signature, or likeness for commercial purposes.

Then there's the case filed by an aggrieved Johnny Carson against the porta-potty rental company run by a Mr. Earl J. Braxton. The portable toilet czar was fantastically creative in selecting a memorable name and slogan for his business, but it so infuriated Carson that he set out to crush the man's dream. Braxton called his enterprise "Here's Johnny," and dubbed himself "The World's Foremost Commodian." Yes, commodian. Get it? Johnny told his lawyer to flush the portable potty plutocrat's parody of his professional personage. The 1987 case immortalized as *Carson v. Here's Johnny Portable Toilets, Inc.* was in the courts through years of litigation and appeals. Legend holds that it took something close to a half-million dollars in legal fees for Johnny to eventually collect just $40,000 in damages and, more importantly, to protect his right of publicity.

A funny parody that Johnny Carson considered no laughing matter.

There's a great kicker to this story. Braxton waited almost thirty years for Carson to die and then, in 2006, he tried again to register the phrases. Braxton's argument was that there was no protection for "post-mortem rights of publicity." The Trademark Trial and Appeal Board ruled that those rights did indeed exist, and had passed to Carson's estate. With that final ruling the porta-potty prince's dreams went down the drain. I can imagine his face was flushed upon hearing the verdict. You could say that Braxton was full of shit.

In most settings and situations these days the benign sprinkling of a few choice profanities is often generally considered an acceptable and effective way to make language more colorful. However, having never worked as a longshoreman, when newly hired onto my first national TV series I hadn't yet adjusted to what passed for appropriate language in this industry's workplace. The first nugget of overheard cursing was shocking not so much by what was said, but rather because it came so matter-of-factly from the otherwise cultured mouth of a proper and professional lady executive. Plus, it was within the confines of a meeting of the mostly female production staff where I thought such vulgarities would rarely, if ever, be uttered. Clearly, I wasn't as worldly as I thought I was.

A few minutes after wrapping the day's taping I was on my way to the associate producer's office to return my signed contract. The usual post-mortem discussion that follows a show was echoing down the hall. The brain trust was discussing one of the many hunky soap stars who are happy to be booked on a program that's popular with their daytime audiences. Between a natural gift of charm and the pre-interview prep this stud-du-jour was unusually interesting and entertaining. He was a guy so 1980s-macho (think Tom Selleck), so oozing with pheromones and testosterone that he was probably born with chest hair as thick as the fairway on the third hole at the Lakeside Country Club golf course.

The well-respected Patty Gary-Cox was hosting this producers' assemblage, although I don't believe she was one of the people I overheard. The usual informal reflections included stuff like, "Guest X was a great booking. She was very funny and had great chemistry with our host, blah, blah, blah…" The chit-chat at that moment had turned to Mr. Soap Hunk. Approaching the office I heard, "… oh, he was great TV, so telegenic." "Goddammit, he's hot!" To which a third member of the group nonchalantly added, "Well, all I know is if he walked through that door right here, right now, I'd drop to my knees and give him the blowjob of his life."

I froze! I couldn't believe what I'd just heard, so casually rolling off an otherwise genteel tongue. I did the quickest 180-degree pivot ever because it was ME who was just about to step through her door, right here, right now. I'd had no idea about the estrogen-soaked locker-room talk that went on when not a single jockstrap or sports bra was anywhere to be found. Sadly, just about the time I became proficient at pitching my own share of outrageous sexual innuendo, the politics and legal oversight of the workplace did its own 180.

So quickly did things change that less than a decade later I found myself face-to-face with an NBC attorney trying to explain some acceptable circumstance for my having crossed the new line into post-modern inappropriateness. I learned that, unlike libel or slander, where there is no actionable offense if what was printed or said is true and offered without malice, veracity is no defense against a harassment charge. I also learned that what constitutes harassment is so nebulous as to ultimately be determined by the person who feels they have been harassed.

As a warm-up personality it sometimes feels like I'm expected to be a joke jukebox with a quip always locked and loaded. With a silly comment to a co-worker I'd unwittingly stepped over the hazy line of good judgment with a wisecrack about the audience wrangler. This was not a network or production company page, but an employee of an outside contracted vendor that supplies paid bodies to fill audience seats. The rumor mill had already carried the not-very-stealthy word that the wrangler was sleeping with the show's director who was several decades older. However, when my light-hearted remark to a third party about the coziness was repeated to the wrangler, I had unwittingly created what is known as a "hostile work environment." Under California law I would be guilty if the statement was judged to offend a person's protected characteristic, in this case "gender expression," and was found to be "severe."

There was no hostile intent on my part, and I never expected that my comment would be repeated. It was just a bit of benign dishing of the latest gossip and, hey, it was true. If anyone was exercising questionable judgment it was the two who were in full-body horizontal Bluetooth pairing mode. It was eye-opening to learn how easily a flip remark could have made defendants of me, the network, the show, the producer, and seemingly everybody down to the rent-a-cop at the guard gate. I received a severe verbal bitch-slapping, was sincerely contrite, truly remorseful, and very apologetic, as well as greatly appreciative of the network's leniency in allowing me to continue on the job.

I can only imagine the pandemonium that would have been unleashed if I'd said anything about anyone dropping to their knees to give a blowjob. Certainly, I can't be the only person who would benefit by having a personal built-in seven-second digital delay system, complete with the all-important "dump" button.

Chapter 8

Somehow television survived its first decade before there was tape to edit. One of the times some post-production magic literally saved an ass is among the best and most widely repeated stories. It's true, even if the man in the middle of it swore it never happened.

I wasn't there. In fact, I was nowhere near. I take the liberty of including this outrageous tale by virtue of having had my own private telling directly from the star of the story, Bob Eubanks. It involves a bit of history that he curiously wiped from his memory. Asked about it countless times, Bob dismissed the incident as nothing more than urban myth, and he remained steadfast in that belief for decades. So sure that it never happened, I was told that Bob even offered cash to anyone who could prove him wrong. It all changed in an instant when he was confronted with video proof some 30 years after the moment. Hidden away in storage for decades was a clip excised from an original episode of *The Newlywed Game*. It was unearthed when compiling one of those "greatest game show moments" specials.

I was the announcer for the initial seasons of the most recent incarnation of the venerable *Newlywed Game* and had always been fascinated by the fact that the show is a product of the minds behind what was TV's very first hit series, *Howdy Doody*. Roger Muir had helped create and served as executive producer of the 1950s kid favorite, while Bobby (Nick) Nicholson performed several of the character roles. Together, they'd written the premise for their simple game on a piece of paper they passed to ABC-TV executives: "Husbands predict wives. Wives predict husbands." The network gave those six words to *The Dating Game* wunderkind Chuck Barris to develop.

When the mad scientist of game shows mounted a presentation of his idea for *The Newlywed Game* it was the stuff dreams are made of. Among his four sample newly-nuptialed pairs were up-and-coming comedian Dom DeLuise and his wife, actress Carol Arthur. They had the ABC brass laughing, but the big moment came when another couple's wife, one Bob Eubanks described as "a drop dead gorgeous blond" disclosed that her husband's nickname was "numbnuts." That's when the network buyers motioned for Chuck to follow them as they walked out of the Vine Street studio.

As couple number one, Dom and Carol Arthur DeLuise added laughter to Chuck Barris's presentation of *The Newlywed Game* to ABC's programming executives. Barris left the network's studio at 1313 Vine Street that day with a series commitment. Photo courtesy of Fred Wostbrock.

It was a rare instant sale. They not only wanted the show but they wanted the run-through emcee, Bob Eubanks, who had not been Chuck's intended host. Oh, they also wanted what they saw to start on-air immediately. *The Newlywed Game* went straight to series without a pilot, with a host who admits he had no idea what he was getting into. The 28-year-old local radio DJ suddenly became network TV's youngest emcee, and says that he was so nervous at the first taping that Chuck told him he had the look of a deer in headlights, swearing he fronted the entire episode without blinking once. Bob claims he then taped a note to his podium reminding himself to blink.

The show was bold and edgy, perfect for 1960s viewers on the younger side of the widening generation gap. There was plausible deniability when Chuck Barris was accused of lowering America's moral standards with his generous dose of suggestive and double entendre questions. Feigning innocence, Chuck and his staff deflected the charge to the newlyweds who clearly were responsible for how they responded to the show's queries. It was true. Even if the questions occasionally walked the couples right up to the line of good taste, that last treacherous step was all theirs.

So it was with merely a suggestion of titillation that Bob Eubanks posed the question, "Where, specifically, is the weirdest place that you personally, girls, have ever gotten the urge to make whoopee?" Among the writers' anticipated responses were the backseat of a car, the balcony of a movie theater, or perhaps an airplane bathroom. Anything close to those answers would have generated the treasured audience tittering that was the show's number-one ingredient for devilish fun. Nobody could ever have anticipated one newly-married wife's response to "Where is the weirdest place that you ever got the urge to make whoopee?" With only a hint of embarrassment she stepped way over the line of good taste with, "In the ass!" Now, how can anyone say that television isn't educational?

"It never happened," insisted Bob, until the clip was found among the endless racks of decades-old tapes Sony had acquired from various production companies. Yes, she said it. The audience howled and Bob nearly fainted. Maybe that momentary loss of blood flow to the brain is why he swears he had zero recollection of the event. Once confronted with the tape Bob could no longer claim it didn't happen, but he then insisted that it never aired.

Incidentally, the audio of "in the ass" had been censored by being muted on the copy of that moment from the ancient *Newlywed Game* taping. I'm told it was the only copy that could be found from the long-ago likely-destroyed master. If you ever see the clip and actually hear the word "ass," it would be the result of the audio being re-recorded and synched to the contestant's lips. They're clearly her words, but her voice was recreated decades later as all searches to that point for the original unmuted moment had been fruitless.

Spending time in an editing bay to clean up language or make video fixes is the last thing most producers want to do. It cuts into profits. For Chuck Barris, working around that single line of unacceptable content was no big deal considering what he'd already been through. His first successful series strayed so deeply into tastelessness that he was forced to deep-six an entire dumpster full of video. Thousands and thousands of dollars worth of work went down the crapper when the complete first week of *The Dating Game* was too blue to be rescued in editing.

The work that went into those two-and-a-half hours of program content was wasted because the moment the lights came up and tape rolled, the demure bachelorettes and clean-cut young bachelors on all five episodes transformed. Each of the 40 Dr. Jekylls became a Mr. or Ms. Hyde. Despite their having used TV-appropriate language in their auditions and run-throughs, after spending hours sequestered together backstage, Chuck recalled it all quickly went to hell. He explained. "They said, 'I'll suck yours if you'll suck mine.' 'I'll tell you the size of my titties only if you tell me the size of your cock-a-doodle-doo.' Every other word was bang, boff, hump, diddle, dicky, twat, pussy, dong and dork."

If you wanted to binge watch all of the surviving tapes from the thousands of ABC's daytime and nighttime *Dating Game* episodes of the 1960s and 70s you'd either be in luck, or out of luck, depending upon your point of view. If you didn't need to see the slowest-motion transformation of fashion on a week-to-week basis, you'll be happy to know that, in total, fewer than half of those tapes still exist. The slightly more than 1,000 from the original run that remain are more than enough to provide point-and-laugh opportunities as the miniskirt and shorthaired collegiate look of the mid-1960s transitions through the long-haired hippie-freak flower-child era, which leads to the braless polyester bell-bottomed loud print disco regalia that our parents somehow survived.

At the beginning, the networks were still regularly reusing the expensive reels of videotape without any consideration that the time-filling silliness they held could ever have any value beyond documenting a sociological curiosity of the era's Homo sapien mating rituals. According to Game Show Network's archivist David Schwartz, all of *The Dating Game* early black and white daytime shows are missing. Even fewer of *The Newlywed Game* tapes survive, as it appears that with the exception of a few scattered shows, pretty much all of the episodes of post-nuptial twosomes between 1966 and 1972 are nowhere to be found.

There's an alternate explanation for why only about 75% of the *Dating Game* tapes from 1967 and later exist. The missing episodes are not from any particular years but seem to create holes as random as those in Swiss cheese. Is it possible they were purposefully pulled from the library for their specific content?

Chuck Barris's idiosyncrasies and peculiarities have been so extensively documented and discussed, even by people who never met him, that it seems no behavior attributed to him could raise an eyebrow. Well, try this one. Legend holds that when the 1987 sale of Chuck's company was imminent, the video impresario was interested in creating plausible deniability for some of the more outrageous and highly-criticized programming he'd fed America in his wilder days. Think *The Chuck Barris Rah-Rah Show, The $1.98 Beauty Show, The Family Game, The Game Game, Leave It to the Women, Comedy Courtroom, How's Your Mother-in-Law?* and the cavalcade of kooks you love to hate, better known as *The Gong Show*.

While only nature could eventually erase the memories that possibly haunted Chuck, he could at least destroy the evidence by loading up a rented barge and personally dumping a ton of embarrassing tape into the Hudson River. Yes, that's the story that has circulated, without an explanation of how or why all that videotape would have made it from Hollywood to New York. Chuck's reputation as a radical had become so entrenched that it made even that wild scenario seem conceivable. For years it's been rumored to have been true, but could talk of such a wild escapade have actually been based on fact? File it along with the mastermind's own claim that *The Dating Game* was designed to help facilitate his secret globe-hopping assignments as an undercover CIA agent.

One of those many missing episodes from the original run of *The Dating Game* is said to have cost Chuck a lot of lost sleep and an untold sum of money. It also adds a gem to the crown that Chuck will forever wear as the showrunner with the longest list of most incredible escapades. This one involved the long-hoped-for discovery of a couple that ended up married after meeting on the show. Finally, there was such a pair. The happy surprise was to be revealed when the twosome returned for a *Dating Game* Valentine's Day special episode.

It all went horribly wrong after the engaged but yet-to-be-hitched lovebirds taped their return in advance of the February 14th airdate, and in advance of their actually exchanging vows. The wedding and reception were scheduled during the intervening weeks. Perhaps the couple suddenly decided they wanted a bigger chocolate fountain at the dessert table but, for whatever reason, they unexpectedly elected to extort a dowry of dollars from Chuck. They demanded $50,000 to go through with the wedding.

With the special episode featuring the announcement of their having just been married already in the can, as well as a promotional campaign in the works, the couple assumed that Chuck would simply pull out his checkbook. Hey, the $50,000 would pay for a hell of a honeymoon and it's merely chump change for a millionaire television executive, right? A producer like Dan Enright might just kick them out of his office with a litany of curse words, while Mark Goodson would likely puff on his pipe a few times and then call his lawyers, but Chuck was far more hands-on. The former street-wise kid from Philadelphia met with the betrothed pair, convincing them to agree to a plan only the eccentric showman would think to personally execute.

In exchange for not reporting the blackmail attempt and for a substantially smaller check to be handed over the following Monday, Valentine's Day of 1966, Chuck personally drove the couple to Tijuana for the weekend. There, he witnessed their wedding and, to defend against an instant divorce or annulment, he then stayed in a hotel room with the newlyweds pretty much nonstop through their honeymoon until the pre-taped celebration of their recent wedding aired. As the credits rolled, Chuck handed over the money and blessed their marriage, or their divorce, their choice. Whether or not he stopped payment on the said-to-be $20,000 check after returning to Los Angeles is uncertain.

The version of *Newlywed Game* that Carnie Wilson and I worked nearly a half century later had evolved in content from vaguely suggestive questions to now include a record number of double entendres per episode. Our risqué queries set up the couples to tickle the audiences' prurience with responses about all manner of sexual and excretory activity. I was assured that the thinly-veiled creative euphemisms made the show relevant for our 2009 debut.

The author teamed with the multi-talented Carnie Wilson in 2009 for GSN's reboot of *The Newlywed Game*. Created by *Howdy Doody* alumni Robert "Nick" Nicholson and E. Roger Muir, a version of the series had been in production during each decade since its 1966 ABC debut. Photo from the author's collection

On our first day in the studio I remembered hearing about Barris's problem with language from the prospective hook-up partners on his first week of *Dating Game* shows all those years ago. While there are no applicable FCC standards governing indecency or obscenity on cable, I already knew that the only thing blue Sony wanted to see on their family-friendly channel was in the pixels on their big-screen TV sets. There'd be no place for any seriously salacious material in their program content.

If we'd have fallen into the same trap that Chuck did the first time around and a week of our *Newlywed Game* had to be re-shot, the extra money in my pocket would be just a tiny fraction of the huge financial hit to the tight GSN budget. Hoping to avoid spoiled episodes, I wondered whether anyone had given a thought to history possibly repeating itself. On our first tape day I saw that both the network and our veteran producer Vinny Rubino already had it covered. We had one thing going for us that Chuck and his hosts, Bob Eubanks and Jim Lange, didn't. It was a secret weapon named Al Rosen.

Al was a delightful, easygoing light-hearted, and friendly guy, and the only person I ever heard of who came to television from the furniture business. He was 70 years old if he was a day. In our joking he enjoyed my observation that the only way we could be sure about his age would be for the lab at UCLA to carbon-date his farts. After a lifetime worrying about selling armoires, who wouldn't love to be behind the scenes in the magic act of making television entertainment? He enjoyed the studio milieu—bright, talented, funny people, and all the free food you can eat. In this second career Al worked for Sullivan Compliance. That's the company that provides the standards and practices oversight for a great many cable and syndicated shows, including the all-mighty *Jeopardy!* and *Wheel of Fortune.*

Traditionally the networks assign their in-house legal staffs for their own shows while third party contractors, like Sullivan, do the policing on non-network productions to keep them kosher. That was Al's gig, keeping it kosher. He looked the part too, like an old rabbi on hand to bless the proceedings. As our secret weapon, Al's responsibilities included briefing the contestants on the standards that were applicable to our show. There was far more to what sounds like a simple task. It was all about subtext, and Al was masterful in this unique role.

You see, with the benign intent of simply insuring that the show's language wasn't blatantly offensive, Al was also actually arming the couples with acceptable ways of including all manner of implied soft-core indecency. He was broadening their horizons to include a whole universe of euphemisms, many that hadn't occurred to the players before their heart-to-heart talk with Al. I loved to be within earshot as this soft-spoken, senior citizen went through his litany of acceptable language for each tape day's new crop of contestants.

Grandfatherly Al would say, "We don't use 'fuck' or 'intercourse,' instead we say 'whoopee' or 'the deed.' We don't say 'eat pussy' or 'suck cock,' we say 'pleasuring' or 'going south.' We don't like 'going down,' but 'going downtown' will communicate the same thought and it will also get a laugh. 'Cock,' 'dick' or even 'penis' is not good. We go with 'maleness,' 'unit,' 'package' or 'his little man.' We stay away from 'vagina,' 'pussy' and 'vulva,' but we like…" And on it went for every conceivable body part, sexual act and excretory function. I could never get enough of an Al Rosen briefing!

All of that potty-mouth seems to have endless entertainment value for both studio and home audiences. In addition to *The Newlywed Game*, it also contributed to the reinvigoration that has made the over 45-year-old *Family Feud* format more successful than ever. Among the families competing on ABC's *Celebrity Family Feud* a few years ago was a star known as an outspoken activist with well-founded partisan views about government. That includes the politics at the Screen Actors Guild where he served as president in the early 1980s.

Ed Asner had always been ready to espouse well-informed political insights when asked. Otherwise, when operating in default mode, he was wickedly funny and wonderfully foulmouthed. That made him a perfect patriarch when the Asner family appeared to be stumped by emcee Steve Harvey's *Feud* question, "Name something a girl may get from a boy on a date." Flowers, chocolates, and jewelry were all covered by other players. With two strikes and only one guess remaining there was a single unknown answer on the board that nobody had been able to discern. Ed's turn came and he blurted, "A social disease!" Not only the funniest moment of the show, it was the correct answer.

Always a winner, Ed Asner with family scoring opposite Vicki Lawrence's clan on ABC's *Celebrity Family Feud* (2015). Photo from the author's collection.

It was proof that Ed was just as frisky as he had been almost 40 years earlier when he and his successor as president of the Screen Actors Guild, Patty Duke, were celebrating at our sister union, AFTRA's 50th anniversary picnic. There, amazingly, these two took turns as the attraction at a carnival dunk tank. When dry, both of these TV stars and union leaders generously shared their passion while fighting for their brethren in support of increased wages, health and retirement benefits, and improved working conditions. However, that day Patty and Ed each allowed a bunch of us fellow union performers to fire fastballs that repeatedly knocked them from their perches, dunking them into a huge barrel of water. Each time Ed came up he was laughing and cursing. Similarly, over and over again Patty surfaced dripping and snorting, and always smiling. Real troupers.

Many years later, at a 2018 celebration of John Wayne's birthday at the Gene Autry Museum of Western Heritage, Ed and I shared a laugh about that memory still vivid for the nonagenarian. Amazingly, Ed still had much of the passion he had when running SAG. He was back on the ballot again and won a seat on the board in 2020. The last time our paths crossed was in 2021 at a play reading where his 91 years had taken their toll. It turned out to be mere days before he passed away.

That night Ed needed assistance walking and he was obviously suffering with arthritic hands as he struggled to turn script pages, but his mind was crisp and clear. That was obvious when, once again, our conversation meandered to a mention of dear Patty Duke. We agreed that it didn't seem that our endearing, honest, vulnerable, and delightful mutual friend had been gone more than five years already. Patty's story is a triumph of the human spirit in which a troubled child star grew to overcome tremendous challenges to eventually find peace, live an outstanding life, and continue to enjoy a fruitful career. It's also another example of the reason former *Donna Reed Show* child actor Paul Peterson had been so dedicated to his cause, "A Minor Consideration." The work he's done advocating for underage performers has been a long-running miraculous gift to the industry with many success stories that Paul was usually far too modest to publicize.

Patty was a bright, precocious, endearing little trouper. By the tender age of 12 her acting resume already included more than 50 TV appearances. Her natural talent, enhanced by a full regimen of classes and training, propelled the budding star to unprecedented accomplishments on stage, in movies, and on television. One of her lesser-known appearances was as a game show contestant on *The $64,000 Challenge*, one of the dozen-plus rigged quizzes of the 1950s. Patty was victorious in her category, music. She told me she was frightened to death on live television trying to remember all the practiced answers while in a hot isolation booth that she remembered was "98 degrees, if not more."

Following her game show appearance, the young actress had one performance that was even more emotional than her debut as Helen Keller on the Great White Way. That booking was before a Congressional committee on November 3, 1959, just two weeks after her Broadway premiere in *The Miracle Worker*. When called to testify in closed executive session at the hearings into game show rigging the 12-year old lied, saying she'd not been coached. Patty delivered a very credible and detailed narrative about her primetime win and how she accomplished the feat entirely on her own.

When she finished, one of the Senators looked her in the eyes and quietly asked, "Now Anna Marie, have you told us the truth?" Patty remembered breaking down in tears, admitting that she had been clued in advance about the material. "I spilled my guts," is how Patty described her recanting. It was later revealed that Shirley Bernstein, composer Leonard Bernstein's sister, had been the staff producer who helped Patty prepare by quizzing her with the same questions she'd be asked on air. Shirley testified that was standard practice, she explained, "either because the contestant was very nervous or the sponsor had requested a particular outcome of a match."

Patty Duke in her dual role on ABC's *The Patty Duke Show* (1964). A year before the series debut the gifted actress became the youngest person ever to win an Academy Award in a competitive category for *The Miracle Worker*. Four years earlier she gave an award-worthy performance at the Congressional hearings into game show rigging.

Named Anna at birth, Patty was a brilliant kid being raised in a psychological hell. Patty's parents split from each other, as well as from their daughter. Her alcoholic dad and severely depressed mom had signed all authority over her upbringing to an unscrupulous couple, and she was forbidden from seeing her mother for years. Patty's throat tightened, her voice cracked and she fought back a tear remembering the moment, at age eight, when she said farewell to her mother. "She told me I had to go, and I had to be a good girl." Hearing Patty tell this story, no doubt my face revealed both my incredulity and sadness. Rather than curse her misfortune, Patty surprised me by saying that her mom was basically a sweet person, "very warm, very bright, but very naive."

Patty explained that her parents' relinquishing her care and custody was the result of her mother's insecurities being cunningly manipulated by talent managers John and Ethel Ross. Once legal guardianship was theirs, Patty's life was tightly controlled by a couple whose sole concern seemed to be grooming her to be pimped out into the entertainment business. They dominated every aspect of her life, "Everything from what I wore, to when I slept, to what I ate," remembered Patty. She recalled that within a short time Ethel announced, "We're gonna change your name. Anna Marie is dead. You're Patty now."

The child was subject to all manner of physical exploitation. She recalled two separate occasions when John and Ethel each tried to fondle her in bed. "My response both times was to vomit," she said. The sexual harassment ended, but the emotional abuse continued. In the hands of the Rosses her life was regimented and entirely focused on work. Along with the less desirable things they did to her, Patty generously credits the couple's mandated acting lessons and workshops with making her a star.

After the teenager was celebrated for carrying the lead role in the first of a two-year Broadway run of *The Miracle Worker* she brought Helen Keller's story to life in the movie version. Patty was feted with the Academy Award for Best Supporting Actress for that moving portrayal. At that time she was the youngest person to receive an Oscar in any competitive category. An Academy Award is the supreme hallmark of a successful career in show business, isn't it? It surely didn't feel like success. Ironically, as her fame increased the Rosses' mistreatment became more and more torturous. "When I became successful, their fear that I would leave them became so great," she remembered, "that they became rather twisted in their behavior with me."

In the turmoil, Patty battled anorexia all the way down to a weight of 76 pounds. She also began drinking heavily and taking Valium, repeatedly landing in the hospital having overdosed nearly a dozen times. Still undiagnosed with what was then called manic-depression, it was the seemingly dual personalities resulting from Patty's bipolar disorder that actually inspired the concept for her sitcom. Yes, the idea for *The Patty Duke Show*—identical cousins with contrasting personalities—was born from the seeming duality in Patty's disposition and temperament caused by her untreated bipolar mood swings. The show's creator, Sidney Sheldon, came up with the sitcom's hook observing Patty's behavioral quirks on a day she spent with his family.

In pre-production it quickly became apparent that portraying two characters with at least one in virtually every scene, *The Patty Duke Show* would be labor-intensive for the 16-year-old actress. Then and there the choice was made to film in New York because, as Sheldon said, "California has too many laws about kids on the set. New York doesn't care if you work them to death."

Understandably, Patty welcomed the change in her legal status that came with her 18th birthday in 1964. With the star now able to work longer hours in Los Angeles, a few episodes returned to the MGM lot in Culver City where the pilot had been shot. ABC wanted to make that move permanent. United Artists and Patty's managers agreed, but with her new independence and legal autonomy, the show's star made it clear she wanted to stay in New York for the planned fourth season. She exerted her newfound authority and, as a result, the series wrapped prematurely. For the first time Patty was now sufficiently empowered to derail plans she found objectionable. She finally broke free of the Rosses' control only to ultimately discover that the couple had squandered most of her sizeable earnings.

With *The Patty Duke Show* wrapped after 104 episodes, and work as an adult not forthcoming, Patty fell deeper into the downward spiral of substance abuse and worsening mood swings. On the heels of her 18th birthday Patty impulsively married a man 13 years her senior. It was more stable than the next knot tied with Michael Tell, a rock promoter who had been subleasing her apartment. Bridesmaids were still combing rice out of their hair when the newlyweds separated.

In the seven short years following her TV stardom Patty was on her third of four marriages. With nearly a half-dozen partners at the time she learned she was pregnant, her son Sean Astin was never sure who his father was from among three prime suspects, Desi Arnaz Jr., actor John Astin and Michael Tell. Although Astin and Patty raised Sean as their own, a later DNA paternity test revealed that Tell was his biological father.

Finally, in 1982 a psychiatrist diagnosed the condition that had wreaked so much havoc, manic depression. Once stabilized on lithium Patty's life began anew: "It saved my life and it gave me life." With her 1987 autobiography Patty revealed her psychological challenges and soon became a courageous advocate for mental health.

I first met Patty the year after the book hit the shelves, when she was a guest on a talk show I was working. During a stopdown in the taping I asked Patty a question I presented as being for the audience's benefit, but it was much more to satisfy my own curiosity. With *The Patty Duke Show* then running nightly on Nickelodeon, I wondered how it felt when she caught a glimpse of her teenage self on reruns of the series. Perhaps more than any other kid star she was truly miles from the person she was then.

Patty took a moment in thought before responding, "I do occasionally run across the show while flipping through the channels. I know it's me and I can remember doing the work, but it was such a different me that it feels more like I'm watching another person." To my ear, Patty seemed to take a brief pause before speaking those last two words that had become an all-too-familiar phrase associated with her, "another person." She told me in a later discussion that she'd heard those words all during her childhood from others who were trying to understand and reign in her flighty moods and behavior.

I admired Patty and enjoyed her company on the occasions when our paths crossed at SAG functions. In addition to being a huge talent she was such a quality human being—courageous, empathetic, cheerful and very bright. There was inspiration to be drawn from Patty's tenacity in vanquishing her demons. She overcame so much to survive and thrive in later years, and was so open about her turbulent life as part of her advocacy for mental health. Dear Patty passed in early 2016 of sepsis resulting from an intestinal perforation. Beyond family and friends, it was a huge loss for the Screen Actors Guild, where she'd dedicated herself to improving the lives of her performing brethren.

While even today the vast majority of the merged SAG-AFTRA's membership is anonymous to even the most compulsive readers of credits, they along with every single high-profile movie and TV star all carry the same card in their wallets. It helps to create an instant affinity with even the Guild's lifetime achievement award winners, including Ernest Borgnine.

Chapter 9

Ernest Borgnine was an Oscar winner for his film role as *Marty*, and earned early TV credibility for repeatedly surviving the rigors of acting in ambitious live dramas. Between his television debut on *Captain Video and His Video Rangers*, and his final role performing as Mermaid Man in *SpongeBob SquarePants* video games, there were over 200 performances that helped to make his a household name. How I came to spend an entire afternoon sitting next to Ernie was a rare case of serendipity as it began years of occasional conversations that helped demystify the world of show business while providing some wonderfully entertaining stories. Always with a twinkle in his eye and in his voice, Ernie contributed great tales from decades of Tinseltown television.

Ernie helped anchor the 1980s adventure series *Airwolf*, and the 1990s sitcom *The Single Guy*. I was a much bigger fan of his 1960s enlistment as Lt. Quinton McHale on *McHale's Navy*. The series was born from an *Alcoa Premiere* anthology episode titled *Seven Against the Sea* and aired complete with an introduction by none other than Fred Astaire explaining the backstory. The subsequent scripts were entirely formulaic, but for mindless wartime sitcom hi-jinx fun they were in good company with the writing for *The Phil Silvers Show*, *Hogan's Heroes*, and the more meaty *M*A*S*H*. By the way, was there any war during *Gomer Pyle, USMC*? Other than the war between Gomer and Gunnery Sergeant Vince Carter, that is.

Never mind that a visit to Universal Studios reveals that McHale's lagoon is just barely larger than William Howard Taft's White House bathtub. The cast is what made the show transcendent. Ernie played straight man to Tim Conway's crazy antics and Joe Flynn's exasperation as Ensign Charles Parker and Captain Wallace Binghamton respectively. That was a breakout role for Conway, as only a matter of months earlier he was working in TV near his hometown, Cleveland, with that city's local legend, Ernie "Goulardi" Anderson. That's the same Ernie Anderson who later became the voice of ABC. Think, "*The L-o-o-o-o-v-e Boat.*"

Tim Conway subtly hamming with co-star Ernest Borgnine on the set of *McHale's Navy* (1962), one of a dozen TV series on which he was a regular.

Ernie Borgnine confirmed that it was comic actress Rose Marie who helped Conway make the Hollywood connections that propelled his career. They met when Rose was visiting WJW-TV during a promotional tour for *The Dick Van Dyke Show*. "I met him, I said 'You're funny,'" Rose remembered. "I said, 'Do you have anything on tape?' He deadpanned, 'I have a band-aid on my foot.'" Tim then put together a composite of some of his best bits and mailed it to Rose. Before long, Tim and Mary Ann Conway trekked west.

The couple's first L.A. apartment was just a few blocks away from his benefactor's home, and Rose would often cook dinner for the Conways as she continued to support the comedian during his early pursuits. Tim's first break was a job Rose helped him land on Steve Allen's show. Tim never forgot her kindness, recalling shortly before his passing, "She told me about the business [when] I would go over to her house for dinner. I've never had so much food in all my life."

Today Tim is best remembered for his wild characterizations on CBS's mega-successful *The Carol Burnett Show*. "What a difference an hour can make" would be an apt tribute to describe the brilliance Carol saw from the young comedy cut-up every week. You see, like many variety shows at the time, Carol's program was performed twice before two different live audiences with only a one-hour meal break in between. The first was officially called a dress rehearsal, but footage would often be used from both performances in editing the final cut of the program.

Tim played the comedy much as written during that first taping to be sure there would be a straightforward usable version of the sketches in which he performed. Then, after dinner, Tim would embellish the same skits with his own outrageous flights of fancy. The enhancements he brought to the second performances were the fuel that sparked the show's funniest moments. When Harvey Korman appeared to be nearly wetting his pants in a scene, it was an honest reaction to Tim's comedy brilliance. It was all obviously sport for Tim as he said in 2009, "Harvey never knew what I would do next, and I could not wait to get to work to give it a go. One way or another, I always got him."

Perhaps the best remembered from among the hysterical moments that the two friends shared was in what's been called "The Dentist Sketch." It first aired on March 3rd, 1969, and as many times as you may have seen it, another quick trip to YouTube will guarantee another laugh. In 2019, just months before his passing, a writer on the show, Roger Beatty, still remembered that tape day in Television City's Studio 33 and recalled Harvey's resolve not to crack up. Roger told me the two comedians even had a bet to see if Harvey could keep a straight face through the entire scene. As written, the skit had Harvey visiting a dentist on his first day of practice on a human after training with animals. It was funny, but it exploded into hysterics when Tim took flight with a series of adlib mishaps that he said were motivated by an actual experience he had, when an Army dentist preparing to extract his tooth accidently stabbed the Novocain needle through Tim's cheek and into his own thumb.

The adlibbed sight gags that followed reached a high point at the moment when a fly is heard buzzing into the scene. If you remember, it's when Tim goes to swat it with his Novocain-numbed hand that Harvey falls apart. Tim had a secret weapon that virtually guaranteed he would win the wager. You see, there was no fly called for in the script. The only two people who knew it would wing into the scene were Tim and sound effects engineer Ross Murray. Tim had asked Ross if he could find the sound of a buzzing fly. Easy. Then, before taping, Tim told Ross exactly when to introduce the sound effect, and the rest is history. Tim didn't appear to be joking when he said his pal actually did experience what he called "unwanted moistness" during the sketch.

Another favorite clip from Carol's show is proof that no member of the cast was immune from Tim's ability to break up scene partners. It's the "Mama's Family" skit with Dick Van Dyke in which Tim tells his co-stars about the Siamese twin elephants that were joined at the trunks, and the time they sneezed. There was indeed a scripted passing reference to an elephant in the dress rehearsal, but nothing like what the cast heard in the second performance. Although Carol had a firm rule for her cast to always remain in character, there was no way to be on stage listening or watching Tim's gift for absurdity without losing composure.

In fact, "Mama" herself, Vicki Lawrence, remembers how in that scene it was none other than Carol who broke first, and hard. Vicki reported that the star had tears in her eyes as she bit her lip to regain composure. It didn't help, as it was impossible not to surrender to Tim. The cast's only advance warning came from the director who told them, "Good luck!" after Tim privately hinted at what he was prepared to bring to the second taping. Carol giggled recalling those moments: "We prided ourselves on being trained theatrically, but there were times you couldn't [help it]. It was like giggling in church or the library."

You'd think a comedic mind as brilliant as Tim's would have had a wonderfully successful career, but before being hired for Carol's show almost all of his TV projects came and went quickly. Sporting the license plates "13 WKS" was the comic actor's self-deprecating reminder that, other than his successful hitch aboard McHale's PT-73, he set sail fronting sitcoms and variety shows that all promptly sank during their initial 13 week outing. The quick cancellations of *Ace*

Crawford, Private Eye and *Tim Conway's Funny America* were nothing when compared with ABC's single-episode failure, *Turn-On*.

Although it's highly doubtful, Tim repeatedly claimed that his hometown Cleveland affiliate cancelled the sketch comedy show during its first commercial, preferring to play canned music than subject viewers to the rest of the atrocious program. The cold response from other eastern stations served as a warning to several west coast affiliates that turned off *Turn-On* before it even started. Tim remembered that the launch party doubled as a wrap party. Despite the involvement of comedy legends Albert Brooks and Chuck McCann, as well as the pedigree of being conceived by the mind that birthed *Laugh-In*, George Schlatter, this flop was no laughing matter. *TV Guide* immortalized the February 5, 1969 single broadcast of *Turn-On* as "The biggest bomb of the season."

Ernie Borgnine was all too happy to talk about Tim. They'd remained friends ever since being paired as Captain and Ensign aboard McHale's PT 73, and ultimately worked together again a half century later voicing *SpongeBob SquarePants* characters. There was a lot to like about Tim. When our paths crossed he was friendly, kind, joyous, and warm with a surprisingly subdued off-stage manner. He got the first laugh with a twisted pronoun when we were introduced, "It's a pleasure meeting me." It was.

Equally memorable were the times on both coasts that I encountered Tim and Ernie's sitcom co-star, the vaudevillian who played McHale's crewmember Seaman Gruber. That actor was Carl Ballantine aka The Great Ballantine, vaudeville's celebrated bumbling magician. We exchanged greetings in New York at the restaurant The Forum of the Twelve Caesars, and enjoyed a few minutes in conversation upon arriving simultaneously, he with his daughter, for a function at Hollywood's Magic Castle. In talking with Carl about his own half-century in show business I learned that his four-season enlistment in *McHale's Navy* came when the show's supporting roles were cast in New York in order to get some fresh faces and fresher attitudes.

Before earning his gold braid as Captain Merrill Stubing, commander of *The Love Boat*, Gavin MacLeod was another lowly seaman, Joseph "Happy" Haines, scouting the south Pacific with McHale's crew. In a Television Academy interview he revealed that he enlisted for the gig because he specifically wanted to work with Carl Ballantine. As a child during the twilight days of vaudeville he had been enraptured by the magic of The Great Ballantine.

The on-set camaraderie was everything he'd hoped for but, with barely a couple of lines in each week's script and no billing at the top of the show, the tide turned for Gavin during his second year with McHale. He feared that his career had run aground. It led to a deep depression that he self-medicated with generous doses of alcohol. He confessed that, one night while driving L.A.'s notoriously twisty Mullholland Drive, the thought of suicide was compelling him to steer off the road and into the deep ravine below.

Gavin said some force stopped him in the last second. Shaken, afraid, and drunk, he immediately drove to pal Peter Falk's nearby home. Peter's advice was to see a shrink, and recommended his own psychiatrist. Gavin did, and explained that the hours on the couch helped him crystallize the reality that he needed to quit the series that was stifling his aspirations. Although locked into a three-year contract, the urgency of his request led to his being released without penalty—an honorable discharge from McHale's crew. As with many stories of personal triumph, when one door closed another opened. Gavin said the phone rang with a new opportunity within hours.

The actor's face became more familiar as he guested on a number of series. He knew his career was back on track the day he auditioned for the role of Lou Grant, Mary Tyler Moore's boss at the WJM newsroom. After reading for the role that Ed Asner ultimately played, Gavin explained to producers that he felt better suited to play Murray, the writer. Auditioning with that supporting player's lines felt like the right fit for all involved, and he became the very first to be cast to star with Mary.

As an aside, casting the part of Lou Grant proved to be difficult. The character had a heart of gold that was buried beneath a blustery, harsh, sharp-tongued dismissive boss. Being a bully, too mean to sweet Mary, would have killed the show by making him unsympathetic and unfunny if not outright hated by audiences. Even Ed Asner couldn't pull it off on his first attempt. Ed said on his second audition he substituted a benign craziness for anger. He won the role by reading the part loudly with grandiose gesturing, but without being angry, demeaning, or threatening. It helped to make Ed the male celebrated with more Emmy awards for acting than any other at the time.

I heard the most about Gavin MacLeod, Tim Conway, Carl Ballantine and the nautical nuttiness that afternoon while sitting next to Ernie Borgnine, the commanding officer of *McHale's Navy*. The event was an annual World Championship Chili Cook-Off competition. There's only one, and it's sanctioned by the apparently prestigious International Chili Society. For hopeful gold-ribbon winners you could say this was a bread-and-butter event. Ernie was an established and respected authority on all matters chili, but it was only 10 years before our 1990 meeting that he claimed he'd never even heard of a chili cook-off.

Although considered a competent chef, Ernie was clueless about these competitions until Peter Marshall's sister, actress Joanne Dru, opened his eyes. Those eyes were soon weeping from the chili powder and onions as Joanne and her husband at the time, a fellow named C.V. Wood, invited Ernie and his taste buds to a new experience. He was helicoptered to his first chili affair by Mel Larson, an amateur pilot whose real job was as an executive at the Circus Circus Hotel and Casino in Las Vegas. Thereafter, the chopper became part of Ernie's deal.

With a mass of humanity watching his landing in the huge open field in the northern reaches of Los Angeles County, I realized this was indeed a big brouhaha on the beef and bean circuit. The chopper's rotor wash stirred up a medley of aromas from the simmering stockpots being tended by more than 100 chefs. Each had been cooking all day, backtiming for the moment of peak flavor to coincide with the four o'clock start of the judging. They each had high hopes of becoming the big cheese atop the chili world.

Ernie, I, and our brethren on the panel of celebrity gastronomic adjudicators donned the aprons festooned with the ICS logo and our names. The guy with "Borgnine" emblazed on his apron made the rounds meeting his fellow connoisseurs, including this new guy with "West" across his chest. When we sat down, Ernie was next to me. Frankly, being the local radio station's morning personality was a comparatively poor excuse for being considered a celebrity, but on a disc jockey's salary the lure of free food was irresistible.

Between reminders to spit out each chili sample after tasting, the ebullient actor and I chatted for hours. Tim Conway's brilliance was a top topic of conversation, but hearing about James Garner's successful legal battles with the studios ran a close second. Garner was among the first to prevail in the courts in challenging the film industry's notorious bookkeeping practices. He sued for unpaid compensation from playing both Bret Maverick for Warner Bros. and Jim Rockford for Universal.

The story went that the actor's *Maverick* pay had been suspended during a writers' strike, with the studio claiming that the work stoppage allowed them to withhold salaries under a force majeure contract clause. Garner prevailed by proving that Warner Bros. had no fewer than 15 writers working in secret during the same strike weeks for which his pay was suspended. Two decades later and less than a couple of thousand feet away from Warner's iconic water tower, neighboring Universal was unwilling to open *The Rockford Files* financial files. Ernie told me enough of this tale to whet my appetite for researching the details.

Garner ran up $2.2 million in personal legal fees as the studio dragged him through delays with hopes that he would simply give up on pursuing $16.5 million. That was the balance he claimed was his rightful 37.5% share of profits. After eight long years when all postponements, continuances, and stalling tactics had been fully exhausted and Universal would finally be compelled to open the books on their dubious accounting, the studio negotiated an out-of-court settlement. Garner said he was satisfied with the undisclosed payment, especially after reimbursement for his $2.2 million in legal fees were added.

Would the studios really stiff their all-important fan-fave talent? Take the case of one of Warner Bros. most admired performers. Generations of audiences know and love Mel Blanc's work, some even consider him a national treasure. As the voice that first breathed life into the studio's famous mascots his is still the heart and soul that enables Bugs Bunny and the whole rat pack of animated characters to continue ringing Warner's cash register to the tune of over $10 million a year.

Producer Chuck McKibben worked directly for Mel and his son Noel Blanc as their choice to engineer all studio recording at the production company the Blancs owned in the 1970s. He reports that after his former boss's death, Noel filed a lawsuit against the studio for his father's unpaid TV residuals. The resulting settlement bound Noel from seeking any further remuneration, and forbid his making any public disclosure of Warners' payment. The compensation accepted for all past and future television use of Mel's voice characterizations in the filmed cartoon shorts totaled approximately $670,000 plus decades of interest. Noel privately confirmed the details as recently as 2017. In 2021, at age 83 himself, and with his father dead for over 30 years, Noel closed the final chapter on Mel Blanc's life and career by putting all of the keepsakes and personal mementoes from the man of 1,000 voices up for auction.

Ernie Borgnine blew me away with another surprising revelation, this one about casting. He said he'd been on the short list to play Don Vito Corleone in *The Godfather*. Ernie explained that, at first, Paramount nixed Francis Coppola's choice of Marlon Brando. Then, after the director's other pick, Laurence Olivier, declined the role, Ernie apparently became a candidate on the studio's short list that he remembered also included Edward G. Robinson, Richard Conte, Anthony Quinn, Carlo Ponti, George C. Scott and, interestingly, Danny Thomas. Unable to picture the nightclub comic-turned-producing mogul in the role, I later heard that the studio was hopeful he'd bring cash to the project if given the plum gig. Originally envisioned as a current-day drama budgeted at a down-and-dirty $2.5 million, Paramount had started looking for a partner to help cover what eventually became a $6 million period piece.

Coppola prevailed after assurances were made in deference to Brando's ego and salary demands. There's comedy mixed with the drama of *The Godfather* once you know to watch for Brando's turning away from the characters he talks to. While the Don appears to be choosing his words Brando was, in a way, doing exactly that. The legendary actor was actually looking to the vast array of cue cards placed all around the set to glimpse the next of his un-memorized lines.

Ernie was too humble to want to talk about himself despite having countless fascinating experiences. That even included a few claims to fame for this Academy Award winner in the lowly world of game shows. Uber-fans will remember that Ernie was the original center square in the giant 17-foot tall grid on the debut week of *Hollywood Squares* in 1966. That's before Paul Lynde rode that chair to his greatest fame for most of NBC's run of 3,500-plus shows. Ernie also participated in an elaborate stunt for *I've Got a Secret* in which he intentionally riled the anger of the saucy redhead panelist, Jayne Meadows. Disguised as a taxi driver, Ernie picked up Jayne at her uptown Park Avenue apartment for her trip to the show's midtown studio. Ernie, whom Jayne didn't recognize under his cabbie's cap, deliberately drove in a series of wrong directions running up the fare while she ranted from the back seat.

Among his more compelling recollections of Hollywood movie making were those from shooting the incredibly gory, gritty, and controversial 1969 western *The Wild Bunch* with its all-star cast and the fantastically inebriated director Sam Peckinpah. Ernie remembered that his gun-loving alcoholic director was such a maverick that he fought with Warner Bros. during post-production about their adding generic gunshots from the studio's sound effects library. He demanded each pull of a trigger be "fresh as a pretty girl just noticed," insisting each one be unique and appropriate to the weapons in the firefights.

Talk about an actor with range, within months of that bloody cinema shootout with the Mexican federales, Ernie spent three years touring as co-star in a production of *The Odd Couple* opposite Don Rickles. "How was that experience?" I asked. He let loose with the heartiest belly-jiggling laugh I ever heard. Rickles played the fastidious fussbudget Felix Unger while Ernie inhabited the Oscar Madison role, the sloppy sports writer best remembered from Jack Klugman's portrayal. It was a bigger stretch for Ernie than for Jack. Like the fictional Oscar Madison, Jack was a frequent guest at the racetrack and was very fond of playing the ponies.

I was with Jack Klugman at a Screen Actors Guild seminar about career building. Jack spoke to our small group, answering questions about the industry with solid advice that was delightfully spiced with humor. Questions from several of us started to steer Jack toward sharing his fascinating anecdotes from a lifetime in the business. Despite the challenges of a weak and raspy voice following throat surgery, Jack completely enthralled us with reminiscences. One was all about Ethel Merman.

Despite feeling uncertain, anxious, and tentative through the casting process, Jack won a role in the 1959 original Broadway production of *Gypsy* starring the grandest leading lady of American musical theater. "The Merm," as she allowed some to refer to her, was charmed by Jack's innocence, honesty, and vulnerability. While an experienced actor, this was to be Jack's first major musical comedy role. It required he perform the seemingly impossible task of singing a duet with Merman and actually being heard over her famous decibel-abundant belting voice.

Broadway musical newcomer Jack Klugman with the era's first lady of the Great White Way, Ethel Merman in *Gypsy* (1959).

Jack remembered candidly explaining to the star that he was intimidated by her reputation and experience, and that he had apprehensions about singing with her. Merman immediately reassured Jack, "I'm going to work with you on this." Indeed, Jack said he was invited into her dressing room pretty much every day. There she helped him with his singing, gave him performance advice, taught him theater history, and serenaded him in private. They also took to sharing bawdy jokes and tall tales of backstage lore.

Through all of this Jack said he was still calling her "Miss Merman" out of respect for her fame and the difference in their ages—Jack was fourteen years her junior. Merman told him she wasn't "playing star" with him and that he needed to finally loosen up. Jack said he was naïve to Merman's motivation until the day she matter-of-factly announced, "You know Jack, I've fucked all of my leading men and I've started to include second-leads. Are you almost ready?" Jack remembered he was speechless. Merman's mouth had a well-earned reputation for its ability to be as uncouth as it was loud, but this was a whole new side of her that Jack had yet to see.

What he didn't tell us that day at SAG was whether or not the two consummated their friendship. He made it clear that they had "a love affair during the production, and for years and years after. I loved her. We just loved each other." He then added as an afterthought, "It was platonic." I wonder. There are published accounts of Merman's sexual escapades extending from leading men down through the ranks to chorus boys, to theater staffs, and to restaurateurs. Most notable from that latter realm was Sherman Billingsley, owner of the legendary Stork Club. You can add at least one woman to that resume of romances. If gossip columnist Cindy Adams is to be believed—and she usually was—Merman enjoyed a lengthy lesbian relationship with famed author Jacqueline Susann.

The true measure of the chanteuse's attitude toward conforming to social mores is best summed up by her behavior on a visit to Twentieth Century-Fox. Merman signed to do a movie at Fox and was being wined, dined, and toured around the lot. Entering the sound stage where supposedly straight-laced Loretta Young was preparing to shoot a scene, Merman spied the set's massive staircase that ascended nearly up to the grid some 35 feet above the stage floor. "Where the hell does this go?" Hearing the question, Ms. Young came forward shaking the coffee can into which anyone who swore in her presence had to drop a coin or two as a penalty to be donated to charity. Having heard from Carole Lombard that Loretta Young was every bit as bad a girl as Merman was, The Merm reportedly said, "Tell me Loretta, how much will it cost me to tell you to go fuck yourself?"

So how much did Ethel Merman and Jack Klugman love each other? Years later, when casting TV's *The Odd Couple*, showrunner Garry Marshall wrote in his autobiography that he told Jack at his audition, "I saw you in *Gypsy*. You did a scene with Ethel Merman and I was impressed because, as she was singing to you she was spitting a lot and it was getting on your clothes and your face and in your eyes. You never even flinched." Jack told Garry, "I loved her." Garry responded, "Love her or not, when I saw that, I said to myself, 'Now that's a good actor!'"

Chapter 10

Nature or nurture?

There's a long list of temperamental people who migrated to show business with that attribute already well developed. Others became temperamental and spoiled, as their self-doubt and moodiness were increasingly indulged. That uncertainty and anxiety seem to be inevitable consequences of a life spent in a whimsically unpredictable business, continually seeking security amid endemic capriciousness. Stated simply, living with the continuing angst of constantly seeking approval has made some talented people so nutty that they can induce the anaphylactic shock of a peanut allergy at 50 yards.

Despite his healthy ego and a well-litigated interest in one pretty co-worker, Bob Barker is not among the prima donnas. However, consummate pro that he is, there was one Monday morning when Bob seemed to be suffering with a very rare case of diva-itis. After a lifetime as a reliable trouper, including some 6,000 episodes of *The Price is Right* taped without a significant incident, here was Bob, alive and well, in the building, all dressed, coiffed, and fresh from make-up, refusing to start that day's taping. What could suddenly usurp Bob's decades of dedication to getting the job done?

For years and years the door to the beloved host's dressing room in Studio 33 at Television City was adorned with a decorative wooden plaque bearing the letters "W.G.M.C." It stood for World's Greatest Master of Ceremonies. The fact that it was a gift from an audience member makes it a little more charming than a simple object of crass narcissism. I suppose it set the tone for appropriate respect from all who crossed his threshold. It did for me.

That star dressing suite is nothing elaborate, merely two rooms with a bathroom. It was pleasantly furnished, but far more functional than glamorous. It was Bob's for the first few days of most weeks. At other times it was home to the various headliners who worked in that studio. Over the years that included everyone from Jack

Benny to Carol Burnett to Pat Sajak, Red Skelton, Vin Scully, Bill Maher, Diahann Carroll and Tom Bergeron. The list also included Bob Eubanks when he taped *Card Sharks* there, and that's who was responsible for Bob's unwillingness to perform.

Both the show's producer, Jonathan Goodson and Eubanks himself, have shared the story of the weekend when the mischievous *Card Sharks* host removed the "W.G.M.C." sign from the door and hid it under the couch as a prank. Eubanks said he went home and thought little of it, until Jonathan called Monday in a tizzy. For about an hour most of the *Price* crew and a handful of CBS personnel had been frantically searching the studio, dressing rooms, and prop storage cabinets for the missing plaque. Although Bob was being charmed, cajoled, and coaxed to start taping while the search continued for the missing sign, the world's greatest master of ceremonies would not budge. No sign, no show.

Doing his best Sherlock Holmes impression, Jonathan was investigating to establish a timeline which might lead to the plaque's recovery. Dialing the Eubanks home he was told the host was out on his ranch property and would call back. Claiming there was an emergency brought Eubanks to the phone. He was intrigued by the anxiety in Jonathan's voice when he asked about the last time he'd seen the sign. Questioning why this was apparently so important, Eubanks was amused to hear that Bob Barker wouldn't perform until his sign was located and restored to its rightful place. An emergency, indeed!

In recounting the story years later Eubanks told me he found it laughable, and remembered wanting to leave it all a giant unsolved mystery. He said it was very tempting to play ignorant, just for laughs to see how this crisis would play out. Jonathan was having none of that and insisted that if Eubanks knew anything he had to come clean. The plaque was retrieved from where Eubanks had hidden it. Once returned to glory on the dressing room door, Barker started the day's taping of back-to-back episodes of *The Price is Right*. The requisite cars, refrigerators and Turtle Wax were given away and the universe returned to normal. Bob Eubanks recently shared that on another day at another studio he'd once hidden the star that adorned fellow host Allen Ludden's dressing room door. He claimed it had the same result— Ludden refused to perform until it was found.

I know these emcees to be as sane as any performer can be. In Barker's case, the "W.G.M.C." sign was more an indulgent lucky charm than any mystical pictogram. Just the same, Eubanks still thinks the plaque was a ridiculous pretension, that Bob Barker had been under the lights too long, and the entire incident funny as hell. It's those kinds of Defcon Three calamities that kick some producers' best problem-solving skills into high gear, as it did with Jonathan. Others simply seem to take the crises in stride, calmly allowing time and space for problems to resolve themselves. Those who are unable to do either don't last long.

Working with Bob Barker, I came to appreciate the depth of his insight into the art of facilitating a television show. Not only could he precisely anticipate how an adlib would play with an audience, it seemed he was continually writing and editing before he spoke. Little came out of his mouth before he had instantaneously calculated the value of each potential comment in the dual goals of enhancing a guest's moment in the spotlight and further advancing the show's forward momentum.

Bob Barker in a pensive moment on the set after the taping of one of the thousands of episodes he helmed of CBS's venerable *The Price is Right*. Photo courtesy of Fred Wostbrock.

That awareness made him a rare judge of talent in others. When hiring emcees for a show his mother created—*Lucky Pair*, airing on CBS's local KNXT—Bob spotted those gifts in two different performers and was responsible for their very first jobs as hosts. They were local radio DJ Geoff Edwards and comic actor Richard Dawson. Talk about picking winners. From Bob first spotting their previously-unexploited hosting talent they both rose to the top of the game.

During my season with the master I also learned more about the extent of Bob's unwavering support of animal rights. In addition to excluding meat from his diet, he also avoided wearing it. His shoes and belts were never leather, and his activism against using animal fur and skin for clothing have been well documented. Less known is the non-negotiable stance Bob once took against something as wholesome as a Thanksgiving turkey dinner.

In 1996 Bob and Shirley Jones appeared as visiting parents in an episode of the ABC comedy *Something So Right*. The plot centered on a family's Thanksgiving dinner; it was all just typically innocuous sitcom silliness. Bob first saw the script on the day of the initial table read at Universal Studios. He soon excused himself for giving such short notice as he announced that he could have nothing to do with any storyline that involved planning a turkey dinner, much less eating a bird. That also included any related allusion about how a turkey ends up in a supermarket meat section.

With any lesser fan-favorite guest star than Bob, or any less collaborative producers than Judd Pillott and John Peaslee, this impasse could have been as hopeless as trying to negotiate with North Korea's Kim Jong Un. This Thanksgiving fable had a happy ending, however. The episode was re-written to exclude a scene in a butcher shop and to include a vegetarian dinner. It was enough to warm your giblets.

Here's one more Bob Barker story I can confidently guarantee you never heard. It's a classic and it stars another TV personality who also enjoys multi-generational popularity, Marc Summers. Marc's been a friend for decades, but I still had to wrestle his approval to share this tale. Marc's name came up during a 2018 lunch with his agent, Richard Lawrence. Among other things, we were lauding and applauding the popular host on his return that year to a reboot of the show that first put him on the map, and how he'd prevailed over a long-hidden personal challenge.

As emcee of the perennial kidvid fave *Double Dare*, Marc was often splattered with the overspray from gooey slime by the end of each episode. While those were the moments his smile was widest, those were also the moments when his anxiety rose to nearly intolerable levels. You see, Marc has obsessive-compulsive disorder. His necessity for cleanliness and order in a germ-free and controlled environment would have been an insurmountable obstacle for most people in pursuit of a successful career in the world of slime.

Amazingly, Marc was able to hide his tormenting battle with OCD for years. I consider him a masterful entertainer, but his co-starring with slime was an award-worthy performance of which his legions of fans were none the wiser. I enjoy watching when they meet Marc. They're always happily surprised to learn that there's little separating his true personality from his public persona. The guy is pretty much what you see. Dig deep enough however and you will find the usual amount of inner turmoil that we all carry. The difference: Marc wouldn't call it turmoil. His word is tsuris.

Beyond his amazing strides in minimizing the symptoms of his OCD, Marc's rightfully proud of the many accomplishments that have added up to quite a remarkable career. It showed no signs of cooling as he breezed past the age of Social Security eligibility. For a kid who got a foot in the door as a studio usher he worked hard to ultimately become an on-camera icon to an entire generation of kids who followed him into adulthood. Marc's work, both on-camera and as a producer, has been outstanding. His programs for the Food Network helped to boost that channel's viewership and cachet for many years.

In 2019 Marc's triumphant return for a second season of Nickelodeon's rebooted *Double Dare* proved there's no justification for ageism. Marc was just as sharp, quick, witty, and entertaining as ever. In fact, that role earned him an Emmy nomination. The 2017 documentary that chronicles his decades in the business is a joy to watch. *On Your Marc* starts with a young Bob Barker introducing an even younger Marc Summers. His association with Bob has been Marc's biggest and longest-playing source of both inspiration and tsuris.

The relationship started when Marc was an admiring teen who babysat audience members as a CBS page in the early years of *The Price is Right*. It also included work on Bob's *Truth or Consequences* as well as moonlighting as a writer for some of Bob's side work. While some years the friendship included little more than a call to Bob on his birthday, at other times Marc participated in events honoring the man who epitomized the polished on-camera professionalism to which he aspired.

Bob had long been a source of encouragement, even saying that Marc had the talent that could make him a splendid successor at *The Price is Right*. The up-and-coming host remembers hearing Bob offer, "When the time is right, I'll recommend you to the network." In the middle of this seemingly idyllic relationship Marc says he was surprised to suddenly find himself the target of Bob's disdain. He came face-to-face with a surprising measure of mercurial moodiness.

After the speeches and toasting on the day in 1999 when Bob was honored by the Television Academy with a lifetime achievement award, a photographer from *The Los Angeles Times* asked to grab a shot of Bob and Marc. Readying his camera, he suggested the picture could be captioned "two generations of fan-favorite hosts." Bob cringed. Nobody wants to be reminded how old they are, and some stars are even reticent to share a frame of celluloid with any younger mortals. Marc remembers that Bob instantly shot down the idea of any photos with an "Absolutely not!" To avoid an unpleasant public moment he acquiesced and agreed to a single flash. Marc says that Bob then struck a pose in which he all but turned his back on his young friend. That moment was a reminder that Bob sported a healthy ego with more than a pinch of vanity, and could instantly turn off the charm at will. Rude? Perhaps, but the *coup de grace* was yet to come.

In 2003 I announced both CBS's daytime and primetime celebrations of Bob's 80th birthday. That's when I first heard him mention retirement. Giving away refrigerators and cars during an energized, occasionally-manic, non-stop hour had become sufficiently exhausting that only one episode was now being scheduled for most tape days. While more expensive for the production company, it was an accommodation earned by virtue of his having awarded enough Rice-A-Roni, "the San Francisco treat," to fill that city's bay.

Having reached the pinnacle of his chosen profession, and with sufficient wealth to both endow his favorite charities with ongoing million dollar contributions as well as enjoy any pursuits that interested him, Bob had nothing more to prove. His nearly 50 years of service to the TV tube more than justified the privilege of a life of leisure, but he was understandably reluctant to call it quits. Bob told me, "I'd love the first few weeks, but I know I'd soon come to miss the job. Besides, I really think it helps keep me young." He then acknowledged, "Some days, doing the show is the best hour of my day."

Bob Barker avoiding the dispersing audience members and fans by making his usual exit through the loading dock and past the CBS commissary to where his Cadillac is parked under the nameplate "Mr. Smith" (2003). From the author's collection.

Two and one-half years later a day that had been dreaded at Television City finally arrived. Bob Barker announced that after a half-century on television, 35 years of which were on *The Price is Right*, he would retire the following June. CBS and the current caretakers of Mark Goodson–Bill Todman Productions' most valuable property embarked upon a lengthy search to find just the right new host to continue the tradition as well as draw a new generation of eyes.

The stakes were high and a number of potential successors joined me at the long-running stage show *The Price is Right – Live* in Las Vegas to hone the hosting skills specific to this beloved hit program. The likely and unlikely candidates who came to share the 1,000-seat showroom stage made for a diverse group. The hopefuls included actors George Hamilton and Doug Davidson, game show pros Todd Newton, Mark L. Walberg, and JD Roberto in addition to Marc Summers. There was KTLA weatherman Mark Kriski, New York-based CBS weatherman Dave Price and the show's host in Mexico, Marco Antonio Regil. Others in contention included John O'Hurley, Mark Steines, Mario Lopez, and a young man who was then working frequently as a segment producer and sporadically as a cable host, Michael Richards. You may remember Richards from the months in 2020 and 2021 during which he stirred up controversy and shook-up the status quo on the sets of *Wheel of Fortune* and *Jeopardy!* after being named executive producer at both, and naming himself host of the latter.

Tom Bergeron says he was flattered to be approached by CBS to talk about his interest in emceeing *Price*, but turned down the offer to audition because he was already busy fronting two series for ABC. He was also sensitive to the risk of being overexposed to viewers. He philosophized, "Whatever it was that made you interesting to these people in the first place, you don't have it anymore because you're exhausted. And that little creative flame is now just an ember."

Meanwhile, Rosie O'Donnell seemed to have nominated herself to succeed Bob Barker in what the Hollywood trades characterized as a "bid" and "campaigning." Longtime producer of *The Price is Right* Roger Dobkowitz confirmed that the show's executive, Syd Vinnedge, supported Rosie's overture, as did Bob when first interviewed on the matter at the 2007 Daytime Emmy Awards. CBS and Fremantle initially considered the idea even after hearing how she wanted to re-format the legacy program. *Price* producers were told to prep for taping a test episode as Rosie envisioned the program—halving the number of games from six to three, to be interspersed with musical and entertainment elements. "I just wanted to 'gay it up,'" she told *TV Guide* in July of 2007 for a story that projected her getting rid of "Barker's beauties" in favor of a chorus line of Broadway hunks, confetti, musical bumpers and a much-needed set makeover "so the colors actually match." I was told that Rosie's public lobbying for the gig generated unsolicited negative mail addressed to Television City.

CBS then abandoned the idea of having her audition. Rosie told the press that she withdrew her bid because the show was unwilling to relocate to New York and she was not keen on transplanting her family. Casting doubt on that account, Bergeron reported that during his discussions with the network the idea of moving the show to New York was mentioned as a possibility. Indeed, Rosie later told *TV Guide* that CBS nixed the prospect, "They thought I was too controversial to host the game show."

Roger Dobkowitz knew of Marc Summers' long relationship with Bob, and he knew that Marc had his eyes peeled on the job since the days long ago when he wore one of the CBS pages' blue blazers—matching the fabric on the seats in the studio, they were blue before they were red. Marc remembers the producer calling him with the suggestion he invite the soon-to-retire host to dinner. Marc said he did just that and was surprised to hear a long silence on the phone before his idol responded to the invitation with "So, you want my job? Who put you up to this?"

In the face of that unexpected off-putting reception Marc fumbled a few words before admitting the idea to call came from Roger. The sentences that followed left no question in Marc's mind that, not only did Bob have no desire to go to dinner but he had zero intention of endorsing or supporting Marc in the quest to fulfill his lifelong dream. Marc had held on to Bob's promise to recommend him from years earlier, and suddenly losing what had been his ace in the hole left him devastated. There was love and respect for the man whom he considered a friend and mentor for over 30 years. Now there was also shock, anger, and hurt at the unexpected abandonment by his benefactor.

It was hard to reconcile the dichotomy of emotions, and Marc's next move fully reflected that ambivalence. He recalled Bob's acceptance speech at the TV Academy event in which he mentioned his interest in an important historical figure from the years that he himself was in uniform as a World War II fighter pilot. Who knew that Bob was fascinated with the life of the British statesman and army commander Winston Churchill? As host of a series on the History Channel at the time, Marc was in a unique position to amass an extensive library of DVDs documenting every aspect of the life and career of the former British Prime Minister. Marc boxed the exhaustive collection with a note that reminded Bob of the evening he had discussed his fascination with Churchill, and explained that he was delighted to be able to assemble this reference material as a gift.

Marc has always been generous and thoughtful. He forgives easily, but his mind is too sharp to forget. He has a sterling reputation in the industry as a cooperative team player and it has propelled his career through some fantastic successes. Just the same, being human makes us all vulnerable to being hurt, and the slight from Bob had cut Marc deeply. He couldn't stop himself from expressing that hurt along with the generous gift. Marc says he closed the very cordial note to Bob with a most un-cordial choice three-word phrase that couldn't have made his feelings any clearer.

Marc Summers with the author, backstage following a performance of *Double Dare Live*. After more than 35 years, fans of the original Nickelodeon game show still can't get enough of Marc and the show's ubiquitous slime (2019). From the author's collection.

Shocked? Don't be. Hollywood can sometimes feel like the epicenter for broken promises, and where not all of the public smiles and loving embraces among performers are heartfelt. There are so many clever deceptions, illusions, and ironic unseen truths to be found just out of frame. A 100 year-old story of the world's master illusionist Harry Houdini illustrates how the partnering between seemingly cooperative co-stars can be quite different than it appears.

Magician Penn Gillette is a passionate and knowledgeable student of the magical arts and their history. His wife is a fan of *The Price is Right* and together they came to our *Price-Live* production in Las Vegas. On that occasion Penn told me about a huge frustration that the great Houdini suffered at the height of his international fame. Among the celebrated illusionist's most fantastic tricks was making a giant elephant disappear in clear view of his audience. It was a spectacular part of his act; however Penn said that Houdini came to hate performing that massive misdirection because of the elephant. He grew to hate its look and its smell, and resented the accommodations that he had to make to feed and transport the giant. Each and every day that he faced that pachyderm upped his aggravation, and he came to believe that the elephant had grown to hate him in return.

The master conjurer and escape artist had already amassed incredible wealth; he was beholden to no man nor beast, elephants included. However, Houdini chose to suffer for his art knowing that no other animal could ever be as dramatic in his illusion. That cursed wrinkled gray monster stayed in the act, and his fans never sensed Houdini's intense disdain for the creature. He feigned affection for the benefit of his audience but, in time, hiding his disgust for his wrinkled co-star became the most challenging part of the trick. It's been the same with other successful professional pairings, even when the scene partners are both humans. You need look no further than Vivian Vance and William Frawley, or Joan Collins and John Forsythe.

If you follow the feuds then you already know of other on-screen friendships that disguised off-screen animosity. They include Rose McGowan and Alyssa Milano from *Charmed*, Kate Mulgrew and Jeri Ryan of *Star Trek* fame, as well as Debra Messing and Megan Mullally who were seemingly so in tune with each other on *Will and Grace*. There should be no surprise that there was more than just anger between *Anger Management* stars Charlie Sheen and Selma Blair. Likewise, there was no delight, joy, or glee between *Glee* actresses Naya Rivera and Lea Michele. I heard that Stana Katic and Nathan Fillion made the set of ABC's *Castle* a warzone, and David Duchovney now attributes all of his hostility towards *X-Files* co-star Gillian Anderson as proof that, as he restated, "familiarity breeds contempt." The full extent of Sharon Osbourne's wrath over being booted from *The Talk* has not fully been aired, as she's promising to fill a podcast episode with her disdain for Sheryl Underwood with whom she clashed on-screen and off.

We've all smiled through anger, feigned friendship, and laughed at our boss's lame jokes. There's truth and wisdom behind the old wisecrack, "Once you can fake sincerity, you've got it made." While not every comedian is hiding a different reality behind Thalia, the ancient Greek mask of comedy, some are indeed living the life of the sad clown portrayed in the Italian opera *Pagliacci*. In higher numbers than most of us, comedians have had more than their fair share of psychic suffering. Indeed, pain, fear, and anxiety are often the seeds from which comedy blossoms.

Take stand-up's masterful David Brenner. He was funny before he started being paid to be, back when he worked with Tom Snyder writing, producing, and directing documentaries at Philadelphia's KYW television. *The Mike Douglas Show* taped in the same building, and David was given a shot at filling five minutes on one day's episode. It led to his claim of ultimately becoming the most frequently booked TV talk show guest of all entertainers. That tally includes 158 appearances on *The Tonight Show*, still leading as the most of any guest in the show's nearly 70 year history.

With advancing cancer soon to take his life, David vented the apprehension he felt while preparing his will. It simultaneously assured he'd be funny even after he was gone. His bequeaths filed in Manhattan Surrogate Court shortly before his 2014 death have the makings of a monologue. As they say, always leave 'em laughing:

"I request a very modest burial, no fancy box, no pillow (you think at a time like this I'm worried about a headache?), no special suit (jeans and a nice shirt will be fine, but make sure my high-top sneakers are tied properly)."

"All I want is a small stone on the grave site with these words; 'Here lies David Brenner. He lived, he died, but MAN DID HE LIVE!' On the flip side I want 'If this is supposed to be a joke - I don't get it.'"

"Place one hundred dollars in small bills in my left sock (just in case tipping is recommended where I'm going)."

"I give my full permission to any comedians who may think of a funny line while at the funeral to use it in his act, for I know how difficult it is to write good material. However, if any comedians are overheard doing any of my lines at the funeral, they are to be put in the box with me."

Under the heading "Personal Farewell" he wrote, "To those who have been kind to me and have loved me, I thank you. To those who were not kind to me and didn't love me, I hope you're next!"

Some other comics' venting are honed to a sharper edge to where the delightfully-mocking cynicism and deliciously-biting sarcasm in their humor barely disguise the anger. David Letterman comes to mind. His career began to ascend when emcee Allen Ludden was on a 1974 promotional tour for *Password*. Allen found Indianapolis a refreshing break from the routine repetitive questions asked by most members of the media. That's where David Letterman was breaking into the business as a local broadcaster, and he had Allen laughing through his free-wheeling radio interview. After they wrapped their rap, Allen encouraged Dave in his desire to take a shot at Hollywood for a career in comedy, promising to help him make key contacts after he arrived.

Once in town, producers Ron Greenberg and Bob Stewart saw the same spark that Allen had. Each of the three had a hand in casting Dave for pilots. In 1976, Hollywood's new arrival was a celebrity panelist on Ron's *Word Grabbers*. The following year he did pilot panel duty on the Allen Ludden-hosted *The Smart Alecks*. Later, he was a celebrity player on Jack Barry's *Decision, Decisions* pilot. It was Bob Stewart who tapped David for his first hosting gig on his sample episode of *The Riddlers*.

Host Allen Ludden (left) introducing his discovery David Letterman to the audience on the set of the unsold pilot *The Smart Alecks*. Far right are David's panel mates Pat Carroll and Don Meredith (1977). Photo courtesy of Fred Wostbrock.

Dave's talent was undeniable, but his internal whirling joke machine twirled with too much horsepower to be reigned-in for game show hosting. He clearly overpowered the format and the civilian players. However, it revved at a righteous rate to be a celebrity player on *The $20,000 Pyramid, Hollywood Squares, Password Plus* and *Liar's Club*. Years after making the rounds on these classics Dave cemented his status as an acceptable clue in the category: Former game show personalities who have been embroiled in scandal.

Long after establishing a successful beachhead in late night talk, Dave was victimized in one hell of an embarrassing indignity. He handled the situation with as much class as anyone can be expected to muster while being unwittingly inducted into a hall of shame. In 2009 the story broke that CBS news producer Joe Halderman had attempted to extort cash from Dave after finding the host's name in the pages of his live-in girlfriend's diary. In addition to her hook-up with Joe it seems that Stephanie Birkitt had a sexual relationship with Dave while working on *The Late Show*. It was an affair which she apparently chronicled in embarrassingly graphic detail. After boyfriend Joe confronted Stephanie with the diary accounts she promised to break from Dave.

Many Thursday nights, after pre-taping his Friday show the host had been driving the former intern from the program's midtown theater to her Connecticut home. It wasn't too far out of his way from his own weekend retreat in the Nutmeg State. That continued, but it seems it wasn't as completely platonic as promised. On one subsequent Thursday night boyfriend Joe said he spied the pair parked in Letterman's car at the end of his and Stephanie's street, apparently embracing. Perhaps they were simply sharing a kiss, or perhaps Dave was—as the saying goes—driving her home, again. The boyfriend freaked.

Joe Halderman demanded $2 million in hush money with the threat that he was prepared to drag Dave's name and reputation through the mud. Specifically, news accounts indicate that he threatened that Dave's world was "about to collapse around him." Instead of whipping out his AmEx Black card the victimized host contacted his attorney who set up a sting with the Manhattan District Attorney's office. As instructed, Dave gave the would-be blackmailer a bum check. After depositing it into his bank account, Halderman was charged with attempted grand larceny. Bang, six months in jail.

Harder for Dave than explaining the extramarital affair to his viewers, I'd imagine was explaining it to his new wife of only several months. The marriage survived, and apparently his coming clean with a heartfelt, contrite on-air explanation and apology was sufficient for his audience. We'll never know how much the trauma and embarrassment from that incident may have contributed to Dave's declining passion for his late night show, and his subsequent decision to retire a half-dozen years later.

Chapter 11

With apologies to *Star Trek*'s United Federation of Planets, I suggest that death, not space, is the final frontier. Here are three documented instances in which a well-known comic killed, and then actually dropped dead, ceasing to live while their audiences howled with laughter.

The hysterical Albert Brooks and his real-life brother, Bob Einstein, better known as "Super Dave" Osborn, lost their father Harry Einstein under just such strange circumstances. Performing as the Greek-dialect comic character Parkyakarkus on Eddie Cantor's and Al Jolson's hit radio shows helped the senior Einstein become a popular comedian whose fame extended to movies. On Sunday night, November 23rd, 1958 he was getting big laughs from a crowd of 1,200 partiers at a $100 a plate Friars Club roast for Lucille Ball and Desi Arnaz, or as he was calling them, "my very close friends Miss Louise Balls and Benny Arnaz."

He finished one of the best-received comedy bits of his career and started to return to his seat on the dais in the Beverly Hilton Hotel ballroom. As Einstein was passing behind his chair toastmaster Art Linkletter announced, "Every time he finishes, I ask myself, why isn't he on the air in a prime time…?" From behind Milton Berle in the next chair Parky interrupted with, "Yeah, how come?" That's when he collapsed. He passed out and fell against Berle.

The audience erupted with more laughter at what they thought was a pratfall and a seemingly-faked loss of consciousness. Berle recognized the grave reality and cued Art Linkletter to ask for anybody with medical experience to please help. His cliché question, "Is there a doctor in the house?" reportedly started a second wave of laughter. In the midst of the hilarity emcee Linkletter again leaned into the microphone with a second plea for medical help, specifically asking if anyone had nitroglycerin tablets. A hush instantly swept across the room before some guests started calling out the names of doctors they knew to be in the ballroom. Others shouted medical advice. Ed Wynn, who was seated at a nearby table ran to the dais with the suggestion, "Put his head down, put his head down."

Einstein' wife, actress Thelma Leeds, knew it was no joke. She rushed forward and placed several nitroglycerin pills into her husband's mouth, but he was already unconscious. Berle, George Burns, and actor John Bromfield then moved Einstein's body from view as five physicians from the crowd gathered around him. While the doctors started working on the lifeless comedian, toastmaster Linkletter tried to carry on with a semblance of the program. Years later he described what happened next as he looked to singer Tony Martin and said, "'Tony, this is no time for humor. Come up and do a song for us.' Tony came up and the orchestra was ready." The crooner made the worst choice from thousands of possible tunes. Linkletter remembered, "You know what he sang? *There's No Tomorrow!*"

To the strains of that most inappropriate choice for a musical interlude the doctors used a pocketknife to slit open Einstein's chest. While they performed a manual heart massage that briefly revived him, a cardiologist in the group was actually preparing to try administering an electric shock using the bared wires from a lamp's electrical cord. Despite their heroic measures the doctors were unable to rouse any further response from the patient. Ultimately, Danny Thomas stepped out from the shadows and relayed the news that the beloved comedian's heart had stopped. Guests in the packed ballroom froze, motionless, and silent.

Finally, Desi Arnaz stood, picked up the award he'd just received and softly said, "This offering meant so much to me. Now it means nothing. Please, everyone, pray to your own God that he will be saved." Lucy stood to speak but was at a loss for words. She added only, "I can say nothing." Desi shook his head and said to Linkletter and the crowd, "They say the show must go on, but why must it?" That night it didn't.

Comedian Dick Shawn was a brilliantly creative performer. His most memorable film roles may have been as Lorenzo St. DuBois (L.S.D.) the actor who gets hired to play Hitler in Mel Brooks' original *The Producers*, and as Ethel Merman's crazed surfer son in *It's a Mad, Mad, Mad, Mad World.* Shawn was performing at the University of California at San Diego on April 17, 1987 for an audience of approximately 500. As was usual for Shawn, his material was far more avant-garde than a simple series of mother-in-law jokes. Marty Ingels explained, "He was the world's most insane performer. He never used any formulas or jokes per se. He had no routines. He'd just get up with a stream of consciousness and sometimes he was brilliant."

Indeed, Shawn's act was often very esoteric and his presentation especially theatrical. He opened this performance appearing as a disembodied head resting on the top of a table. In that tableau he shared dialogue with another actor who entered and sat at the table as if eating dinner. Then, a blackout. When the stage lights came back up Shawn reappeared for a second scene. He was miming a routine in which he moved erratically, out of rhythm to recorded dance music.

At about 25 minutes into the show, the comedian put his microphone on the stand and asked if he could be heard without it. He then started a loud rant about the end of the world in which there would be almost no survivors, "Nobody except the 500 people in this theater!" he shouted. "And I would be your leader!" Then Shawn suddenly dropped face down on the stage where he remained immobile and silent. The unpredictable nature of his act made it all the more difficult to know whether or not his collapse was part of his routine. At first the audience laughed, then applauded. After the last guffaw and claps faded to silence, things grew increasingly awkward.

The crowd's fidgeting and whispering increased the longer Shawn laid center-stage. Heard over the hushed murmuring were quips including, "Take his wallet!" Slowly, as the audience fell into an uncomfortable quiet stillness it became apparent that the act had crossed the line beyond avant-garde theater. During an interval that was estimated to be between three and five minutes, a stagehand came out and approached Shawn's body, reportedly several times before asking the proverbial question "Is there a doctor…"

A few MDs came forward from the crowd, flipped the lifeless body onto its back and began to administer CPR. Simultaneously the comedian's son, Adam Shawn, had already raced down from the lighting and audio controls to look for his father's second cousin, a heart surgeon who came along that evening. He found his cousin in the lobby and they both sprinted to the stage. The crowd remained as the doctors worked on the apparent heart attack victim. Finally came an announcement asking audience members to leave. They slowly wandered out as Shawn was carried to an ambulance where he was pronounced dead just before 10 p.m.

Finally in this bizarre trifecta is the odd tale of Redd Foxx. After years of grabbing his heart and crying "This is the big one," as his character Fred Sanford did each week for laughs, it was ironic that the actor's true demise would mimic that comedic shtick. The successful run of *Sanford and Son* was the crowning moment in the performer's long career, cementing him as an important influence cited by Richard Pryor and Chris Rock, as well as Jamie Foxx, who took the comic's last name for his own as homage. All of America loved Redd Foxx's portrayal of cantankerous junk dealer Fred Sanford. The sitcom rocketed in popularity from its January, 1972 premiere, and remained among Nielsen's top ten shows for five of its six seasons.

Producers Norman Lear and Bud Yorkin were surprised to find their *Sanford and Son* occasionally surpassing the duo's ratings king, *All in the Family*, that had debuted the previous January. Despite an ever-escalating salary, Foxx remained chronically dissatisfied over a perceived lack of respect. Perhaps intoxicated with his success, during the show's run Foxx famously battled with the producing pair and with NBC for money, ownership of the series, prestige, and perks.

While his show was a hit, the network never considered him a team player. Foxx seemed to love nothing more than firing filthy jokes at the people least likely to appreciate them. Virginal Sandy Duncan was placed adjacent to Foxx in Peter Marshall's *Hollywood Squares* grid until she'd had more than her fill and insisted she be moved. Emcee Jim MacKrell has no idea whether or not it was purely random that on his *Celebrity Sweepstakes* set this connoisseur of carnal comedy was seated next to the wholesome Captain Kangaroo.

The most infamous of Foxx's battles with the peacock was his non-negotiable demand for a window for his dressing room. After being told no other room was available, the star became adamant that the building be altered to create a window where none existed. Foxx was still harping about his window at NBC when he was moving to ABC, telling America during a Barbara Walters interview, "I've got to have freedom for my eyeballs because, you know, that controls what my body feels." Then the petulant child within the comedian raised its head by adding, "It's not asking too much as the star of the network. Is that asking too much when they give other people organs and automobiles and have their homes wired? I never got any of that."

In that same NBC studio building with an insufficient number of windows Tom Snyder was said to have indulged his own architectural obsession. By cajoling members of the maintenance crew the talkmeister gained access to dressing rooms late in the evening hours, after taping his nightly show. They say he was secretly measuring other performers' shower enclosures to be sure his was at least as large as other stars', Johnny Carson's included. Fact or fiction, that story was part of the legend and lore that circulated among the facilities' employees, shared with me and I assume others who befriended the old-timers.

Celebrities whose insecurities are magnified by booze, pot, or cocaine can develop a seemingly insatiable hunger for narcissistic indulgences. Snyder was clean and sober, but Foxx was abusing all three. In fact, drug use was the reason cited for the production's inability to get its star insured. It's a predicament that usually results in re-casting, but for *Sanford and Son* Lear and Yorkin chose to roll the dice, relying instead on their own deep pockets to cover any losses that might result from their lead actor's incapacitation. It was a gutsy play for a performer with such a checkered past.

Their gamble paid off. Redd Foxx in his role as Fred Sanford drew viewers like moths to a sweaty wool suit. However, the star's series of immutable demands was the source of growing conflict. Things became so contentious that Bud Yorkin said he almost pulled the plug on the money-minting hit. NBC was fully willing to accept that fate after documenting that Foxx "appeared at the studio flaunting a pearl-handled revolver." One network executive said that, in retrospect, he wished they'd gone with their original choice of actors for the lead in *Sanford and Son*: Cleavon Little.

Redd Foxx finds love as Fred Sanford, starring with Lynn Hamilton on the April 7, 1972 episode of NBC's *Sanford and Son*.

Production wrapped at NBC after 136 episodes when the comic fled in 1977 for greener pastures, to host an ABC variety show. The conjecture was that the lucrative offer was made simply to lure the star away from NBC in order to end the long run of the ratings powerhouse, with less concern about the success or failure of the new venture. Beyond the cash, part of the attraction for Foxx may well have been the longed-for window which he reportedly got when the short-lived variety show taped at Television City's Studio 43. In 1980 Foxx was back on an NBC sitcom, *Sanford*, which taped at Metromedia Square, a safe distance from the network's lot.

Six years later the comedian was back at bat in *The Redd Foxx Show*, which shot on ABC's home turf. One member of the studio facilities crew joked that Foxx's dressing room needed to be just a few panes of glass short of a greenhouse. In reality, a window was added to his digs above Studio 55 on the Prospect lot. All three attempts to attract audiences crashed and burned soon after their debuts, and for years the obviously patched wall above Studio 55 served as a reminder of the strikeout. Redd Foxx's television career was cold for about a dozen years.

Eventually the sitcom gods again smiled at the veteran comic and he returned briefly as Al Royal in CBS's *The Royal Family*. His final day was on that show's set during a sweltering Friday afternoon, October 11, 1991, when L.A. temperatures climbed above 100 degrees. The air conditioned Stage 31 at Paramount was comfortable as the cast and crew rehearsed the episode that would tape the following evening. Spirits were high as the new series' first three broadcasts had been well received. Co-star Della Reese remembered *Entertainment Tonight* was on set, interviewing Foxx. Others recall the visiting crew being from *Lifestyles of the Rich and Famous*—it doesn't matter.

The *Lifestyles* or *ET* Q-and-A was stopped so that Foxx could join the cast to nail down the blocking of a scene. Other than his being annoyed by the interruption, the mood was light. The star was getting big laughs in the rehearsal as he approached Della, delivering his scripted joke. Walking past her, he unexpectedly fell to the ground. As Della remembered that moment, "Redd said, 'Ah, give me a break' and reached for the chair and did what we thought was a pratfall, 'cause he did that all the time. And we all stood there laughing while he was lying on the floor." Those on-set chuckled at the surprise move as it seemed to be a bit of inspired improv, perhaps for the benefit of the visiting crew. The producers looked at each other with affirmative nods, hoping Foxx would be willing to repeat it for the cameras.

Della said she bent down and heard her co-star say, "Get my wife, get my wife." She yelled out for someone to call an ambulance, and you know what happened? Nothing. It sounded like it was part of the joke. Members of the crew were first to realize that Foxx was truly ill and the call went out for help. Della said she leaned over Foxx's body and prayed. She remembers her co-star was first pronounced dead there on the stage floor before rallying briefly at the hospital, where he was pronounced again. It was outside the emergency room, with the body still warm and the widow in earshot, that an ill-timed reaction to the sad news was spoken a bit too loudly by the producers: "What do we do with this week's script without Redd?" Della overheard the question and all but lost it in a loud and angry rage, responding to what she felt was incredible callousness. It was highly inappropriate, as that dilemma clearly should have been discussed out of earshot.

Like any other commercial enterprise, management's focus was on delivering the factory's output. It was another harsh reminder that it's not show business; it's the business of show. Seeking return on the millions of dollars invested in a series that showed promise just a few weeks into its run, CBS pre-empted three of the next four weeks' episodes while new scripts were written and produced. Foxx's character was killed off, and on November 27th the audience learned that Al Royal died at a bowling alley when his funeral is attended by many of his old friends, including a couple of characters from *Sanford & Son*. Ultimately, *The Royal Family* continued airing until May 13, 1992. It was a full seven months after Foxx died before the series was finally pulled, leaving two unaired episodes that were never monetized.

Foxx's fascinating backstory helps to elucidate some of his obstinate nature. The young John Sanford ran away from his family home in St. Louis at age 13, drifting through Chicago before arriving in New York where he and Malcolm Little—the future Malcolm X—ran scams, hustled, fenced stolen clothes, and peddled drugs in their younger days. Among a litany of misdemeanors, in 1949 Foxx was busted for selling reefers to an undercover cop. It led to the discovery that he and his wife were growing a sizable quantity of pot in their New Jersey backyard.

Biographer Michael Seth Starr reports that the inventive comic managed to engineer a 4F medical deferment from serving in the military by inducing heart palpitations, purportedly by eating half a bar of soap before his draft board physical. Foxx himself admitted to joining the Communist Party with the sole motive of participating in their social events after learning they served food and had pretty women to dance with.

Foxx came to show business directly from that life on the streets. Chitlins would be offended to hear that he performed on the so-called "chitlin circuit," likely believing they are higher up the pig intestines than those seediest of nightclubs and dives. Playing one-nighters in the joints that catered to black clientele in the days of segregation was like hand-to-hand combat at the front lines of show business. Foxx and his fellow entertainers considered it a good night if a fistfight didn't break out during their act and if they actually got paid for the gig. Foxx was bitter about being relegated to that world and, in 1961, said, "I see a lot of white comedians working a lot of good rooms, and I know I'm better and more original than most of them."

Although singer Dinah Washington had given Foxx a huge break in 1959 by insisting he be her opening act, he was unable to transcend into the mainstream. Another opportunity came and went the following year when Count Basie had him on the bill at The Crescendo in Hollywood. On both dates Foxx's material was considered overly risqué with much of it downright raunchy. Redd was too blue for white America.

After years of being denied well-paying prestigious bookings, in 1966 Foxx helped to finally break a color barrier when he was among the first African-American solo performers to headline a mainstream Vegas strip hotel. With the newfound bankroll from that gig he purchased a nightclub, The Redd Foxx Club, on L.A.'s tony west side adjacent to Beverly Hills. The comics who played the room reported that Foxx was the worst businessman they'd ever known. Exhibit A: the piles of unpaid bills scattered all around the office. The club didn't last long.

Through it all, the comedian's skewed view of the world was undeniably funny, and his live comedy party albums became a mainstay in many black households. Because of their salacious nature, the records were relegated to being sold from behind the counter. *Wild Party, Laff of the Party, Naughties but Goodies, Sidesplitter* and others were considered too racy to be on display in most record stores. Just the same, his 15 LPs sold a total of over a half-million copies. Cash from a string of 45-rpm singles, simply excerpts from his albums, filled the dollar bill tills at record shops another quarter-million times.

The veteran comic had a long tough climb to mainstream acceptance, followed by an unprecedented rocketing to stardom portraying junk dealer Fred G. Sanford. Most observers agree that Foxx's life changed faster than he could adapt. Friends reported the comic's struggles never ended, even at the height of his apparent success. He was resented by club owners after claims that he occasionally walked off the stage rather than perform to small unresponsive crowds.

Norman Lear hired Foxx for *Sanford and Son* perhaps not knowing the extent of the comedian's ornery rebelliousness and disregard for traditional norms. Co-star Demond Wilson echoed crew members' reports that Foxx would regularly snort cocaine at the weekly table reads. For that matter, with both Richard

Pryor and George Carlin contributing each week to Flip Wilson's show down the hall, drug use was beyond flagrant during the two years that Foxx and Flip shared NBC's Burbank facility.

With Flip in Studio 2, his old friend Foxx lobbied for a move from the other wing of the building to Studio 4, located just across the hall from his pal. Adding to the insanity, director Alan Rafkin recalls Foxx and co-star Wilson both carried guns: "They would get stoned and start to play with their guns. I was scared somebody was going to get killed." Comedian Bill Kirchenbauer remembered the time Wilson was so angry that a dollop of shaving cream from a prop pie landed on his suit that the actor left the studio at a taping of *Make Me Laugh* to get his gun from his car. Security kept the comics safely locked away until Wilson was removed from the lot.

The publicist for *Sanford and Son*, Kathleen Fearn-Banks, reported that Foxx had perfected a move any magician would be proud to master. She remembered, "He had this way of patting a woman on the back and in that one pat he could undo a bra strap through whatever clothes she was wearing. I mean, he was doing it all over the studio." One staffer filed a formal complaint and, predictably for those days, she was fired. To twist an old proverb, "When a replaceable force meets an immoveable object…" There was no removing the man who was generating millions in profits.

Foxx's adlibbing through scenes to cover un-memorized scripts often generated more laughs than the written dialog. His small talk with the studio audience during breaks was a whole other matter. Try as they did, the powers that be at both the production company and the network were unable to reign in the use of his endless reserve of raunchy nightclub material. Foxx insisted that getting the biggest laughs was his only goal, and nothing else mattered. Producer Aaron Ruben attempted to explain to the star that even those who found the off-color jokes to be funnier than they were offensive would only become less receptive to the script's tamer, and often lamer jokes.

Director John Rich shared one of Foxx's lines that he remembered shocked the audience. It was the story of a man and a woman steaming up the windows of their parked car. As their kissing escalated the woman became so aroused that she begged her partner, "Kiss me. Kiss me where it smells." As the audience gasped in unison, Foxx hit them with the punchline, "So I drove her to El Segundo!"

Foxx refused to be constrained and the outrageousness of his chats with studio audiences escalated. Bob Einstein, the comedian who found his greatest fame performing as "Super Dave" Osborn, shared another Foxx-ism which he said he'd never forget. With a break in taping, the star walked towards the audience with the greeting, "How many people washed their assholes this evening?"

Despite the popularity of the character he created, Foxx was unhappy. Even copious drug use failed to sedate his chronic dissatisfaction. Likewise for the demanded salary bumps that grew to far exceed his contracted compensation. Two years into *Sanford and Son* his character was written out of the season's final half-dozen scripts as long-simmering disagreements boiled over. Norman Lear and Bud Yorkin's Tandem Productions filed a $10 million suit against Foxx and Wilson, charging that the two lead actors walked off the series.

To counter that accusation the star's physician claimed Foxx was suffering from "nervous exhaustion, claustrophobia, and calcification between the fifth and sixth vertebrae in his back," all somehow linked to his work on the show. The standoff was resolved in 1974 with a monumental ring of Tandem's cash register. From a starting salary that matched that of Carroll O'Connor's first season—a weekly $7,500—Foxx was ultimately bumped to $25,000 per *Sanford and Son* episode, plus a healthy slice of the producers' net profits.

As to the true nature of Foxx's ongoing rumbles and rants, one former crew member pieced it together for me. In essence, he explained that the comic was incensed over the fact that Lear and Yorkin were making infinitely more cash than the star could ever demand. Rather than seeing them as the owners of the show that was making him rich, he viewed the relationship more akin to plantation life where he was the slave working to make his masters exceedingly wealthy.

On that issue of race, *Sanford and Son* writer Ted Bergman remembers Foxx objecting to a script that called for Fred Sanford, son Lamont, and friend Grady Wilson to be playing a game of Monopoly. "Black people don't play Monopoly," Foxx huffed. It led to another scribe's unconfirmed recollection of Foxx's repugnance over not having enough black writers on staff, demanding his entire creative staff of comedy veterans be fired and replaced with black writers. After fewer than a handful of weeks Foxx allegedly threw down his script at a table read and said, "This sucks! Bring me back my Jews!"

The IRS hounded Foxx, obsessed with retribution for his practice of filing each year's tax return without remitting a single dollar. On November 28, 1989 they cleaned out his house and garage in a seizure that brought the comedian to tears as he watched. News footage from that day shows Foxx standing in front of his Las Vegas mansion in his underwear, shaking his head in disbelief while the IRS looked to settle the bill they computed to total $755,166 excluding penalties and interest.

Parading down his driveway went his classic 1927 Ford model T, a 1975 Panther J72, a 1983 Zimmer, a Vespa motor scooter, a dozen guns including an Uzi and a semiautomatic pistol, the watch Elvis Presley gave him, a roomful of imported Asian furniture, his ukulele, records, photographs, the pictures off the walls, $12,769 in cash, and even the jewelry from around his neck. Foxx lamented that the IRS "took my necklace and the ID bracelet off my wrist and the money out of my pocket." He never recovered. When Foxx died less than two years later on the sound stage at Paramount, Eddie Murphy had to step up to settle his affairs. As he revealed to *Vanity Fair* in 2020, "I buried Redd Foxx… I had to physically pay for his funeral, and buy his headstone, and do all that stuff."

Comedy meets tragedy. Seen asking for donations, Redd Foxx never recovered after the IRS finally swooped in to his Las Vegas home in 1989 attempting to settle the comic's overwhelming tax debt. Less than two years later the comedian died penniless.

When I first worked at NBC the halls were still reverberating with the saga of Redd Foxx's demands. He won many of those battles but he didn't get everything he wanted, especially what he wanted most of all. Writer-producer Mark Evanier confirmed that Foxx asked for a guarantee that he be among the substitute hosts of the network's prestigious *Tonight Show*. It seemed a reasonable request as a sizeable list of greater and lesser performers were then being booked for fill-in duty. When the idea was relayed to Johnny Carson, who by this point in his reign owned and fully controlled the show, the answer was an instantaneous "No." Johnny had no particular issue with Foxx, but he was quick to slam the door on the idea of the network being able to include that kind of perk in any performer's contract negotiations. He wanted to avoid relinquishing any of his hard-fought autonomy.

NBC came back to their sly Foxx with a compromise. They pledged that when Johnny stepped down, the star of *Sanford and Son* would be given serious consideration as the next host of the franchise. Once it was formalized as part of his contract, the promise placated Foxx. Years later, when Johnny finally did step down, NBC had the legally binding obligation to consider the actor as successor to the late night throne. There was a very short contemplation that the network summarized in a formal note for the files to satisfy their legal requirement. It was a quick and easy decision not to use Foxx, as he had died a few months earlier.

As mercurial, confrontational and demanding as Redd Foxx could be, the first lady of television was the complete opposite.

Chapter 12

Betty White was indeed TV's first lady. Her image first flickered on the tube during a 1930s closed circuit experimental video display located in a downtown L.A. car dealership long before the ever-improving invention was taken seriously. Years later, when Los Angelenos started to look to their tiny TV screens for companionship and entertainment, Betty's was the most-seen face in their living rooms. In 1951 she fronted a variety show that ran five-and-a-half hours a day, six days a week. During an amazing four-year stretch she was on the air no fewer than 33 hours a week. Some weeks, many more.

"That was in the early days of television," Betty recalled, "and the people in charge thought TV would operate like radio. . . you know, give someone four or five hours to fill at a time. I worked with Al Jarvis, who had been a disc jockey for 18 years. He believed he could do on television what he had done on radio. . . so we tried playing records on our first program. That experiment lasted one day. Al and I just stood there doing nothing while the music played."

Live television was fleeting and disposable. The pictures drifted on the wind like clouds in the sky, viewed by few, then never to been seen again. It was all done on the cheap, often in spaces hurriedly converted for video. Most were without adequate air conditioning to beat the heat of the intense lighting required by the early camera technology. Betty remembers, "We worked in a small studio that had a door leading directly to the street. People passing outside would hear strange noises and open the door. As soon as they peeked inside, they were on camera. We never knew what to expect."

At the beginning the pay was meager. Betty recalled that as TV became profitable, talent looked to unionize. "Since most performers were on the air only 30 to 60 minutes each week, they tried to establish a half-hour pay scale. They had to make an exception for me. If I had gotten paid by the half-hour I would have become a millionaire." Betty explained, "By this time I was doing a nighttime show in addition to the afternoon marathon." A skit on that nighttime show called *Alvin and Elizabeth* eventually developed into Betty's first network series, *Life with Elizabeth.*

Betty next jumped to another romantic comedy role on *Date with the Angels* which lasted 39 weeks. "I hated that show," she said. "It seemed like we were doing *Life with Elizabeth* all over again. I'd look at the scripts each week and think, 'Oh no! They can't be serious.' But they were. I was glad when the show ended. The trouble with a lot of situation comedy shows is they take a joke that can be told in five minutes and puff it up to a half hour."

Her third series, *The Betty White Show*, started its short run on ABC in 1957. "I decided to freelance after that," she recalled. Next came a steady stream of filling seats on Jack Paar's old *Tonight Show* and other talk fests, panel programs, parades, telethons, game shows, and variety programs in addition to commercials and summer stock. Eventually Betty found her most lasting success with a return to series television in the 1970s. On *The Mary Tyler Moore Show* Betty turned a planned single guest appearance into a co-starring role as Sue Ann Nivens.

It seems as though all of America loved Betty, and the admiration was well deserved. I've seen her be tremendously kind and patient greeting members of the public at all manner of functions. She's always been terrifically gracious and sweet at each of the dozen times we've been in contact since as far back as 1981. That was the year her beloved Allen Ludden and my father both passed away, each after protracted periods of declining health. After seeing Betty so emotionally raw eulogizing Allen on a talk show, I was moved to reach out as a stranger with a simple note of condolence. I was surprised to receive a hand-written response.

Betty and I exchanged a few letters, hers filled with heartfelt thoughts to ease our mutual grieving. Following our brief pen pal-ship, she continued to be so emotionally accessible from the very first meeting. Our final contact was 35 years later on the set of her last series, *Hot in Cleveland*. Approaching her 94th birthday then, Betty effused the same charming, sharp, funny, and playful guise. Physically however, time had begun to take its toll. After a long evening of taping, Betty confessed to being thoroughly exhausted. While she now allowed for a bit of assistance when walking, her mind hadn't seemed to slow. We enjoyed a laugh over the ancient joke that her late husband used to tell about Betty's TV career starting so early. Allen called her a pioneer in silent television.

The author with the cast and guest stars of Betty White's last series, *Hot in Cleveland*. This 2015 episode, "What a Joy," was from the sitcom's final season, airing within days of Betty's 93rd birthday. The actress engendered nothing but love throughout the production. Photo from the author's collection.

On one of the occasions that she and I had contact, I unwittingly and momentarily displeased dear Betty, and I don't think I'll ever get the discomfort of that moment out of my mind. I was a presenter at the 2009 Game Show Congress event where the large group of attendees was giving a posthumous award to Allen. I was getting a great response from the crowd saluting Allen with a mix of accolades and gentle joking while reviewing his career. Betty was smiling ear-to-ear in the front row.

Despite the audience's chuckles, the smile instantly drained from Betty's face when I joshed, "… and that's when our honoree became a household name—you know, like Brylcream, and Drano." It was an old joke and offered without malice. The audience laughed, but not Betty. My heart sank as she grimaced, until

Betty White upon accepting the Bill Cullen Career Achievement Award from the author on behalf of her late husband, Allen Ludden at the 2009 Game Show Congress. Photo from the author's collection.

her smile returned a moment or two later. I still don't think it was inappropriate, but I'm sad to have fleetingly chilled Betty's joy during her beloved Allen's posthumous moment in the sun. Continuing with the tribute, I thought to myself, "C'mon Betty, lighten up. You know better than almost anybody about a little judiciously-used benign humor."

If I had intended even an ounce of offense, I would have considered mentioning those nude photos Betty is said to have posed for when she was first looking to get noticed. Did she also do what many young stars-to-be have done? Betty unequivocally said it's not her. While the photos of Betty's doppelganger are artistic, they are revealing even by today's standards. As for my toasting Allen, all's well that ends well. After accepting the award, Betty hugged me. Good, because like all of America, I loved Betty. Any opportunity to be in her presence was a gift, but I never did get the chance to join in her weekly poker game with producer Bob Stewart and other lifelong friends. As she was with all games, Betty was said to have been quite a player.

Betty White was thrice married, twice divorced. Her first pairing was with Army Air Force pilot Dick Barker in 1945, but it lasted only a few months. In 1947 she married Lane Allen, a talent agent, only to divorce again just two years later. Then Jack Paar introduced Betty to Phil Cochran, a director who shot the aerial scenes for the Howard Hughes film *Jet Pilot*. They were dating when Bob Stewart booked Betty as a celebrity player on his hit *Password* with emcee Allen Ludden.

With much in common, the two performers hit it off immediately. Betty didn't know that these were the darkest days in Allen's life. He had been running between the studio and the hospital where his wife was in her final battle with cancer. She died within days of his meeting Betty. Despite his sadness from the loss, Allen has said that immediately upon meeting Betty he told Bob, "I'm going to marry that girl." While it was a case of love at first sight for the new widower, it was not the case for Betty and she deflected a series of proposals.

Betty had been single for more than a dozen years, and added one more to that tally while Allen pursued her. The couple finally tied the knot in 1963, and it meant some very significant lifestyle adjustments for them both. The first was the geography. Each had roots on different coasts, and Betty had no desire to relocate to New York. She turned down that opportunity other times as well, including one very sweetheart deal offered by NBC to co-host *The Today Show*. Betty told me that her passing on that opportunity opened the door for the child of a well-known, well-connected New York nightclub operator, Lou Walters' daughter, Barbara.

Betty came to believe that their allegiances to two different coasts was just one of the differences that, maybe more than their commonalities, contributed to the strength of Allen and Betty's partnership. It was an open relationship with outside experiences, pursuits, and passions. Once brought home to share with each other, Betty's and Allen's diverse interests, active careers, and varied relationships kept their marriage fresh and allowed both to grow. In one newspaper profile Allen explained, "We thrive on our individual pursuits. I like the idea of Betty having a life of her own."

America's love for Betty was matched by the high esteem in which she was held within the Hollywood community. Game show producers for whom she regularly appeared could usually rely on Betty to make herself available for their pilots—ready, willing, and able to help sell their new concepts. After appearing on the panel of Goodson-Todman's *Make the Connection*, Mark Goodson wanted to have her host his next creation, but the network said "no" to the idea of a female host in the 1950s. It took nearly 30 years, but Betty holds the rare first Emmy awarded to a female game show host for her 1983 outing with NBC's *Just Men*. After Betty, it took another 22 years for a woman to win television's top honor in that category again. In 2005 Meredith Viera won the first of her two Emmys for her work on *Who Wants to Be a Millionaire*.

The opinion seems to have been unanimous that Betty was simply a joy to work with. It's almost unanimous. Almost. You see, there's one person with whom Betty clearly locked horns and for whom, she didn't mince words in private, and occasionally in public. There was turmoil on the set of *The Golden Girls*, and Betty places the responsibility squarely on the broad shoulders of "that obnoxious broad." That's what she called Bea Arthur. Betty and Bea were two women who, like oil and water, ultimately couldn't mix for any length of time. There was no emulsifying agent that could overcome that disparate chemistry. It was only their professionalism that kept any hint of their skirmishes under the radar of even the most discerning home viewers.

(l-r) Rue McClanahan, Bea Arthur, Betty White, Estelle Getty. Through seven seasons of ground-breaking and gut-busting comedy from the mind of Susan Harris, *The Golden Girls*' tarnish never showed on the screen (1985).

At a Television Academy event, Betty offered a kinder comment: "Bea and I didn't have a lot of relationship going on. Bea is a very, very eccentric woman." Betty's most common quote on the subject was simply, "Bea was not that fond of me." It hadn't always been that way. In the first season of the series, both faced the common challenge of watching their mothers' health decline until they passed away within one month of each other. As a mutual friend recalled, "There was a lot of hand-holding and condolences." Bea and Betty lived near each other and in those early days the two even commuted to work together, but once the camaraderie soured, it was as rancid as month-old milk.

Personality conflicts are common, but a battle between two stars of their magnitude and maturity, each so highly respected as professionals, was curiously unusual. While TV viewers were not as aware of Bea's pedigree as they were familiar with Betty's, Bea was also a long-time trouper. While Betty was blazing a trail in video, Bea's home was on the stage. Long before earning a Tony Award on Broadway, she traveled the country by train as Tallulah Bankhead's understudy in the prestigious Ziegfeld Follies.

According to co-star Rue McClanahan, Bea's negativity started even before she signed to do the show. The character named Dorothy was described from the very beginning as "A Bea Arthur-type," and Bea seemed happy to read for the role. "I thought it was brilliant," she told a Television Academy interviewer. "I thought it was one of the funniest, most adult, hilarious, sophisticated, terrific, delicious things I had ever read." Bea Arthur and Rue McClanahan were friends from working together on *Maude*, and the latter remembered things very differently.

Rue recalled Bea was reluctant to take the gig. Susan Harris, the show's creator, asked for Rue's help in persuading her former co-star to sign on for the role after she'd repeatedly refused. Rue remembered her call to Bea: "I said, 'Why are you turning down the best script that's ever going to come across your desk as long as you live?' and she said, 'Rue, I have no interest in playing 'Maude and Vivian meet Sue Ann Nevins.'"

As to the show's formulaic casting Bea did have a point. You see, at first Rue McClanahan was hired to play the scatterbrained Rose Nylund, and Betty White was envisioned as the promiscuous Blanche Devereaux. For Betty it would have been little more than an encore of her lustful Sue Ann Nivens homemaker character from *The Mary Tyler Moore Show*. It was an Emmy-winning audience favorite, but old hat. Likewise, Rue would have been much as we'd seen her as Bea's neighbor on *Maude*. Respected director Jay Sandrich's pedigree goes all the way back to *I Love Lucy*, and he's the one credited for sparking the idea that the casting be switched.

Rue became the man-crazed Blanche, a character that had not been written to have a Southern accent. Rue added that flavor later and it helped to further differentiate this golden girl from the actress' previous work. As Betty sized-up the transformation, "Rue, my god, she took Blanche out into orbit where I would have never dared to go. So I just think it worked out beautifully. If I had half the sex life Blanche had I would have been dead from exhaustion."

Reflecting on her own transformation, Betty said, "I knew Blanche. That would have been easy. I didn't exactly know how to play dumb." To play a character oblivious to insincerity, irony, or metaphor, she ran with Susan Harris's explanation that Rose "took everything at face value," and Jay's idea of "terminal naivety." Betty explained, "The best advice I got was, again, from Jay Sandrich. He said, 'Rose takes every word for its literal meaning. She knows no sarcasm, no nothing. If somebody said Rose could eat a horse, she'd call the SPCA.'"

During the time that Bea remained on the sidelines, Broadway veteran Elaine Stritch auditioned for the part of Dorothy. Stritch was no stranger to TV sitcoms having pioneered in the 1950s as the first Trixie Norton in the earliest sketches of Jackie Gleason's *The Honeymooners*. In remembering her *Golden Girls* audition, Stritch claimed that the writers didn't like her very much: "I didn't get the job." However, a mention in her one-woman show reveals that she sabotaged herself in pursuit of the role. After the producers asked her to read the audition lines as written, for whatever reason Elaine still chose to embellish the part with a number of four-letter words. As she remembered, "I blew a multi-million, zillion dollar, international, syndicated, residual-grabbing, bopparoni, smasharoni, television situation comedy."

It was only after Betty and Rue decided to switch roles that Bea committed. Thereafter, you can be sure there were many times Betty thought Bea should be committed. Idiosyncrasies aside, Bea's eldest son Matthew Saks told *Country Living* magazine in 2017, "My mom was the real deal." He said, "I think she felt she was more of an actress than Betty. Mom came from Broadway. Betty starred on a game show." That's harsh but, indeed, Bea did come from the stage and was steeped in the classic traditions of the theater. She would remain in character during the breaks in taping, and found her co-star's informality off-putting. Betty would pitch a joke to the audience on the occasions when she flubbed a line, and would regularly walk downstage and off the set to make small talk with the audience during stopdowns. As to doing battle with Bea, Betty said, "I just make it my business to get along with people so I can have fun. It's that simple."

Barrie Wellman was a network page from a more golden age of television and remembers, "Many of the famous actors and comedians I worked with at NBC were incredibly kind and generous with their comments to the pages and production staff… none kinder and more friendly than Betty. She hated to stay in her dressing room and would roam the studio hallway looking for people to make happy." She enjoyed people. Indeed. It seemed to be just that simple.

With television being a more intimate medium than movies or the stage, the strangers in the *Golden Girls* audiences at Sunset Gower and later Ren-Mar Studios felt like they already knew Betty. Their friendly reception and lovingly informal interplay with her during the set changes and between the takes ignited a slow-burning resentment in Bea. "I think my mom didn't dig that," son Matthew explained for *The Hollywood Reporter*. "It's just not the right time to talk to fans between takes. Betty was able to do it and it didn't seem to affect her. But it rubbed my mom the wrong way." Many say Bea was simply jealous of Betty's easy and breezy rapport with the evening's new friends in the bleachers. It seemed to some that her disapproval stemmed less from any perception of proper protocol than from the hard-to-believe reality that Bea was actually a very shy and private person.

In 2015 Matthew stipulated, "My mom wasn't really close to anybody. I'm not saying she was a loner, but she just liked to go home and read the paper." As strange as it may seem to those who have confused the actress with the characters she'd portrayed, the creator of her starring vehicle *Maude*, producer Norman Lear is among those who have confirmed that Bea was actually very insecure and immensely shy when not performing. Similarly Rue described Bea as "a very close, quiet, rather timid person, very gentle."

Gentle is not to be confused with soft, compliant, accommodating, or yielding. Hollywood's esteemed publicist Harlan Boll was among the many to see that distinction firsthand, "I once placed them together at a table during a Tony Awards after-party and both Betty and Bea, individually and with quiet discretion, each asked me to move them to another table." There's a chance that request was less hostile towards Betty than it was benignly quirky, as Bea did indeed have several peculiar eccentricities. Rue recalled how the actress could hardly tolerate people who chewed gum, in some cases reportedly asking that repeat offenders be fired. Stranger still, Rue added that her co-star hated birds. As to the cheesecakes the characters ate frequently, only Bea found that a distasteful part of the job. Bea freely admitted to also being "terrified of flying."

Finally, there's this golden girl's well-documented distaste for wearing shoes. It's indeed documented, as Bea's contract stipulated that she could walk around the set barefoot, agreeing not to sue the producers, production company or the studio, holding them harmless if she was injured as a result. More than anything else, her friends say Bea was misunderstood, painting the picture of a woman who made many sacrifices in a career that, although successful by almost all measures, never allowed her to realize her original dream. Bea explained that her height, voice, and swagger forever kept her from the roles she had originally envisioned for herself which she described as "a blond starlet." That was not a joke, but a brutally honest admission of a lifetime's unfulfilled dream.

If you think that's all psychobabble mumbo-jumbo, you'll appreciate Joan Rivers' simple explanation for Bea Arthur's sometimes cool, detached, aloof, and introverted nature. In her best Marcel Marceau miming, Joan raised an invisible cup to her lips, drank, shrugged her shoulders, cocked her head to one side and said, "She was a lush." Joan explained that Bea was sufficiently intoxicated at the one and only dinner party to which she invited her, that Bea threw a ladle full of gravy with such force that it hit the ceiling before dripping to the carpeted floor in her entirely off-white dining room. Joan swore it was true. She's also far from the only person to reference Bea's enjoyment of potent potables.

There's no denying Bea's incredible gift. One leering scowl from Maude Findley or Dorothy Zbornak spoke volumes. Despite all the internal and external strife, looking back in her later years Bea expressed great appreciation for the professional life she'd been able to live and to those who helped her along the way. Once retired, Bea indulged her joy of cooking by increasing the frequency with which she held small dinner parties for friends. She was also gracious and thoughtful when it came to her fans, leaving a lasting legacy with several charities that she generously endowed.

Playing fiercely against her true type—a shy introvert who successfully portrayed a couple of in-your-face extroverted characters—is a dichotomy that earned Bea high praise within the Hollywood community. In similar fashion, it added luster to Betty White's already golden image when she "played dumb" as Rose. It certainly didn't hurt Julia Roberts' reputation when she convincingly portrayed a convicted murderer on *Law and Order*, nor did it damage Whoopi Goldberg's prestige when she guested on that franchise's *Criminal Intent* spinoff as a foster mother who manipulated her children to murder on her behalf.

The converse turned out to be disastrous when a hidden dark side was seen through the cracks in the veneer of what appeared to be a good-natured warm-hearted, humble and gracious award-winning actress-comedienne. So it was for Ellen Degeneres in 2020. Finally, the reports of mounting behind-the-scenes animosity engendered by the charismatic talk show star began to make sense. It seemed thoroughly incomprehensible to all but perhaps the most cynical to consider that it all might have been an act.

Ellen certainly found a multi-billion dollar niche for herself, for Warner Bros., for NBCUniversal, and for the various other entities that had a piece of her chat-fest action. Debuting in major markets on NBC-owned stations in 2003, it took only one year for her syndicated daily talker to begin hauling in Emmy statues beginning with 2004, 2005, 2006, and 2007 wins. I was the voice of the Daytime

Emmy awards the year her streak began and there seemed to be nothing but love for this young, energetic and sincerely funny star-on-the-rise. Both she and her mother were charming and fun throughout the ceremony, and while table-hopping during the dinner that followed.

That's why it was so strange to hear Ellen's crew members bad-mouthing her on the days I'd be with them working on other sets. The din from their bitching got louder with each season. The supposed policy for subordinate staffers to not speak to her when she was in the office is certainly off-putting, despite the fact that Ellen is not the first with that sort of decree. Eventually as many as a dozen friends' buzzing included damning stories about what they termed her show's hostile work environment. That only got louder when *Ellen* moved from NBC Studio 11 to a multiple-stage compound on the Warner Bros. lot. That was where Australian radio host Neil Breen had what he called a "bizarre" encounter in 2013 when producers instructed him not to look at Ellen before his interview started. Kathy Griffin, Lea Thompson, and Brad Garrett were among the celebrity guests who later came forward with their stories of backstage dysfunction at *Ellen*.

Apparently it took 17 years for word to begin to spread that the senior producers of this seemingly charming, incandescent bundle of joy's program must be spending much of the 23 remaining hours of the day pissing off those who helped Ellen shine so brightly. Under the added stress of the Covid-19 pandemic, halfway through 2020 the dam began to leak as staffers started going public.

Trade paper reports state that the dysfunction started with anonymous complaints of sexual misconduct, harassment, assault, racism, intimidation, a culture of bullying, and a series of "microaggressions." There were allegations that employees had been fired after taking medical leave or bereavement days. Then a core group of about 30 crewmembers reported that they initially received no written communication from producers about the status of their working hours, pay, or any responses to their inquiries concerning their mental and physical health during the Covid-19 pandemic.

Warner Bros. confirmed that internal investigations found many of the complaints to be credible. Fingers pointed to three executive producers whose heads were quickly placed on the chopping block as human sacrifices at the altar of public opinion. Ellen's apology was convincing to everybody who hadn't worked on the show. Among some of those who did, the venom boiled over with the star's assertion that she had no idea what was going on. One production team member said she rolled her eyes while reading her boss's memo promising renewed sensitivity and respect for all.

Within hours of hearing of her employees' angry and skeptical responses to her apology, rumors began to swirl that Ellen wanted to walk away from the entire enterprise. After 18 years on the air, Ellen DeGeneres announced in May of 2021 that *The Ellen DeGeneres Show* would indeed be dancing off television screens for good in 2022 after 19 seasons. She told Savannah Guthrie on *Today* the show was ending because she's "bored." She echoed the sentiment for *The Hollywood Reporter*, attributing her pulling the plug to her desire to find "something new to challenge me."

Warner Bros. had millions of reasons to keep her dancing, while Ellen had millions of reasons in the bank to consider walking. Comedy is a big, serious business.

Chapter 13

Comedy is indeed a serious business, and the smiles from the audience at some shows far outnumber those seen backstage. In an unlikely twist, one actor who seemingly never smiled on-screen got big laughs behind the scenes. There was near zero comic relief when Robert Stack played the all-business crime-busting G-man Eliot Ness on *The Untouchables*. Likewise, he showed not an ounce of levity hosting the interstitial segments of *Unsolved Mysteries*.

It was in the guise of that film noir-inspired character that Stack was booked at a corporate event wearing his law-enforcement sneer. It was accessorized by a classic trench coat with upturned collar and a fedora, looking much like Bogart's interpretation of Dashiell Hammett's Sam Spade. Onstage in the ballroom at the Century Plaza Hotel, they even had mysterious plumes of steam to make the street scene complete, as if Stack was standing on a New York City manhole cover at twilight.

A half-dozen of us lowest-level thespians trying to make a living were hired to crawl around a make-believe murder scene, flashing cameras and buzzing about some dastardly deed that Stack was talking about. It was all based on some inside corporate joke we weren't, and didn't need to be privy to, unless you're a strict method actor. In that case, you'd need to know what the make-believe murder victim had for breakfast.

It was backstage that Robert Stack was all laughs and smiles, but who wouldn't be when picking up several grand for a silly 10 minutes in cop drag. I mentioned to him how much I loved the gritty and stylized production of *The Untouchables*, including the staccato narration from the then-defrocked but once dynamic superstar broadcaster and controversial columnist, Walter Winchell. Robert shared how surprised he was that the production remained so true to the tone of the book on which it was based. The gruff and violent nature seemed incongruous with the perception of Desi and Lucy's family-friendly Desilu, *The Untouchables'* production company.

For most of those working on the lot, Desilu did have a family vibe. After all, it was a mom-and-pop operation with mom and pop—Lucy and Desi—present and actively involved. When Lucy would drive through the gates, if the youngest kids from *My Three Sons* were on a break outdoors, they enjoyed getting in her car for a quick ride. Nicknamed "Bub," William Michael Francis O'Casey was the boys' maternal grandfather on the show. Grumpy co-star William Frawley took that grandpa role to heart, escorting the kids offsite to enjoy restaurant lunches.

The child actor who played Chip Douglas, Stanley Livingston, remembers that as Frawley drank through his noontime meal break, they'd be favored with an entirely different and ever-darkening view of life that they couldn't hear anywhere else. In return, the kids would try their best to get the booze-infused actor back to the set sometime close to schedule. It then became the production company's job to keep Frawley from nodding off during scenes. That magic trick was accomplished by having a stagehand lie on the floor just out camera range to tap old Bub on the foot when the camera rolled. Frawley's Bub disappeared and William Demarest's "Uncle Charley" arrived after the actor's drinking diminished his health to where he was no longer able to pass the annual insurance physical.

Although it had been years since Frawley shared the stage with his *I Love Lucy* nemesis, Vivian Vance, the ill will hadn't fully faded. During some of his *My Three Sons* years, his former co-star was on the lot filming *The Lucy Show* which gave him the chance to exact further revenge. On occasion, Frawley could be found sneaking through a back door onto the *Lucy* stage with an armful of empty 35mm film reels. Unseen, he'd wait for Vance to begin to deliver a line, then heave the reels into the air. They'd land with the loud crash of a dozen cymbals interrupting her dialogue, to which she'd scream, "BILL!!!!" After all, who else could possibly be that hatefully disruptive?

Another of the Desilu kid stars, Jon Provost, remembers that while he and Lassie were filming on Stage 9, Bing Crosby Productions' star Vince Edwards was in medical drag saving lives as Dr. Ben Casey on Stage 10. Then, in the combined Stages 11 and 12, lives were lost almost daily as rival mobs Tommy-gunned each other and shot at G-men on a faux Chicago street. Jon loved watching the action scenes so much that actor Abel Fernandez, one of Eliot Ness' FBI agents, would drop in at *Lassie* to see if Jon was available when the more exciting stunts were about to be staged.

TV's original *Untouchables* from the 1959 *Desilu Playhouse* pilot. Only Robert Stack as Agent Eliot Ness (third from left) and Abel Fernandez as Agent William Youngfellow (second from right) remained on the elite crime-fighting team when picked-up by ABC for series that fall.

Robert Stack explained how the *Untouchables* lead role came to him last minute without the usual lead time to thoroughly familiarize himself with that stark and dark approach, and without the lead time for much contract-negotiating foreplay. Initially, actor Van Heflin had topped the list to play Eliot Ness, but turned down the role. Soon after, Van Johnson was apparently on board for the lead. On board, until his wife pulled a classic Hollywood classless cliché maneuver just days before filming was to begin. It's an old ruse utilized by the less scrupulous to wrest more money. For producers, it's nothing more than infuriating bullshit.

One of the happiest moments for a showrunner has to be when writing, casting, staffing, the rental of studio facilities, and the myriad of details are all finally coordinated with the stars' availability. There are so many variables that locking down pre-production and shooting schedules can be as challenging as solving Rubik's Cube. Once all the loose ends are tied, each "i" dotted, and every "t" crossed, no production company wants to unravel the package. That's when some people take a shot at extorting a little extra cash.

First in this subterfuge, hammer out a deal and agree to the terms with a firm verbal "yes" but delay returning any signed agreement, the longer the better. Then, create some last minute sob story about the agent screwing up (it's never the talent's fault). Perhaps it was some miscommunication about available dates. Then apologize profusely before miraculously finding a way to fix the fictional problem, if the deal could somehow include a little extra cash. Some have extorted loot under the premise that they would be suffering lost income from having to cancel another commitment. The requested bump in pay may be couched as an incentive to not retract their "yes" for a better paying opportunity, or it can be suggested as a signing bonus to cover the cost of supposedly adjusting the star's schedule. Perhaps it's cash requested for first-class airfare to return from some imaginary location shoot.

Producers will see right through whatever story you come up with, but just may throw a stack of Benjamins on the table anyway. What's a few more bucks in order to avoid twisting Rubik's Cube again? It's blatantly dishonest and thoroughly transparent, but it has worked. Robert told me that Van Johnson's wife was acting as her husband's representative in the *Untouchables* deal and was clearly out of her league with a ham-fisted last-minute attempt to play that game. She insisted that her husband's pay be doubled! The $10,000 per episode that had been agreed to would now need to be $20,000. Well, no sale. Desi Arnaz wasn't having any of it. Van was out, leaving Cliff Robertson, Jack Lord, and Robert Stack remaining on the short list. Robert got the call on a Friday night to play the lead role less than 48 hours before rehearsals began for the pilot.

That night's conversation with Robert at the Century Plaza was delightfully free-flowing, but he had nothing to add to a story that had fascinated me for years. It's the strange connection between his employer on *The Untouchables* and a convicted murderer—murderer or patsy, that is. Surprisingly, there was just one small degree of separation between Desi Arnaz and Robert Kennedy's assassin, Sirhan Sirhan. Beyond a reported friendship between the two, that relationship included Sirhan's working at The Granja Vista del Rio, a horse ranch that Desi co-owned in

Corona, east of Los Angeles. Robert confirmed that Desi did indeed own a horse breeding ranch somewhere around Corona, but he had no other insight into Sirhan and Desi's relationship.

The Emmy-winning actor then had me mesmerized as he steered the conversation to the real off-screen *Untouchables* drama. It started when word first spread from the Hollywood production community to members of organized crime that a plan was in place to bring the 336-page tome *The Untouchables* to television. It was bad enough that Oscar Fraley and Eliot Ness had co-authored the 1957 memoir that named the names of people who preferred to remain unnamed. The idea of bringing even fictionalized accounts of their prohibition-era lawlessness to a vast network audience was met with cigar-chomping sneers by some very serious characters. It sparked serious backroom talk about how to put an end to the series before it began.

By the way, there has always been a *sub rosa* pipeline of information between Hollywood and the highest levels of the underworld. It goes far deeper than the oft-told true tale of Billy Wilkerson, founder of *The Hollywood Reporter*, partnering with members of the Mafia who tapped the Teamsters' retirement fund to develop dusty Las Vegas into a gambling mecca. Among the most direct links between movies and murderers was a Chicago gangster named Willie Bioff, a personal friend of Al Capone and Frank "The Enforcer" Nitti.

The 1930s were the golden age of motion pictures, when the studios each cranked out dozens of mostly-profitable features every year. It made them ripe targets for extortion. Bioff was sent to Los Angeles to be the muscle for mob-controlled labor leader George Browne. When Browne became president of the stagehands' union, IATSE, Bioff was right there assisted by "Handsome Johnny" Roselli, coercing cash and extending the mob's influence. The Hollywood trade papers reported that the studios then informed 12,000 of their 30,000 employees that they were required to join one of four IATSE crafts locals, or be fired.

After members of the newly-bloated union found their paychecks lightened by a two percent surcharge things really heated up, eventually burning the mob. Investigations, kickbacks, indictments, payoffs, strikes, and death threats, plus more than one bloody free-for-all eventually led to jail time for the luckiest of the extortionists. Among the unlucky, Nitti was found shot to death. Some conjectured it was a suicide, after finding himself set up as a sacrificial lamb and dreading the thought of serving another prison stretch. Roselli went to the slammer, while Browne drank himself to death. After living in quiet anonymity in Arizona, Bioff's exit was courtesy of a classic old reliable, a car bomb that decorated his neighborhood with debris and body parts when he clicked his truck's ignition.

Reached through his home state's powerful political machine, President Harry Truman was allegedly compelled to quietly arrange a parole for movie mogul Joseph Schenck who was in prison for tax evasion related to this caper. In this web of lawlessness, incredibly, when Johnny Roselli was released after a four-year hitch behind bars he was rewarded with a deal to produce a couple of movies at one of the studios he helped victimize. What a business!

The two films were 1948's *Canyon City* and *He Walked by Night*. Interestingly, Jack Webb played a forensics specialist in the latter, a cop drama, before donning L.A.P.D. badge 714 to become radio and TV's top crime buster Joe Friday on *Dragnet*. As for "Handsome Johnny," Roselli remained active until 1976 when he testified before a U.S. Senate Select Committee about the Mafia's potential involvement in a conspiracy to kill President Kennedy. Soon after, his decomposing body was found floating in a 55-gallon steel drum in the waters off Miami.

Why should the mob stop at IATSE stagehands when the movie czars had the far deeper pockets? The history of demands for protection money from the studios by various gangsters forms an intricate overlapping and interlocking web of payoffs and reciprocating favors. Among them was a 1936 brazen demand for 50% of profits which was answered with a counter-offer from virtually every studio. Paramount, MGM, 20th Century-Fox, and Warner Bros. all agreed to a down payment of $100,000 each to be followed by annual $50,000 inducements to keep the film factories free from interference. The story goes that within three days of acquiescing to this shakedown, MGM's Nicholas Schenck and Fox's Robert Kent personally delivered the first of the studios' initial installments. After carrying a suitcase packed with $1,000 bills to New York's Waldorf Astoria, they waited while a trio of thugs counted the two hundred Grover Clevelands on their room's twin beds.

Other huge payments re-opened targeted theaters in Chicago owned by RKO, Warner, Paramount, and Loews that mysteriously had gone dark as a sample of what was possible on a national scale. It was a classic protection racket. Production and exhibition would continue smoothly provided tribute was paid as agreed. Estimates of the racket's total take range from $3 million to more than $6 million, over $120 million in today's dollars.

Before movies, nightclubs were notorious for being operated by the mob. Even above-board owners were almost always beholden to the wise guys in a tangled web of reciprocity. I was tipped off to much of this by a broadcaster whose previous career included managing a New York nightspot. He explained how dishware and glasses had to be purchased from only the approved mob-connected supplier. Likewise, the laundry service that cleaned tablecloths, napkins, and uniforms was syndicate-controlled. You certainly couldn't buy your produce from some random supplier or wholesale market. Already so deeply in the nightclubs' doors, one industrious *caporegime* figured that it made sense to also control the entertainers.

Comedian and game show personality Orson Bean was touring the small showrooms as a standup act at the time and told me, "I found the Mafia guys to be interesting and pleasant. If you crossed them, you'd wind up with your feet in cement, but if you didn't cross them they were generous." The crime families' requests of talent usually weren't very taxing. All they wanted from Joey Bishop was for him to emcee the wedding of Sam Giancana's daughter, which he most certainly did.

Comedian Shecky Green has spoken about the time he had to turn down Frank Sinatra's request to perform at an all-star benefit the crooner was organizing for a church. He shared with Sinatra the details of his conflicting booking on that same weekend at some distant club. An hour later Shecky's phone rang. Sinatra explained that the comic's shows were gladly un-booked by the venue's owner so Shecky could be part of the benefit.

The multi-talented Peter Marshall worked for what some called The Outfit and summed it up for author Kliph Nesteroff: "working for the mob guys, that was the best." Why? "When you worked for the mobsters you were treated like royalty." Other performers had an infinitely less cordial relationship after being tapped to tithe a portion of their earnings as tribute and for protection. Most were happy to cough up the cash when reminded of what happened to successful singer-funnyman Joe E. Lewis in 1927. Already playing at Chicago's Green Mill Cocktail Lounge, he was lured to also do stand-up at the New Rendezvous just down the street. Both clubs were mob run, but Joe E. didn't know they were operated by rival factions. That act of treason was met by a throat slashing that the comic miraculously survived, but left him barely able to speak—his stock-in-trade. Joe E.'s story was later made into a motion picture, *The Joker is Wild*, where he was portrayed by Frank Sinatra.

Mafia kingpin Sam Giancana proudly owned up to being the muscle for that knife job when he was a kid. He convincingly came clean naming "Machine Gun" Jack McGurn for giving him, along with "Needles" Gianola, "and another punk" the assignment to visit Joe E at his hotel room. Giancana bragged, "We beat him to a pulp and pistol-whipped him real good. Shit, we cut his fucking throat from stern to stern. His goddamned tongue was hanging by a string." Word traveled fast. "There isn't a star alive now who'd turn us down," he added.

There were parallels among the ranks of musical performers when country-pop singer Jimmy Rodgers suffered brain damage from a beating after pressing his record label's president Morris Levy for overdue royalties. Tommy James of The Shondells tells that story and his own tales of life under the thumb of the mob at Levy's Roulette Records. Warner Bros. executive Joe Smith says he was required to bring $20,000 in cash to an address on Ninth Avenue in Manhattan to buy Van Morrison's contract from organized crime.

Crooner Al Martino's daughter, Allison, tells a far more complicated story of the Mob's relationship with talent. It started with the Mafia buying her dad's contact from his manager, Bill Borelli, without the singer's knowledge. Then, when Martino wanted out of the deal, the Mob demanded $75,000 as a down payment on what they saw as their cut of his future earnings. Unable to come up with the cash to buy his way out of the contract, and with Mob musclemen then threatening to kill him, in 1953 Martino hid in England for seven long years. The story goes that after Albert Anastasia, the boss of Murder Inc., was himself butchered in a Manhattan barbershop, Chicago kingpin Sam Giancana, along with Angelo Bruno of the New York crime family and Pennsylvania mob boss Russell Bufalino, successfully negotiated permission to allow Martino to return home. Bufalino was the inspiration for the character portrayed by Joe Pesci in the Martin Scorsese film *The Irishman*.

In a related Hollywood footnote, Martino initially turned down the part of Johnny Fontaine that he ultimately played in *The Godfather*. He didn't want to cross swords again with members of La Famiglia as this was a controversial role. Frank Sinatra, concerned that audiences would think the movie's washed-up Johnny Fontaine was based on his life, wanted the character scratched entirely. Conveniently, Giancana just happened to be married to Martino's pal, Phyllis of the singing McGuire Sisters. She's said to have helped assuage Sinatra's concerns, while also advocating for Martino's replacement to voluntarily bow out of the film.

Vic Damone had been booked to play Johnny Fontaine after Martino first turned down the part. Damone did indeed step aside when Mr. and Mrs. Giancana convinced Martino to reconsider his decision. Martino later claimed that taking that gig brought repercussions because his casting was consummated despite objections from director Francis Ford Coppola. "We convinced Coppola that I should stay in the movie," the crooner said. As a result, "He ostracized me when I was on the set."

MCA, later the owner of Universal Studios, was first established as a talent agency. The company was said to have worked hand-in-glove with the various mob families in booking a great many of the bands, singers, and comics performing on the nightclub circuits. There's been much written about several government investigations into MCA's alleged infiltration by organized crime and illegal cash transfers. There was no deep probe needed in another case, as it was common knowledge that the underworld was running the American Guild of Variety Artists. It was so obvious that a 1962 Congressional subcommittee easily ferreted out that link. Some of the most interesting performers carry AGVA cards in their wallets, including The Radio City Music Hall Rockettes and Cirque du Soleil cast members, as well as theme park, Las Vegas showroom and cabaret acts.

As to *The Untouchables*, the conversation with Emmy-winner Robert Stack became hushed when he ever-so-briefly mentioned organized crime's intervening with executive producer Desi Arnaz's early plans to bring the hard-hitting crime drama into living rooms. He left me to dig for many of the details on my own. L.A.'s crime boss Jimmy "The Weasel" Fratianno made it easy to do that research as he didn't take this, or many other stories to the grave. As an informant, "The Weasel" had lots to say before he entered the Witness Protection Program.

Fratianno testified that upon the first word being mentioned about *The Untouchables'* pending small screen dramatization the news was immediately sent upstream, directly to Al Capone's widow Mae Capone. Mrs. Scarface was already furious about the book's biased and sensationalized portrayal of Eliot Ness and his G-Men emasculating her proud husband while destroying his bootlegging empire. Mae felt that more than enough had already been said of Al Capone's harassment, capture, and subsequent tour of several federal prisons. It certainly didn't need to now also be played out coast-to-coast each week on ABC.

Numerous accounts have Mae Capone actually speaking directly to Desi Arnaz, imploring him to cancel his studio's plans for the two-part episode *The Scarface Mob*, the lead-in for the series *The Untouchables*. When Desi wouldn't accede, Mae was apparently prepared to do whatever was necessary to snuff production before the first frame of film was exposed. Numerous published reports have Mae asking Sam Giancana for help. He in turn contacted his friend Frank Sinatra who paid a post-midnight visit to Desi in Indian Wells, near Palm Springs. The conversation became so heated that it almost came to fisticuffs before Sinatra backed down and left. Within days, Sam Giancana, with his pals Anthony "Joe Batters" Accardo and Paul Ricca, had a contract out on Desi's life. As the saying goes, Capone's widow "pushed the button."

In a conversation with Johnny Roselli that's quoted in Fratiano's book, *The Last Mafioso*, it's revealed that San Diego hitman Frank Bompensiero was primed for the job:

Roselli: "Millions of people see this show every fucking week. . . a bunch of Italian lunatics running around with machine guns, talking out of the corner of their mouths, slopping up spaghetti like a bunch of fucking pigs. They make Capone and Nitti look like blood-thirsty maniacs. The guys that write that shit don't know the first thing about the way things were in those days. Elliot Ness, my ass. The tax boys got Al, not Ness. And what did he ever have to do with Frank Nitti?"

Fratianno: Nobody pays attention to that shit. It's like a comic book, a joke. Who cares?

Roselli: I'll tell you, Jimmy. Sam cares. Joe Batters cares, Paul Ricca cares, and I care. Jimmy, what I'm about to tell you has been decided by our family. The top guys have voted a hit. I've already talked to Bomp about it. We're going to clip Desi Arnaz.

Al Capone's widow was suspected of intervening to veto the hit. Fratianno confirmed it was canceled two weeks later, saying of Desi, "He never knew how close he came to getting clipped."

The studio head also heard from Capone's son. Believe it or not, Albert Francis "Sonny" Capone and Desi Arnaz already knew each other. They were far more than simple acquaintances, as they had gone to school together. Desi was one year older than Sonny Capone and was enrolled at St. Patrick Catholic School in Palm Beach, Florida upon emigrating from Cuba in 1934. In addition to being schoolmates for a couple of years, several biographies report that Sonny and Desi had a close relationship.

A couple of decades after their school days the younger Capone was now imploring Desi not to go forward with the project. According to Robert Stack,

Sonny's plea was along the lines of "Everything about dad has been buried. Let it rest." Book or no book, the history and mythology surrounding the bootlegging era was all in the public domain for exploitation by anyone. Sonny asked "Why you?" Desi responded that *The Untouchables* saga would only be produced by someone else if he backed out.

The Capone estate filed a multi-million dollar lawsuit against Desilu Productions, CBS, and sponsor Westinghouse. The case was dismissed on appeal with the ruling, "What a man does while alive becomes a part of history which survives his death. Comment, fictionalization and even distortion of a dead man's career do not invade the privacy of his offspring, relatives or friends, if they are not even mentioned therein."

When not doing battle with the Capone family, Desi was under attack on another front. Robert Stack and I laughed at the capper to a story he shared about the time The Sons of Italy became outraged over the issue of continuing negative portrayals of Italian-Americans. As the show's plotlines of the gangster rackets in 1920s Chicago were inspired by true-life stories, they included a great many Sicilian, Italian, and Italian-American names and characters. The explanation that these were fictionalized portrayals of actual historic figures fell on deaf ears. Desi was reticent to cave on the matter but finally acquiesced, just a little. There was contrition when a memo came down from Desi and Lucy's executive offices requesting that the fictional character in one episode, Rocco Balboni, be renamed. With that directive, Rocco Balboni became... Seth Balboni! As if that were better. Robert swore it was true.

He went on to recall that an unlikely alliance was formed over the issue. There was likely only one concern capable of uniting Frank Sinatra, Cardinal Spelling, Senator John Pastore, and J. Edgar Hoover. Each of that odd foursome had also taken note of all the Italian-sounding surnames attached to the criminals in the weekly scripts. By the final season of production Italian names were all but gone. In the attempt to skirt any further animosity some of the heavies were even given Chinese names.

There was little I could add to the actor's great stories of his days at Desilu as I'd not yet heard about a surprising confrontation between Desi Arnaz and

Rob Reiner. It was 1967 and Desi had the old *I Love Lucy* writers turning out scripts for his short-lived NBC comedy *The Mothers-in-Law* starring Eve Arden and Kaye Ballard. It was a funny series with two great comediennes, a couple of veteran comic actors as their husbands, and a parade of familiar-faced guest stars. The casting was wonderfully incestuous with dozens of friends and an extended family of instantly recognizable 1960s sitcom actors. Desi, his son Desi Jr., and daughter Lucie Arnaz were in various episodes, as was Carl Reiner's son, Rob, a few years before he became famous as Archie Bunker's "Meathead."

Rob was about 20 years old at the time and was back in front of the cameras to play the archetypal hippie, as he'd done guesting on *Gomer Pyle, U.S.M.C.*, *The Beverly Hillbillies* and a bunch of other series including Garry Marshall's short-lived *Hey, Landlord*, and Andy Griffith's even shorter run 14-episode series *Headmaster*. Indeed, it was young Rob's portraying variations on that longhaired liberal that eventually led to his breakout role on *All in the Family*. His showdown with Desi on the set of *The Mothers-in-Law* was on a Wednesday, a rehearsal day before Friday's filming of the episode "The Career Girls." Rob, playing the part of a director, was improvising his lines as they walked through a scene.

Everything was mellow until Desi walked onto the set. Within seconds of watching his actors the boss's anger erupted. He was soon screaming and cursing at Rob, accusing him of being unprofessional for not sticking with the scripted dialogue. Rob was being less than repentantly apologetic and recalled suddenly being pinned against the wall with Desi's face inches from his. Although Desi kept calling Rob his "amigo," he continued to shout, berate, and curse him. The stereotypical Latin temper from hell was raging as Desi screamed, "We pay $10,000 a script! I don't need you fucking around with the fucking lines!"

Physically trapped between Desi's arms and with his back against the wall, fearing for his safety, all Rob could think about was getting the hell out of the situation. With a vein in Desi's forehead throbbing and his face turning crimson, Rob now began to apologize profusely while explaining that another actor would clearly be better suited to the role. He extricated himself from the ugliness as gracefully and professionally as he could, only to find himself painted as an uncooperative hothead when word was leaked to gossip reporter Rona Barrett. Miss Rona, as she was known, is said to have been responsible for spreading the story far and wide that Rob had amateurishly walked from the show.

In addition to a career as a performer, Desi Arnaz oversaw production at the television industry's largest independent studio, responsible for producing more than two dozen series during the 1950s and 1960s.

I wish I'd heard this story years earlier, as it would have had Robert Stack doubled over with laughter—he'd already alluded to Desi's penchant for occasionally erupting with fiercely argumentative outbursts. He would have also appreciated another, even more recently confirmed postscript that vindicates Desi. Desilu film editor Bud Molin remembers that, unlike Rob, Desi knew every word of each week's script, "All those years, Desi Arnaz never once ever blew a line or missed a shot… he never once fluffed. It was amazing that he could go that long and never screw up."

You'd think that Rob might have learned a lesson in the crosshairs of Desi's rage, but when sitcom specialist Hal Kanter stepped in to produce the 1975 season opener of *All in the Family* he also found Rob's playing fast and loose with the writers' carefully-crafted dialog. Kanter didn't know or care that Rob had been doing that since the series began, he considered it unprofessional. After instructing the actor to deliver the lines as written, he remembered facing Rob's sullen pout for the remainder of the table read.

A few hours later came a call from Norman Lear who agreed with Kanter's sensibilities, but not his failure to pamper and pander to his performer. Rob had gone home and Kanter was now required to call with an apology lest Rob decide to stay home indefinitely. Sally Struthers had already started that season refusing to perform over a contract dispute. With all the intrigue at some shows, sometimes it's a wonder that anything ever actually ends up in viewers' living rooms.

The evening skulking around a make-believe murder scene on-stage at the Century Plaza Ballroom remains memorable for its introduction to two now-long-time favorites, Robert Stack the actor, and Grey Goose the vodka. Say, let's grab some Grey Goose right now and mingle.

Chapter 14

Working or partying in Hollywood means meeting a potpourri of personalities—the famous, the wanna-bees, the has-beens, the once-were's and the never-will-be's—the happy as well as the miserable. It quickly becomes crystal clear that some people's lack of joy eclipses even their brightest spotlight and biggest paycheck. Those who live under an internal dark cloud feel unloved even when they're already adored by a spouse, family, friends, and a fawning public. They can have the production staff falling over themselves, stocking snacks and perfectly icing their favorite beverages in their dressing room, even running personal errands for them, all to no avail.

Troubled performers are indulged, pampered and catered to because producers know they need to feel confident and supported to give their best performances. Yet even with all of that mollycoddling some are barely able to tolerate another day. Perhaps worst of all, misery loves company. Damned if the whole set doesn't soon feel like it's in hell—hell, but with air conditioning. The energy is sucked out of the room, the usual camaraderie evaporates, and everybody spends the rest of the day looking at their watches.

There are a few examples of people who embodied that negativity in these pages, including several of their sad downfalls. Unfulfilled, a chronic sufferer of unsuccessful-itis starts to find fault everywhere. The frustrations include such trivialities as not being waved through the studio gate fast enough. Their control issues can escalate to establishing overreaching rules for how others are to behave. Steve Harvey's legendary memo to his staff and crew is a classic example; it's in a later chapter.

According to disgruntled employees, Ellen DeGeneres is among the stars who set rigid limits on making direct eye contact, insisting that nobody greet her unless she greets them first. "I don't know where it started," was Ellen's response. "Please talk to me. Look me in the eye. It's crazy, just not true. I don't know how it started. [It's] not who I am." Jessica Alba came away from a small role on *Beverly Hills 90210* saying she was contractually forbidden from making eye contact with Tori Spelling or Luke Perry, "You wouldn't be allowed to talk to them unless they spoke to you first."

The New York Post reported that Barbra Streisand insists hotel workers face the wall when they are in the room with her. Tom Cruise purportedly forbade extras on the set of *Magnolia* from looking him in the eye. Bob Eubanks reports that his son was an assistant director on the JLo-starring movie *The Wedding Planner* where each day's call sheet carried the headline, "Do not make eye contact with Ms. Lopez." Then there's the narcissism of demanding changes in lighting and camera angles to enhance one person's appearance without regard for another's. I watched one superstar of old Hollywood spend 15 minutes directing a lighting crew, only to leave the studio when her insecurity and vanity must have outweighed her desire to be celebrated by the audience. Of course by that point in her life, and considering her post-stroke limitations, the beloved Bette Davis had earned every accommodation.

A variation of that senior star's anxiety about sitting for an interview had a very different ending. With a record-setting four Oscars awarded over an amazing 48-year span, Katherine Hepburn had long been on many talent bookers' most wanted lists. That included the casting team at Dick Cavett's old ABC late night show, but the star never committed to appearing on any talk show. Unexpectedly on the Tuesday afternoon following the 1973 Labor Day holiday the actress sauntered into the old Elysee Theater on West 58th Street. She told the crew that was busy prepping for a taping that evening how she'd never been on a television show and just wanted to look around the studio. That news instantly reached Dick Cavett who was on the stage in seconds. He remembered, "She checked the cameras, the lights, these chairs, the temperature in the studio, she pronounced the carpet ugly and then she surprised me by suddenly saying, 'Why don't we just go ahead and do it now?' And we did."

Well, they almost did. The show's director, Arthur Forrest had just arrived home, back in New York from producing the all-night all-day Jerry Lewis MDA

Telethon in Las Vegas. He remembers the phone call that preempted his planned nap: "They said get down here right away.... Katherine Hepburn's in the studio and she's willing to do an interview right this minute!" Arthur arrived just in time to find the 66-year-old rearranging the on-set furniture. Tape rolled and the long chat that ensued became two episodes, the first of which aired 10 days later.

On September 4, 1973, 66-year-old Katherine Hepburn unexpectedly arrived on the set of *The Dick Cavett Show* and announced that now would be a good time for an interview. The actress gave Dick three hours of compelling television.

When stars talk about talk show hosts there's one master of the genre whose name has popped up more than any other, likely because he's interacted with more of them than any other person in the entire history of the business. Nobody was bigger on the small screen than Johnny Carson. With 4,531 nights behind the desk over the course of his nearly 30-year run as number one in late night, he seemingly played host to more guests than Hilton and Marriot combined. He certainly hosted more visitors than anyone ever on the tube, and all were subject to his no-talk policy.

For years, impressionist Rich Little had a standing invitation for a monthly guest spot on *The Tonight Show*. He says that during dozens of visits he and Johnny never once exchanged more than a few strained words while sitting together in the on-set chairs during commercial breaks. First-time guests were told by their talent coordinators not to try to talk with Johnny during those cutaways, but for guests who knew him socially the silence always felt awkward. Still, there was rarely little more than a nod or a smile until the lights came back up with the cameras and microphones hot. Billy Crystal says he dared to break that silence on one occasion by asking simply "How's it going?" "It's going pretty good" was the terse response as Johnny suddenly became deeply occupied drumming with his pencils.

Johnny's longtime friend Dick Cavett explained to a crowd at Chicago's Museum of Broadcast Communications on June 21, 2014, "[Johnny] had the band play loud music so he wouldn't have to talk to the guests between [segments], which was not only typical for him but not a bad idea." Cavett was a fellow Nebraskan who, like Johnny, started entertaining as a magician, eventually writing comedy for established headliners. Where early in his career Johnny wrote for Red Skelton, Cavett wrote for Jack Paar, Jerry Lewis, Jack E. Leonard, Groucho Marx, and for Johnny Carson early in his *Tonight Show* years. The two formed a solid bond that continued even during the years that Cavett's show was his competition on ABC in the 11:30 time slot. It begs the question of whether Johnny and Joan Rivers could have remained friendly during her years at Fox had their communication not broken down before her debut.

Those who had more than merely a passing familiarity found Johnny to be a complex man who, many say, was only truly happy for the daily hour or so he was being loved by a live audience. Most nights when the lights dimmed, so did his charm, along with most of what made him so popular. Cavett summed it up with, "Johnny was very tense off camera... hardest person to talk [with] easily that I ever met." As a man so shy in the company of all but a handful of those who earned his confidence, Johnny sought solitude. Among his strategies for avoiding social contact was bringing every afternoon's lunch to work in a brown-paper-bag to be eaten alone.

On both coasts it was always a sight when fans lined up hours in advance to see the Johnny they came to love watching from their beds. In New York that queue would start as early as 5:30 a.m. as hopeful would-be audience members waited for seven o'clock. That's when they could climb the stairs to the once-opulent mezzanine at NBC's headquarters to claim one or two of any remaining

Tonight Show tickets not already distributed for that evening's taping. When those were exhausted, there was still excitement as blue stand-by tickets were next to be dealt to adoring fans. Numbered consecutively, those who scored a low number seemed happy to hang around midtown for the next ten hours, waiting to find out if sufficient no-shows would result in them having a coveted seat in Studio 6B.

The Holy Grail for those not sufficiently wired-in with the network, affiliates, ad agencies, or sponsors. The energy in NBC's Studio 6B in New York was electrifying when the band played Johnny's Theme at the nightly taping of NBC's *The Tonight Show*. From the author's collection

That love was reflected in the ratings, and Johnny wielded his Nielsen numbers to greater and greater advantage over the decades. He skillfully leveraged his popularity to advance from a salaried performer to the CEO of a multi-million-dollar production company. His ratings and the income they commanded from advertisers afforded Johnny the prized perk of successfully negotiating for ownership of *The Tonight Show*.

His Carson Productions also shepherded several other talk series and sitcoms to air. You can either admire Johnny's business acumen or curse his ever-expanding demands for increased compensation and control. During contract renewal talks in the 1970s, NBC's executive vice president for programs did the latter. A member of the network brass who decades later is now a friend, says he clearly remembers being in the room when VP Irwin Segelstein told a fellow executive, "Johnny Carson is a vicious prick."

I can't speak with any authority about Johnny being a prick in negotiations, but I'm confident in confirming that his organ of the same appellation lived a very active life. There's no great mystery behind his serial divorces. The man was simply unwilling or unable to be monogamous. Apparently Johnny shared one-nighters and extended affairs with dozens of partners. A game show emcee who taped his daytime series across the hall from *The Tonight Show* remembers one staffer whose sole function, he claims, seemed to be procuring starlets for the king of late night. On both coasts a great many women who found themselves within flirting distance of Johnny report that he seemed to always be working his charismatic magic with the clear-cut goal of securing another romantic rendezvous and conquest.

His targets included a lovely actress friend of mine who was on Johnny's couch twice. That's the couch in the studio, the one on the show's set. As for the couch in his ultra-private basement dressing suite at NBC, she never answered affirmatively to his overtures. A less principled performer might have been tempted to acquiesce to the invitation for a toss in the hay with the charming Nebraska farm boy. This actress was no dope then and still isn't. She knew that, had she acceded, it could only have led to an awkwardness that would be enough to end the calls to book her as a guest.

Others were not as withholding. By some exaggerated accounts, you could flip through the Academy Players Directory of ingénue actresses and find a veteran of the late night king's exploits on most pages. Sweet Sally Field, 20 years younger than Johnny, recently told Andy Cohen on *Watch What Happens Live* that she didn't know how to deflect the star's advances. In dishing about Johnny's hands-on approach and her naivety, Sally characterized their romantic trysts as "the octopus and the little guppy."

Trying to find a way to end the seductions, Sally eventually told Johnny that she needed to be hospitalized for mental instability. True. She told the octopus that his guppy would be unavailable for an unknown length of time because she was being institutionalized. "I couldn't figure out how just to say 'I really am just not into this,'" she explained. In addition to Sally, the tabloids had Johnny hooking-up with Angie Dickinson, Dyan Cannon and Morgan Fairchild. No, not on the same night, but that's a fanciful fantasy.

There's a wonderful story about a pre-*Three's Company* Suzanne Somers' chance 1973 meeting with Johnny at the NBC commissary. The yet-to-be-crowned queen of the Thighmaster was waiting to hear the results from her audition for the sitcom, *Lotsa Luck*. She remembered Johnny sauntered over and saying, "Hello, pretty lady." They spoke, she appeared as a *Tonight Show* guest pitching her book of poetry, and their friendship blossomed, allegedly into full bloom. Oh, as to her audition, Somers won that guest shot playing a femme fatale in the short-run sitcom's penultimate episode.

The vivacious actress Teresa Ganzel was a frequent guest and sketch performer with the Mighty Carson Art Players. She was another targeted would-be conquest, but when Johnny asked her out on a date Teresa turned him down. It was a gutsy move considering she was working on an NBC sitcom, *Teachers Only*, that was owned by Carson Productions. The almost-affair started in 1982 when she was invited on *The Tonight Show* to promote the series. "I was overwhelmed with stage fright," Teresa remembers. "But Johnny treated me like a million bucks and actually held my hand during part of my interview. It really was sweet." The next morning Teresa was fielding calls from friends who had seen the show. When she heard "Hi, Teresa, this is Johnny Carson," she assumed it was a friend doing a hell of a good impression. Indeed it was Johnny, calling for a dinner date.

Teresa says, "You have to remember, I was only 25 and he was more than 30 years my senior. I turned into a stuttering mess on the phone. 'D . . . D . . . D . . . Dinner? Er. . . I . . . Um. . .'" Johnny was gracious, started laughing and asked if the problem was that she had a boyfriend. She jumped on the explanation, "Yes, that's it, Johnny. I have a boyfriend!" Teresa smiles with the memory. "As he was getting off the phone, I realized I was being an idiot to turn down the date. I followed with 'And don't worry Johnny, lots of times I DON"T have a boyfriend!'"

Even though Johnny was laughing, Teresa figured she'd just guaranteed there'd be no encore for her one and only *Tonight Show* appearance. Surprise! Teresa says, "A couple of months later I was shocked and delighted to be asked to be a guest again. And that led to many more appearances, including all the 'Tea Time Movie' and other sketches which I adored doing. He was so wonderful to me that had he asked me out again, I in fact would have said, 'Yes.'" At the time Johnny was dating and soon married the beautiful Alex, Mrs. Carson number four, but Teresa is not that easy to forget. She recalls, "Ten years later we were doing his very last sketch together. As the audience was cheering and applauding our final bow he gave me a big hug and said, 'You know, I'd still like to fuck your brains out!'"

The love affair that wasn't, didn't end there. Teresa explains, "A few days later a delivery person came to my door with a small package I was asked to sign for. As I was turning to go back in [the driver] asked, 'Can I see what you got? You know, that package was insured for $10,000 so maybe you won something!'" Well, it was a hell of a prize. Teresa says, "I tore open the envelope. It was a lovely thank you note from Johnny saying how much he had enjoyed working with me. In the box was a beautiful watch inscribed on the back, 'To Teresa. Love, Johnny.'" Teresa smiled and added, "My story is not one of sexual harassment. Johnny was a class act from beginning to end, and I loved him for it."

Teresa Ganzel has the comedy chops and improv skills to co-star as
The Matinee Lady with Johnny Carson as Tea Time Movie host Art Fern
in one of the fan-favorite recurring skits on *The Tonight Show*.

Far more fantastic in forging a female affiliation was the night when Johnny and fellow broadcaster Dennis James were in Miami Beach for a movie premiere. Dennis's son, Brad, explained that as guests of the same company, his parents were given the hotel room next to Johnny's. That gave Dennis an unexpected front row seat late that night when Johnny was out on the balcony serenading a young lady he'd picked up earlier that evening. Dennis reported that Johnny was stark naked—the only thing between him and his date was a ukulele. The next morning Dennis explained to his wife what he'd seen and she gave him hell for not waking her up for the show.

All good things come to an end. That's true for both Johnny's balcony musical revue as well as his reign in late night. There's been much written about Johnny's involuntary retirement. It was indeed orchestrated in great part by Jay Leno's manager, Helen Kushnick, although she initially denied doing so when Jay asked her, point blank. In early 1991, when Jay was only being hired a week at a time as Johnny's guest host, Kushnick told a *New York Post* reporter that CBS had interest in her client. She had indeed met with a couple of the network suits simply to solicit a preliminary bid for Jay to put CBS back into the late night talk show race. In reality, apparently her true goal was to squeeze NBC into a commitment.

Kushnick promptly brought CBS's offer to NBC, indelicately ruffling the peacock's feathers with a threat to make Jay NBC's competition if they didn't sign him to be the next permanent host of *The Tonight Show*. Johnny had no intention of vacating the throne anytime soon, but NBC buckled to Kushnick's strong-arming. Jay was locked-in for the gig, effective whenever Johnny Carson chose to sign off. Although Jay's salary was eventually boosted to over $30 million, Kushnick's only goal at the time was to secure the deal and she agreed to a bargain-basement minimum starting salary of $3 million.

There are few secrets in this business. As Charlie Barrett, NBC's *Tonight Show* publicist at the time described it, "Johnny could hear the grass grow." Indeed he'd heard about Kushnick's deal for Jay, felt the heat, and saw the hazy handwriting on the wall. Johnny wasn't satisfied with NBC's lukewarm denial that he'd suddenly become the peacock's lame duck. He retaliated for what he viewed as betrayal by shocking the network and the press with a surprise announcement.

Without any advance hint the 65-year-old gave his one-year notice to the world, publicly announcing a May, 1992 date for his retirement. It blindsided NBC as he casually dropped that bombshell from the Carnegie Hall stage at the 1991 affiliates meeting. The word was instantly disseminated to every TV, newspaper, magazine, and wire service newsroom in America before the peacock's publicists had a chance to formulate any spin.

Johnny joked, "I like Jay Leno, and as a matter of fact he is very concerned for my health. In fact, he suggested that I jog through Central Park about midnight tonight." He then walked off the stage and out of the building without any explanation. With a perverse elegance befitting his image Johnny's message to the network was a crystal clear, "Fuck you."

Few outside the business knew Johnny as being anything but the joyful carefree jokester they saw on the tube. It's a fact that some who worked with him for years never truly understood his complex nature. He confessed to Mike Wallace on *60 Minutes* that, when away from the studio he was pretty much a loner. He also confessed to having been what's generally referred to as an angry drunk. Indeed, there's a colorful history of arguments, fistfights, and at least one beating from Johnny's earlier days of frequent boozing in Manhattan watering holes.

The two most lasting memories of Johnny Carson from my New York fanboy adolescence combined to create the first inkling I had about the chasm between some performers' on-camera and off-camera personas. I regularly ditched school, unable to resist the lure of exploring the nooks and crannies of NBC's Rockefeller Center facilities—it was my Disneyland. By today's standards it's impossible to imagine the nearly nonexistent security that presented virtually no challenge once a visitor finessed himself past the lobby checkpoint.

I was on the sixth floor, waiting for the elevator during one of my expeditions. When the doors opened, there was the living and breathing Johnny Carson. For a split second I froze and likely blinked my eyes a couple of times. When they opened he was still there, in living color and far larger than the 19 diagonal inches that was his maximum measure at home. As I stepped into the elevator car, before I could form a sentence that would likely have included the word "Hello," Carson looked away and began humming to himself.

It must have been obvious from the surprised look on my face when my eyes locked onto his that I intended to say something. He instantly withdrew to such an extent that it was almost as if he was no longer physically present. He put up an invisible shield, a force field, a black hole of time and space so powerful and distancing that it was impossible to address him. He became unapproachable in some sort of disappearing act. It defies description, and it was performed so spontaneously that I suspected it had been perfected over many years. We rode together for just one floor, the seventh, where the *Tonight Show* offices were. Even after he exited I was still nonplussed.

The same Johnny who magically vanished during our five-second elevator ride was entirely unlike the Johnny who was bathed in the spotlights only a couple of hours later. He now welcomed and encouraged my sudden adlib when I called out from the audience. I had watched the show so devotedly that when Johnny said, "Boy, it was cold today," with Pavlovian reflexes I alone shouted: "How cold was it?" These days an entire audience will do that instinctively, but I still have the audio tape from the 1960s when only one daring soul had the audacity to steal what had been Ed McMahon's sole purview.

Ed and I responded almost simultaneously. He stopped after "How," and said, "OK, go ahead." The audience laughed as Johnny smiled warmly, raised his eyebrows, leaned forward and cupped his hand behind his ear making the universal sign for "I'm listening." I delivered the line and there was a generous helping of spontaneous laughter, a smattering of applause, and a chuckle from Johnny. He appeared so easygoing, friendly, adaptable, and welcoming of the intrusion. He was a completely different man.

Who did Johnny Carson think he was to act so aloof and be so off-putting to some adoring kid in an elevator? Well, *The Hollywood Reporter* estimates that at about that time *The Tonight Show* was the single most profitable program in all of television, grossing a cool $60 million a year for the peacock's stockholders. Adjusted for inflation that's $250 million today, a lot of feathers indeed. I guess that earned him the right to be unsociable, but the late night king wasn't putting on princely airs. The adjectives most often ascribed to Johnny were aloof, cold, painfully shy, intensely private, and uncomfortable in his skin. He's remembered with far more respect than warmth. Even staffers who worked with Johnny for many years are on record sharing the same observation that one-on-one contact was palpably uncomfortable for their boss, and often the fewer words exchanged the better.

It was primarily an intense case of shyness that made even the simplest greeting from this stranger unwelcome, if not outright painful. Our elevator moment came at about the same time his heart was being broken by his second wife, Joanne. A kid then, I never stopped to think about Johnny as a complete person with an entire off-air existence. Despite what *TMZ* and the rest of the privacy-invading gossip media reinforce, I'm among those who believe entertainers only owe us their performance without having to be on 24-hour selfie avail.

When Johnny moved *The Tonight Show* from New York to Burbank in 1972 things didn't change much. If anything his isolation intensified, as I later saw him regularly being accompanied by a uniformed security guard for the moments it took to walk between the second floor offices, his basement dressing suite, and the ground floor set. I'd say it was unlikely anybody was going to attack Johnny in that little-used backstage stairwell. It seemed obvious that the guard was there to insulate and defend the star from unwelcome overtures by distancing, discouraging, and subtly intimidating anyone who might want to initiate an unwelcome conversation. One friend who pierced that protective barrier waving a 30-year-old ticket from Johnny's *Who Do You Trust* found the star happy to engage in a few sentences and willing to autograph the ticket. When it came to protection from true security threats, the guard shack at the entry to his home was manned 24-7. Plus, according to his longtime personal assistant, Helen Sanders, Johnny was among a number of high-profile celebrities who carried a handgun at all times when in public.

There was only one time when Johnny was happy to engage in unlimited small talk. Guests say it was at the wrap party that he threw at his Malibu home at the end of his long run. Everybody who worked the show, NBC pages included, was welcome to bring their spouse or partner to eat, drink, and be merry, dancing to the live music of Les Brown and his band of renown, and chowing-down on chef Wolfgang Puck's finest. It was also an opportunity to engage their boss in small talk as they never had before. Johnny was celebrating a television career that began nearly 50 years earlier on the day in 1949 that Omaha's WOW-TV first signed on. It ended with this retirement blowout where his guests' most common observation was that their host appeared to be relieved, as if a great burden had been lifted. *Tonight Show* producer Peter Lassally said the transformation was permanent, "after the pressure of the job was gone."

During the nearly 30 years as America's late-night nightlight Johnny was indeed an extreme example of a performer's duality. With the exception of his closest confidants and tennis partners, during 23 hours of most days he was so introverted and detached that even some who considered him a friend didn't stand a chance trying to read his moods. That was the case for someone who guested with Johnny countless times, and claims the rare distinction of being his substitute host on no fewer than 37 occasions over the years, Rich Little.

The author with impressionist Rich Little. Outstanding in his field (2018). Photo from the author's collection.

Although Rich won Johnny's confidence as a performer, the host remained a perplexing riddle. At a Pacific Pioneer Broadcasters lunch in 2018, Rich Little explained, "There was no Johnny Carson. . . he never talked to anybody, he was a loner, he was always in a bad mood, he was a drinker…" Just the same, Rich thought he would always enjoy at least a cordial professional relationship with Johnny. Then, suddenly in the early 1980s, it turned ice cold.

Rich told the story in his autobiography much as he explained it to me: "… to this day, I don't really understand what happened. All I know is that after numerous appearances on the show, both as a guest and as a guest host, they stopped asking me. It just suddenly came to an end." Quizzed further, Rich told me he'd once heard a rumor that he had somehow insulted *Tonight Show* director Bobby Quinn. He didn't put much stock in it but, just to be safe, he visited producer Fred De Cordova to clear the air and make any needed apology.

Rich remembered being given a classic Hollywood shuffle, complete with a giant smile, a pat on the back, and some line of bullshit. "We just don't book impressionists anymore, but if we start again I'll call you right away" is how Rich remembered it. Laughable. He'd been in the business too long to have been taken in by De Cordova's Tinseltown two-step. I conjectured that maybe Johnny felt he was being mocked by Rich's impression of him. That suggestion elicited Rich's amazing capper to this mystery. Yes, wait. It gets better!

After 10 years of an unexplained total freeze-out by the powerful star-maker, Rich was again mystified when approached in a Malibu restaurant by a now humble and unassuming post-retirement Johnny Carson. Here's how Rich tells it: "[Johnny] said, 'Rich, you're still performing aren't you?' I said, 'Yeah, all around the country.' 'I guess you don't do me in your act anymore,' he replied. 'Of course I do!' I responded. 'It's one of my most popular impressions.' 'But I haven't been on TV in years. Do they still remember me?' I told him, 'Johnny, people will always remember you. You're a legend.' 'You're kidding?' he said. 'You're really still doing me?' 'Of course,' I replied. 'Well, thanks for keeping me alive.'"

Of course Johnny's still alive in the memories of millions of nostalgic viewers. Just the same, few are aware that it's a whitewashed and sanitized memory. Beyond the well-publicized marital disharmony, Johnny was in the middle of generations of family dysfunction. He blamed his mother for many of his problems, cursing her as cold, heartless and "the harshest son of a bitch I have ever known" for the love and approval he claims she withheld. Despite the overabundance of success it appeared the beloved comedian enjoyed, Johnny and Ruth Carson never came to peace. He didn't even attend her funeral.

Relationships were also far from ideal with his three sons, all of whom are from Johnny's first marriage. The youngest, Cory Carson, is a guitarist and songwriter who recorded several albums in the early 2000s, and has worked as a session player. Middle son Ricky became alcoholic and suicidal while serving at a remote Alaskan outpost for the U.S. Navy, landing in the military psychiatric ward of the Bellevue Hospital. Johnny reportedly never visited and, although the two remained distant, Johnny was devastated when Ricky died at age 39 in a car accident while pursuing his passion for photography.

With his eldest son, Christopher, Johnny faced an issue that few if any other people, public figure or not, dealt with as he did. For decades the reigning late night king provided financial support for Christopher while the young man sought to develop his golf game for an entree into the pro leagues. He played well, and worked for a while as a resident pro at Florida's Plantation Golf Club. Other than an occasional gig he lived a comfortable life entirely off his father's continuing stipend. Suddenly, Johnny threatened to close the spigot on that cash flow and totally disown Christopher the moment he found out that he would soon be the grandfather of a bi-racial child.

During the 1980s, Christopher had a secret 10-year relationship with a black girlfriend, Tanena Love Green. Tanena was six months into her pregnancy with Christopher's daughter, Christal, when Johnny learned he was soon to be the grandfather of a child he wanted no part of. Wielding the power of the purse, he convinced his son to immediately walk away from the entire situation. From that moment on, both father and son each refused to ever acknowledge the mother's or the daughter's existence. They also withheld any financial or emotional support. In fact, Christopher then went out of his way to deny that he ever fathered Christal.

News accounts confirm that eight months after the baby's birth in 1987 Tanena took Christopher to court seeking child support that she claimed was necessary to keep her off the welfare rolls. Indeed, mother and daughter were reported to be nearly destitute, surviving on Medicaid and public assistance, living in a trailer in Ft. Lauderdale. Their attorney Jeffrey Miller claimed, "The child is living in a hovel. I mean she is living in abject poverty. I have photos of this child with rodent bites." The younger Carson's attorney offered a mere $50 a week, saying the sum would be more than adequate. The Broward County Circuit judge was only slightly less parsimonious in awarding temporary support of just $500 a month. Christopher paid, but time did nothing to soften his heart. In 2003, when Christal was 16, Tanena took her to see her dad at his home. The former girlfriend and lover claimed that Christopher ordered her and their daughter off his property, telling them to "never come back."

Johnny's heart never softened either. When he died in 2005 the host's estate was valued in the neighborhood of $450 million. There were sizeable bequests for his widow Alexis, his surviving two sons, and for several charities, but not a penny was earmarked for Christal. Tanena Love explained that the then 18-year-old was "a Carson by birth and she got cheated all these years. It's about time she got what she deserves. With all the millions Johnny had, you'd think he'd have given his only granddaughter something."

Tanena's pleas remained unanswered when she died in late 2021 at age 70. Daughter Christal wrote, "My mother perished in an accidental fire within her home… I want to ensure that I honor my mother's wishes and give her a proper burial." Without any inheritance and still struggling, Christal turned to social media for contributions. Apparently, even after Johnny's death when concerns for being disowned had passed, Christopher Carson never came back into Tanena or Christal's life, even if only to help to bury his ex-lover.

Almost as surprising as this entire sordid affair is the fact that viewers were never aware of any of this ugliness. I didn't know, did you? There's lots we never knew. Read on for another slice of surprising TV reality.

Chapter 15

Among the great mysteries of the 20th century: Did a UFO crash in Roswell, who killed JFK, and how did Fred Silverman manage to program not one or two, but all three major networks? Well, that last one is really simple. When he was hot, he was hot. When he was not, well…

Fred green-lit more than a few abysmal series and stepped on more than a few toes, especially in his later years. He earned his first network corner office by making magic with limited budgets at WGN, Chicago and WPIX, New York. Nobody could present an old movie that had been rotting in the basement with more panache and promotion. As he described it, "a case of packaging, and really good marketing, to take crap and make it look like gold."

Inheriting the reins from vice president of programs Mike Dann at CBS in 1970, Fred's appointment marked the start of the "rural purge" that quickly wiped some audience folksy favorites to present a sleek new line-up of Madison Avenue-appealing more upscale series. Fred gave CBS founder Bill Paley bragging rights to ownership of nine of Nielsen's top 10 rated shows for the 1973-1974 season. America's favorite *All in the Family* boasted a 31.2 household rating. *The Waltons* was runner-up at 28.1. NBC's juggernaut *Bonanza* was cancelled mid-season, but the peacock's *Sanford and Son* at 27.5 in its second year kept CBS from an overall clean sweep for the season. *M*A*S*H* was next with a 25.7, then *Hawaii Five-O* at 24.0. *Maude*'s 23.5 led both *Kojak* and *The Sonny and Cher Comedy Hour* which tied at 23.3 each. *The Mary Tyler Moore Show* and *Cannon* tied with a 23.1 rating for each, rounding out CBS's impressive dominance.

Just two years later Fred was off to ABC to compete with that seemingly unbeatable lineup of blockbusters. He made it look easy by targeting a less sophisticated audience. As he put it, "We were appealing to an urban, lower-middle-class audience, it was a working-class audience." Instead of *M*A*S*H* think *Mork and*

Mindy, and instead of *The Waltons* think *Welcome Back, Kotter.* Of course there were a fair share of "what was he thinking" blunders. One was imagined while Fred and his wife were vacationing in Hawaii. It was where for almost half a century entertainer Don Ho rivaled Diamond Head as Waikiki's main attraction.

Fred returned from the islands gung ho for Don Ho, and gave the musician a 30 minute slice of daytime with Hawaiian steel guitars and hula dancing as an improbable lead-in to the soapy *All My Children.* Transported from a dark nightclub to the sunny outdoors, amidst the palm trees, colorful leis, and floral print shirts, the 1976 variety show featured a parrot said to have such amazing peripheral vision acuity that the bird could win every time playing the shell game. Indeed, a pea could be placed under one of three bell-shaped covers, and those covers could be quickly switched around with such dizzying speed that it seemed no man nor beast, parrots included, could follow the action. Somehow the bird found the pea every time. Some of the show's audience members won or lost a $25 dollar prize depending upon how they bet on the outcome of the game. It went on for weeks during which dozens of vacationers from all around the world played.

No, the bird didn't have the ability to follow the pea. The secret was eventually leaked that the parrot was trained to indicate the one of the three bell-shaped covers that had a tiny, almost imperceptible marking at its top. As long as the human placed the pea properly it would be discovered by the parrot no matter how fast and furiously things were switched around. Nobody on the production staff saw this as much more than a fun recurring bit, but back on the mainland, far from the Mai Tai cocktails, it was recognized as the unfair contest that it was. The game was stopped immediately and dozens and dozens of checks for $25 had to be sent all around the world to the past participants. To help cover the network's ass in the event of an FCC inquiry, the low-rated show saw a premature pink slip. It opened up a time slot for a program that could quickly be readied for air. The sets and game electronics for Bill Carruthers' recently piloted game *Second Chance* were still intact, and the show won the timeslot for only so long as it would take for Mark Goodson to develop the concept for a title that had previously piqued Fred's interest, *The Better Sex.*

Once having succeeded at besting the CBS primetime lineup he assembled, in 1978 Fred was wooed from ABC by NBC for a $1 million a year gig as president. It seemed he then wasted no time in alienating the top money-maker in all of television, the proud peacock's biggest boast, TV's MVP, Johnny Carson. Fred was quoted in the press complaining, "I wish Johnny was on more." Interviewed in the next century Fred back-pedaled, claiming his words were taken out of context. He now professed that, instead of complaining about the star's copious vacation time, his comment was meant as a compliment. "I wish Johnny was on more" was meant as a wish, not a criticism, he explained.

Nice try. At the time there was little doubt about what Fred meant and the late night king didn't take well to the new corporate suit dissing him, in public no less. Johnny responded by telling UPI in March of 1979, "I am having discussions with the network about leaving the show before my contract expires in 1981." He had his attorney call the network to say that their number-one attraction was indeed planning to ankle from NBC. Fred said that upon hearing that news he could hardly keep his lunch down.

The programmer's punishment included being lambasted in monologue jokes. Public humiliation seemed a fair penalty to impose for Fred's failing to show appropriate respect when speaking about the network's golden boy. How much gold? Fred had disparaged the man who, that year alone, was single-handedly responsible for an estimated $60 million in gross income. It was Johnny's contribution to the bottom line that took some of the sting and shame from Fred's having tapped the coffers for losers such as *The Runaways, Harris and Company, Highcliffe Manor, Presenting Susan Anton, Hizzonner*, the infamous *Supertrain* and, to a somewhat lesser extent, *Hello, Larry*. It also went a long way towards offsetting the massive losses from the cancellation of 150 hours of coverage that was to be broadcast from the 1980 Moscow Summer Olympics. That anticipated tsunami of advertising revenue suddenly dried up after President Jimmy Carter pulled the U.S. team out of competition in retaliation for the Soviet invasion of Afghanistan. After paying $87 million for the rights and logging hundreds of thousands of man-hours in preparation for the coverage, NBC sports was the biggest loser in those summer games. Insurance and tax breaks reduced the hit to $22 million.

Fred did further penance for dissing the deity. He was soon forced to sing Johnny's praises to an all-star audience at the New York Friars Club dinner at the Waldorf Astoria where Johnny was being honored as Entertainer of the Year. Minutes after the night's insightful host, Bob Hope, joked about just how much NBC was buttering up the star to keep him, Fred was prepared to do exactly that. "All NBC's top brass are here," Hope said. "I'm sure you've seen them refilling Johnny's glass, cutting his steak, kissing his ring. Next year he's got a sweeter deal." Hope then tickled Johnny's fantasy with, "All he has to do is come in once a week and pick up his messages."

On a dais that included Lucille Ball, Kirk Douglas, and Jack Benny, when Fred's turn came he paid homage to the magnitude of Carson's TV presence. He feted the star with accolades, "Johnny, you're more, much more, than Entertainer of the Year. You're the entertainer of our time. You're the best friend TV ever had." That best friend was soon embroiled in months of sometimes less-than-friendly, occasionally-contentious negotiations with the network. The squabbling culminated on May 2, 1980 with Johnny winning his unprecedented sweetheart deal.

In exchange for $25 million a year he need only perform one hour a night, three nights a week, 37 weeks a year. Carson Productions would also control the one hour timeslot following *Tonight*. Most importantly, leveraging a veiled threat that he was considering defecting to ABC, Johnny won the ultimate perk, ownership of his show. That victory instantly scored the easiest $26 million of Johnny's career. That was the take for delivering 130 half-hours of sliced and diced excerpts from old shows to Columbia Television as *Carson's Comedy Classics*.

The humiliation of caving to that magnanimous deal must have left a very bad taste in Fred's mouth because he was still bitching about the late night king a full five years later. When his company launched *Thicke of the Night* as competition in Carson's timeslot, Fred told UPI he planned "to knock the comedian off his late-night catbird seat on *Tonight*." That jab was only half of Fred's one-two punch as he added, "Late-night programming is soft and vulnerable… Carson's audience is very old."

After that new series barely managed to limp through a single season its star, Alan Thicke, explained, "*Thicke of the Night* was supposed to challenge Johnny Carson. They said it couldn't be done and I was the guy they chose to prove it.

The show was ahead of its time... it should've been on in 2084, when all of us are dead." Fred focused the blame on the popular Canadian host he imported saying, "Alan Thicke left his talent at the border," and later reflected *"Thicke of the Night* [was] probably the nadir of my career." Johnny Carson had the last laugh, having buried yet another of many pretenders to the throne while also besting the show's mastermind, his nemesis.

So Johnny and Fred were not friends, but that's not to say that the programmer wasn't a great pal with other people. One respected NBC radio executive working directly under Fred—now a syndicated radio host—was among those who saw another side of the often-celebrated and often-maligned programmer. He remembers one day in particular when he shared the sad news that his family was struggling financially through a very difficult period. Fred came to the rescue without being asked. He sent a sizeable check with a note in which he was emphatic that the lifeline was not to be repaid. It was the kind of generous move that won his friend's continuing loyalty that understandably persists to this day.

Overall, Fred enjoyed many successes and is credited with several significant innovations during his career. Promoting his network lineup was no longer relegated to a live booth announcer reading over the closing credits of programs. Fred is said to have pioneered in borrowing from the way motion pictures were sold. He upped NBC's game with flashy produced promos that teased the coming attractions using the briefest of clips woven into a high-impact assault on viewers' eyes and ears. The voices behind the peacock's dozens of weekly promos changed periodically over the years since the 1980s. Among the top talent announcers who took turns as the network's primary image voice were Casey Kasem, Danny Dark, and Townsend Coleman. It's hard to pinpoint who was the very first to adapt network on-air promotion to resemble the movie trailer model, but it was revolutionary for the time and served as a template for all networks for decades to come.

Fred's best years were at CBS and ABC where he lived up to the appellation "the man with the golden gut" for his instinctive ability to sniff out the shows with the potential to live long and prosper. That's mere sleight of hand when compared with one of his greater mystical wiles. Fred seemed to be astoundingly intuitive with an innate gift for instantly assessing the public's reaction to a show mere minutes into its debut airing. It was as if he was clairvoyant. How could he ascertain a program's popularity in real time? The little-known secret behind that magic act was deceptively simple.

In the days before cable, when three networks ruled the airwaves, during the primetime hours after sunset Fred could peer from the window of his Central Park high-rise to the windows of the dozens of apartments visible in the adjacent buildings. From the light leaking through those windows, Fred could get an approximate idea of what percentage likely had their TVs on. Then, by using his own television as a reference, the changing colors of the glow from those homes clearly indicated whether each was tuned to his network or to another channel. On a few occasions when these instant ratings were so skewed against his programming choices, he'd call to have west coast affiliates alerted to air a rerun of some other more popular show rather than chase the audience away with a bomb that was poorly-received among Central Park-adjacent high-rise viewers.

One story told to me by NBC network game show host Jim MacKrell illuminated an 86-proof side of the programmer I'd never heard about. Following his corporate tenures, in 1982 Fred hired former NBC daytime programmer Lin Bolen to head creative affairs at his independent production company, InterMedia Entertainment. On this one particular afternoon Fred and Lin were preparing to present a fully-staged demonstration of their original game show to CBS network honcho Bud Grant. It was a role reversal as after being pitched countless program ideas, Fred was now on the pitching mound.

Fred and Lin's format had evolved through months of development and the game played magnificently in run-throughs. Hopes were high for hitting the jackpot. The stakes were indeed significant, as even a minimum 13-week run would mean a healthy payday for everybody involved. Hell, even a pilot deal alone would open CBS's checkbook. Always a total pro, Jim says he was well rehearsed and confident that he could present the game in its best light. He remembers the moment Fred walked onto the set. The boss was drunk.

The booze must have failed to vanquish some deep insecurity about the chances for success, because Fred didn't waste a moment as he began to revise the entire game, undoing months of work. There was no changing his mind, he owned the company. With the clock ticking down to the big presentation everyone was suddenly trying to unlearn the format, rewrite the script, and cram like C-minus students on the night before the SATs. Needless to say, it all went to hell despite Jim's best effort to smooth the rough edges. There are no consolation prizes when you leave a network presentation having blown the rare chance to have a show greenlit. It's a long walk to the car.

Pissing off your staff and a hired host in a self-destructive fit was small potatoes for a man whose volatile personality had earned him at least as many detractors as his neighboring peers did during his network days. At CBS, ABC, and at NBC, then all headquartered within a three block stretch of New York's 6th Avenue, saying "no" far more often than "yes" was no way to make friends. The same held true for changing the course of careers by canceling a series or continually changing its timeslot. As such, it's a time-honored tradition for talent to covertly curse network programmers. However, a performer overtly feuding with a fellow performer, one who was formerly a valued ally, is a whole other story. Few mêlées were as infamous as the 180-degree flip between fellow funsters Johnny Carson and Joan Rivers. It's likely the most publicized in the history of television.

Early on the two shared a deep mutual respect, despite coming to comedy from very different worlds. Johnny was a farm-belt Methodist, and Joan a suburban New York Jew. The two could certainly be considered an odd couple, which made one of Joan's last mentions of Johnny's name all the more titillating. In the final year of her life, long after the late-night king had passed away, Joan made the provocative and dubious assertion that she and Johnny had a sexual encounter back in the 1960s. She referred to it as a "one-night bounce."

Was it true, or just a way to garner press? Could there have been a romantic connection between the two? It would not have been shockingly out of character for Johnny to bed a young female guest. If they did do the horizontal hula it would place Joan as one among dozens of Johnny's extramarital dalliances. Was Joan also a "player" in the swinging sixties? All that's certain is that during the duo's good years their professional relationship had been as close as any that Johnny enjoyed.

The star-making host appreciated how tough it was for a woman to find a balance in maintaining her femininity while wielding a razor-sharp tongue. Likewise, Joan praised Johnny at a 1972 UCLA lecture explaining, "Any of us could talk to Orson Welles. Johnny talks to morons. That's tough." Few comedians were ever made of tougher stuff than Joan. During hard times, struggling for acceptance in a male dominated world, Ed Sullivan was likely the only other established tastemaker to give her such a generous helping hand.

That largesse started with Ed throwing her $500 on several occasions to write the dialog he shared with his little mouse puppet, Topo Gigio. He also gave Joan regular exposure on one of weekly television's most watched hours when it was still very early in her pursuit to become a headliner, which helped blaze a new trail for female comics. Often, before performing stand-up on the Sunday night showcase, Joan was sent to Bonwit Teller or another Fifth Avenue headquarters of high couture to pick out a complete ensemble for the appearance. Ed paid for the outfit, and allowed her to keep the clothes.

Altruistic as the old stone-face could be with Joan, he showed no favoritism when it came to his requirement to preview and approve every word of his comedians' acts. Some remember performing in Ed's six-room suite on the 11th floor of the Hotel Delmonico while the arbiter of good taste was sitting in a bathrobe with his hair still dripping from a shower. No comic was spared the Tuesday or Wednesday review of their act, with the sole exception reportedly being his occasional golfing buddy Alan King who logged a total of 37 appearances on the show. Joan recalled the time Ed refused her repeated requests to allow her use of the word "pregnant" on one appearance when she very obviously was.

Between shifts on various survival jobs Joan was focused on building her career, considering every offer as an opportunity to advance. She remembered writing for Phyllis Diller's short-lived ABC sitcom as well as playing clubs as part of a threesome, Jim, Jake & Joan. While still in her 20s Joan became a member of Allen Funt's repertory company, setting-up the marks who were secretly "caught in the act of being themselves" on his *Candid Camera*. Through most of those years she was also honing her craft by working in Greenwich Village clubs for as little as $6 a pop. The motivation was not the meager carfare. Joan was refining her skills and building an act in relentless pursuit of every comic's goal, scoring an appearance on *The Tonight Show*. Johnny's small stage was the springboard from which many landed prestige bookings. Joan claimed to have auditioned on seven different occasions, being rejected each time.

Joan Rivers paying dues and learning the craft, partnered with
Jim Connell and Jake Holmes, third-billed as Jim, Jake & Joan.

It was Bill Cosby's manager, Roy Silver, who signed Joan and worked to get her that first important guest spot with Johnny. She killed that night and every subsequent time she did the show. Johnny became such a supporter that he offered to do a huge favor reserved for very few. Johnny boosted viewership of Joan's short-lived 1969 syndicated talker, *That Show*, by appearing as a guest. In a 1986 newspaper op-ed piece Joan wrote of her debt to Johnny, "He was the first person in power who respected what I was doing and realized what I could become. He handed me my career." Likewise, she told *People*, "Johnny was the one person who said, 'Yes, she has talent; yes, she is funny.'"

Naming Joan as his sole substitute *Tonight Show* host in 1983 was an even greater magnanimous kindness, but it's been whispered to also have been a gift

Johnny gave himself. Ever insecure, as Johnny aged he wondered whether the exposure he was giving to up-and-coming comedians by placing their butts in his chair in his absence might be hastening his own demise. Indeed, it was Jay Leno's fill-in time on *The Tonight Show* that helped his manager to ultimately secure the coveted gig for him years later, albeit earlier than Johnny had intended. His solution was to give the ever-expanding number of vacation nights to someone that the network would never hire as his replacement, Joan Rivers.

Then and even now, the traditional thinking has always been that late night is no place for a female host. Cable, maybe; network, no. Add to that NBC's inevitable concern about how much of the country might be alienated by such an overtly New York Jewish replacement for their beloved Methodist Midwest corn-fed Carson. Johnny also mentioned to one of his poker pals that he had done so much for Joan that he felt secure he'd won her eternal loyalty—she would never steal the gig from him. For those reasons Johnny felt he was bulletproof from any possible encroachment by Joan. That's why her acceptance of the gig to go opposite his show on Fox in 1986 was seen as an ill-mannered act of ultimate impertinence, the supreme slap in the face.

The struggling fourth network's deal was incredibly lucrative. Could you turn down $15 million for three years? Joan did hesitate briefly while considering the fallout and said she took the leap only after NBC refused to give her anything but short-term renewals for her *Tonight Show* fill-in duty. It's credible to speculate that Johnny would have been able to advocate for Joan on that contract issue, but there's no evidence that he did. Hollywood columnist Sue Cameron chimed-in on that part of the story. As an author and one-time guest on Mrs. Carson's talk show, *Joanne Carson's VIPs*, Cameron is adamant in her claim that Johnny actually was behind NBC's short-term commitments. In that version, Joan was purposely kept on a short leash and already marked for extinction by Johnny because the ratings on her fill-in nights were regularly higher than his.

The given in all scenarios is that Johnny believed he had all the power, the way he liked it. He confidently assumed that Joan wouldn't walk from the high-visibility, low-paying but prestigious gig as his pinch hitter, short-term contracts or not. Johnny's attorney, Henry Bushkin, asserts that Joan and her husband, Edgar Rosenberg, were correct in their assessment that Johnny hadn't supported them in their attempts to get a meatier commitment from NBC. That might have been because Joan's usefulness was considered limited. Bushkin wrote that his famous client felt, "She can't sustain for more than a week at a time because of the nature of her act." The lawyer explained Johnny's point, "People are going to get tired of it, annoyed with it. They're going to want a break." Bushkin's claim that Johnny and others felt, "she didn't wear well," reinforces the presumption that Joan would never have inherited *The Tonight Show*.

Members of the Carson and Rivers camps were in agreement on one point, that Joan already had a good thing going. Her long-time advisor, agent, and manager, Sandy Gallin, said, "I thought she had the perfect setup." He argued that, as Johnny's pinch-hitter Joan had all the exposure and support she needed to garner top-dollar for large-venue concert dates, weeks in Vegas, or pretty much whatever she wanted to do. "But she was always pushing ahead, always striving to do better, always looking for the next thing, always looking to improve a deal, always looking to do something new," Gallin explained. "She was incredibly ambitious." Joan's take on it: "I was smart enough to go through any door that opened." It was a guiding philosophy that she repeated again for NPR's *Fresh Air* near the end of her life.

So, Joan and Edgar pulled the trigger and accepted Fox's offer. Her most encouraging friends say it was a sound decision, admitting however that it was poorly executed. How poorly? The TV community is even smaller than Andy Griffith's Mayberry, and everybody knows what everybody else is up to. It's such a tiny, incestuous business that word travels like lightning. The serious players are all only one or two degrees of separation from each other, and everybody seems to instantly learn about every important deal. Remember NBC publicist Charlie Barrett's assertion, "Johnny could hear the grass grow."

Decades later, Barry Diller, the Fox-TV head honcho who championed Joan's show suggested that NBC's Brandon Tartikoff was the one who whispered the news to Johnny. That may have been nothing more than misdirection as there was a far more direct route. Small world—Fox's Diller himself regularly played poker with Johnny in those days. He's on record as having suggested to Joan that she reach out to Johnny first, to break the news and ceremoniously ask for his blessing. When she and Edgar chose not to, it might well have left Diller as a prime suspect for secretly whispering the news to his friend.

Could Diller have revealed Fox's corporate secret to the competition and then convincingly deny it? We already know he sported a world-class poker face by virtue of holding one of the coveted seats of honor around the most elite round table since the 12th century when only the best knights of England could gather in the court of King Arthur to sit at his circular table. The present day knights who gathered at Hollywood's most revered poker table with Diller were Johnny Carson, Steve Martin, Carl Reiner, Neil Simon, Chevy Chase, film mogul David Chasman and movie producer Dan Melnick, who was responsible for establishing this Wednesday night game back in the 1960s in New York. Standby seat fillers for absent regulars at this showbiz summit have included the likes of Tom Hanks. Chevy's inclusion is proof that Johnny was able to forgive and forget after the SNL alum tweaked the *Tonight Show* host to where he publicly declared, "Chevy Chase couldn't ad lib a fart at a baked bean dinner."

Johnny claimed he'd learned of Fox's plans for Joan Rivers early on. As there were nearly three long months between the time the deal was signed and its announcement to the press, the ill will must have been mounting and the anger festering with each day that Joan failed to call the man who indeed felt he had "handed Joan her career." The comedienne's silence was a counterintuitive move that she claimed Edgar had insisted upon. He was adamant that she not break the news to Johnny until the last minute before word of her Fox show hit the street. He predicted that she'd be dropped from *The Tonight Show* the moment Johnny knew, and feared her profile would suffer from the months of lost exposure.

Joan repeatedly questioned Edgar's judgment on that strategy, and insiders say he responded with a lie. He assured her that *Tonight Show* producer Freddie De Cordova was fully aware of the situation and was "handling Johnny" for them in the interim. Joan became more and more uncomfortable keeping a secret that was very likely no longer secret, living in limbo, knowing she was long overdue in calling her benefactor directly. Although Diller might have thought it was premature, Joan couldn't wait any longer. At her and Edgar's insistence a date was set in May, a full five months before *The Late Show* was to debut, for officially breaking the news that the comedienne would be leading Fox's foray into late night. When she finally reached out to Johnny the night before the press was to get the story, he considered that call too little and far too late. Joan said he hung up on her, twice. You know the rest. Johnny refused to ever speak with her again. Joan claims that was the case even after she broke the silence to reach out with condolences following the death of Johnny's son.

Joan's Fox show debuted opposite *The Tonight Show* and she remembered the ratings being what she described as "better than fair," and pegged the show as "profitable." Just the same, the entire experience turned into a nightmare. Edgar, who was already exercising a Svengali-like control over his insecure wife's career and home life, began to micro-manage every aspect of the production. While he may have felt he was being supportive by freeing Joan from distractions and allowing her to focus on the show's content, he failed, repeatedly alienating the network. Legend holds that the only thing more combative than Edgar's increasingly argumentative relationship with Barry Diller was Edgar's struggle with the owner of all things Fox, Rupert Murdoch. Sources say it came to a head behind closed doors when Joan was given the ultimatum she recalled as, "You can stay, but your husband can never come on the set again."

Chapter 16

Few would argue that Joan should have chosen the show over Edgar, but her decision to remain loyal to her husband brought a swift response from the network. Fox's death knell was delivered with even greater insensitivity than is typical for television. Looking to make it clear that they were done with her, Joan claimed that Rupert Murdoch and Barry Diller delivered the word shortly before her having to put on a smile and generate the laughs for her penultimate taping. Indeed, Joan said she remembered being fired in her office on Thursday, May 14th of 1987 with a simple, "Tomorrow is your last show." Diller adamantly denied that cruel timing.

It left Edgar to carry the responsibility for having poisoned his wife's career. He knew Joan would now be branded as an abject failure in late night, and that the stench from such a high-profile firing could take years to dissipate, if ever. Edgar understood that beyond crashing Joan's career he had cost the family untold millions of dollars from the Fox gig alone. The couple's already rocky relationship suffered, with friends describing the pair as "estranged."

Happy days for the family. Edgar Rosenberg, Joan, and Melissa Rivers at Fox TV in early 1987, a few months into the new network's *The Late Show Starring Joan Rivers*. The tide turned quickly that year. Joan's last night on the show was May 15, 1987. Three months later Edgar ended his life. Photo courtesy of Fred Wostbrock.

Joan and Edgar put on happy faces for the benefit of their daughter, 19-year-old Melissa, while the family vacationed in Europe that summer. Once home, Melissa returned to the University of Pennsylvania for her junior year, working towards a Bachelor of Arts degree. Then, exactly three months to the day after Fox fired Joan, Edgar shocked the family by committing suicide in a Philadelphia hotel room. It's easy to guess why he traveled 3,000 miles from home to off himself. He likely made the trip to where Melissa was at school in order to talk with her one last time. After that visit she stopped speaking to her mother. One can only wonder what Edgar might have said that apparently poisoned Joan and Melissa's relationship.

With her husband gone, her reputation in shambles, her daughter refusing to talk to her, and suddenly unable to support her high lifestyle, Joan recalled the night she sat with a gun in her hand, contemplating her own suicide. When her pet Yorkshire terrier jumped on her lap, Joan said she realized she was loved, if only by a dog. Her life had never been bleaker. "I was $37 million in debt," Rivers confessed to Esquire in 2007. Not at all a sad story, this is a tale of triumph.

Joan began to tap into the unshakeable strength that had carried her through the lean years, the years during which she almost starved before career success. Against all odds, she bootstrapped herself back to prominence. Unable to return to Murdock's good graces or score with another network, Joan faced the daunting task of having to re-start her career. She clawed her way back by playing clubs, working the road, writing books, doing a nightly radio show on New York's WOR, and generating other opportunities for herself in the low rent world of cable. By reimagining the decades-old red carpet interviews that accompanied film premieres as far back as the silent movie era, Joan became a sensation in the forecourt at award shows.

The New Hollywood Squares played a major role in rehabilitating Joan's career and helping her swim through the red ink. In a reported $1 million deal she joined the series prominently featured as the game's center square. With her impeccably-timed razor-sharp delivery of both adlib and prepared zingers it seemed the twice monthly weekend tapings were all laughs. It was no laughing matter however, the first time Joan tried to get to the show's studio on the old Fox lot in Hollywood.

It was her first attempt to return to the facility where she'd been so humiliated by her firing from *The Late Show*. She was humiliated again when, following the instructions that were still in effect—the guard at the gate refused to grant her access.

When *Squares* wrapped, Joan immediately segued into a syndicated daytime talk series for Paramount. The five year run brought Joan an Emmy and was a great boost in helping her to recover from debt. "My career was over. I had bills to pay," she told the *Staten Island Advance* in 2004. "In those days, only dead celebrities went on [QVC]." Still driven to a level that some observers characterized as desperate, in 1990 Joan became willing to tirelessly pitch jewelry and fashion creations on the home shopping outlet. Surprisingly, she hit the jackpot when the QVC partnership grew to ultimately move over $1 billion in merchandise, of which Forbes estimated her cut to have been $250 million pretax during the remaining 24 years of her life.

With dogged tenacity Joan regained her stature and rescued her career, although a network's late night slot was still seen as no place for a female host. Reflecting on that challenge just one month before her death in 2014, Joan told *Entertainment Weekly*, "What Johnny should've done—and it's so theatrical—after the whole thing, after I left the show, and after I was fired from Fox, and after Edgar committed suicide, Johnny should've had me back on the show and said to me, 'Where you been?'"

The *coup de gras* came long after Johnny Carson's death, when Joan finally busted through what she referred to as a decades-long blacklist that she believed the late night king had instituted against her at NBC. She made a one-time long-hoped-for return to *The Tonight Show* on Jimmy Fallon's premiere episode. That's right, the former substitute host hadn't returned to the show for years, even after Johnny was long gone. As to the many months that Jay Leno had kept Joan from those cameras, the comic said, "I didn't want to [have Rivers as a guest] while Johnny was alive out of respect for Johnny. I don't think he wanted to see her on the show and that's why we didn't do it." As to her continuing absence during the nine years that Jay hosted after Johnny's death, he was quoted telling Howard Stern, "I think it would be awkward and uncomfortable, and she'll just sit there and slam Johnny, and I don't want that on my show."

Way before all the bad blood, back when Johnny was championing Joan's career, there was a first skirmish between the two from which they recovered. It was back in December of 1972 when Johnny was chosen to be feted with the dubious honor of being Dean Martin's very first "Man of the Hour." Back then, with the show only 30 minutes long, Johnny was the "Man of the Week." He was the subject, or victim, of what became the decade-long endless series of weekly roasts that replaced the crooner's variety show. For the debut, Dino's spotlight focused on the king of late night after a rigorous selection process: Johnny was in the building.

When producer Greg Garrison hooked Johnny to premiere the new vehicle for Dean, the roastee had only one request. He wanted his dear Joan to appear as one of the roasters. Simple, right? Well, although Joan would walk hot coals for Johnny then, she refused to have anything to do with the show. Dean's longtime music director, Lee Hale, knew where the bodies were buried and was the only source I found who was able to recount the tale of Garrison's bad karma returning to roost at that roast.

Try as he might, Joan would not agree to fete her friend, Johnny. Behind her refusal was the memory from years earlier when Joan had auditioned for Garrison. Confident in herself and her well-honed act, she was shocked when the producer turned her down cold. She demanded to know why, and the tactless Garrison repeated the criticism she had come to resent: "You're too New York and too Jewish." Joan vowed revenge and, finally, this was her chance. Garrison could leave an empty chair in her place if he wanted, but Joan wouldn't spend a day on his dais, even for Johnny.

Despite truckloads of schmoozing, Joan stood firm, and it left Garrison with the dirty work of explaining to his man of the half hour why he couldn't deliver on the roastee's singular request. When Garrison conveniently failed to explain how he had alienated Joan years earlier, Johnny thought the snub was a slap in the face Joan was directing at him. It was a momentary hiccup in the professional lovefest that quickly healed, only to eventually sour so publicly.

Dino did more roasting than a South Carolina roadside Cracker Barrel, as the format helped to prolong his lengthy reign on NBC's Thursday night air. Ultimately his cancelation was inevitable, as it was for a number of his contemporaries. As the senior small-screen stars' legacy series continued year after year the average age of their audiences ticked another notch higher, and each renewal brought another hike in the licensing fee. They inevitably priced themselves into oblivion, beyond their value to the networks.

The science of demography was corrupted to become Madison Avenue's new curiosity-turned-obsession. Ad agencies wanted to tell their clients not only how many people were watching the shows they sponsored, but who those viewers were in relation to their products. Age, education, income, recent purchases, homeowner or renter, urban or suburban or rural, and as much other data as companies like Nielsen and Simmons Research could extrapolate from the few they actually surveyed. Suddenly the focus was on quality, not just the quantity of eyeballs.

This new deep dive for data was no passing fad. It's evolved to where our lives are now open books, with our most esoteric information bought and sold among a slew of corporate entities. Early in 2019 *The Hollywood Reporter* told the story of a 22-year-old computer whiz who was suddenly worth $60 million after crunching a payload of smartphone data. His analysis was so meticulously detailed that manufacturers, retailers, and researchers threw money at his feet because, as the article put it, he "can tell companies how many Visa cardholders order Domino's before watching *The Big Bang Theory*."

More than anything else, the pinpoint targeting of programming to attract audiences of Madison Avenue's most desirable consumers was the downfall of many of TV's first generation of variety artists. The folks your grandparents watched that had ruled the ratings as TV royalty year after year now choked on the new buzzword. "Demographics" was the death knell for George Burns, Pat Boone, Perry Como, Andy Williams, Dinah Shore, and other perpetually popular personalities. In the vernacular, these performers "skewed old." In television it's perhaps the most egregious of all sins.

Along with Dean Martin, even network blue-chip troupers Red Skelton and Jackie Gleason faced extinction. The Great One's reign ended when CBS refused to raise the show's production budget. Lothian Skelton, widow of the beloved clown reflected in 1990, "He was heartbroken when CBS let him go because of demographics, and that was because of the change in comedy at the time." That undoing of *The Red Skelton Show* was an especially sad loss among the employees at CBS. It wasn't the program's broadcast that engendered such loyal devotion, it was the rehearsals that the crews loved. Red consistently delivered the biggest insider yucks of any star for the network's backstage and office workers. It made him the most popular citizen in all of Television City.

With the exception of a few years at NBC, at Desilu, and a couple more at the old Charlie Chaplin studio lot which Red owned briefly, for close to two decades his rehearsals at CBS were legendary. On every series' camera-blocking days talent walks through the scenes and routines while the director choreographs camera movements and lines up shots. Red took this opportunity to adlib around the skits' scripted dialogue. It kept the jokes fresh for taping, while providing an outlet for his more prurient creativity.

Because this Tuesday afternoon blocking rehearsal could be far funnier than anything he ever performed for air, it became a highly anticipated weekly event that attracted more and more employees from adjacent studios and the upstairs offices. Word would spread through the building, and the 330 seats then in Studio 33 would quickly fill. Encouraged by that audience of insiders, Red replaced his writers' lines with increasingly obscene material. His lewd and lascivious language, un-gentlemanly gestures, X-rated rants and general debauchery are remembered as the funniest act ever seen by those in attendance. Their enthusiastic laughter only served to spur Red to new heights of depravity. Not for squeamish spectators, Red shared some of the most colorful humor to be found outside of a locker room.

The staff at the network's Standards and Practices office could watch these raunchy rehearsals on the in-house video system that carried feeds from all of the studios. Newly-hired staffers working under William Tankersley, CBS's chief censor, would be stupefied in horror at their first viewing. Each who alerted their boss with a panicked warning about that week's Skelton show soon learned that it was just Red's run-through routine—simply business as usual.

Dick Smothers was among those who visited from his set across the hall and remembers, "He would put on the dirtiest shows you've ever seen! And during the live show, Red had a thing of laughing at his own jokes. He was laughing at all the dirty jokes they didn't say!" Indeed, no other star on the tube laughed more at his own punch lines and could be any more relied upon to break himself up with his characterizations. Nobody seemed to love his Clem Kaddiddlehopper and Cauliflower McPugg more than he did.

Red was on television as well as in television, as an investor. In addition to briefly owning the lot now occupied by Henson Productions, he owned and rented remote broadcasting vans, was a booster during the development of color, and was even a part owner of *Lost in Space*. Red generously gave a struggling actor a break when he hired a young Jamie Farr to help write and perform for both his on-air and personal appearances. Paying the future *M*A*S*H* star out of his own pocket enabled the up-and-coming actor to remain in Hollywood, instead of leaving the business to return home to support his recently-widowed mother. Jamie still remembers some of his mentor's deliciously raunchy rehearsals. Among the tamest gambits was a question shouted from the lighting grid, "Hey Red, how's your boat?" Red responds, "I don't own a boat." From the grid, "Your wife told me you had a small dinghy."

One of 20th century America's favorite burlesque, vaudeville, movie, radio, and television funnymen, Red Skelton was a shrewd businessman with investments in early color TV technology. Red was performing in Las Vegas when he learned that CBS had canceled his long-running variety hour. His reaction, "My heart has been broken."

The self-proclaimed clown had worked as a medicine-show pitchman and traveled the burlesque theater circuit before radio gave him national exposure. He first stood at a network microphone in 1937 on crooner Rudy Vallee's weekly show, before advancing to his own NBC program in 1941. Red's G-rated comedy routines so impressed President Franklin Roosevelt that the mirth-maker was made the official host of FDR's birthday celebrations. Red so appreciated the lady who coached him and others in radio technique, Lurene Tuttle, that he made her a regular on his series. For her contribution to both his career and his show, Hollywood mythology holds that he gave her eight fur coats, one for every year she was on his radio program.

After Lurene made the move to television with Red, she recalled how the comic used to play fast and loose for radio audiences back when they were first teamed: "He got steamed up, and the half-hour show didn't really satisfy him, so he kept the audience there afterwards… he did at least an hour, sometimes an hour and a half." That after-show was a bit racier than his broadcast, but still acceptable for the civilian audience of the era. To the contrary, the TV City routines evolved to where they were not for the public nor the faint of heart.

For a guy who ended every broadcast with the sign-off, "May God bless," Red Skelton had an ungodly gift for gross vulgarity. In comedy parlance, Red worked blue with seemingly little self-imposed limits on sexual and scatological content. During breaks in rehearsal Red maintained the mood with random stories from what seemed to be an endless archive of jokes involving a parrot in a whorehouse, a nun who runs into two sailors on shore leave, an especially accommodating hooker with a blind man as a client, and other delightful characters.

Nearly fifty years later I can still evoke memories of those riotous afternoons with Red among the surviving old-timers at the CBS Retirees group that call themselves The Frogs. They joke about having worked during TV's golden era, knowing that these days the same behavior would fill an HR department's file cabinets and motivate more lawsuits than laughs. Red's deliciously-crude language could be uncomfortable for some, and actually brought at least a couple of co-stars to tears. One of them, *Bathing Beauty* star Esther Williams, was no puritanical prude. Despite spending countless hours in pool water every day while filming her MGM aquacades, once home Esther often enjoyed a swim. It was a nude swim, often with invited guests. Just the same, the bathing beauty is on record saying, "I think I learned every four-letter word I've ever heard from Red. He used the filthiest language on the set imaginable. He'd shock me so, I'd go back to my dressing room and cry."

Comedy cohort Steve Allen got a dose of Red's blue-hued ways as early as the 1950s, before the scatology seriously escalated. Steve wrote, "He did a dress rehearsal of the program in front of a full studio audience, which largely consisted of women and some children. Despite their presence Red did a number of vulgar, raunchy lines." Long-time entertainment reporter James Bacon bestowed upon the Skelton rehearsals the dubious honor of "the filthiest hour you can imagine."

Bacon also wrote of Red's proclivity for unspooling what were called "stag films" from the era before VCRs made porn an open and ubiquitous billion dollar business. Red believed in sharing—his projector would be aimed and focused to display the movies on his neighbor's white garage door. Listening carefully you could almost hear the neighborhood property values dropping. To say that TV's favorite clown of the era was a nonconformist is to understate Red's rebelliousness. Just below the G-rated happy-go-lucky veneer that viewers saw, there was deep sadness. Dick Cavett remembers Groucho Marx telling him about Red Skelton in an off-camera moment, "He holds total contempt for his audience."

Like so many comedians this NBC Tuesday night star was said to be hiding a disheartened, depressed, and angry side to his personality. Groucho saw the dark Red, blacker than any maroon paint chip at Sherwin Williams. His writers said his heart—if ever found—would be black. Producer Lloyd Schwartz recently told me the story of how his father, celebrated sitcom creator Sherwood Schwartz, was promoted to head writer on *The Red Skelton Show*. The previous chief of the writing staff had quit after an epic confrontation with his boss. In the heat of an argument, Red allegedly pulled a gun and shot at the writer's feet.

When the job was next offered to Sherwood, the scribe took the gig with the proviso that he never had to meet with his boss. As he told the producer, "I like my feet." After he took the gig, Sherwood indeed never did come face-to-face with Red. In October of 2002 Sherwood vented about his boss having listed himself as one of the writers on a submission for an Emmy award his show ultimately won: "The truth of the matter is that Red was never in a room with the writers... my condition of employment with CBS was that I never had to meet with Red about the script. Red and I had a pleasant sort of arrangement where we could discuss the weather... or the weather... or the weather, but we never talked about the script... It was very difficult, I'm sure, for CBS to get Red to agree to this arrangement which, in effect, made me his executive producer. Red never even knew what character he was going to play from one week to the next."

Sherwood had enjoyed an entirely different relationship working for other stars, such as Bob Hope. Of Hope, Sherwood said that the boss enjoyed his gag men and spent hours writing and editing elbow-to-elbow with his small army, "He didn't care if you were Chinese or black or Jewish, you wrote a good joke and he would love you."

Not so with Red Skelton. Even from afar the comedian was still able to wound his top scribe. Despite seven years of feeding the material that delivered number one ratings, Red told a talk show's national audience how "Every week, when I get those lousy scripts from the writers I yawn. And the voice of God tells me how to fix things."

Sherwood heard the insult and recalled, "So the next day I went to CBS and I said, 'Goodbye.'.... I said to my brother [who was also on staff], 'Al, when I leave, you're going to be fired... because Red Skelton is about five years old emotionally. The only way he would have at getting back at me [for quitting] is to fire you because you're my brother.'.... all [Red] said in reference to me leaving the show, which I had put in the top ten for seven years, was, 'Fire that other fucking Schwartz!'"

To begin to make sense of Red's unconventional existence and Sherwood's observation of his arrested emotional development you need look no further than his earlier life. His father died of alcoholism two months before Red was born, leaving his mother and three brothers penniless. As a child, Red slept among the rats in the attic of a vaudeville theater, clowning for the public's tips from his youngest years to help keep the family fed. He next followed in his father's shoes working as a circus clown. Survival preempted school. It was said that through his entire life Red was never able to read above a grade school level. As scarring as that kind of childhood can be, Red faced continuing challenges as an adult. In 1958 at the height of his career, his son died of leukemia just days before his tenth birthday. Red was crushed.

"I have never known a successful comedian who was not somewhat neurotic. The unsuccessful ones must be in even worse condition," Steve Allen mused. "A difficult early life seems to be an essential requirement for admission to the ranks of the eminent clowns." Trust Steve as he's been down that road himself. His father also died young, when Steve was an infant. He ran away from home to live on his own while still in his teens. It was during the depression, and Steve remembered surviving by begging and dumpster diving for scraps of food.

Steve also knew infinitely more comedians than you or I would ever want to. By his assertion that there's a history of dysfunction behind their clowning, I guess anytime we think we found an exception among the ranks of funsters, it probably just means we haven't dug deep enough. That's the case for me with Ronnie Schell, a standout standup and sitcom veteran best known for playing Duke Slater on *Gomer Pyle, U.S.M.C.*

Ronnie was a part of the mid-century groundbreaking San Francisco comedy scene that also helped to birth the careers of Mort Sahl, Lenny Bruce, and Godfrey Cambridge. Ronnie was a bubbly, manic, laughing bundle of chuckles when we first met, auditioning together for a commercial at William Morris, our common talent agency—our "ten percentary," as *Variety* would say. Ronnie was so damned funny that I still remember his best gut-busting joke from the monologue he performed that day in 1985 in Beverly Hills for an audience of one, me. I told the joke back to Ronnie at a party in Sherman Oaks in 2018, more than 30 years later. As a man now approaching age 90, his laughter was more subdued. The twinkle in his eye had dimmed and his demeanor had been attenuated by the years, but he was genuinely amused. He remembered the line and appreciated the memory. The impact of the quickie was all in his delivery: "Did you know Duke Ellington was Canadian? 'Take The Train, A?'"

I guess I don't yet know Ronnie well enough to see any signs of the neurosis or bitterness that Steve Allen spoke of. Then again, his snide and insulting comments about a young pre-*Laugh-In* Goldie Hawn, his co-star in the 1967 sitcom *Good Morning, World,* may have been the tip of that iceberg. "Goldie was a go-go dancer out of Baltimore," Ronnie explained. "She was discovered after she appeared on *The Andy Griffith Show* and some executive said, 'Gosh, she's great.' So they put her on the sitcom with me." Ronnie felt Goldie's lack of experience and dedication were dragging down his chances for success with this important starring vehicle.

Ronnie Schell and Goldie Hawn (pictured) starred with Joby Baker, Julie Parrish, and Billy De Wolfe in *Good Morning World* (1967). The series was canceled by CBS after a single season despite being birthed and produced by masters of the sitcom art form, Carl Reiner, Sheldon Leonard, Bill Persky, and Sam Denoff.

"Every night we rehearsed in my apartment. She would get tired and say, 'I don't want to overdo it,'" Ronnie remembered. "One night I said, 'Goldie, you're not going to make it because you don't have discipline. You give up before you even start.'" Then, with the classic Ronnie Schell delivery he deadpanned the punch line, "Two years later she won the Academy Award for Best Supporting Actress for the film *Cactus Flower*, while I was working a toilet bowl in Omaha."

By "toilet bowl in Omaha," Ronnie was no doubt referring to any one of hundreds of random small-town low-pay seedy nightclubs. There's only one comic who seemingly worked every single one of those dives, Jay Leno.

Chapter 17

While Johnny Carson was known for suffering through only the most unavoidable social contacts, his successor was always welcoming to any and all, civilian or star, who wanted to share a quick exchange. A possible exception to Steve Allen's axiom, Jay Leno appears eternally at ease, thoroughly informal, and seems delightfully comfortable in his own skin. Even the occasional on-set disagreements I saw at *The Tonight Show* were brief and muted.

Jay said that his regular-guy manner, with his ability to charm NBC's brass and the network's affiliates, were significant factors in his victory over David Letterman for the coveted late night gig. It was while working on the road, making the coast-to-coast circuit of comedy clubs that Jay laid the foundation for fulfilling that dream. "What got me *The Tonight Show*," Jay remembered, "is that I would visit every NBC affiliate where I was performing and do promos for them. Then they would promote me in turn. My attitude was to go out and rig the numbers in my favor." Jay told me it felt like he had visited every one of the over 200 peacock-linked stations, personally inviting their managers to the local clubs to see his act. It was such a shrewd move that even his competition had to give what seems like props to Jay for his business acumen.

After telling a *Playboy* interviewer, "Leno… fuck him," Jimmy Kimmel said, "I believe he's not just a smart politician but also a smart guy. I haven't met anyone who knows more than he does about how ratings and the business of late-night television work. . . I always feel bad if I hurt anybody's feelings, but I don't believe Jay Leno has actual feelings, and he doesn't seem to be that worried about other people's feelings." I think there was a compliment buried somewhere in there.

Every comic has an opinion of the brethren they once competed with for stage time at Mitzy Shore's Sunset Boulevard landmark. The Comedy Store was a launch pad for the careers of David Letterman, Jay Leno, Richard Pryor, Robin Williams,

Jim Carrey, Tom Dreesen, Sam Kinison, Paul Rodriguez, Sarah Silverman, Chris Rock, Dave Chappelle, David Spade, Bob Saget, Howie Mandel, Joe Rogan, Jimmie Walker and so many others. They all had their eyes on the same prize, a guest shot with stand-up star-maker Johnny Carson.

The short drive over Laurel Canyon for five or six minutes on *The Tonight Show* would usually result in a wealth of club bookings as soon as the next morning. For some, a six-minute set propelled their careers into the major leagues from which they scored their own sitcoms. That's why the night when Johnny personally visited the L.A. Improv to check out new talent became an indelible memory for the young up-and-coming Jay Leno.

Johnny had come to the Improv at the urging of Harvey Korman. Harvey used to drop in regularly after becoming an investor with owner Budd Friedman at a time when he was planning on opening additional clubs across the country. Harvey specifically wanted Johnny to see Jay. His son, Christopher Korman, was kind enough to share the story his father told about that night, taking his gray Rolls Royce to pick up Johnny at his home at the time, 400 St. Cloud Drive in Bel Air. Just in case Johnny might change his mind last minute, Harvey hadn't told Budd they were coming. You could hear a pin drop when they walked in the club.

Jay remembered, "It sent an electric current through the place. Johnny was in the house!" After doing his act Jay stopped at their table to say thanks for coming. He recalled Johnny was very genuine saying, "That was funny stuff, but you're not quite ready… you're getting good laughs, but you need more jokes." Jay confessed, "I was hurt by that, but I'd go home and watch what he did, and he did 15 jokes in three minutes, and I looked at my act, and I did 15 jokes in 25 minutes."

Always going for the laugh, Jay twisted the story when interviewed by author Jay Walker. He told Walker that Johnny panned his performance by telling the newcomer, "You're just not right for the show, not very good." In the embellished version Jay claimed he was so peeved that he grabbed a basket of eggs from the club's kitchen and bombarded Johnny's car. Not true, but it does make for a better story than Jay simply going home and watching TV.

A couple of years later Steve Martin caught Jay's new and improved act and promised to put in a positive word for him with Johnny's talent booker. Jay got his break on March 2, 1977, and nobody, Jay included, would have believed that a dozen years after that first *Tonight Show* appearance in a creased green suit he'd be inaugurated as the new resident pitch hitter by the comedy god who didn't think he had much of an act. In a strange twist of fate it was his old friend Joan Rivers' jump to Fox that created the opening. Although the crown was slightly tarnished by its previous owner's hasty exit, Jay shined it up as he made the guest host gig his own. Then the wager with even longer odds would be that 17 years after his *Tonight Show* debut, Jay would inherit the franchise in its entirety.

Once behind the desk at NBC Burbank's Studio 1 Jay did indeed make the show his own. After years of playing small clubs the audience seemed too far away and, unlike clubs, the crowd was separated from the host by a waist-high physical barrier. That buffer was emblematic of Johnny's desire to keep people at bay, a safe distance, physically if not also emotionally. When Jay asked about some kind of a makeover the network asked which venues he'd worked felt most comfortable, and why. The *Saturday Night Live* configuration was one he mentioned for the hosts' intimacy with the closest guests.

The result was a complete remodeling of Studio 3 across the hall. The layout was spun 90 degrees within that twin facility. Instead of having the stage and audience each being narrow and deep, the new configuration had Jay on a wide stage playing to an audience that filled far fewer rows, but was seated as wide as the studio walls allowed. As it was at *SNL*, Jay delivered his monologue to guests seated on the stage floor, some almost at his feet. There was a small protruding retractable extension called the "tongue" that put Jay even further into the audience during the monologue. Those who were closest were instructed to stand and approach as Jay entered, and shake his hand. It's impossible to imagine Johnny Carson in that scenario.

Jay's fanciest footwork was his ability to dance around the minefield of dysfunction created by his longtime manager, Helen Kushnick. He stayed above the fray and out of the shitstorm while Johnny Carson's assassin continued her spiteful spree, pouring gasoline on the rivalry among Jay, Arsenio, Dave, and Conan. The competition for dominance in late night talk turned ugly, especially between Jay and Arsenio after Kushnick contacted agents and managers to fire the first shot in a booking war. Respected talent manager Ken Kragen passed away during the final days of 2021, but not before he explained how his refusal to un-book singer Travis Tritt from Arsenio's show for an appearance with Jay enraged Kushnick. She not only banned Tritt for life, she also canceled a confirmed booking for another Kragen client, singer Trisha Yearwood. NBC was then shocked and embarrassed to suddenly hear Kushnick on Howard Stern's show refuting that charge from Kragen and ranting about Hollywood's sexist conspiracy against her.

The discordant relationship between Kushnick and the network grew increasingly heated. When NBC served her with a gag order after her interview with Howard, she returned that slap with a letter of intent to file a sexual discrimination suit. Faster than you can change channels, on September 21st, 1992 NBC responded with a public statement: "Effective immediately, Helen Kushnick will no longer…" She was asked to permanently leave the premises that very afternoon, and did.

With NBC's suits understandably worried that Jay might follow her out the door, the shrewd host quickly allayed all fears by pledging his loyalty to the network. He later remained in the peacock's good graces even after he was bumped from *The Tonight Show* to accommodate a contract clause NBC had agreed to years earlier with Conan O'Brien. The network would have to give Conan the coveted 11:35 slot or forfeit a massive sum of cash, north of $40 million. Jay remained a team-playing company man, struggling with a new show at 10 o'clock. After the ratings tanked on Conan's late-night watch, the tall redhead received his multi-million dollar buyout, and Jay returned to again helm the venerable *Tonight Show* franchise.

Jay had succeeded in distancing himself from the public relations hell Helen Kushnick created to now find his image suffering for whatever role people believed he played in Conan's ousting from *Tonight*. As Joan Rivers put it, "He fell off of many people's Christmas card list." Those in the trenches with Jay remained loyal, especially after he volunteered to take a pay cut instead of having staffers fired during a round of NBC belt-tightening.

For a while when he was at the top of his game, I saw a lot of Jay Leno. In the early 2000s my multiple gigs at NBC earned me a wonderful perk. I was given the key for exclusive use of one of the simple dressing rooms along the hallway that *Tonight Show* guests called home for a few hours. Unlike his predecessor, I saw Jay meeting, greeting, joking, and schmoozing his celebrities before each day's taping. It meant that he and I regularly squeezed past each other in the narrow hallway. Jay was quick to make anybody feel like a friend. That meant that I was usually offered a selection from the rolling bar that served lip-loosening libation to his guests before the show. It was a decades-old tradition, and I always respect tradition.

As an example of Jay's generosity, I remember one particularly long tape day of doing warm-up on the set of *Weakest Link*. We were in Studio 1, across the hall from the remodeled *Tonight Show* digs. I had stepped back to my dressing room for a quick moment to answer nature's call while the pages replaced some applause-weary *Link* audience members with fresh victims. As Jay was walking down our shared hallway I asked if he had a minute sometime over the next couple of hours during which he might be willing to just walk in and say "Hello" to our audience. I knew showing his face for even a few seconds would be a treat that would generate excitement and energize the crowd of 300-plus people, some of whom had been sitting almost long enough for rigor mortis to set in.

It was the kind of thing you could never ask of many performers, but predictably Jay instantly said, "Sure!" I assumed he'd wait until he was dressed and energized for his own taping and might cruise in for a quick round of applause on the way. Instead, he headed straight for the studio double doors. Wearing his unofficial uniform of jeans and a blue denim shirt, Jay walked into the audience's view, speaking loudly so as to be noticed: "I knew there were people in here, I could hear the breathing next door. How is everybody?" Instead of a quick quip or two, Jay did three or four minutes of an impromptu monologue and then entertained questions from the audience.

I couldn't believe how generous he was being with his time and energy, chatting about everything from cars to current events. One person asked about the charitable work his wife was involved in, some overseas effort to help empower women fighting against cultural discrimination. Instead of offering a quick answer, Jay turned to one of the family of NBC staffers we shared: "Would you mind taking a look for Mavis? She's probably with one of the guests."

Soon Mavis and Jay, together, were happily chatting on and on until it became clear that Mr. and Mrs. Leno were delaying the *Weakest Link* taping. I'm still amazed by Jay's instant willingness to spread some good cheer and help carry some of my burden in keeping the audience entertained. I guess I shouldn't have been that surprised as everybody who knows him says that's just Jay's way. Everybody who knew Johnny Carson knows that if I'd tried this a decade earlier the story would have had a very different ending.

It was in this same spirit of friendship that Jay engaged me in conversation about some of the cars he drove to the lot. There was a different one every day from the hundreds of classic and antique vehicles that Jay owned, restored, and lovingly maintained. The 199 cars and 168 motorcycles he owned at the time ran the gamut from steam-powered prototype horseless carriages from the turn of the previous century, to the earliest electric vehicles manufactured by companies long forgotten, and all the way to archetypical muscle cars and a few recent exotic vehicles. It was obvious just how much Jay loved these classics and loved to talk about them.

Thinking erroneously that my passing curiosity about some of these rare cars qualified me as a full-fledged motorhead, Jay called me over one day while we were both on the wide lane of pavement at the old NBC Burbank lot referred to as the midway. He pointed to a pre-release prototype of some massively tricked-out BMW motorcycle to be introduced for the next model year. It looked like something out of the future, designed to help Arnold Schwarzenegger fight crime in the 25th century. Jay described a few of its unique features and then surprised me by offering me a ride. At first I thought he meant for me to hop on behind him and hang on for dear life while he put the bike through its paces. That sounded very cool.

No, Jay offered me the bike; he meant for me to drive it! I don't know squat about controlling a motorcycle and especially wanted no part of the responsibility for one so valuable. The only thing worse than me taking a spill and cracking my skull open would be to scratch, fold, bend or mutilate this magnificent machine. Jay insisted. He was adamant: "Ya know, this here is the ahhh, throttle and ahhhh, you kick here to shift gears." He wouldn't take no for an answer. "C'mon, it's nothing!" I don't know what the hell I was thinking, but I got on the bike. I squeezed the clutch, Jay kicked it into first and, following his direction I very slowly released the clutch while barely twisting my wrist on the throttle. I left my stomach back at the starting line and made it to the end of the long midway without tipping over. I couldn't believe I was still vertical. Because I was too intimidated and ignorant about shifting, the bike was still in low gear, When I released the throttle it quickly slowed on its own. Great, because the pavement ended at the side of a set storage warehouse down by Studios 9 and 11. I was too baffled to be confident about which of the levers, buttons, switches, and grips was the brake.

I made a wide U-turn with my feet dragging on the pavement, inching along as I finished the 180. Then I fed some gas and almost threw myself off the bike as I came back up the midway. I released the throttle, squeezed the clutch, and the bike rolled slowly enough that I could hand it off to Jay. I started to breathe again as he said, "Well that's an interesting approach, you never shifted out of first gear." I laughed it off, slapped him on the back, said thanks and quickly headed inside to thank the TV gods for not having crashed the bike.

Jay had always been that generous, even going back to his days before his star rose into the firmament as a top-rated late night host. Comedian, television host, and motivational speaker Ross Shafer remembers when he and Jay were a couple of comics working the road. On one particular day in Reno, Jay was neatening-up the hotel room they shared for a scheduled interview by some journalist neither of them had ever met. Opening the hotel room door they were surprised to find the person who knocked was a kid no older than 13, a junior high school student. Jay welcomed him in and, while Ross watched in amazement, Jay gave the kid his complete attention for no less than 20 minutes, answering even the junior journalist's most insipid questions. After the kid left Ross asked something like, "Jay, why the hell are you wasting your time?" Jay shrugged, grinned and said, "Hey. You never know."

OK, I can hear you asking, "If Jay is such a gracious, generous, and genial good guy what the hell is he doing in this Godforsaken book?" Well, in Jay's drive to succeed in the hand-to-hand combat of the standup comedy world, he ventured into show business's seediest nether regions where even a straight-shooter encounters some curves. That included filling stage time between strippers in the sleaziest of bump-and-grind joints.

At one of the Boston clubs he played, which included one simply called "Nude," Jay was struggling in handling a heckler. In the legend that Jay has perpetuated, one of the two naked women who were taking sponge baths in giant martini glasses behind him came to his rescue. A hardened, seen-it-all busty old pro with a stage name like Ineeda Mann got out of her oversized glass, walked downstage to the loudmouth and cold-cocked him with her fist. Not only did she break his nose, Jay remembers that with one well-placed punch she knocked the guy unconscious.

Another adventure in Beantown's Combat Zone left burn holes in Jay's suits. He recalled how patrons at one hellish dive showed their disapproval of his act by tossing lit cigarette butts at him. Beyond all the dimly-lit smoky roach-ridden toilets, Jay told me he actually performed in a real live Boston whorehouse. He'd work any room because he was reduced to being nearly destitute and homeless in the dogged pursuit of his dream.

Jay apparently never forgot those dues-paying days. When the Hollywood Chamber of Commerce's Walk of Fame selection committee asked if he had a preference for the location of his prized pentagram to be installed in April of 2000, somewhere along Hollywood Boulevard or Vine Street, Jay didn't select some prestige site to be immortalized in terrazzo and gold. Instead, he requested a well-traveled low-rent square of sidewalk in front of the Ripley's "Believe It or Not Odditorium." Why there, at the downscale tourist attraction next door to a McDonald's? Because when Jay first came to California to pursue a career in comedy it was at that very spot that he was arrested for vagrancy.

Mistaken for a drug dealer, Jay was busted and indelicately shoved into the back of an L.A.P.D. black-and-white. Instead of whining to the cops with some tale of woe, Jay performed standup—actually sit-down comedy—while in the back seat of the patrol car. As he put it, "An audience is an audience!" The cops were so enjoying his adlib monologue that they drove him around for hours while he cracked wise about everything they saw. It was the purest form of observational humor, and Jay admits that he was on a roll that night. At the end of their shift the cops were still laughing and decided to cut Jay loose without booking him. The pair of L.A.P.D.'s finest was among Jay's first and most encouraging California audiences. In the vernacular of comedy, he killed. In cop-talk that would be a 187.

Like most who come to Hollywood without a firm job commitment, Jay's early days were all about survival. In 1972, after he scraped some money together he didn't rent a place to crash. Instead, for $350 he bought a 1955 Buick Roadmaster. It gave him a place to sleep as well as transportation. He said he used to sweet talk waitresses into letting him take a shower at their homes, and then approach others for help with a free meal or an occasional night on a sofa. When all else failed, Jay slept in the downtown missions and shelters, as well as under the stairs at the Comedy Store.

While it sounds like an insane life, Jay was no idiot. By almost living at Mitzy Shore's comedy landmark he quickly learned the ways of the business. It was a fully-immersive fast-track education at the old nightspot that had become the most vibrant club in America for standup. The Comedy Store was ground zero from which comics launched into the next echelons of success, some of whom helped Jay hook up with writing gigs and a few TV guest shots. One of those was on Dinah Shore's afternoon syndicated talk show. Jay's memory of that appearance struck me as perhaps the funniest story he ever told.

Jay was to perform a few minutes of standup and then join Dinah for the customary chit chat. As part of the pre-interview with his segment producer Jay was asked for his outcue, the last words of his monologue so that the band could jump right in with his play-off before the laughter died down to an awkward silence. It's standard practice, but Jay was so new to TV that he'd never been asked. Thinking on his feet he responded, "How about if I just say 'thank you' twice. It will be 'Thank you, thank you very much.'" So the producer writes down, "Thank you, thank you very much" to pass along to the director and band leader. Great.

The show starts. Jay's backstage. He hears his intro from Dinah. The stage manager cues him, a crewmember pages the curtain for his entrance and Jay takes center stage. The audience is hot and extremely generous with a laugh for his very first line, "I'm from the United States. Are there any other Americans here?" The silly opener never got such an enthusiastic reaction before. Surprised and pleased, Jay basked in a few seconds of unanticipated laughter and said, "Thank you, thank you very much."

The band leader instantly looked up and dropped an armload of sheet music and the drummer lunged for his sticks, while the horn players dropped their cigarettes and grabbed their instruments. They started playing him off! Bah da, dat da tetah da…! He's been on stage for 15 seconds, told one almost-joke, they heard the outcue and think he's done. Dinah hears the band, drops her notes, stands, straightens her dress, smiles and starts applauding. The audience is baffled, but once Dinah starts applauding they also start clapping. Jay joins Dinah who says, "That was some of the freshest material I've heard in a long time. Very funny." Obviously nobody was paying attention, and the whole damn show was on autopilot.

Jay still works the road, although it clearly isn't for money. His great indulgence is classic cars, but otherwise the perpetually denim-clad funnyman seems to live a very simple life, in the same home he's had for decades, and without the trappings of great wealth. That's clearly how almost everyone knows him to be, but apparently we're all wrong. We never knew about Seafair, the 15,861-square-foot Louis XIV-inspired 1936 chateau that he bought on impulse. Jay says while in Rhode Island visiting family in 2017 he took a drive along scenic Ocean Avenue through posh Newport. He spotted one estate's driveway electric gate opening as he passed by. He says he took it as a sign, pulled up and rang for the caretaker. Jay drove the long motorway through the massive lush manicured lawn to the main house.

With his easy-going everyman charm he learned from the caretaker that the immense nine acre property had a tennis court, an infinity pool, a carriage cottage, a six-car garage, and private beaches along some of New England's most spectacular coastline. The main house is on the tip of a peninsula overlooking the Atlantic with 12 bedrooms, 13 bathrooms and features a paneled library, a formal dining room, and a chef's kitchen. Jay nodded his head a few times in thought and then asked if they could get the owner on the phone. Jay remembers asking, "Will you sell the house as-is, with everything, all the furniture, the ketchup in the refrigerator, the salt shaker, and just walk away?" At $13.5 million, without a beat Jay said, "I'll take it."

Yes, he and Mavis love the estate despite the fact that they rarely visit. Jay jokes, "It's big. I've yet to flush every toilet in the place." He spends over a half-million dollars a year maintaining the property, but don't worry about the price tag or the upkeep. If he were ever in a bind, he could cover all the estate's expenses by selling just one of his 199 cars. Jay says, "I bought my McLaren F1 in 1998 for $800,000; the last offer I got was $17.5 million." Good news, Jay. Prices are up. A McLaren F1 sold in 2021 for $20.5 million.

Chapter 18

While TV personalities are buying $13 million dollar homes, there are people sitting as few as 10 feet away earning minimum wage by watching the mega-millionaires. They have a job that didn't exist until around the turn of the 21st century. It's a gig you might like and it's fairly easy to get. All you have to do is watch a television show. However, unlike watching at home, you have to wear pants. You also have to laugh and clap. Here's how this both loved and hated job came to be.

The number of minutes it takes to tape a TV show has expanded exponentially with each advancement in technique. Under the old real-time live, or live-to-tape zeitgeist the math was easy. It took 30 minutes of production time to get 30 minutes of finished product. Likewise, an hour show took 60 minutes. What could be simpler, sweeter, neater, or cleaner? With the new paradigm of start-and-stop production for pick-ups, alternate takes, and re-staged moments, the process has come to resemble feature film production.

With many tapings now measured in hours rather than in minutes, few tourists are willing to stay for it all. Who could blame them? We're no competition for the allure of Disneyland. Producers used to rely on school groups, Boy Scout troops, senior citizen klatches, and even patients on rehab centers' field trips to happily fill seats when ticket distribution was low. Not anymore. It's finally come down to where even the delightful and loyal women of the Red Hat Society can rarely be coerced to sit for as long as necessary. Unlike Maxwell House coffee, audiences think watching the production of a show that's brewed by this slow-drip process is not good to the last drop.

With the ever-decreasing pool of willing civilians we entered the era of the paid audience. A job sitting, applauding, laughing, and smiling certainly beats bussing restaurant tables. That's reason enough to sign on for the gig, but some who do aren't completely grounded in reality. Movie star Lana Turner was indeed discovered sitting at a soda fountain counter 80 years ago. It wasn't Schwab's, but actually the Top

Hat across the street from Hollywood High School. Some hopeful would-be stars and starlets seem to think their celebrity appeal is ripe for being similarly spotted. Could their big break come as a camera quickly pans their face in a crowd of like-minded seat-fillers? Maybe the fantasy is that the emcee will suffer a heart attack and, instead of asking for a doctor a producer, will yell, "Is there a host in the house?"

With $15 an hour being about the going rate for this mindless task it's an easy way to pick up a few bucks. An even faster way to pick up those bucks is to find where the supervising page from the audience booking company hid them, and steal them. With a handful of wranglers trying to manage several hundred folks with light wallets, while also babysitting the problem children among the group, I'm surprised it only happened once in my presence.

Despite being repeatedly told that snack times and bathroom runs would only be accommodated at supervised scheduled intervals, nobody can convince a strong-willed audience member dancing with what appears to be an uncomfortably overfull bladder that you'd rather mop up after them than allow them to trot to the closest exit on their own. Then there's the smartphone addiction which has recently raised the stakes to where all audience members' electronic devices are now confiscated and held by security during tapings. Even without those distractions there's still plenty of random activity and disorder in some studios. A few strays can sometimes be found strolling around unsupervised, needing to be corralled. The audience page job has become more and more like trying to herd cats.

I never knew what the standard procedure was for cashing-out these hired pairs of hands at the end of the hours of slapping them together. On one memorable day in 2009, south of Hollywood at Meruelo Studios the contracted audience company was robbed. This is no longer the practice, but a runner had delivered the cash towards the end of that tape day to be ready for doling out to a crowd anxious to hit the road. Minimum wage for seven or eight hours for each of two or three hundred people is way too large for someone to carry around in a pocket. Some kind of bag, satchel, brief case, attaché or backpack was stashed somewhere the audience wranglers could, in theory, try to keep an eye on it. Apparently it proved to be a sufficiently easy target for some desperate ne'er-do-well who had likely watched and learned the routine on previous tape days. I didn't have a clue what had gone down until a very worried-looking page asked if I had seen anything unusual. Hey, it's television. Some days everything that happens is unusual.

If the temptation is too strong for people to resist the lure of maybe 20 grand, it's freakin' insane to bring two million dollars anywhere near the public, but that's what we did about a dozen times at NBC. It had to present a temptation for even God-fearing, church-going former Eagle Scouts and Campfire Girls. Even in Las Vegas casinos where they're as expert as anyone on the planet at managing tantalizing piles of beaucoup bucks just inches away from viewers' naked eyes, the displays of masses of cash are fictionalized. I worked in Caesars Entertainment's showrooms for years, trust me. It's all an illusion.

However, it's an illusion so realistic that some damn fool actually busted the glass that separated him from a display labeled to be $1 million in the walkway between the Bally's and Paris hotels. He grabbed what he could and ran, his attempted getaway captured on almost as many video cameras as coverage of the Super Bowl. Casino security guards laughed as they handcuffed the smash-and-grab bandit knowing he could face felony charges for what, in reality, was more like a couple of thousand dollars than a million.

Two mountains of cash at the 2000 reboot of the legendary quiz show *Twenty One* was the lure behind my single craziest moment on a set. The new version of the 1956-1958 headline-making series taped in the cavernous Studio 1 at NBC in Burbank. You've likely seen the audience section on camera at least once or twice over the years, probably on the old *Tonight Show*. It's the huge room that was designed with Bob Hope in consultation with architect John C. Austin and RCA's top acoustic engineers of the 1950s.

The height of the ceiling and the sharp vertical angle of the audience seating was unique for the time, affording nearly 500 guests totally unobstructed views from seats that rise to a dizzying height. Any taller stadium seating configuration and the visitors in the top rows would need oxygen—there'd be St. Bernard dogs carrying brandy casks. Rod Roddy had the best line about working in that studio's audience section: "It's a great room… if you're a Billy goat!"

Soon after Jack Warner sold 35 acres of Burbank property to NBC in 1951 construction began on an advanced engineering facility for color, the future of television. Studio 1 was built to a soaring height of 42 feet with unobstructed sightlines and state-of-the-art acoustics. The audience section's sharp rake took full advantage of the room's massive space. The stage's nearly 10,600 square feet was the network's largest on the west coast. Being constructed simultaneously, two studios at CBS Television City would best those stage dimensions with an additional 1,400 square feet.

Big money game shows were back in a very big way in 2000 when NBC looked to answer ABC's success with *Who Wants to Be a Millionaire* by reviving the infamous *Twenty One* with Maury Povich hosting. Lavish production in Studio 1 and massive cash awards never translated to ratings.

In addition to utilizing about 400 of the permanent audience seats, another 200 or so chairs were added on the stage floor for tapings of this highly-promoted primetime weekly extravaganza. During a stopdown with taping to resume momentarily, I could see a few people, their faces indiscernible, in the highest altitudes moving in the dark distance. I was in full warm-up mode joking with the accessible audience members on the stage floor but still playing it large for the entire house. I continued watching curiously with one eye as it became clear that a couple of the guests in the furthest rows had stood up and were now pushing each other.

Holy crap, there's a fistfight starting in the audience. It seemed to be quickly escalating as two or three others nearby stood up. They were exchanging words and perhaps ready to exchange a couple of blows. I'd never seen anything like it. What is there to fight about, a disagreement over the right answer to some question on the show? I kept doing my shtick in order to keep the focus from moving to the altercation, and risk compounding the madness into a full-fledged rumble. I caught the eye of stage manager Robert Ferkle and nodded to where the action was. He saw it and immediately called for help on his headset.

A couple of the regular studio guards started the steep climb up the audience stairs, soon followed by several added plainclothes security personnel who I guess were assigned to protect the cash. Unfortunately, all the activity seemed to exacerbate the problem by refocusing some of the audience's attention in the direction of the brawl. Then, all of a sudden, simultaneously, all the cops froze in place. Instantaneously, time stood still. Word had spread on earpieces, headsets and walkie-talkies, likely warning that this fight at the furthest reaches of the studio might be a purposeful distraction designed to draw attention and protection away from the cash. Most of the uniformed and the black-suited security personnel suddenly spun around and started back to the stage. It was not the least bit subtle, and even the most clueless of the 600 audience members was now aware that something might be very, very wrong.

In this era before visitors were paraded through metal detectors there was a very real possibility that any pre-meditated scheme to cop some cash could have included weapons. It sounds extreme, but of the countless banks and supermarkets that have been robbed at gunpoint, few likely ever had anything close to $2 million in currency on hand. It was tense. None of us on the stage floor had any idea whether we were witnessing a simple altercation among a few audience members, or a diversionary tactic in a pre-planned full-on armed robbery attempt. I knew it was my job to keep people calm in their seats and to try to diffuse the sudden anxiety with humor. Oh, and in the event of gunfire it was also my job to avoid getting shot.

As the running stopped, I started the joking. "Wasn't that fun? That was one of the new NBC employee aerobic breaks designed to keep studio crews in tip-top condition. It seems like everybody's exercising these days. You know, if God wanted me to touch my toes, he'd have put them higher on my body. The executives on this show are so rich, they pay people to go to the gym for them. I like the gym and all those machines, but I hate that there's no ashtray on the Stairmaster. My favorite machine at the gym is the candy machine…" I could feel the anxiety slowly mellowing as I continued, "My mom says walking is great exercise. Last month she started walking two miles every day. It's been three weeks and we have no idea where the hell she is." Soon, tape rolled again, and all was happy and clappy.

I never did find out for certain exactly what had happened. One staffer later said a guy who rested his foot on the seat back in front of him had planted his boot directly on the sweater of the woman in that seat. Her boyfriend, defending her honor and her wardrobe, said something that offended the guy connected to the foot and they were soon battling. Nobody knew who these people in the audience were, what was on their minds, and what might be in their pockets. I'd always thought we should have had metal detectors for the audience. Eventually we did, soon after September 11th, 2001. Maybe we need *mental* detectors, as well.

Maury Povich remained totally unfazed by all this craziness. He was soon back on the set and we were playing the game again. Coming from decades of live television, dozens of times he'd likely been challenged to concentrate despite some random event within his peripheral vision. I love that about the pros. They're focused, aware but single-minded, and ready to deal with whatever might happen. They know it's all about getting the show on the air or in the can, on schedule, and getting out the door. Maury seemed to always get everybody home on time, despite the predictable unpredictability of creating television.

On some of these tape days Maury wasn't headed home. He was likely even more dedicated to wrapping on schedule the times his wife, news star Connie Chung, came to the set with the long-wed lovebirds no doubt heading out for the evening. Connie and Maury's 1984 marriage wasn't made in heaven, it was a marriage made in a newsroom, and the matchmaker was a news director. Although their relationship started at WTTG in Washington, their romance blossomed after they were both hired individually at Los Angeles' local CBS station where they ended up as co-anchors in the late 1970s. I wonder if they were playing footsy behind the anchor desk.

The audience's reaction upon spotting Connie in the studio was another reminder of how appearing on television somehow seems to imbue anyone who has stared down the camera lens with some special magnetism and compelling presence. For those who grew up in recent decades, regularly shooting then instantly watching their own video on all manner of screens, it must be hard to fully appreciate television's earlier power. With cameras the size of refrigerators and the majority of Americans watching their choice of, at best, only four or five channels, the stars on the small screen were bigger than life.

There's magic that seems to transform how people are perceived by the public that results from the simple fact that they were scanned by the cool, unblinking image orthicon tube, and had their image flung into the vast electronic ether. It's as if their essence, their DNA, their very being has been altered to give them a special transcendent quality. The gods of television have smiled upon them, imbuing these mere mortals with a mystical aura and the illusion of credibility, power, charm, and limitless authority. The most trusted man in all of America in the 1960s and 1970s was a very imperfect news anchor. Walter Cronkite was a college dropout.

Apparently all of this being held in such high esteem can be both a blessing and a curse. Oprah Winfrey has shied away from countless events lamenting, "A party with people with their cameras is not really a party for me. You're on display and you're just literally selfie-ing the night away. And if you do one, you've got to do everyone." That inconvenience is a tiny part of the curse that comes from a life on television; ask anyone who's been stalked.

Oprah has also experienced the blessings of celebrity. In 2019 she told interviewer Lacey Rose, "I was at [the] Apple [store] the other day and this young girl just started shaking and crying. She said, 'But you don't understand.' I just took her by the arms and I said, 'Are you OK?' And she said, 'You don't understand.' I go, 'Yea I do.'" The kid kept insisting that Oprah couldn't comprehend what it meant for her to see the TV star in person. Finally, Oprah nailed it in this dialogue: "I raised you. You came home from school and there was nobody home, right? Every day, four o'clock, I was there." "Yes, yes, you raised me," the fan agreed. Oprah's reply, "That warms my heart."

There are also viewers who hold a romantic fascination with some on-camera personalities who, if not for their time on the tube, wouldn't be given a second glance. Ah, the countless passionate pursuits of love-starved, obsessed fans and fanatics. Among many, there's one story that is too fantastic to remain untold. It's the 100-percent true tale of an Emmy-winning television personality who extricated himself from a mantrap with such guile that it deserves an award of its own. I guarantee you never heard this one as it's a deep dark personal memory, and not a proud one, for a gentleman who wouldn't even consider my mentioning his name.

Unmarried at the time, our handsome young broadcaster took advantage of occasional romantic trysts that were generously offered and emphatically declared to be without any expectation of further entanglement. There seemed to be no shortage of these hook-up opportunities for him, including one with a spectacularly attractive lady. As they were from distant cities the consenting adults' half-dozen or so rendezvous took place at hotels all across the country, usually coinciding with the guy's travel. By the time of their meeting in Las Vegas the affair had taken an unexpected turn.

This sexy young flirt who had willingly shared her charms suddenly became fixated on getting married to her casual friend-with-benefits. Smooth talker that all broadcasters are, our pal dodged the repeated references to a wedding until it became clear that this lady had come to Vegas with the sole goal of taking advantage of that town's specialty—performing marriage ceremonies at the whim of any and all comers. The noose tightened over the several days of this deluded fan's visit until it seemed there might be no way to get rid of her without marrying her. Our TV-boy was unable to think of a way to get out of this alive.

He called another on-camera personality, a game show emcee, who despite being long-married and past dating age had the most incredibly creative solution. His advice was to arrange for one of the city's many willing wedding officiates to perform a non-binding "commitment ceremony," much like those that were being offered to gay couples when they were still being denied legal marriages. The almost bride-to-be was ecstatic with what she believed to have been the fulfillment of her dream. All smiles, the attractive couple walked down the aisle of a Vegas wedding mill and vowed to forever love, cherish, and respect each other. Not a legally binding word such as "marriage" was uttered, nor was it printed on the certificate they gleefully signed. That all went unnoticed by a mind filled with fantasies of living the rest of her life in some kind of TV bonus round. The couple celebrated with an ersatz honeymoon, and the pretty groupie returned home to begin planning the domestication of her new hubby.

During her flight, knowing that her phone wouldn't receive his call, the almost-husband fully explained the entire situation of unrequited infatuation in a voicemail message. He reminded her of the long-standing nature of their pre-Vegas relationship, clarified how they actually had not been legally married, wished her well, and made it clear that she was not welcome in his life again. After several months of unanswered calls, unreturned messages, ignored letters and unopened greeting cards, her advances finally ended. Unwilling to be tamed, trained, and housebroken, our handsome friend managed an escape that would have impressed Houdini. Unkind, you say? Indeed. Sure, he was a miserable heart-breaking cad, but I doubt there's a gracious technique for backing away from a deluded fanatic struggling single-mindedly, dead set determined to turn a fantasy into a reality.

For some fans an actor or broadcaster's time on television is the ultimate aphrodisiac. The stalking cases in the L.A.P.D. files are the proof. The targets include stars and bit players alike, in all parts of the city—Kendall Jenner in the Hollywood Hills, Paris Hilton in a Malibu beachfront compound, Selena Gomez in Calabasas, and dear Dawn Wells of *Gilligan's Island* fame who was terrorized during her final years living in her San Fernando Valley home. In that case, there eventually was some justice as her stalker was ultimately ordered by the courts to pay over $11,000 to her estate. It's a living hell for stars as well as some up-and-comers, like a 21-year-old actress living in the Fairfax district in 1989, the late Rebecca Schaeffer.

The former model being cast in her first sitcom, CBS's *My Sister Sam*, suddenly changed Schaeffer's life, not all for the better. The concept of successfully achieving your goals becomes far more ominous than joyful when you learn she was ruthlessly murdered at the street level entry to her second floor studio apartment. Her obsessed 19-year-old fan had hired a private detective to get the actress's address. It was an unnecessary expense as the information was part of the DMV's public records for anyone who wanted it. Schaeffer's legacy includes California's passing of America's first anti-stalking laws in 1990, and the California's Driver's Privacy Protection Act of 1994 which is unofficially named The Rebecca Schaeffer Law in her memory.

Living the dream, so it seemed. Oregon native Rebecca Schaeffer bounced between New York and Hollywood, building an acting career that included the soaps *Guiding Light* and *One Life to Live*. Finally, after being cast in a primetime sitcom it all ended tragically with her murder on July 18, 1989.

It's no wonder faces that become familiar soon spend more of their hours at home. The week before her movie *Spencer* opened in theaters in 2021, I spoke with Kristen Stewart who admitted she missed the days when going to Starbucks or the mall were even remotely possible. The greater the fame, the higher the gates and fences. It's been more than 30 long years since the Rebecca Schaeffer case tragically illustrated that long gone are the days when it was possible for a recognizable personality to feel safe in a random studio apartment.

Studio apartment. That's such an unusual combination of words. The idea of a studio apartment conjures a mental picture of a building in which each resident's unit has theatrical lighting, cameras throughout, an "on the air" light in the living room, and maybe an "applause" sign over the bed. Studio apartment. What else could that mean? Well, there is one domicile that truly lived up to the full grandiosity of the term.

Chapter 19

Far from a studio apartment's traditionally tiny floor plan, there was one unbelievably spectacular apartment constructed in a building full of TV studios. I stumbled upon this grand residence one of the first times I worked at CBS Television City while grabbing a few moments of fresh air and sunshine at the rooftop helipad. The structure added atop the building had obviously been vacant for many years. With a long, nearly-seamless glass wall facing north it appeared this add-on might have been designed as a studio that would allow for a live skyline to be seen behind some on-camera action.

Ever since *The Today Show* pioneered the window-on-the-world background at the dawn of television, that design has been borrowed at various times by all three networks. I thought this may have been the remains from one of those studios. The problem with that idea is that when it was built in the 1960s a skyline shot of Los Angeles on most days would have been little more than a brown horizontal swath of haze. Neither smoke nor fog, the appellation "smog" was coined somewhere along the way to describe the colorful air that crossed the Hollywood skyline in the era of unchecked emissions. The joke was to never trust air you couldn't see.

The mystery of this top-floor addition was solved by a celebrated former CBS program executive, Michael Dann. He remembered how drafting its plans started after signing Danny Kaye for his own variety show for the 1963-1964 season. Kaye was a musical comedy star of radio, films, records, and television who excelled at performing rapid-fire intricately-rhymed original lyrics. It was early rapping. Most of this brilliant special material was written by his talented wife, Sylvia Fine. Among Danny Kaye's many fans was a 10-year-old George Carlin. George often credited the mid-century comic actor as the primary influence behind his fascination with words, although Kaye was not the source for the seven dirty ones the comic became famous for.

The heat was on Danny Kaye briefly during the witch hunt for Communists and other un-patriotic insurgents that began in 1949. All it had taken was to associate himself with Helen Keller and actor Fredric March in a group critical of America's growing nuclear arsenal. Unlike others who were blacklisted, Kaye's popularity wasn't permanently diminished. By the late 1950s the star was again a top-tier talent as evidenced by the fact that all three networks had been after him for years to star in a weekly series.

Kaye wasn't holding out for money or creative freedom, his reticence was based on a righteous concern for burning through his trove of prime material. He saw how the video beast chewed through people and remained insatiable for the last crumbs of their creative output. "Any medium that has to use as much talent as TV does is cannibalistic," he mused. Kaye had even turned down $2 million for five years of periodic specials. Eventually he softened, and his agent at MCA solicited bids for a weekly variety revue. CBS responded first, offering an irresistible production budget of $160,000 per episode. That would make it the era's most expensive regularly-scheduled weekly hour in all of broadcasting.

Of course the occasionally-temperamental star had a couple of requests to be fulfilled. Mike remembered, "Danny complained that his dressing room was way too small, not just for him to change between acts, but also to accommodate his colleagues and friends who would drop in at all times, night and day." According to Mike, at the time there wasn't a single unassigned dressing room or office of sufficient size, nor even two adjacent rooms of any kind that could be refurbished into a suitable accommodation.

Mike didn't recall whose idea it was, but he remembered jumping on the suggestion that a rooftop penthouse might do the trick. "In those days, there was never a question of cost," Mike explained. "$75,000 was a small price to pay for a happy star." For what it's worth, *The Danny Kaye Show* producer Perry Lafferty priced the perk at $150,000, equivalent to $1.4 million today. CBS even indulged Danny Kaye's additional request for a new kitchen in his Beverly Hills home to match the one the network was to install in his new apartment. Both were custom chefs' kitchens specially designed to accommodate his penchant for authentic Chinese cooking.

Kaye loved his new digs at first sight, and delighted in staying overnight as well as entertaining there during the four seasons his show emanated from Studio 31. His luxurious 1,386-square foot home-away-from-home sat atop the adjacent Studio 33 and featured that professional-grade full-sized Asian kitchen, a waiting room with secretary desk, a large living room with a grand piano, a bedroom, two bathrooms, and a patio with a barbecue, all with a private entrance. It was one hell of a perk. If this were some trashy torrid tell-all book I would include that Kaye's longtime intimate buddy, the eminent thespian Laurence Olivier, was reportedly among his most frequent overnight guests.

Singer Nancy Wilson guest starred with Danny Kaye on his January 20, 1965 show. In addition to a roster of comedy stars, top crooners Tony Bennett, Peggy Lee, Nat "King" Cole, Andy Williams, Harry Belafonte, Ella Fitzgerald, and Louis Armstrong guested during the four season run.

Kaye moved in during the summer of 1963 and tape rolled for the first of the season's 32 programs on August 10th. Harvey Korman and Joyce Van Patten were featured supporting players in a variety format developed with celebrated television writers Larry Gelbart and Perry Lafferty. The network was proud and hopeful, despite the fact that their star was nervous, insecure, and difficult to work with. "Danny had a lot of anger in him," Lafferty recalled. Danny's wife Sylvia was a very witty lyricist, composer, and producer, but had proved to be so headstrong, demanding, and off-putting that she was quickly barred from being on the lot. When *The Danny Kaye Show* debuted its audience was the largest for the time period, but it scored down the list of the season's top shows at number 30. Spending big for a hit variety hour with a long run was never an issue, but through several renewals the series never broke the magic 30-share threshold. Having more than one-third of the viewers in the three-network universe would have assured continuing renewals.

With NBC's counter-programming of popular movies and, later, *I Spy*, Kaye's viewership declined slowly and steadily. By the variety hour's fourth season Bill Cosby and Robert Culp's sleuth series had risen to the week's number 13 show, while Danny Kaye had slipped to number 79. His joy in the apartment was never shared by the numbers crunchers at the research department; likewise among the accountants. In the spring of 1967 Kaye vacated the deluxe apartment in the sky. Here's the takeaway television tenet: the talent of the tenant did not transform a tepid telecast. Sorry, I couldn't resist.

The penthouse's next star residents were the brothers Smothers. Mike Dann claimed Tom and Dick made good use of Kaye's custom kitchen by baking marijuana-laced brownies. The brothers had CBS subdivide the apartment to accommodate approximately 20 offices, which included cubicles for their staff of renegade writers. There were old-guard Jack Benny alumni, as well as voices from across the generation gap that included Steve Martin, Rob Reiner, Lorenzo Music, Mason Williams and Bob "Super Dave Osborn" Einstein. Tommy Smothers remembers the first time he saw the set-up: "We walked across the roof... hot mopped in gravel on either side of a wooden path... there was a whole suite of offices there, and it was just exciting... starting off on a new adventure."

The same season that Danny Kaye began living the highlife above the CBS eye, Judy Garland was also signed for her own network variety show. Undisputedly an A-list talent, concerns about Judy's mental health and her substance abuse were laid bare in the executive conference room. Exhausted, over-medicated, and in desperate need of cash, 1963 was a bad year for Judy. Her marriage to Sid Luft had become an on-again off-again source of heartache. His sizeable debts further challenged her bank accounts which were already overwhelmed by IRS claims for unpaid taxes, and by the yet-to-be-discovered embezzlement by agents David Begelman and Freddie Fields. A call from CBS was the first bit of good news she'd had in quite a while.

Judy would be happy to follow-up her recent periodic specials that had scored strong ratings for the network. However, CBS president Jim Aubrey didn't want more specials, he demanded a weekly show. Judy was seduced by the $24 million offer despite the fact that she herself had well-grounded doubts about the workload. She was not alone with that concern. Mike Dann told me that he and others at the network knew that Judy's emotional health was a precarious balancing act. Sadly, that fragility would soon become common knowledge. In trying to paint Judy as an unfit mother in the custody battle for their two kids, Luft publicized her history of no fewer than 23 suicide attempts, including one in which she almost successfully slit her throat.

Dann was worried that Judy would be over her head trying to keep up with the grind of a weekly show. Just the same, he was required to do president Aubrey's bidding. So, a weekly series it would be. He remembered, "Our biggest concern was that Judy might not make rehearsals on time, if at all. So, even though Judy recently bought a house in Brentwood, [Producer George] Schlatter pleaded with us to provide some sort of incentive, similar to Danny Kaye's penthouse, to ensure Judy turned up for work each day." The result was a spectacular installation. A 440-square-foot mobile home was finessed by a crane to the second floor exterior deck at Television City as its centerpiece. It was placed within staggering distance of Studio 43 allowing for the shortest walk possible when the star was escorted between center stage and her new temporary getaway.

No perk was considered too lavish when it came to keeping CBS stars feeling appreciated. Judy Garland was initially enthralled by the special accommodations prepared for her arrival. Photo courtesy of Charles Cappleman.

CBS art directors and construction crews went all out turning a motor home into a fully customized environment at the end of a yellow brick road for Judy Garland. Photo courtesy of Charles Cappleman.

By some accounts this was the most elegant house ever built on wheels. Designed to pamper CBS's new Sunday night superstar, the interior was decorated in the style of Judy's new Brentwood home, equipped with a piano and every luxury. It was all highlighted by theatrically-inspired pink lighting, and the exterior was accented in red and white. The entire affair was landscaped by the network's artisans with a lawn of artificial grass traversed by a yellow brick road that led from the studio to her front door. There hung a star and a plaque with the words "The Legend." Judy loved it.

CBS put out that most elaborate welcome mat and was initially prepared to give Judy her creative freedom. However, within the initial two weeks of taping the suits were already nitpicking Judy's performance. Their critiques included mention that they thought she didn't sing enough, that she touched her guests too much during duets, and generally appeared neurotic and edgy. Mel Torme was on the staff composing original songs and writing special lyrics for the show. His book *The Other Side of the Rainbow* confirms what Mike Dann told me about the events during one week in particular.

Judy's daughter, Liza, was a guest on the third episode which taped in July to air on November 17, 1963. Judy tried hard to hide her anxiety as well as the sting from the network's criticism. She was a trouper, but obviously a bit off her game. Her condition was made worse by the recent addition of amphetamines to her regimen in an effort to drop a few pounds. With their great tact, the executives had seen fit to include a mention of her weight in their critiques. Liza could see the angst through Judy's facade, as could Mel.

He wrote, "After the taping, Judy disappeared. There was no little gathering in her trailer, no drinks with the cast or crew, no goodnight kisses, No Judy. It was perfectly understandable. She had been a good soldier that whole week. She had kept up her spirits for the sake of Liza, and it had no doubt been quite a strain." As the pro that she always was, Judy returned for episode four and continued to pour her heart into her work. She was inviting friends and coworkers to join her in watching the show's broadcasts at her home on Sunday nights. Costume designer Bob Mackie was among the rotating guests.

As skillful as producer George Schlatter was in dealing with talent, he experienced his share of the behavior that had earned Judy the reputation as being difficult as far back as her MGM days. He shared the story of one wonderfully successful intervention on a day when his star was complaining about seemingly everything—the sets, the lights, the script, the camera angles. At a loss to find words to tame the negativity, he just started singing *Somewhere Over the Rainbow*. Judy whirled on her heels demanding to know what the hell George thought he was doing. After eight more bars of the tune he responded, "If you're going to produce, I'll sing!" Judy laughed so hard that the two of them fell to their knees at center stage in hysterics.

While the tension could occasionally be relieved, it's irrefutable that the deck had been stacked against Judy from the very beginning. She had been slotted into the time period from hell. With her talent backed by a proven producer wielding a respectable production budget, the weekly musical and comedy spectacles were the ammunition in CBS's star-studded salvo intended to drown NBC's seemingly unsinkable Sunday night stalwart, *Bonanza*.

In retrospect it's clear that expectations for Judy to tame the Ponderosa were unrealistic after so many other worthy challengers had failed to unseat the Cartright clan. CBS was unwilling to surrender in the ratings battle and continually tried to retool Judy, tinkering with the heart and soul of the show. They had bought a star, but soon wanted to remake her as the girl next door.

George Sunga, at the time CBS's newly promoted production supervisor, recalled in one of our 2019 conversations that George Schlatter was fired after five episodes and that at least three different showrunners came and went. Second among them was the renowned Norman Jewison who, only a few years later, began to bring a string of major movies to the big screen starting with 1967's *In the Heat of the Night*. Despite the fact that he was wearing the chef's hat, like excess cooks in a kitchen by late summer a gaggle of programming personnel had invited themselves to help stir the broth.

Convinced that the recipe needed more comedy, they adjusted the roster of supporting cast members and spiced up the list of guest performers, only to later reverse that decree in favor of focusing on Judy's singing. As Mike Dann told the press at the time, "We have decided that [Judy] should never appear in sketches and never play any character but herself. And she'll be singing more songs, more medleys, more standards. Songs are her babies. We told her what we think and she's listening."

Indeed, Mickey Rooney guested on the December 8, 1963 broadcast for a musical tribute to their days at MGM. Judy opened the hour with *I Feel a Song Comin' On*. Mickey shadowed with *When I'm Not Near the Girl I Love, Girls Girls Girls,* and *Thank Heaven for Little Girls*. Duets were followed by the pair looking at old photographs, reminiscing about their youth. Judy closed with *Old Man River*.

Mickey Rooney on a 1963 music-filled episode of *The Judy Garland Show*. Backstage Mickey offered needed support and encouragement to his lifelong friend, and discussed the film *It's a Mad, Mad, Mad, Mad World* which was released that November. Judy had turned down the opportunity to co-star with Mickey as Mr. and Mrs. Crumpin in the blockbuster comedy. Those roles went instead to Sid Caesar and Edie Adams. Mickey was recast as Buddy Hackett's friend, Ding Bell.

Although there was a respectable audience for the beloved star, "The Legend" and her guests were handicapped by being broadcast in black-and-white. For early adopters of the new technology who wanted a return on their investment in a color TV set, a gray Judy couldn't match the allure of the Nevada wilderness presented in the peacock's living color. Although it had been marked for cancellation after its first 13 episodes for being drastically over budget, *Bonanza* was destined to reign as TV's number one attraction for many years to come.

Armed with fresh reams of research, the generals in Jim Aubrey's army met at CBS's new imposing gray granite New York headquarters best known as Black Rock. Soon after, a formal sit-down with the star was scheduled—Judy was being called to the principal's office. As they do today, network notes in the 1960s often bordered on the irrational. The opinions of researched civilians and a few random affiliate station managers could be coalesced with the casual input from executives' wives, golf buddies, an occasional neighbor, and miscellaneous conversations overheard on the commuter trains from midtown to the Connecticut suburbs. The resulting incongruous mélange is often in conflict with the show's original concept.

Judy was again told that test audiences were made uncomfortable by her frequent hugging and hand-holding with some of her guests. In 1963 this was likely code for objections to interracial contact. Black and white TV was no place for blacks and whites to show affection. On the third season premiere of *The Martha Raye Show* in 1955, when Broadway star Tallulah Bankhead embraced 12-year-old Gloria Lockerman, an African-American spelling champ who had won on *The $64,000 Question*, all hell broke loose. Even as late as 1968 the issue remained too hot to touch, literally. While singing a duet, Petula Clark innocently and naturally touched Harry Belafonte's arm toward the end of their song. Doyle Lott, a vice president from the show's sponsor, Chrysler, was on-set and objected to what he described as "interracial touching." His demand for the scene to be reshot was honored simply to placate the stuffed suit. However, the controversial moment aired as first taped and Lott was subsequently fired over the incident.

In a related bit of television history, actress Nichelle Nichols confirmed for *The Hollywood Reporter* in recent years that when her *Star Trek* character, Lt. Uhura, engaged in that series' first interracial kiss with William Shatner as Captain Kirk, there was a back-up contingency added in the event that NBC decided to chicken-out at the last minute. With the show already slated for cancelation there was little to lose, but the network was afraid of repercussions beyond the limited scope of that one series. It wasn't to be TV's first interracial kiss, but it was still considered to be highly controversial.

During the filming of the scene the actress reported that Shatner took liberties in requesting additional takes of the kiss before filming the alternate version in which the two actors embraced without consummating the lip-lock. At the very least this version could be incorporated into special edits of the show that would be made available upon request, predictably by affiliate stations in the South. Shatner said it was a chicken-shit move and did all he could to thwart the plan. "We did a few takes, but Bill was deliberately trying to flub it," Nichols remembered. "At one point he even crossed his eyes to make me laugh." In another account, Ms. Nichols claimed that the director couldn't see during filming that the one and only seemingly usable non-kiss take was intentionally ruined by Shatner's subtle mugging. The surprise came when the dailies were projected and it became apparent there was no viable alternate version of the scene.

Shatner has his own slightly different account in one of his autobiographies. However, when I dared to ask him about it, he told yet another variation of the facts. Regardless of how it actually went down, Shatner ultimately won. The network gave up trying to get a clean take of the less-controversial version and broadcast the full kiss, coast-to-coast. Somehow, life in the galaxy continued without disruption.

Like Shatner, Judy Garland wasn't acceding to any of her network's nitpick about her touching and hand-holding with African-American guests. Judy fired back that she'd played to enough audiences to know what made her public comfortable and uncomfortable. As the disagreement escalated, she looked around the conference room for a telephone. On the spot and in the presence of network chief Aubrey's henchmen, Judy called her good friend, President John F. Kennedy. It took only moments to get the leader of the free world to pick up the phone for his Hollywood chum. She put the call on speakerphone.

The executives were dumbfounded by the fact that, in just moments, Judy had the most powerful man in America on the line, talking about her–their–television show. Judy asked if Jack and Jackie had seen the previous week's program, and then asked how comfortable the President and First Lady were with her performance. Kennedy said the show was delightful and that he had seen nothing that made him feel even the least bit uncomfortable. The CBS suits exchanged looks as Kennedy went on about how he and Jackie both thought Judy was as entertaining as ever, and that they looked forward to seeing next week's show.

The conversation wrapped with a few pleasantries before Judy hung up. She then sat silently and expressionless. She'd made her point. Judy had won the battle, but she lost the war. When told about the call to the U.S. President, CBS president, founder, and CEO, William Paley, considered it a supreme act of insubordination. Several published sources report that he said of her, "I don't want that cunt bringing down my Sunday evening!"

Then the unthinkable happened. On the heels of that conversation Kennedy was assassinated. It left Judy despondent. She and the President had been good friends. After she sang at the 1960 Democratic Convention it had become a delightful custom for him to call her from the White House several times a month, usually asking her to sing *Somewhere Over the Rainbow* over the phone, which she would. With Judy's emotions raw following the assassination there was yet another showdown with the network. Her desire to stage a musical tribute to the fallen President was met with blank stares. She was told that her proposed words and music would constitute the kind of political commentary that was the purview of the news department.

Again Judy wouldn't take "no" for an answer, but the compromise that was hammered out left her precious little to work with. CBS would allow Judy to sing only *The Battle Hymn of the Republic* provided that she not change any lyrics, dedicate the song, or make direct mention of John Kennedy. Forbidden from appropriately honoring her friend the last of Judy's autonomy, joy, and creative fulfillment were doused. Her anger was vented in a highly emotional performance of the classic anthem, with Judy spitting out the words and flailing the microphone cable like a whip. It was electrifying. By the end of the performance the entire audience, members of the band, and studio bystanders had all risen to their feet, some crying. Judy had connected and gave voice to the outrage all of America felt in the aftermath of the young President's senseless murder.

Seen as an act of rebellion, the programming department's last flame of pleasure and pride from having the prestigious star on their air was extinguished. While still taping the balance of the season's episodes Judy was told her contract would not be renewed, and that the budgets had been cut for the remainder of the 26 shows. Everybody at Television City knew she was a lame duck, and Judy was demoralized. If there was ever to be a time that she would become the no-show that was feared early on, it would happen now. To the contrary, there's universal agreement that she then did some of her best work.

CBS's Sunga remembered Judy's reluctance to finish the final episode and leave the studio for the last time. He said she repeated performances of her songs and asked for additional retakes. The crew was understanding and compassionate, even though the work continued well past midnight with no end in sight. Sunga had an idea. He knew there were always a few hardcore fans waiting at the artists' entrance for a chance to get an autograph or simply see Judy when she left after tapings. Despite the late hour and inclement weather, indeed there were a half-dozen hearty souls who so loved Judy that they were camped-out that night.

Understanding that his star needed encouragement, confidence, and approval, Sunga went down to fetch the small gathering of groupies that he called "bench ladies." He took them up to Studio 43 and seated them in the empty audience section. Their applause and outpouring of love for their cherished Judy was exactly what she needed. That final night of shooting wrapped close to 3:00 a.m. Judy said her goodbyes and left exhausted but with a heartfelt smile. She was proud to have finished the season, proving the naysayers wrong.

Then, there was one more parting indignity. It came when CBS indelicately cut Judy's final episode. The electrifying farewell rendition of the emotional Tin Pan Alley ballad *By Myself* that she'd worked on into the wee hours of that last night never made it to air. The stated reason was that it was "too dark." Apparently no public display of sadness or even ambivalence could be tolerated, not even in the closing number of a series finale.

A performance of a tune from a previous episode that ran close to the needed time was clumsily plopped into the show. That final edit added to the legacy of hatred for CBS president Jim Aubrey, as he once again reinforced his repute as The Smiling Cobra. It also sparked Judy's cursing of the luxury trailer and the yellow brick road which she had joyfully accepted only a few months earlier as tokens of the network's undying appreciation. Even old friend Mel Torme turned on Judy. He filed a lawsuit for the value of the remaining number of guest appearances that were guaranteed in his contract, then wrote a book about the whole debacle. Many critics panned his tome for what they said was its unwarranted negative tone as well as his poor taste in allowing for its release in 1970, the year after Judy's death.

Even with the best of intentions and a hand outstretched with what they believe is a loving gesture, the businessmen and businesswomen of show business so often fail to successfully embrace the special species of sensitive souls known collectively as talent. Catering to the even smaller sub-set of those who have achieved stardom is such a specialized skill that NBC had a highly respected, highly regarded, and highly paid senior vice president who spent 20 years responsible for nothing more than placating talent.

Dave Tebet had an incredible knack for keeping celebrities happy. It wasn't a measure of NBC's respect for its headliners as much as it was an investment in keeping them motivated to put forth their best efforts while manufacturing entertainment on the video assembly line. Tebet played a vital role in the network's relationships, rallying team spirit among top-line stars like George Burns, Johnny Carson, Angie Dickinson and Bob Hope, as well as the up-and-comers. That included the early casts of *Saturday Night Live*.

In 1974 Don Rickles dropped his insult act long enough to tell an assemblage of NBC affiliates, "Dave Tebet is a guy who every actor has admired and loved… the kind of guy who takes you in his arms and says, 'Hey. Win, lose, or draw I'm your friend.' And when you fail he sends you a gift. That's unusual. And I tell you David Tebet, you're a beautiful man."

With incredible charm and diplomacy, Tebet could massage celebrity egos, cool stars' rivalries, solve performers' financial challenges, occasionally fix minor legal problems and, in at least one instance, have a Mafia hit called off. His tools included a seemingly limitless expense account for luxury dinners and gifts, as well as the ready cash needed for solving all manner of inconveniences. Talk about living large, when in L.A. the guy resided in a suite at the swanky Beverly Hills Hotel, taking meetings and treating VIPs to meals at the famous Polo Lounge. As big-budgeted as his activities sometimes were, Tebet's work was considered vital to the network's success.

In the late 1950s and early 1960s Tebet had a favorite extravagance that he generously lavished on performers, their families, and their friends. It was the brand-new large-screen-for-the-time color TVs when color was first being introduced. They were especially favored gifts when the new sets were temporarily hard to get due to high demand. NBC's parent company, RCA, cranked them out day and night on conveyer belts from which its VP of talent could pluck a seemingly unlimited supply. Tebet's treasured talent was tranquilizing troubled troupers.

Chapter 20

Phil Rosenthal, co-creator and showrunner of the mega-successful *Everybody Loves Raymond*, unabashedly admits to being a member of the generation raised and deeply impacted by the alternative reality of family life portrayed on sitcoms like *The Brady Bunch*. He confessed in 2021, "It was this beautiful gentile world of niceness. I dreamed of that life." Indeed, the dozens of series that projected a romanticized version of the all-American nuclear family were profoundly impacting for those who grew up in the era when they were the mainstay of the networks' primetime schedules.

Adding to the mid-century ubiquitous host Art Linkletter's reminder that kids say the darndest things, they also do the darndest things as they put the "com" in America's beloved vintage sitcoms. One or two, or sometimes eight is enough to contribute both the comedic shtick and heart-touching moments. Impossibly cute and precocious children have always been key in crafting plots of puerile playfulness and parental pathos. That's despite the fact we've known for decades that for some of those kids, off-screen life was nothing to laugh at.

Likewise, their idealized television mothers, virtuous as they may appear, have their own lesser-known angst-filled moments triggered by Tinseltown trepidation. Take the otherwise gracious former farm girl Donna Reed who played Jimmy Stewart's empathetic wife in the Christmas classic, *It's a Wonderful Life*. She enjoyed an eight-year run as Donna Stone on ABC's *The Donna Reed Show*, where her character was envisioned as such a superlative homemaker that the network actually considered titling the series *Mother Knows Better* to trump the long-running classic *Father Knows Best*.

Donna was a World War II pinup who graciously danced with hundreds of servicemen at the Hollywood Canteen years before television presented her as a charming and benevolent domesticated mom. In reality, Donna focused a heap of hidden wrath on the industry with ferocity that belied her on-screen image. The actress returned to primetime TV in 1984 portraying the mother of J.R. Ewing on CBS's *Dallas*. It was her first significant television opportunity in about twenty years, and instead of being embraced by audiences as she had been during the run of her eponymous sitcom, viewers mostly yawned at her work on the Southfork Ranch. That's why Donna disappeared from the Ewing estate. At least that was the story.

Hollywood insiders speak of a different reality in which Donna was sent packing from *Dallas* for what apparently was no other reason than star Larry Hagman's reluctance to have a bigger name on the show. As both an Academy Award winner and the beloved prototypical TV mom audiences grew up with, Donna Reed was a double-threat to the series' lead actor when it came to the public's and the press's adoration. Similarly, her presence refocused attention around the set. With Donna's status as both a big and small screen star, many on the cast and crew saw her as royalty. Larry was not happy to have his dominance eclipsed. So, between the two, the lead character J.R. and the supporting role of J.R.'s mom, who do you think prevailed?

When his characterization of J.R. Ewing became a breakout fan favorite and the key ingredient in the big-budget highly-profitable international sensation, it gave Larry the leverage to have his mercurial whims indulged, his misbehavior tolerated, and grandiose demands catered to. As big as Larry portrayed J.R.'s ego, his was apparently even larger and it was being fully coddled. As it was said most cunningly back in the day, "He has trouble getting that ten-gallon hat on his eleven-gallon swelled head."

Those are reports from the *Dallas* set, and they echo much of the dysfunction that *I Dream of Jeannie* co-star Barbara Eden attributes to Larry's behavior from an earlier decade. In all fairness however, they should be taken in the context of friends' stories of Larry's kindness and generosity when away from the cameras. They include a well-known ABC newsman who sings the actor's praises as a big supporter of his son's private school. Another defender is one of Hollywood's premier production designers whose life Larry changed when he offered to sponsor his visa so that he could work in the United States.

So, Donna Reed was written out of the show after a single season. Her predecessor, Barbara Bel Geddes, who had retired after undergoing heart surgery, was lured back to return in the role for the following fall. Despite the veteran's thorough understanding of how the industry works, Donna was hurt by being cast aside through no fault of her own. So, following her discourteous farewell you could say that Donna became a prima donna.

In 1985, the year TV's now-infamous Les Moonves joined the *Dallas* production company, Lorimar Television, Donna filed a $7.5 million breach-of-contract lawsuit. She sought a court order that would immediately stop production of any *Dallas* scenes that included her character. Her lawyer said the Oscar-winning star "has certain principles and class. . . . She intends to stand on them." Don't be shocked, but this girl-next-door actress already knew how to play hardball. Thirty years earlier Donna sued Universal for relegating her to "B" movies.

Class and principles notwithstanding, Lorimar was fully prepared to continue paying her weekly $17,250 salary for the next two years, per the terms of her 1984 three-year deal. However, Donna claimed that her exposure on *Dallas* was worth far more than the wages. She was described as "mad as hell," and her venomous retaliation over being written out ultimately yielded an out-of-court settlement reported to be over $1 million. If you believe that festering anger, indignation, and unchecked all-consuming outrage take a toll on the body and soul you won't be shocked to hear that Donna was dead just a few months after her $1 million-plus payoff. Healthy enough to pass the insurance physical the previous year when she started work on *Dallas*, tragically she was dead from cancer on January 14, 1986, at age 64.

Another TV mom was an Oscar winner in motion pictures and a bona fide Broadway star. Of course Shirley Jones will always be most beloved by TV fans as matriarch of *The Partridge Family*. For the uninitiated, Shirley played the mother of her real-life stepson, David Cassidy, lead singer and teen idol in the sitcom that was based on a real singing family, the Cowsills. It's so Hollywood that the real Cowsills were considered for the roles of playing themselves but were deemed to not be "right" for the parts. How more "right" do you have to be when the character is you?

The telegenic Cowsills accept a gold record award for their debut 1967 hit *The Rain, the Park and Other Things*. There was too much real-life dysfunction among the Cowsills, but the idea of a singing family was irresistible for television.

When the Cowsills smashed onto the scene in 1967 with their first record, the instant million-seller *The Rain, the Park & Other Things*, Columbia-Screen Gems executives fell in love with the youngest of the clan, Susan. While they felt she had the potential to be a breakout star, two of the brothers were judged to lack much personality. After watching their performance, one of the producing team observed the boys "stood there like stick figures." The widely disseminated cover story was that the Cowsill kids were a bit too old for the kind of naive nonsensical nuttiness that was to be written for the youngest members of the family sitcom. It's a questionable claim as young Susan Cowsill was 11 years old when *The Partridge Family* debuted. The kid who scored one of the brother roles, Danny Bonaduce, apparently wasn't deemed to be too old. In fact, he was the same age, born just three months after Susan. Of course, he remembers hearing the true story.

Danny remembers that Papa Cowsill was at the center of the extreme dysfunction that made him, and thus his family, *personae non grata*. Let's start with William Joseph "Bud" Cowsill, Sr. disapproving of the plan to have a name star play Mama Cowsill, insisting that the non-actress Cowsill matriarch, Barbara, carry the lead role. That would be a deal breaker on its own. Never mind a film camera, Mrs. Cowsill was so nervous in front of a microphone during the recording session for The Rain, The Park, and Other Things that she couldn't deliver her background harmonies without son Bob standing and singing with her. Her family revealed that in live performances her timing was so off that she regularly came in a beat or two late with her parts. As Barry Cowsill recently reflected about the unrealistic expectations placed on her, "Mom was just a housewife who sang while she did the dishes."

Scratch deeper and you'll find the more damning reasons for the Cowsill clan being so thoroughly divorced from the show that they inspired. Daddy Cowsill, "Bud," was described by his own kids as "a tyrannical, sadistic, mean-hearted physically-abusive angry drunk." A gentle milking of the Cowsills for more insight suggests that those are just some of the nicer comments for a dad who the kids say brutally beat his children, whose daughter says he sexually assaulted her, and who, allegedly, regularly accosted their maternal aunts with unwelcome sexual advances. Now, doesn't that have all the makings of a delightful family sitcom?

Then there was Bud's run-in with Ed Sullivan on October 29, 1967. The industry was impressed by the group's instant meteoric blastoff after signing with MGM Records, and the host of America's great Sunday night hour of vaudeville especially loved the wholesome appeal of a singing family. He signed a 10-appearance contract for the Cowsills, rare for an act with such a short history. The guaranteed exposure was of incalculable value, but it turned ugly on their very first night. There was an audio problem. The kids were singing, but couldn't be heard until the microphone levels were corrected some 20 seconds into the performance of their big debut hit. Rather than roll with the disappointment of an unintended glitch on a live broadcast, Bud got into a screaming match with producer Bob Precht which precipitated the show dropping eight of their dates. The Cowsills returned to the Sullivan stage only once, eight weeks later on Christmas Eve.

After earlier turning down the mom role on The Brady Bunch that went to Florence Henderson, Shirley Jones signed on as the matriarch of the Cowsills-inspired *Partridge Family*. With that lock, the series was added to ABC's schedule of 1970 fall season new debuts. The cutest Partridge plot played out before the show was even in production. Shirley was present when producers were seeing prospective young actors who were finalists for the role of Keith Partridge, her eldest TV son, when in walked her real-life stepson, David Cassidy. Shirley recalled that David was about to be signed when the uncertain producers thought it best to bring them together to discuss any possible reservations either might have about working with a family member.

David had a less plausible but infinitely more entertaining version of that face-to-face with Shirley. He claims that the producers were clueless about the Jones and Cassidy acting dynasties being related. "They had no idea," David explained. "So I said, 'What are you doing here?' She looked at me and said, 'What are you doing here?' And I said, 'Well, I'm reading for the lead guy.' I said, 'What are you doing here?' She said, 'I'm the mother!'"

Jack Cassidy and Shirley Jones in 1961. The couple married five years earlier and had three sons, Shaun, Patrick, and Ryan. David Cassidy was Jack's son from a prior marriage. Crediting him as her true love, Shirley was loyal to Jack through his many infidelities and bisexual affairs.

Jack Cassidy, David's father from the actor's first marriage, was a terrifically gifted performer who perished tragically in 1976. He was burned alive in a fire he accidentally started while smoking. An afternoon during which Jack stopped his Rolls Royce at Rodeo Drive and Santa Monica Boulevard with an offer to help a college kid whose car had stalled, turned into Jack's last day of living large. A few hours later, after sampling the Beverly Hills nightlife with stops at a few bars, Jack returned home to his West Hollywood penthouse apartment.

Stretched out in the living room, Jack fell asleep that night with a lit cigarette that ignited his Naugahyde couch. His body was so badly charred that positive identification could only be made days later, after comparing dental records to his remains. During that intervening time Shirley and her sons hoped against hope that the deceased was someone else, grasping tightly to the word that Jack's car wasn't in the garage that night. The family was devastated when, finally, the identification was confirmed. No words were needed. Friend Marty Ingels' face fell after answering Shirley's phone and hearing the crushing news.

Some uber-fans point out a thread of supposed cosmic synergy. During filming of the first season of *The Partridge Family* another fire also disrupted Shirley's and David's lives. A 1970 blaze destroyed the shell of the house located on Blondie Street at the Warner Ranch in Burbank that served as the fictional Partridge home for exterior photography. The sixth episode of the series was reportedly delayed while the house was rebuilt. The blueprints provided all that was needed to match the original construction, but there were no blueprints for the landscaping. The show's loyal devotees say that the tree in the front yard magically disappears after the first five shows.

Shirley, who divorced Jack two years before his death, was the actor's second wife. Together, the couple gave birth to David's half-brothers, Shaun, Patrick, and Ryan. I met Patrick in 2016 at his mom's home. He was a teenager when Jack died, and is blessed with a striking family resemblance. Patrick shared with me that his father had been diagnosed as bipolar and had suffered secretly for decades with an assortment of psychological demons. Exacerbating Jack's anguish were jealousies. Shirley wrote in her autobiography of the fallout from *The Partridge Family*,

"The stratospheric success of the show took its toll on my marriage to Jack. His overriding sense of inferiority in the face of my success drove him into the arms of other women even more often than before."

Son David's sudden fame, sparked by the success of the sitcom, was also tough for Jack whose own career was cooling. That jealousy of his son's triumphs as a white-hot actor and arena-packing recording artist were whispered to be only part of Jack's envy. Groupies' reports published in a fan rag, combined with a quiet confirmation I gleaned from co-star Danny Bonaduce, confirmed that David was a young man well-endowed with an attribute beyond his singing and acting talents. As she had been with comedian Milton Berle, word is that Mother Nature was unusually generous. Supposedly this Freudian factor somehow also played into Jack's neuroses.

Talented, sweet, and delightful as Shirley Jones is, Patrick volunteered that his mother had her own personality quirks. He said the beloved actress, this charming dear woman, had a long history of being attracted to men suffering with emotional issues. Three years after divorcing Jack Cassidy in 1974, she married comedian and actor Marty Ingels whom she'd first met at a party at actor Michael Landon's home. Dear Marty was one of Hollywood's best-known and most troubled geniuses of our times. Despite his challenges the man was often brilliant on and off stage, capable of being charismatic beyond all measure. He was quick-witted and seemingly able to sell anything to anybody. He and Shirley were a devoted couple that shared nearly 40 years together before Marty's death.

Marty said that his first break in show business came while he was in the Army. On leave visiting New York City, he got in line to be in the audience of *Name That Tune*. In uniform, handsome, and with his reddish hair, Marty was spotted by a contestant coordinator who was scanning the line for potential players. After a quick interview, he competed on the next episode where the young soldier remembered decades later that he clowned his way to $6,000 in winnings.

Marty had proven himself a capable stage actor, and after release from the service looked to start a career working in television or film. Like millions before him who have knocked on Hollywood's doors, he found he couldn't even get past the guards at the studio gates. The massive, seemingly impenetrable barrier that protects professionals from interlopers and dilettantes is purposely foreboding. However, those with the tenacity to have succeeded usually reflect back on that obstacle as merely a minor inconvenience.

Marty couldn't score much more than one or two tiny bit parts a year on various TV series. He was in Hollywood, but not for long. He had a plane ticket and was prepared to return home in defeat. He said, "On what was to be my last day in California I tried to get into Paramount Studios, but the guard turned me away. So I went across the street to a restaurant and ordered 12 coffees to go. I paid a waiter to wear his apron and walked back across the street and into the studio carrying the coffees on a tray." It worked. No sane security guard would want to deprive a dozen executives in some possibly high-level meeting what appeared to be their ordered round of caffeine.

Once on the lot, Marty trashed the coffees and the apron, and went looking for Jerry Lewis's office. He sweet-talked secretary Rita Dillon into buzzing Jerry. They met, they talked, they joked, and Jerry gave him a break. That era's box office comedy king took Marty to a sound stage and started rolling film for an instant screen test. Marty went home, sent flowers to the secretary, and went to bed. At three in the morning, after the film was developed and previewed, Jerry called Marty and told him to come right over to his house. They talked through the rest of the night and, by sunrise, Marty was suddenly in big-time showbiz as Jerry's protégé.

It started with a bit part in 1961's *The Ladies Man*; eight weeks guaranteed at $1,000 a week. Marty took ads in the trade papers, got glossy headshots, and began a campaign of shameless self-promotion. There was only one problem. Jerry called, "That's a wrap!" without ever shooting a single frame of his new discovery. When Marty asked about his anticipated role, Jerry told him to wait while he huddled with writer Bill Richmond. They returned with a bit in which Marty is in a fictitious TV commercial for shaving cream and, in pure Jerry Lewis slapstick, the aerosol can endlessly shoots foam until Marty is fully obscured, over his head in lather. Mel Brooks might have been able to come up with something more creative on short notice, but he earlier resigned from his deal to contribute to the film over creative differences with Jerry.

At the movie's premiere Marty anxiously waited for his scene only to find it never made it into the final cut. His opinion of Jerry flipped an instant 180 and, as quickly as they had come together, they were estranged. He kept the bragging rights to calling himself "Jerry's protégé" and never bothered to tell anyone he actually wasn't in *The Ladies Man*. With sufficient talent and charm to back up his bravado, Marty exploited the gig that never was into a thriving new career. Within months he was co-starring with John Astin in an outrageously funny and critically-acclaimed 1962 sitcom. Although created by the mind behind *Sgt. Bilko*, *The Honeymooners*, and *Get Smart*, super-scribe Leonard Stern, the 32 episodes of *I'm Dickens, He's Fenster*–a comic feast–was starved for viewers, canceled, and now all but forgotten.

Marty Ingles (left) co-starred with John Astin, seen here flanking Emmaline Henry, in 32 episodes of the ABC sitcom *I'm Dickens, He's Fenster* (1962). Marty's extensive resume also included guest roles on over 50 other television series and nearly two dozen movies.

Eventually Hollywood learned of Marty's deep, dark, embarrassing secret. He was the victim of a cluster of psychological quirks capable of sabotaging his ability to perform. The whispered conjecture about his bouts with agoraphobia and depression were confirmed when he suffered a massive anxiety attack for all of America to see on no less public a venue than *The Tonight Show*. The gossip mill has grossly distorted the story over the years to include versions in which Marty is guilty of all manner of offensiveness.

Marty's own account is that he performed his standup spot and chatted with Johnny Carson without incident. Then he was hit with a growing sense of anxiety that quickly escalated to become what he called a devastating nervous breakdown. While on the couch listening to Johnny's next guest, Marty said his hand started to tingle and shake, and the sensation then spread through his body. "At first I thought the audience wouldn't notice, but I was quivering… they thought I was doing a shtick… I thought I was having a stroke."

Anxious to get off the set before literally dying on national TV, Marty stood, made a joke about going to use Johnny's john, and started to make a quick exit. He remembered, "I staggered to the curtain, held on just long enough to spin around and fall to the floor backstage." Marty refused any medical treatment despite the fact that Saint Joseph Medical Center is just a block up the street from NBC and has had many unexpected visitors rushed from the studios over the years. Marty could only think about getting home as quickly as possible. According to the story at the studio, two stagehands drove him, carried him into bed, and left. "I went home and spent several months in my house and became a very serious recluse," Marty said. "I went through many years of terrible anxiety."

Patrick shared that at the root of his stepdad's many battles was late-diagnosed manic depression. Now known as bipolar disorder, the condition manifested with disabling fear and dark insecurity. It ripped apart the family on several occasions, including during a period that Marty called his "years of anxiety" when he moved out of the brood's Encino home into a tiny apartment. Patrick remembers that he had no idea where his stepfather had gone.

It was as if Marty had fallen off the planet, until a neighbor notified police of the stench emanating from his tiny flat. Poor Marty was found where he had apparently been for as long as several weeks, lying on a filthy living room floor, semi-conscious amid piles of animal waste. The masses of his un-walked dog's excrement were the only way to estimate how long this bout with debilitating depression and agoraphobia lasted.

Once stabilized on psychotropic medication, Marty worked when he could. He booked guest roles on dozens of series including *Bewitched, The Dick Van Dyke Show, ER*, and even a *CSI* episode. Marty carved a niche in animation and commercial voiceovers and, at other times, was successful getting other actors cast. Several big name performers signed on after he started a talent agency that exploited a very specific niche, representing star clients for advertising endorsements. In addition to brokering deals for Orson Welles, Howard Cosell, Don Knotts, and Farrah Fawcett Majors, it was Marty who put actress June Allyson in Depends… commercials, that is. Then, pissed off with the belief that June had stiffed him on the diaper deal, Marty pleaded no contest to charges that he made annoying collection calls to the actress.

Marty knew his reputation kept him from booking more work. He told author Kliph Nesterhoff, "If you ask people about Marty Ingels they're going to either say 'difficult' or 'insane' or 'unpredictable.' But I tell you, I don't drink, I don't smoke, I'm not a drug person, I don't grope four year olds and I don't have girls stashed in hotel rooms. I'm a solid guy."

The happier ending for Marty was the progress he made in later years. His internal demons were in check and the family was reunited. The once-warm later-torn relationships were repaired. In the final months before Marty passed away in 2015, there was a triumph of love over bruised feelings. Shirley summed up their roller coaster partnership saying, "He often drove me crazy, but there's not a day I won't miss him and love him to my core." If there's a correlation between the heights of one's talent and the depths of one's despair, Marty may well have been its purest personification.

There's no disrespect intended conjecturing about the relationship between performers and their tenuous connection with sanity. It's been a topic of discussion so often and for so long that it's become a cliché. Yet there were decades during which the lifeline of medical benefits that working performers relied upon from AFTRA's health and retirement funds didn't include much coverage for mental health. Woefully inadequate, the help available wasn't near to any parity with the benefits for physical ailments.

While not funny at the time—and still not today—a friend of mine now jokes about a moment in March of 1986 when he called the union's health and retirement office from the locked psychiatric ward at Northridge Hospital. He was inquiring about coverage for his sanatorium stay and remembered how the despair that brought him to the psych ward suddenly deepened dramatically. He was told that in-patient benefits for mental health treatment were negligible. During a lengthy questioning of the AFTRA rep trying to explore how that was possible, he swears the lady ultimately said something like, "Mental health coverage for actors? We'd go broke! You're all fucking nuts!"

Chapter 21

Performers and their tenuous connection with sanity. Academy Award-winning director, producer, actor, and writer Sydney Pollack once jotted a few sentences that are on point:

"Talent has a destructive side to it. I mean, TALENT comes from trouble. . . I've said this before and it's the truth. There is no such thing as a non-neurotic talented person…. It's ALL about dissatisfaction otherwise you wouldn't do it. Otherwise why don't just go live your life? What's the big deal? . . . I've seen a lot of careers end in total self-destruction, I've seen great actors who's (sic) careers ended nowhere. It's not a one way street being talented. . . it's. . . got a (sic) up side and a down side. . . and you have to try and get a hold of the up side."

Pollack was too respected a filmmaker and has worked with too many A-listers for me to refute his opinion, or even correct his grammar. Veteran comedian Robert Klein sums up the dilemma, noting that virtually every comic has had intimate relationships with two familiar partners. "Anxiety and depression are the yin to the yang of comedy," Klein says. With the benefit of age and experience Bob Newhart explained, "For some reason, comedians are still children. The social skills somehow never reach us."

Will Smith was quite articulate in 2022 in talking about the mindset needed to beat the odds in building a successful career. Conveniently, he made no mention of the slap heard around the world that he landed on comedian Chris Rock during that year's live Oscar broadcast. He pontificated, "There has to be a little crazy because you have to believe something that there's no evidence for, and then you have to devote your life to something that is not only invisible, but highly unlikely and potentially impossible. But you believe it wholeheartedly because you can't achieve it if you don't believe it wholeheartedly. So yeah, there's a sliding scale of naiveté to full insanity, and somewhere in there is the sweet spot for dream manifestation."

Actor and stand-up Tony Williams sees himself and his comedy brethren as "neurotic, depressed, cynical types who find it difficult to function in the mainstream… We often have narcissistic or even solipsistic personalities; demanding approval from total strangers on a nightly basis." He acknowledges, "Comedians and depression go together like light and darkness and those vicissitudes can't be avoided." Then there's Mel Brooks who told the *AARP Bulletin* in 2022, "They say comedians usually have a bad childhood, so they make up for it with laughter and love from an audience. That's nonsense!" So what does Mel credit for his comedic brilliance? "Stuffed cabbage!"

Slap recipient Chris Rock concedes, "I have my own demons and dark moods. It's weird." Maybe it carries more weight hearing it from Dave Letterman who's firm in his considered opinion that there's "a general neurosis that motivates people to go into show business." He confesses, "Comedians by and large are not fun people to hang around with. They're dejected and depressed and sullen and nasty and back-biting and jealous, and I'm right in there." That's a few things to think about the next time you're laughing at some stand-up's act.

Instead of the author's bust that's awarded with the Mark Twain Prize for American Humor perhaps the industry could better serve its comedians by handing out bottles of Zoloft. Judging by Pfizer's profits from Xanax, anxiety is not just the purview of professional funsters, there's a full-blown pandemic of angst. All the more reason to respect Shirley Jones, who stuck by the emotionally untethered Marty Ingels through nearly 40 years of funny, unfunny, and high anxiety.

A mention of TV mom Shirley often brings to mind her friend and occasional rival for roles, the late Florence Henderson. As to both being offered the role of Carol Brady mentioned earlier, these two friendly rivals' careers have crossed so many times it seems that TV casting directors considered the beloved performers interchangeable. Projecting similar public images, they're also within a few weeks of being the same age. Being so grounded in reality while also acutely aware of her image, Florence was masterful in delighting audiences by joking against type. That's not to say she's an exception to the Sydney Pollack - Robert Klein - David Letterman rule. In the early 1980s Florence was in treatment with hypnotherapist Dr. John George Kappas for depression and stage fright. Were the sessions successful? You decide. Florence and Dr. Kappas were married in 1986.

Sadly, millions of people struggle in silence and in secret with depression. The several times over the many years that I worked with Florence she was always so upbeat and seemingly at ease that it's hard to think of her ever having battled that occupational hazard. The story that best demonstrates her unflappable spirit is a doozy. It's said that Florence was taping a week of *Password* episodes while nine months pregnant. Although she was still a few days from her due date, her calendar apparently wasn't in sync with God's. Suddenly, she went into labor while playing the game. During the next break she told host Allen Ludden that her third child was apparently in the wings about to make an entrance. Florence remembered, "I said to Allen, 'Don't get nervous, but I am in the early stages of labor.'" Like every comedy skit about parturient women, it's the men who freak out. The host became flustered while the mom-to-be remained cool.

Of course the show was prepared to stop taping so that Florence could answer the call, but she was confident that she still had time. Growing up with nine brothers and sisters herself, much of the mystery and mysticism surrounding childbirth had worn thin. Florence was a trouper. Her only request was for the producers to have an ambulance standing by. She played through the rest of the five days' games as if completely undistracted. When taping was over, she calmly made her exit and rode directly to the hospital in time to greet daughter Elizabeth.

Florence Henderson cavorting with Dean Martin on the crooner's Thursday night NBC variety hour (1968).

I first met Florence around 2002 on very familiar turf, NBC in Burbank, where she'd visited countless times to appear on hits and flops, the latter including 1973's *NBC Follies*. This time the beloved trouper was in Studio 1 where she'd guested with Johnny Carson on the *Tonight Show* and played on *The Magnificent Marble Machine*, just across the hall from Studio 3 where she guested on *Hollywood Squares*. Around the corner in Studio 2 she'd taped cameos for *Laugh-In*, and in the adjacent Studio 4, decades earlier she'd sung and danced with Dean Martin on his weekly variety hour.

Clearly this lady needed no introduction, but that's exactly what I was paid to do when I presented her to the studio audience moments before taping a celebrity edition of NBC's *Weakest Link*. I went for easy laughs taking great liberty in joking about her impossibly pure image as a sitcom mom. She was a great sport. Florence also didn't rebuff my chiding her for her long reign as commercial pitchwoman for Wesson cooking oil, which included over 20 years of her singing the praises of the oil's ability to confer "Wessonality" to foods. It became a theme during that day's taping stopdowns. From her position on stage to my spot in the audience bleachers, together we pitched and volleyed suggestive alternate uses for the oil. I didn't know she always carried a few gallons in the trunk of her car just in case she ends up at a wild orgy. That's what she said, and Carol Brady would never lie.

The fresh R-rated look at TV's straight-laced matriarch of *The Brady Bunch* was a huge hit with the audience. It broke me up, as well. After the taping I took a moment to thank Florence for her good natured participation and to apologize, if necessary, for perhaps taking it all a step too far. *Au contraire*! She was happy to have been part of the fun and congratulated me on keeping the crowd entertained for the lengthy taping. In truth, she'd made it easy.

TV moms have three families—their real-life spouse and biological kids, their on-screen scion, and the sisterhood of similarly cast actresses. That takes us back to Florence's long association with Shirley Jones. When first offered the Carol Brady role that eventually went to Florence, Shirley was anxious to press pause on the travel related to her feature-film work that had taken her away from family for long stretches of location shooting. A chance to stay in L.A. with her young kids would be welcomed, but Shirley's agent and manager advised otherwise.

Her trusted advisors were resolute that TV would typecast and derail her movie career. So, Shirley shied away from the prospect of a life mothering the Brady brood. She walked away from that TV family in 1969 only to find herself as a Partridge parent the following year. The difference was in the scripts. As a Partridge, Shirley said her character would be a working mom with more to deal with than the heartbreak of an overcooked roast.

Florence was next considered to play the domesticated Carol Brady and was ambivalent about committing to the role. For one thing, she lived in New York. She also demurred from the drudgery of weekly television production, although not from the drudgery of TV motherhood. The latter is far easier as the prop department does the dishes while the stage crew vacuums and dusts. It was the long days of shooting film style that Florence was looking to avoid. Single-camera production requires a scene to be performed over and over, first for a master shot, then for coverage of each of the speaking and reacting characters. With a large cast of kids the process would be even more tedious than usual.

In addition to Florence and Shirley, the Carol Brady role was also offered to Joyce Bulifant. She remembers being "signed, sealed, and delivered" for the series saying, "I had been out for two weeks with the wardrobe people to get the right clothes for the show." Then the fates changed, "Friday night, I was trying on the costumes for the director, producer, and [creator-producer-writer] Sherwood Schwartz. I was so excited, but they had a funny expression on their faces." It seems that through all of her reluctance, Sherwood still wanted his earlier choice, Florence.

When the actress was finally convinced to sign on as a Brady, Sherwood had to break the news to Joyce. He fibbed, telling her that ABC's New York brass had made the decision. Joyce remembers having signed a seven year contract, "I didn't sue, because I figured if somebody doesn't want you, that's just the way it goes." She adds, "But I didn't pay attention to the business part of acting as much as I should have."

To the joy of the show's future fans, Sherwood indeed had ultimately succeeded in changing Florence's mind. Florence told me she didn't have second thoughts about initially turning down the sitcom gig. She was fully prepared to pass on the prospect of being a Brady, delighted with her balanced life as mother, nightclub singer, and frequent guest star on TV variety shows. After her agent, Sandy Gallin, implored her to at least talk with the producer she acquiesced.

While initially unenthused, Florence recognized that the blended family idea was admittedly timely. Sherwood explained how he'd recently read that 29 percent of marriages in 1965 included a child or children from a former marriage, opening up what he called, "a wonderful Pandora's box of new kinds of stories." Florence had no idea who Sherwood Schwartz was, but was encouraged by the fact that he'd hit a grand slam with *Gilligan's Island*, had a sparkling reputation among actors as a nurturing boss, and was respected at the networks from his decades of helping to crank out hit comedies. Their meeting was scheduled for the last possible moments before Florence needed to head to the airport for an out-of-town gig. She was booked to sing the very next day at the prestigious Shamrock Hotel showroom in Houston.

Florence headed to the Paramount lot where, within a few minutes of meeting Sherwood, production executive Doug Cramer and director John Rich, the producer, surprised her. He asked if she wouldn't mind a quick screen test—just a few brief moments from a scene in front of a camera. She said it was fine, but only if they could do it now, right now, as she was heading out of town. Without any advance arrangement for a make-up artist for the impromptu filming, Florence said she sat down in the closest manned make-up chair for somebody to quickly paint and powder her.

Giggling with the memory, she told me she found herself sitting between William Shatner and Leonard Nimoy in a seat intended for the next in line of a half-dozen alien space monsters. Florence remembered Shatner's greeting was far from welcoming: "'What is she doing in here?' It was as if I were an enemy Klingon."

Florence surprised Sherwood and director John Rich when she returned looking horrendous. It was a make-up job she described as being more fitting for a Romulan prostitute than for a suburban homemaker. Despite the false eyelashes suitable for a RuPaul protégé, and a layer of pancake thick enough to be part of a Denny's Grand Slam breakfast, Florence aced the test. Two days into her Houston booking the call came for her to film the pilot.

The venue booked Jerry Vale to cover the club dates for Florence after she promised to return, perhaps more famous from the TV gig, at the same rate for a future engagement. Florence remembered, "I did the pilot, never thinking it would sell. Then I went to Europe to film *Song of Norway*. A few months later, lo and behold, the pilot sold." While still on location in Norway, the Bradys filmed the first six episodes around her. Florence arrived back in Hollywood with long days under the lights to catch up, playing mom to children she hadn't yet met.

Sherwood Schwartz mined comedy from the growing trend towards blended families. *The Brady Bunch* brood is seen here in the episode "The Slumber Party" (1970).

At first, it was a happy bunch of newly-cast Bradys at Paramount. The kids enjoyed playing on the *Bonanza* set, and were sufficiently star struck spying *Star Trek* and *Happy Days* cast members who were on the lot during the young actors' first and last seasons, respectively. There were no major conflicts among the brood on Stage 5, but there was one bothersome quirk that only escalated as time went on.

Although Robert Reed was beloved by his TV progeny, Florence remembers her leading man as a complex guy who unintentionally brought disharmony to the set. In short, he could never adequately sublimate his classic Shakespearean training to simply accept the irrationality of the situations in situation comedy. He contemplated even the most esoteric plot points. Would an experienced maid hug a mop with the mop's head on the floor or in her face? Could a broken egg on the kitchen floor really be slippery enough to cause him to trip and fall? In the series creators' world, it was and it did. That would have been enough for most thespians.

Reed's objections and complaints to Sherwood Schwartz repeatedly fell on deaf ears as the producer was open to suggestions for rewording lines and blocking the movement within scenes, but had no intention of fooling with his formula for success. The ongoing clash frustrated both, and only served to cool their working relationship to a deep freeze by the end of the series. Sherwood's son, producer Lloyd Schwartz, remembers, "One time, when a shot ended, [Reed] looked into the camera and said, 'Sherwood, I hope you fry in hell for this!' I never had a nice conversation with him." Lloyd explains, "He wanted to be a leading man; suddenly he was a TV father with six kids."

One time when director Bruce Bilson started a conversation asking, "What are you going to do after *The Brady Bunch*?" he remembers that Reed shot back, "Penance!" Mike Lookinland, who played young Bobby, adds that Robert Reed supplied more drama than ABC's daytime soaps, "When the fireworks started, we were shuffled off to our dressing rooms or the schoolroom. But around us kids, [Reed] was great." Florence told me that her co-star often medicated his frustrations with a drink or two at lunch, occasionally returning to the set late.

Reed's issue had been expressed over the years by a number of his kindred souls—other serious performers who somehow found themselves in the low-brow worlds of sitcoms or kidvid fantasy shows. Trying to inform their characterizations using actors' classic tools of identifying motivation, objective, and conflict only illuminated the silliness of the storylines. The disconnect was their lack of understanding that the escapades of dozens of funny TV families were never intended to be much more than meaningless cotton-candy fluff entertainment, and that the real- life families that gathered in their living rooms had no expectation for the TV screen to reflect much in the way of their actual lives.

I recoil at the resistance to surrender to the realities of the business and simply hit the marks and speak the lines, knowing how many of the other 150,000-plus SAG-AFTRA members, some fully qualified, would kill for one of those life-changing gigs. Reed's frustration with nonsensical circumstances and illogical plots continued all the way to the series' final episode, which was titled *The Hair-*

Brained Scheme. Reed dismissed that show's story as crossing the line into total inanity and chose not to participate. Indeed, he's absent from the series finale.

The timeline for the case of the missing Mike Brady started mere hours before filming was to start, too late to change the script even if there was any desire to. Reed called Sherwood at home with a non-negotiable refusal to perform. The producer recalled he was shaving when the phone rang and later commented on how he wished he had a razor at the actor's throat instead of his own. The situation could have quickly escalated into an angry confrontation complete with threats of legal ramifications with any number of charges such as breach of contract or non-compliance. Instead, Sherwood simply restated and confirmed that Reed was refusing to work. He calmly wished him a restful time at home and then went on about the business of the day.

Outwardly calm once on set, Sherwood started filming the scenes that he could without his M.I.A. actor. Unable to rile his boss earlier, Reed soon showed up at the studio to watch from the sidelines. How could they be proceeding so coolly without him? Sherwood said that for a few moments he entertained the idea of having Reed escorted off the lot by security, but explained that he didn't want to expose the children to a potentially upsetting skirmish. Besides, there was a better way to make his point by simply ignoring Reed, having him remain as a spectator. Sherwood shot around his male lead, first the scenes he wasn't in and then the scenes he was in, just skipping over Reed's lines. It would no doubt make Reed crazy. Well, as he's already an actor let's say crazier.

The crafty producer then started subtly circulating the observation that as Reed had chosen not to perform, the production was saving the cost of his salary without damaging the integrity of the episode. With a little more of his clever guile, some amateur psychology, and an intentionally overheard whisper about Reed's forfeited pay as well as lost rerun residuals, the producer soon had the actor back on the set. Right then and there Sherwood took Florence aside and told her, in confidence, that he'd just made a decision that would change the course of *The Brady Bunch*. If the show returned for a sixth season it would definitely be without Mike Brady. He was done dealing with Reed.

A divorce would leave the door open for possibly having to work with the actor again, so Sherwood decided then and there that he'd have to kill the character. Besides, it would be far more fun and cathartic to ponder the many ways that he could assassinate his nemesis. In a sixth season poor Carol Brady would face new challenges as a widow. That twist might have actually breathed new life into a show getting long in the tooth with the same old trials and smiles. Instead, season five finished with a total of 117 episodes, enough for a profitable sale into the world of syndicated reruns. Mike Brady was reprieved from death row.

When Sherwood Schwartz cast *The Brady Bunch* he had no idea, nor did he care about Reed's sexuality. However, it took no longer than the filming of Mr. and Mrs. Brady's very first kiss for Robert Reed to out himself. After the first take of the scene, Florence remembered she strolled over to Sherwood and asked if he knew that he had cast a gay actor to play the father. How could she be so sure? Florence told her boss, "Are you kidding? I've kissed a whole lot of guys in my life. Believe me, I know!"

As a deeply closeted gay man on a family-friendly show in that unaccepting era, Reed was understandably hypersensitive about appearing natural in the clinches. Florence told me how his anxiety would peak every time the script called for a fleeting moment of romance between Mr. and Mrs. Brady. She claimed on one occasion to be able to see Reed's pounding heart right through his pajama top.

Reed's sexuality was a non-issue on the set. Far more empathetic than any unspoken judgment, Florence said there was true compassion for the actor's need to live a double life. For her, it came with the understanding of how that burden may have contributed to his moodiness and anger. The show avoided scandal as Reed easily passed for straight and there were few outings by the mainstream press in those days, but it could have been an entirely different story. Remember, this was a full decade before ABC's *Soap* created sizeable controversy with a gay supporting character portrayed by Billy Crystal. His Jodie Dallas wasn't a lead, wasn't a father, and was a role played completely for laughs.

It all seems quaint and much ado about nothing, considering the number of LGBTQ characters and actors on the current crop of sitcoms, dramas, and soaps, as well as behind the desks on cable news channels. In recent TV seasons many new shows have gone out of their way to include at least one queer character and/or actor. It's in fashion and likely to stay so, at least for as long as diversity is celebrated. In that sense Robert Reed was way ahead of his time. So many years after his sexuality became known and the world further evolved, Reed is remembered fondly by the members of his TV family, as well as fans of the beloved *Brady Bunch*.

Would the audience have the same adoration for another actor in the Mike Brady role? After Jeffrey Hunter headed the *Star Trek* crew in that series' unsold first pilot, he lobbied to head the Brady crew. It was no sale. Before Reed, Sherwood ran into trouble trying to book his first choice. In his book *Brady, Brady, Brady* he recalled how the studio's research usurped his creativity. They nixed the program creator's choice of a decidedly more macho up-and-coming actor familiar to viewers from a wealth of guest roles on all manner of series. "There were a number of men I wanted to interview, including Gene Hackman." Sherwood wrote, "Paramount wouldn't even okay Gene Hackman for an interview because he had a very low TVQ." Ironically, the year after *The Brady Bunch* debuted Hackman won the Academy Award for Best Actor in *The French Connection* and his career flourished. So much for the reliability of subjective research.

The TVQ 1-to-100 scoring of a celebrity's familiarity and appeal has always been far from a dependable predictor of future popularity. However, networks and studios have treated it at times like the Holy Grail. To this day they continue to pay big money to Marketing Evaluations, Inc. for the continually-updated Q research results, despite the fact that they're based on what is, to my mind, arguably questionable methodology and flawed logic. The score is computed simply by taking the percentage of a national sample that considers a person, program, or product to be one of their favorites. That number is divided by the percentage of respondents in the sample who are at least familiar with the entity being evaluated. Drop the decimal point, and the quotient is the "Q" in Q-Score.

A celebrity, a TV show, or a laundry detergent can only score as familiar and a potential favorite if he, she, or it has already been at least seen by the public.

It would be difficult to find a performer with breakout potential or introduce any person or thing that's cutting edge, mold-breaking or even simply different if it first had to be sampled and scored. An unknown actor will remain forever unknown until and unless somebody casts them in spite of their non-existent TVQ. Casting and marketing seem to be arts at least as much as they are sciences, more right brain than a simple arithmetical calculation.

A couple of last nuggets from the vault of vaunted Brady trivia are just plain strange. Believe it or not, there was one *Brady Bunch* episode with a nude scene—of sorts. There, at the Brady's fictional address, 4222 Clinton Way, in the season four episode *Goodbye, Alice, Hello*, Bobby and Cindy announce that they are going swimming. Cindy says, "The new people at the corner invited us over." When Alice decides to check which bathing suit Bobby is wearing, she opens his robe and discovers that he is as naked as the day he was born.

Cindy is also in her birthday suit! What the hell? Alice, never at a loss for a snappy rejoinder, says, "Who moved in over there, Adam and Eve?" and she puts the kibosh on the swim date. The scene apparently did little to advance any meaningful plot point, as after having been edited out from the episode for reruns the cut has been neither noticeable nor well known. Which leaves us questioning what the hell were Sherwood and the credited writer, veteran Milt Rosen, thinking in the first place? Sherwood's son Lloyd acknowledges it was simply for the laugh from Alice's reaction.

I was impressed by Florence Henderson's dedication. "We believed every word we said, and I don't think you can parody something unless it has been done incredibly truthfully." To that end she recounted the time two young extras were in a scene playing friends of daughter Marcia. Hired as extras, they couldn't speak without being given a boost in pay. That would also end up costing even more money as they would then be subject to receiving residuals with each rerun. Florence told the director, "This is stupid. Kids don't come into your house and not say anything. They would go, 'Hi, Mrs. Brady,' or whatever." When the suggestion of giving the kids lines was courteously declined Florence said, "That's it. Stop." She remembered, "So seldom did I ever raise my voice... I went to the phone and called Sherwood. I said, 'This is absolutely stupid. Let the kids say hi to me and let them act like normal kids. I'll pay for it. I don't want to be in a scene that is so totally unbelievable.' So they let the kids speak, and they paid for it."

By the time the Brady brood went their separate ways, the real life Marcia and Greg Brady, Barry Williams and Maureen McCormick, had secretly celebrated their newfound puberty. Barry had also smoked his fair share of pot. "I thought it would be fun to recreate my character by spicing it up and being off-the-wall." He remembers, "When I got on set and the director said, 'Action!' I went into a deep state of paranoia and froze. I tripped over a bike and pretended I hadn't. I started the first couple of takes by ad-libbing." Nobody commented, he recalls, "They knew. We did the scene again with the straightest performance I could muster."

All good things come to an end, and the Hollywood reality set in quickly for Barry after getting word on a Friday that the show had wrapped. "On Monday I went to the studio to get my things. The same guard that was there for the last five years told me I had to park in the extras' lot. The parking space that had had my name on it on Friday had already been painted over with somebody else's name."

The clan's small-screen portrayals were captured on 35-millimeter film which has served as a catalyst for eternal stardom. *Brady* repeats are in the air, penetrating the atmosphere, bouncing off the ionosphere, and beaming through space, the final frontier, for eternity. Belying her age in Earth years, Florence remained a working pro into her 80s, popular with both the public and within the industry until her death on Thanksgiving Day, 2016.

Nothing will change my high opinion, but there's one detractor who is adamant that I "Take the halo off of Flo's head." That comes from a guy I don't know, but who claims to be Florence's oldest grandson and has heard me talk about this and other sitcoms. He speaks of family turmoil that resulted in the actress's youngest daughter being forced out of college because Florence stopped paying tuition and withdrew her support at the insistence of her second husband. If there's any truth to any part of that story, and if that's the extent of the familial disharmony, I'd say Florence balanced her career and family responsibilities better than most.

In public and backstage, Florence was still as spry and effervescent as ever until the end. The Television Academy held a well-attended star-studded memorial, a testimonial to far more than her acting ability. Florence's story was different from the plight of most senior actresses for whom leading roles were distant memories. Like Betty White's resurgent popularity as a nonagenarian, Florence's advancing years were being increasingly embraced and celebrated right up to the end.

It was while working with the TV Academy that I feel as though I really got to know Florence quite well. We spent the better part of a day together at the 2015 Daytime Emmy Creative Arts Awards. It was the last time I saw her, and I treasure the memory of those hours in her company just a year before she passed. She and Alex Trebek were co-hosts, I was announcing, and we all shared the same dressing suite. We talked about anything and everything while together in our shared digs. Alex waxed nostalgic about his first hosting job, a 1966 Canadian high school competition called *Reach for the Top*, and mentioned how his hiring by Merv Griffin came with an assist by Lucille Ball.

Alex Trebek and Florence Henderson, hosts at the 2015 Daytime Emmy Creative Arts Awards. Two irreplaceable giant television talents.

Likewise, Florence reflected on her early gigs. I never knew that long before Joan Rivers, Florence was the first female substitute host in the history of *The Tonight Show*. Although nobody would know better than she, I still doubled-checked and of course it was true. She was among a number of rotating emcees in 1962, during the period between Jack Paar's departure and Johnny Carson's arrival. Florence also remembered back to 1959 and her first network TV role. It was one also enjoyed briefly by Lee Meriwether, Betsy Palmer, Maureen O'Sullivan and Barbara Walters.

While establishing herself on Broadway, Florence served as a "*Today* Girl," presenting soft news, interviews, weather, and features while sharing adlibs with host Dave Garroway on NBC's *Today Show*. Credit later anchor Hugh Downs for championing Walters' advancement from that subordinate role to full-fledged *Today* co-anchor. As Florence's career goals were more in the realm of entertainment than news, she created opportunities to sing for the show's morning audience. More importantly, she used her hours on *Today* to master the new art of radiating charisma and interpersonal warmth while playing only to impersonal cold hardware.

Some of what Florence saw on the *Today* set blows away the sober and respectable image that NBC crafted for their morning eye-opener.

Florence Henderson found her earliest opportunities on the Broadway stage. It was only a short walk to 6th Avenue and NBC's *Today Show* studios to report on fashion and features for the female audience as a "Today Girl."

Chapter 22

I couldn't resist the urge to ask Florence Henderson about the dichotomy between *Today* host Dave Garroway's on-air lightheartedness and his otherwise increasingly morose existence. There was so much going on off-camera that revealed far more than viewers could imagine. In his public persona Garroway was an incredibly gifted conversationalist with a well-developed talent for projecting warmth, intimacy, and sincerity. "I have never seen anyone in this business who could communicate the way he could," Barbara Walters told *The New York Times*. "He could look at the camera and make you feel that he was talking only with you." Although it appeared to come effortlessly, it was a studied talent.

Before television was wired as a national service, it was dominated by each city's local programs. Garroway left New York for the Midwest in order to break into the new medium. There, on both radio and TV, he came to epitomize the understated, relaxed, more personable presence and delivery that was called the "Chicago Style." Garroway's calm, soft-spoken conversational presentation could wear well for even a long two-hour daily broadcast, one designed to gently ease people into the new day, and that was a consideration in his selection to be the inaugural host of the first national morning broadcast.

The show's creator, Pat Weaver, explained that he wanted someone with sufficient gravitas to handle hard news stories but could also bring humor to the morning audience. Garroway proved to be a true wit. *The Today Show* pioneered as a risky investment in a day part where it was believed nobody would watch. Typically, at those hours folks were dressing and rushing through morning activities with the sole focus of getting out the door and off to work or school. It was then inconceivable to predict the experiment would mature to generate ad revenues that *Variety* tallied for the original first two hours during 2016 at a cool $508.8 million.

I knew from Gene Rayburn and other NBC alumni that Garroway self-medicated his depression with his own cocktails of opiates, amphetamines, and assorted mood enhancers. It was no secret to anyone who was on that *Today* set, as the host was taking flagrant and frequent swigs from a flask throughout the show. Garroway's mixture of liquid Dexedrine and assorted other ingredients, "The Doctor" as he called it, was never too far out of camera range. Barbara Walters joined the show during Garroway's waning days and she also clearly remembered seeing his regular sips of a liquid she described as helping to "pep him up."

Florence Henderson added an element to the story I'd not heard before. In addition to "The Doctor," she said that Garroway would occasionally reach into a small black leather case to retrieve a red or a blue pill. When she asked about the stash, she remembered Garroway answering, "These pep me up, and these calm me down, and I take them together." Mood altering meds may have been especially important to Garroway as TV's first morning host would occasionally stay awake for two or three days at a stretch, engaged in some activity such as working on his car. Another insight from Florence was a shocker. In order to accommodate the host's increasing difficulty waking at 4:30 a.m. to get to the studio and prepare for the 7:00 a.m. live broadcast, *The Today Show* secretly became "The Afternoon Before Show."

Most of *Today* was being recorded in advance, the previous day. Garroway's ratings had made him America's number-one morning man, too valuable and established to be replaced despite the fact that his condition was deteriorating. The temporary fix was to tape the show at a time when its host could function. Among other sources who tell the tale, Florence included that revelation in her book, *Life is Not a Stage*. She wrote, "The viewers at home had no idea. The news readers, either Frank Blair or Jack Lescoulie, were the only ones live, arriving at the crack of dawn, to insert the latest news and weather." Amazingly, that trick was used another time even more secretively, years later at ABC.

Fred Silverman told *The Hollywood Reporter* that he designed *Good Morning America* with a significant focus on pop culture to fill a specific niche, "If you think of the *Today Show* at that point as *The New York Times*, think of *Good*

Morning America as the *Daily News.*" He cast David Hartman and Nancy Dussault to inaugurate ABC's big challenge to NBC's supremacy, but as the November 3rd, 1975 debut approached, Fred was heard lamenting that he had it all riding on "two actors who have no broadcasting experience." His secret solution was to have the first shows taped in advance at 3:30 in the morning. It was all in the can, sanitized with blunders removed, safe and secure before the 7 a.m. broadcast with the exception of timed windows for news breaks to be added live. Although Fred had a full slate of trustworthy pros producing those premiere episodes, he was apparently too anxious to sleep. He lived within walking distance, and network techs say they remember that Fred could be found at the West 66th Street studio in the middle of the night wearing his pajamas, slippers, and bathrobe after removing his winter overcoat.

It took approximately two weeks before Hartman and Dussault were sufficiently in the groove to take *Good Morning America* live. I have no idea how many months of NBC's *Today* shows were covertly pre-taped between an unknown date in 1958 and July 17, 1961, when live broadcasting resumed after Garroway was gone. That's when sidekick Jack Lescoulie, spoiled by the luxury of afternoon tapings, quit the show saying, "I can't face those hours anymore." Hugh Downs became the new morning face of NBC.

The one time I met Downs I asked about how he dealt with the extra-early morning daily ritual, and whether it had become habit to hear the alarm go off when the world was still dark. He said that in the nine years he fronted *Today*, "There wasn't a single morning that it didn't feel like I was waking up in the middle of the night." He shook his head gently, adding, "It never got easier." Just the same, Hugh still had it easier than his predecessor, at least he didn't have to work with a chimp.

Garroway's show reflected the capriciousness of its drug-addled host as well as another challenge. The presence of J. Fred Muggs, his chimpanzee co-host, added another wild card of unpredictability. The 10-month-old simian was brought on as a one-time guest on January 28, 1953, and a week later became an integral part of the program, designed to get kids to start a new habit of turning on the family

TV in the morning. It worked. Muggs' presence continued for four years, even after the chimp reached puberty and his behavior regularly stopped resembling anything close to cute or fun. Muggs eventually took to urinating on the set and drawing blood from Garroway's hands when he began biting the host as well as some guests. He even dug his teeth into *Today* girl Lee Meriwether when he didn't recognize her beneath a Halloween costume. Covering those unpredictable awkward moments often led to the use of the phrase, "More fun than a barrel of monkeys." Then, one morning Garroway arranged for an actual barrel to be on-set.

Sorry PETA but, yes, Florence remembered the wooden keg was stuffed full of live monkeys. As Garroway began to lift the lid there was pure pandemonium. The animals bounded out of the barrel to make the most of the sudden chance at freedom. Once loose, the hyperkinetic chimps went berserk. Instantly, they were climbing into the lighting grid, swinging from the cables, knocking over the scenery, and smashing the props. Florence described what happened next with an air of dignity few could match: "The set became one big monkey toilet, littered in crap."

It was a literal shitstorm, and Florence said she climbed up onto a desk to avoid being in the worst of the crossfire. It was live TV and the show continued with the monkeys still bounding, jumping, running, and shitting until, one by one, a few could be wrangled. Can you imagine what that must have looked like? What did viewers think? How did the pompous network chief David Sarnoff react? Florence's last word on the monkeys was, "They were still up in the rafters when I left. Sadly, I was told later that they had to shoot them to get them down. I hoped that wasn't true."

The backstage Emmy-night storytelling with Florence Henderson and Alex Trebek ended when it came time to don the tuxedos and gown. As we were dressing I asked Florence, "How's your maternal instinct?" She didn't hesitate in responding, "Strong!" I said, "Perfect!" TV's Mrs. Brady was kind enough to help with my tricky cufflinks and shirt studs. For a fleeting moment, I was a Brady. With that thought we left for the stage, laughing. Of course with two pros, Alex and Florence anchoring, the show went off without a hitch. After a night of reading nominees' and winners' names I was looking forward to getting out of the tux and getting home to kick back, but….

Hey, wait! My street clothes are missing! My keys, my wallet! Gone!! Stolen? Not too many people, male or female, have ever been particularly interested in getting into my pants in either sense, certainly not enough to steal them. Florence had a hunch as to what might have happened. While I started to panic, she searched for and found her assistant. He had thoughtfully moved my clothes along with hers to a safer location where he could keep an eye on it all while we were on stage. How wonderfully thoughtful, but I wish somebody had told me before I started to bounce off the walls.

When Florence and I bid adieu, I was looking forward to another opportunity to share good talk, hear her tales, get help with my cufflinks, and maybe have somebody babysit my belongings. Sadly, that chance never came. Beyond her standing as one of television's pioneering performers, dear Florence is remembered lovingly by all who knew her. She had a walk, talk, smile, wit, and style that radiated joy. She seemingly never suffered from the kind of identity crisis shared by many actors who become best known for a single role, despite their versatility and long resumes. As she put it, "If I sat home and went, 'Oh, I can't get another job because everybody thinks I should be Carol Brady,' that would be my fault."

From watching Florence interact with her admirers it was clear she embraced the public's unavoidable identification of her as her character. It was fun to watch their reaction to meeting the actress who many could only relate to as the Brady matriarch. By surrendering to that inevitability I think she found joy that might otherwise have eluded her. I know it delighted her many fans. Call her Mrs. Brady or Florence Henderson, either way, to meet or work with this dear lady was to know that her success was manifested in every aspect of her personality. OK, her "Wessonality," if you prefer.

Within months of Florence's death another beloved star, Rose Marie, made her exit during Christmas week in 2017. Amazingly, Rose had total recall of her life and career to the very end. She quoted conversations, song lyrics, and dollar amounts she earned seemingly all the way back to her debut as Baby Rose Marie at age three. Yes, age three. She was a star with her own national radio show at age four. Ninety-one years later she could still charm a crowd.

Rose's tales of Las Vegas' earliest days working for Bugsy Siegel at the opening of his Flamingo Hotel showroom were priceless. While co-hosting a podcast interview with TV historian Stu Shostak I once asked Rose to tell her fantastic story about singing at the brand new Flamingo. Her incredible memory surprised me again when she said, "I told you that story the last time we spoke!" Of course she had, but that was years before. With a little coaxing she agreed to share it again for the listeners. Rose set up the tale by repeating what people have told her throughout her life, that she "has balls."

It was December 26th, Christmas week of 1946, and Rose was on the Flamingo's opening night bill with her pal Jimmy Durante and band leader Xavier Cugat. "Clark Gable, Robert Taylor, Barbara Stanwyck, Lana Turner, Caesar Romero, Judy Garland, George Raft, Van Johnson, Joan Crawford and Van Heflin. Everyone from Hollywood was there for the opening," Rose remembered. Against the advice of casino employees who feared the wise guys, she dared to confront Bugsy Siegel after being handed her check. She'd been shorted $11 from her $2,750 salary. Having never met him, Rose didn't realize that the man who handed her that slightly-light paycheck for entertaining at the resort's star-studded premiere week was indeed the man whose reputation as a hostile hothead she knew well. As she spoke up about the $11 discrepancy a member of the chorus she was sitting with cringed and tried to stop her from the potentially fatal *faux pas*.

After Rose asserted herself, Bugsy left to check with the back office. It was then that she was told who she had just challenged over a few lousy bucks. When he returned with $11 in cash, the singer changed her tune. Rose backpedalled. She correctly figured that her life, her health, and her ability to work the many mobbed-up nightclubs across the country was worth infinitely more than $11. Bugsy calmly explained that Rose had arrived a day later than expected and that she had been charged back for the empty guest room at the El Rancho—the Flamingo's rooms were not yet completed. Rose explained that there was no offense intended by her late arrival, and that she was delayed simply because all flights from L.A. the day before had been cancelled due to weather.

Rose said that while she was trying to hand back the $11 and persuade Bugsy that the deduction was fine, she was thinking "They'll mail me home in an envelope!" She remembered the mobster saying, "We had to pay the El Rancho, but I'll cover it." In retrospect, she felt that standing up to him won Bugsy's respect and friendship. He later gave her $10,000 in cash to go play baccarat in hopes that she would draw a crowd to the table. Rose turned the stake into $25,000 and couldn't wait to give Bugsy every cent of it, but couldn't find him. She did that evening's show with the cash stuffed into her bra.

When she later found him at the hotel coffee shop and was finally able to hand over the cash, Bugsy smiled approvingly and said, "You're alright." She remembered him promising to book her for a return engagement in the showroom. Three weeks after the opening, the failing Flamingo was shuttered, but six months later Rose was back with a booking that ended on June 16, 1947. Bugsy loved her act, and as she was leaving he told her that he'd be calling her again soon for another appearance. That call never came; Bugsy was murdered just four days later.

Rose then paused to reframe her confrontation with Bugsy, saying that it wasn't a giant leap of impudence as she had been around members of the mob her entire life. "I was performing in Chicago and my father told me we were going in a car to meet someone," she recalled. "I later learned that it was Al Capone. He had seen me perform and wanted to meet me. Most of the theaters were owned by organized crime, so they were my bosses. They were wonderful to me, treated me beautifully." Rose added a new revelation to the story when interviewed by *People* magazine: "My father worked as an arsonist for Al Capone. He used to burn down your warehouse if things weren't going the right way, but I didn't know that at the time. I was a child star and to me, Al was my 'Uncle Al.' My mother used to cook for all these guys."

When Rose passed away at age 94 we not only lost a lovely lady and a walking encyclopedia of showbiz but, I believe, the record-holder for the performer who enjoyed the longest career. On radio at age 3, Rose contributed voices to *The Garfield Show* as her final gig at age 90. Credit producer Mark Evanier for that last booking, and know that it was more than a favor. In addition to everything else, Rose was an off-camera voice actress who contributed characterizations for everything from animated TV series to dramatic motion pictures. They ran the gamut from *Freakazoid!* to Gus Van Sant's 1998 remake of *Psycho*.

As a mature actor with an instantly recognizable face, Rose was invited to enjoy an hour of high jinx on the high seas during several sailings with the crew of Aaron Spelling's *The Love Boat*. While some who appeared actually got to enjoy the sun and the salt air, most were landlocked on a 20th Century-Fox soundstage in West L.A. for their entire voyage. I can't think of another series that welcomed more veteran performers aboard. In fact, as Rose was disembarking in 1983, she passed her pal Lee Meriwether who was boarding for the very next episode. The two had worked together exactly a decade earlier on CBS's *The Doris Day Show*.

Lee was the first Miss America to be crowned on television and she remained royalty through dozens of guest star appearances, as well as being a cast member on no fewer than eight series. She portrayed everything from an "electrobiologist" on *The Time Tunnel* to the matriarch of a motley crew on *The Munsters Today*. That's where I first met this sweet, charming lady. Lee was portraying Lily Munster opposite John Schuck's Herman Munster and Howard Morton's Grandpa Munster in an update of the mid-1960s hit sitcom now re-titled *The Munsters Today*.

Howard Morton, Lee Meriwether and Jason Marsden surround the author during the monstrously funny three-season run of *The Munsters Today*. The series revisited the ghoulish gags from a beloved 1960s sitcom. Photo from the author's collection

I was cast in one of the third season episodes, shooting on the same hallowed ground at Universal Studios where the original *Munsters* filmed. It's also where the many Frankenstein and Dracula feature films that inspired the TV show's characters were first put on nitrate. In the episode titled *The Reel Munsters* I portrayed the smarmy, supercilious host of a hidden camera reality-TV show that had captured the Munster family in all of their eerie weirdness. The name of the fictitious show-within-a-show was something like *America at Home Videos.* My two scenes as Martin Winkdale were pre-taped in the afternoon and subsequently rolled into the show. While I was working, most of the regular cast was in the long process of having their extensive make-up applied—Herman's inspired by Frankenstein's monster, and Grandpa's based on Dracula.

Those iconic looks originally created by make-up master Jack Pierce are now over 90 years old and, somehow, at last check, were actually still under copyright by Universal, although I assume for not much longer. As recently as 2010 Universal's lawyers served a cease and desist letter to an art publisher explaining the studio's ownership of the Frankenstein monster's look as defined by the combination of five visual elements: the neck bolts, forehead scar, green skin, protruding brow and flattened head.

When entering the soundstage I walked past an unrecognizable actor behind the familiar Dracula character now revived as Grandpa Munster. I didn't realize that beneath the ghastly visage and under the flowing cape was the character actor then best known from *Gimme a Break*, Howard Morton. Howard and I had recently become fast friends, but he was so fully disguised that he had to call my name and re-introduce himself. I remained baffled, until he smiled. Not knowing how I'd gotten lucky enough with my audition to score this gig, I thanked Howard for whatever good word he might have offered on my behalf. He said he hadn't advocated for me, and was honest enough to not take any false credit. He motioned for me to follow him. Howard wanted to tell me something confidential that I suspected was likely critical of the show or its producers.

Outside the stage door we found a patch of real estate where we wouldn't be overheard. He lit a cigarette as he started to speak. Just as he was getting to the dicey dishing, one of the Universal Tour trams came around a corner loaded with dozens of visitors—TV and film fans—Hollywood's lifeblood. In full drag as Grandpa Munster, Howard immediately put out the cigarette and walked the few yards to the tram. The driver stopped and the actor generously threw a few funny lines about the Munster family and posed for pictures.

He returned to where we were standing, lit another cigarette and we resumed chatting. Business was good at Universal that day. Bam, there came another load of tourists. Howard immediately put out this second cigarette, walked to the tram which immediately stopped while he, again, graciously regaled the tourists with some Munster family legend or lore. Howard then unfurled his black cape with a theatrical flourish and posed for more pictures. He returned to where we were standing and lit yet another cigarette.

Less than two minutes later, here we go again… lather, rinse, repeat. Respecting his character and not wanting to appear in costume smoking, the number of wasted cigarettes from those few moments in the public eye could have jacked-up his two-pack-a-day habit to a third. We ultimately reconvened to his dressing room for the hot gossip behind the Munster comedy. Vampires have especially juicy stories, but this one is now way past its freshness date and long forgotten.

Howard and I had met only a few months earlier when he was kind enough to be a celebrity player for the presentation of *Chain Game* to CBS. The network had awarded the creative effort of inventing a new game by investing in its refinement and helping to steer it towards pilot-worthiness. Its future was then being decided on the basis of that formal runthrough. I hosted, in part because I knew the game better than any outsider could. It was a format I helped develop, working for months with its creator Mick Kennedy.

Howard Morton's opposing celebrity that day for *Chain Game* was one of the most delightful, fun, vivacious, and may I say sexy females ever to turn the town on with her smile, Teresa Ganzel. Teresa is royalty among game show celebs, a world-class *Pyramid* partner. She's a producer's dream as she loves to play the games; she's smart, witty, and she brings enough energy to light half of Hollywood. You know Teresa. In addition to her many roles on stage and screen she's also beloved for her appearances as the Matinee Lady working alongside super-pitchman Art Fern in Johnny Carson's *Tea Time Movie* sketches. I hope you didn't miss reading Teresa's great memory of sharing the stage with Johnny, a fistful of pages back.

Teresa is a damn good actress who is always working in theater productions between TV and movie roles. I consider her to be among my most-fun acquaintances, and I like to think that the restraining order is just her cute way of playing hard to get—but seriously folks. Teresa was as bubbly as ever and kind enough to bring her smile to my 2018 housewarming. She was so charming that the house is still warm.

Conversation with Teresa is far more fun than the gossiping that others seem to thrive on. While guilty myself, I know those dishing-the-dirt conversations are usually unprofessional for the disher and dishee, and unkind to the person whose ears are burning. Plus, there's always the concern that some hack will try to sell an overheard story to one of those supermarket checkout rags. If you've wondered, "What do the tabloids know?"... well, the answer is plenty. In March of 1981, before Teresa inherited the role of Johnny Carson's Matinee Lady, those magazine racks were warning that the marital misery between Johnny and Mrs. Carson number three was leading to a divorce. Although Johnny vehemently refuted the story on-air, by September he had moved from the couple's Bel Air home to go solo at their beach house. Divorce papers were filed the following spring.

Sure, the tabloids can often stretch the truth thinner than the pastrami at Canter's Deli. Just the same, there's usually at least a seed of verified evidence behind each story in order to make it past the publisher's lawyers. When that seed is fertilized with enough manure, what gets printed can be sufficiently devastating to destroy a career. Most of the enraged subjects who have been smudged by bad ink agree that it's usually best to just let the affronts pass, but there's another fascinating way to avoid victimization.

If you're willing to serve up some even more tantalizing dirt than their original story, I'm told the rags often make deals that bury one celeb's sins in exchange for someone else's bigger embarrassment. The heavyweight champion tale of one star serving up another belongs to Rat Pack-member and actor Peter Lawford, a lifelong friend of the gossip columns' favorite victim, Elizabeth Taylor. According to authors Danforth Prince and Darwin Porter's *Elizabeth Taylor: There is Nothing Like a Dame,* the young actress lost her virginity at age 15 to Lawford. Decades later the two former MGM stars were still in touch, and Lawford was the one person Liz reached out to after disappearing from the public eye. She called to hear a friendly voice, confiding in strictest confidence that she was secretly at a rehab facility and terribly lonely. With his own chronic drug abuse issues Lawford agreed to join Liz, explaining how they could support each other by taking the dry-out detox cure together. No less credible source than the July 19, 1991 issue of the *Chicago Tribune* confirms that Lawford immediately sold the scoop of Liz's admittance at The Betty Ford Center to the *National Enquirer* for a tidy sum believed to be $15,000—double that in today's dollars.

The other option, mounting a libel suit usually accomplishes little more than bringing greater attention to the scandal sheets' fabrications. A former tabloid target, film producer and former concubine of U.S. Senator John Edward, Rielle Hunter, warns that any suit you file would require you to first give testimony in a deposition. Just what you want, one of their lawyers digging deeper into your life with you under oath, required to answer truthfully.

There are exceptions, of course. Liberace successfully sued London's *Daily Mirror* in 1959 after the newspaper strongly implied that he was homosexual. Yes, the great showman denied being gay throughout his career and was somehow able to pass as sufficiently butch to be victorious over *The Mirror* in the wacky UK court system. No wonder we fought for independence from Britain.

In 1984 Marty Ingels and Shirley Jones sued the *National Enquirer* over the rag's headline, "Husband's Bizarre Behavior Is Driving Shirley Jones to Drink." The case was settled out of court for an apology and an undisclosed amount of cash. Carol Burnett, Clint Eastwood, Tom Cruise and Cindy Crawford are among others who've sued, however proving malice or malicious intent in U.S. courts is a high bar to hurdle, especially for a public figure. Tougher than the pastrami at—never mind.

There's such a dichotomy. Working in a milieu that requires everybody on set to be proficient and precise in contributing their expertise usually leads to wonderfully warm friendships with bright and artistic professionals. Just the same, TV can be a treacherous and spiteful sandbox to bring your creative pail and shovel. It seems that way in part because of the sardonic ancient principle appropriated by Hollywood, "It's not good enough that I succeed, my rivals must fail." It's a sufficiently popular precept to have been attributed to everyone from warlord Genghis Khan to novelist Gore Vidal, as well as playwright Somerset Maugham, Broadway impresario David Merrick, tech magnate Larry Ellison, and 17th century author François de La Rochefoucauld, among others.

The industry also often appears cold and harsh because the product being manufactured is so warm and fuzzy. When you get down to the nitty gritty, now more than ever show business is ruled by the same tough realities that govern all commerce. It's true even for the beloved personalities and programs that have risen to the realm of cultural institutions. From what I've witnessed TV has become just another retailer, as unsentimental as Home Depot or Walmart. If it doesn't sell, it's off the shelves.

It was with that thinking that the shelves of the networks' in-house archives and their rented climate-controlled storage vaults were regularly purged. Some old series were orphaned when copyrights were not renewed, or a pencil-pushing bean counter failed to see any return on the investment of paying the continuing storage bills. That was all before, suddenly, content was king and ancient series could again be monetized filling the hours on hundreds of outlets. In addition to the increasing number of streamers respectful to retro entertainment, there are broadcast subcarrier channels like BUZZR, MeTV, Decades, Cozi TV, and Antenna TV that the industry calls "diginets" that have made homes for orphaned classics. Technology was the great game changer and money the motivator when it came to latter-day storage and restoration.

In the interim, sadly, so much of the first generation of television performers' work has been permanently lost, some purposely dumped. Countless hours of video entertainment have joined the half of motion pictures' 100-year history that is never to be seen again. However, there's a huge difference between the two. It was the limitations of technology that doomed early movies. Film stock was nitrate-based, making it unstable and extremely flammable. Before the widespread use of safety film starting in the early 1950s, reels that didn't burst into flames simply deteriorated in the can.

By contrast, television is among the arts for which preservation is comparatively easy. Yet it was apparently the lowest priority during the medium's early decades. With no ancillary markets, TV programs were disrespectfully considered disposable. Expensive reels of two-inch videotape were erased and re-used over and over again. Countless thousands of kinescopes and film prints were dismissed as worthless because, unlike tape, film stock couldn't be erased and re-used. Without any consideration for the content, most landed in the briny waters of both New York Harbor and off the coast of Santa Monica.

Much of the work of prolific producers such as Nick Vanoff will never be seen again. Nick's lost classics include hundreds of hours of the Steve Allen years of *The Tonight Show*, as well as many of his programs with Bing Crosby, Andy Williams, Don Knotts, Sonny and Cher, and Milton Berle. Who is Nick Vanoff, you ask?

Chapter 23

Nick Vanoff was a master showman, a small-screen Ziegfeld and a devotee of grand theatrical spectacles. After dancing on Broadway, his entrée to television was flipping cue cards on *The Perry Como Show*. It wasn't long before he earned an associate producer title there and, soon after, began living the life of an in-demand TV impresario. The producer of prestigious programs such as *The Kennedy Center Honors* as well as Bing Crosby and Julie Andrews specials soon lived the high life in a 9,000-square-foot Beverly Hills villa.

Vanoff was also the creative force responsible for one of the slickest mid-budget variety revues produced for the tube. ABC-TV's *Hollywood Palace* was a program that enthralled many TV fans during its seven season run. Among other claims to fame, The Rolling Stones made their first US television appearance on a 1964 episode and, in 1969 Vanoff gave The Jackson 5 their first shot on national TV, complete with an introduction by Diana Ross.

The Hollywood Palace was as exciting as a Cape Canaveral blastoff from its opening seconds in no small part because of the bombastic hyperbole of announcer Dick Tufeld. Dick was a magnificent talent, known best by TV aficionados for contributing the voice of the robot on *Lost in Space*. There are so many stories about Dick that will have to wait for later pages. When you least expect it, I promise Dick will pop up. Dick Tufeld, that is.

At the end of the 1970s, Nick Vanoff pitched ABC a show that would out-glitz his 1960s *Hollywood Palace*. He even had preliminary plans drawn to rehab the same historic theater for the new production. The network passed on the grandiose scheme of adding a swimming pool below a sliding stage and an ice rink that could be lowered from above, all inside of what is actually a very small old legit playhouse. ABC had already reconstructed that theater at the direction of Jerry Lewis, twice in fact, for what became nothing more than a multi-million dollar write-off from the most expensive flop in TV history. The network was not interested in a repeat of that debacle.

When I arrived in town in 1979 looking to do any job for no pay, a prehistoric concept now known as interning, Nick Vanoff provided my first drive-on pass. He was partnered with Saul Pick, a real estate mogul who specialized in theaters and studios. They had recently plopped down $6.2 million for the ancient Columbia Pictures lot in the middle of Hollywood. The once-bustling studio facility had languished, mostly vacant for so long that a couple of the stages were actually being used as indoor tennis courts. As doggedly as I searched, I was unable to find studio mogul Harry Cohn's old office. I was hoping to catch a glimpse at what was fabled to have been one of the most active casting couches in town.

It appeared as though little had been updated since the days when *It Happened One Night*, *Mr. Smith Goes to Washington*, *Funny Girl*, *The Caine Mutiny*, and the Three Stooges' theatrical shorts were in production. The buildings had been thoroughly pillaged and the lot was home to all manner of vermin—life forms producers would say are even lower than agents.

Even as late a date as the rehearsals for the 1993 Academy Awards, much of the acreage was still a mess. That's when a boa constrictor to be used in the performance of a song from *Aladdin* escaped from its handler. It slithered out of sight, sending the rehearsal into chaos. The snake was sufficiently happy dining on the plentiful population of rats that it didn't reappear for weeks. Another boa constrictor had to be cast for the performance at the Oscars telecast. At the risk of a 15-yard penalty for piling on, I'll suggest that finding another creepy crawling creature wasn't too difficult as it's said there's no shortage of snakes in this town.

Pick and Vanoff had a small part of the lot rehabilitated and leased to a few tenants. That included producing team Sid and Marty Kroft, as well as an overflow of sitcoms from ABC's Prospect lot. Other entities large and small also started to rent space. Having production on the lot was the best way to repay the banks that held the partners' huge mortgages. With cash flow as priority one, Nick Vanoff sold NBC his big 90-minute weekly variety extravaganza first envisioned for ABC and for the *Hollywood Palace* theater a handful of blocks away. With its debut on March 4th, 1980, it was my first series.

Carrying the name of NBC radio's attempt to deflate early television's theft of its audience exactly 30 years earlier, *The Big Show* was a bigger-than-big big deal. The old Stages 9 and 10 on Columbia's former lot were renovated and combined into one giant space. It was outfitted with both the sunken swim tank complete with underground camera portholes, and the ice rink Nick had envisioned. With an added array of computer-controlled fountains that created dancing water effects, *The Big Show* was blue-collar variety TV at its least bombastic. Don Rickles looking like Tarzan in a leopard pattern single-shoulder bathing suit swinging on a vine and falling into the swimming pool, now that's entertainment.

One of the weekly rotating hosts, Steve Allen, generously treated me to some stories of early TV. He recalled being a panelist on Goodson-Todman's *I've Got a Secret* claiming, "We were paid $165 a show and had to supply our own makeup, hairdressing, and wardrobe." I've been told it was much the same for the panel on *What's My Line?* where formal attire was required at a comparable bargain basement scale talent fee. Steve recalled that *Secret* host Garry Moore's salary, "at the beginning was only $500 per program."

The original host of *The Tonight Show* has been called a renaissance man, but not because he was so old that he lived through The Renaissance. It was because Steve Allen seemingly could do everything, and in mindboggling quantities. He claimed to have written 7,900 songs, published 54 books, penned stage shows, scored musicals, created TV series, and so much more. Yet he told me that he could have been far more productive if he wasn't living a cursed life.

What was the curse? Steve said he required a bare minimum of 10 hours of sleep or he couldn't function the next day. The added hundreds of minutes wasted in slumber each night added up to years that he said he would rather have spent in more creative pursuits. How much more productive can any one man be? With such a fertile and creative mind revving at high rpms, Steve also devoted time to a dumbfounding incongruous, little-known enterprise. He owned a Honda-BSA-Vespa motorcycle dealership.

There in West Hollywood, after opening in 1966 at 9000 Santa Monica Boulevard, Steve Allen might drop by on his way between meetings and tapings to check the sales figures for his choppers and scooters. The large showroom garnered ink documenting the unusual décor for a motorcycle shop which included antique church pews and a grand chandelier. During the time he ran the business, Steve was the go-to guy for many producers and stunt coordinators who needed wheels for their movie or TV show. Besides being a regular panelist on *What's My Line?* Steve actually appeared once as a contestant on the show during the 17th season with the secret occupation: "Sells Motorcycles."

That day on the set of the short-lived *Big Show* with Steve, I wasn't able to gently steer the conversation from mopeds and mystery guests to the essential question about *What's My Line?* that lingers to this day. It dwarfs every other quaint tale of the fun and foibles of the original 901 episodes. No, not the oft-told tale of Steve's "Is it bigger than a breadbox?" adlib. Forget Arlene Francis' "Does your job require you to work with your hands?" The biggest unsolved mystery from *What's My Line?* didn't concern any of the approximately 1,000 mystery guests. The only still-relevant burning question is: What, in the name of God and all that is holy, ever happened to Dorothy Kilgallen?!

Hearst newspaper columnist Dorothy Kilgallen (left) joined the *What's My Line?* panel at age 36, playing the guessing game with the same intensity she brought to her reporting. Many believe it was that penchant for passionate probing that led to her demise at age 52.

As he had been a colleague and had been seated on the panel the Sunday night after Kilgallen's death, I delicately tried to bring Steve to the apparently verboten topic. You see, many believe the journalist's demise was almost certainly a part of the enigmatic and unsolvable fatalities that followed the assassination of President John Kennedy. Even in the unlikely event that Steve had a piece of that puzzle, I now realize that he would never have disclosed any of it to a stranger, an inquisitive kid no less, especially while standing on a soundstage with a full crew in earshot.

Just when I thought I would never learn any more about the fate of the respected columnist's demise, I got an amazing earful from someone even closer to her than Steve Allen. By chance, about 15 years later during a leisurely poolside conversation at the massive Oakwood Apartments complex with long-retired Goodson-Todman executive Bill Egan I heard fresh details of the story that have never been adequately explained. Bill was there with Dorothy every Sunday night, including the Sunday night that turned into a Monday morning while they leisurely chatted over drinks, little more than a handful of hours before her lifeless body was discovered.

As Bill spoke I came to truly understand that the connection between Dorothy Kilgallen, the FBI, Jack Ruby's lawyer and various nefarious characters at the fringes of organized crime were not simply part of some conspiracy theorists' fantasy. They were the key players in a story of intrigue that precipitated what many will always believe was the TV panelist's murder. Perhaps her demise could be rightfully categorized as involuntary suicide as it was Dorothy's choice to ignore death threats in her relentless pursuit of the facts surrounding President Kennedy's murder. Two other newspaper reporters working on the case had already paid the ultimate price: Bill Hunter and Jim Koethe.

Dorothy intensified the danger by including provocative revelations and proclamations about the assassination in her widely-ready syndicated newspaper column. Incendiary items like "This story isn't going to die as long as there's a real reporter alive, and there are a lot of them." The FBI demanded to know her sources, and they devoted thousands of man-hours following the trail of the reporter's investigation. The feds did little to protect Dorothy, and once she was gone they were far more interested in finding her missing JFK files than in finding her killer.

The backstory started when the Sunday night guessing game was in its infancy and Dorothy Kilgallen took a permanent seat as a member of the erudite foursome of New York literati. She was a well-respected second generation print journalist following in the footsteps of her famous father James L. Kilgallen, prized as the dean of 20th century American journalism. With her column running in 146 daily *Bugles, Posts, Gazettes, Times, Globes, Journals,* and *Inquirers*, *The New York Post* called Dorothy "the most powerful female voice in America" by virtue of her estimated readership of 20 million. Television had long looked to the ranks of columnists for hosts, guests, and panelists. Besides having something new to say every day, they held the promise of bringing some of their readership with them to the tube.

Ed Sullivan, Irv Kupcinet, Jimmie Fidler, Louella Parsons, Hedda Hopper, Earl Wilson, Drew Pearson, and Walter Winchell were among the mostly-successful crossover talents. Many of them read Dorothy's column as she had an inside track on a number of hot Hollywood stories with which she regularly scooped her colleagues. Among her loyal secret sources for those was her sister, Elinor Kilgallen, who worked at no less a talent agency than the mighty MCA. Elinor handled James Dean as well as other rising stars and was privy to inside information about the hundreds of VIPs, large and small, on the agency's roster.

The Broadway and Hollywood insights in her column kept her readers entertained, but Dorothy's fame, prestige, and circulation fully blossomed on the strength of dozens of exclusives of international significance. She proved herself a tireless investigator on many high-profile stories by making the most of her soft-spoken manner, a demeanor that belied the ferocity with which she wielded the power of the press. Dorothy was the first to pen the story of Project Mongoose, the code name for the CIA's plot to kill Castro. She also helped re-open the Sam Sheppard murder case that resulted in an earlier conviction being overturned in the trial that inspired *The Fugitive*.

Dorothy was also first to publicly hint about the philandering between Marilyn Monroe and the Kennedy brothers. Marilyn was dead within 48 hours of that scoop hitting the street. Immediately thereafter, Dorothy was also first to point out the many inconsistencies surrounding the sex goddess's so-called suicide. In a strange irony, the specifics of Monroe's 1962 death shared several key details with Dorothy's own demise three years later. To sidestep coroners' analysis of stomach contents for residue from the ingestion of pills as well as their futile search for the site of an injection, I'll leave you to ponder the ingenuity of administrating drugs via enema.

Dorothy's "too hot for TV" story of the blond bombshell's likely murder in 1962 exploded at ABC's New York newsroom in 1985. The network's own investigation also led to revelations about Monroe's intimate association with both John and Bobby Kennedy, connections to members of organized crime, and suggestions that another member of the extended Kennedy clan, Peter Lawford, was possibly involved in facilitating her murder. It was a hell of a blockbuster report being produced for their primetime show *20/20*, but the network's news honcho at the time, Roone Arledge, ordered the story killed, spiked as they say in newsroom slang.

Arledge explained the move saying the allegations were insufficiently substantiated and the report was "gossip column stuff." However, most attributed his suppression of the story to his personal friendship with Ethel Kennedy, Bobby's widow. The ABC-Kennedy connection ran even deeper as David Burke, a senior Arledge aide, worked for Ted Kennedy. In addition, Arledge protégé Jeff Ruhe was married to one of Ethel's daughters. Could it get any cozier?

Co-anchors Hugh Downs and Barbara Walters, as well as executive producer Av Westin, were among the high-profile ABC news personnel who denounced Arledge's snuffing the report. Additionally, Geraldo Rivera claimed he was fired from the network's news division over his outspokenness in support of the story's correspondent Sylvia Chase. Chase was a star at ABC news, especially after *TV Guide* dubbed her "the most trusted woman on TV." However, she was so incensed that her completed 13-minute blockbuster video package was being suppressed for political reasons that she quit her gig over the issue.

Dorothy's alluding to President Kennedy in her story about the sex goddess's mysterious death suggests that once she began digging, she was unwilling to hold back in disclosing even inconvenient findings. Undeterred, she resolutely set her sights on unraveling the riddles behind JFK's assassination—what she called "the crime of the century."

While Dorothy would never reveal a source, I'm happy to disclose more about mine. Goodson-Todman staffer Bill Egan had been an integral part of just about every one of the production company's shows from the 1950s all the way to the 1972 revivals of *I've Got a Secret* and *The Price is Right*. Most relevant is that he was associate producer on *What's My Line?* and had assimilated what he'd seen and heard from Dorothy and those closest to her during the panelist's final hours. Bill recalled that she had a thick file folder with her which she waved when making pronouncements about her developing epic expose. In the days before modern photocopy machines, she kept the thick folder of her notes with her at all times when not locked in a safe.

In the minutes before what became her last broadcast on November 7, 1965, Dorothy told Bill, her fellow panelists, her make-up artist and pretty much anyone who would listen that she considered the Warren Commission Report on the Kennedy assassination "laughable," and that her white-hot exclusive was very "cloak and daggerish." She added that she was about to "blow the roof off" the assassination, vowing to "break the real story" and have "the biggest scoop of the century."

The super-sleuth had just returned to New York from Dallas where she'd interviewed Jack Ruby, the man who shot and killed the President's assassin, Lee Harvey Oswald, on live television. Dorothy had a long and mutually beneficial reciprocal relationship with Ruby's attorney, Melvin Belli. Over a period of years he had been feeding her confidential information that she'd print to help sway public opinion in favor of his clients. Dorothy twice had one-on-one conversations with the inscrutable nightclub owner-turned-assassin that could only have been arranged by his attorney. At Belli's request Judge Joe B. Brown granted Dorothy the opportunity to conduct an interview with Ruby in total private. His prison guards stepped far back out of earshot for the eight minute secretive discussion. None of the other 400 reporters covering Ruby enjoyed anything close to that kind of access.

At first, Dorothy's questions for Ruby were part of her research for a book called *Murder One* to be published by panel-mate Bennett Cerf's Random House. However, after hearing what the jailed murderer had to say about the Kennedy and Oswald shootings she became obsessed with fully exposing the conspiracy she believed was behind the assassinations. One of the biggest exclusives of Dorothy's career came when she somehow managed to get her hands on the complete un-redacted 102-page transcript of Ruby's three-hour testimony to the Warren Commission long before it was released to any outsider.

Commenting on that testimony in her column prompted several unannounced FBI visits to Dorothy's apartment at 45 East 68th Street. The feds were trying to ferret out who connected with the Commission had breached security, allowing her access to that transcript. She reportedly told the agents that she "would die rather than reveal her source." Then began the 24/7 surveillance of her comings and goings. Dorothy believed her phone was tapped as well. She confided in her hairdresser that repeated death threats had led to her decision to get a gun for protection.

After Dorothy's death, her friend, Ruby's attorney Melvin Belli, shared a bit of their conversations. Belli recounted that Dorothy was "shocked at the hopelessly inept questioning of Ruby by Chief Justice Warren, and by Warren's failure to follow up on the leads Ruby was feeding him." He called his friend's scoop "the ruin of the Warren Commission." One can only wonder what *What's My Line?* moderator John Charles Daly thought of Dorothy's denouncing the official report of the events in Dallas. Daly was married to the daughter of Chief Justice Earl Warren, namesake of the Warren Commission report.

The unrelenting investigative reporter was especially obstinate in ferreting out the truth behind the Dealy Plaza shooting because, this time, it was personal. John Kennedy was a friend with whom she had dined at the Stork Club and had shared late night phone calls. Kennedy had played charades at her home, and she had taken her son to visit his home, the White House. There, the President graciously took the time to chat with them, give young Kerry Kilgallen a PT-109 pin, and praise his and his third grade classmates' letters to the President.

Bill Egan remembered that on Dorothy's last Sunday night at the CBS studio, just hours before her death, she was elated. She was also not at all discrete in explaining to him, hairdresser Marc Sinclaire, and studio make-up artist Carmen Gebbia, how methodically piecing together the conspiracy surrounding the shots fired at the Dallas motorcade had led to well-known Mafia kingpin Carlos Marcello. Suddenly Bill's voice lowered as he turned on his chaise lounge to look me straight in the eye as he relayed, "She said her next step was a trip to New Orleans to speak directly with Marcello."

Fellow panelist Arlene Francis reflected, "That was the only night in all the years we did the show that Dorothy didn't kiss me on the cheek when she said goodnight." Bill told me that after that final live *What's My Line?* he drove Dorothy, with her files, to P.J. Clarke's for the ritual post-show drink with producer Bob Bach and other staffers. Bill remembered Dorothy telling the group that she had a rendezvous later that night at a midtown hotel with a stranger she provocatively alluded to as "a prospective new beau." She was teasing and playful as she downed her vodka and tonic. Bill said Bob Bach drove her to meet her mystery man sometime after midnight. Bach was the last member of her TV family to see Dorothy alive, accompanying her as far as the opulent piano bar at the Regency Hotel.

Kurt Maier, the piano player that night, said that the panelist was still in the lounge in good spirits when he got off work at 2 a.m. and added, "Of course, Dorothy was with a man. A true lady like her would never come by herself to hear me play." Coincidentally, a contestant from that night's show, an explosives salesperson, Mrs. Katherine Stone from Kentucky, was also at the Regency. She confirmed seeing the panelist who had earlier guessed her occupation. Stone said Dorothy was at a table, deeply engaged in conversation with an unidentified man and appeared to be discussing "very serious business."

That may have been the relatively new man in Dorothy's life who sometimes identified himself as a journalist, but this real-life mystery guest's true role and motivation were never fully clear. In 1979 author Lee Israel disclosed that stranger's name as Ron Pataky, an entertainment reporter at the Columbus, Ohio *Citizen-Journal.* Pataky had been rendezvousing with Dorothy for many months and later confessed to meeting Kilgallen several times in the Regency but denied that he was with her on the night of her death. Dorothy had wondered whether or not he was also an FBI informant or CIA operative. It was suggested that he was actually a Carlos Marcello soldier. What was known is that Pataky was also under surveillance by the feds and likely other pairs of eyes. It's conjectured that the moment Dorothy was first seen speaking with him, her ultimate fate was sealed.

None of the Goodson-Todman family knew who Dorothy met that night, and after hearing of her death, her friends' worst fears appeared to be accurate—that she had been lured into what she believed was a budding romance, or had been tempted by the promise of important details of the JFK assassination by someone who turned out to be her killer. Most who have been trying to solve the puzzle finger Pataky as the most likely suspect in Dorothy's murder, despite his adamant claim that he wasn't even in town that night. Bill told me all that anyone from *What's My Line?* knew for sure was that just a few hours after being escorted to the Regency, Dorothy was gone. There had already been more than two dozen people connected in various ways to the mystery of JFK's murder who had each met their own deaths, and the tally continued to climb during the rest of the decade.

Most deaths are not murders, but the details surrounding Dorothy's leave little room for any other credible interpretation. Those who read the police report or spoke with detectives on the case learned that her personal hairdresser, Sinclaire, found the reporter's lifeless body that Monday morning in bed, in a room in which she never slept. You see, after discovering her husband in the midst of an affair in the couple's bed, sleeping arrangements permanently changed in the five-story townhouse. A stranger wouldn't have known in which room Dorothy slept.

Uncharacteristically, Dorothy was found still in full make-up from her TV appearance, including false eyelashes, a false hairpiece, and earrings, sitting up in the bed, wearing a blouse atop a nightgown. There was a book near her hands, one she reportedly had finished reading weeks earlier, but the reading glasses she needed weren't even in the room. Indeed, it had all the markings of a staged tableau. At first, it was widely circulated that the cause of death was a heart attack. The doctor who performed her autopsy noted in the space for the cause of death "pending further study." Handwritten below he entered "Acute ethanol and barbiturate intoxication. Circumstances undetermined."

It was routine for a few words to be added to a coroner's report later, such as when toxicology studies results were finalized. In Dorothy's case the postscript revealed the presence of barbiturates and a blood alcohol level of 0.15. However, there were no bottles anywhere in the home that contained two of the three barbiturates that were found in her system—secobarbital, amobarbital, and pentobarbital.

While Dorothy's vodka intake that final night of her life was sufficient to bring her to double the legal limit for drunk driving, on its own that was nowhere near deadly. The reporter had been known to liberally imbibe on several occasions, such as when she partied to excess several years earlier on January 20, 1961 at her friend John Kennedy's inauguration. Her chauffeur, Roosevelt Zanders, revealed in 1976 that immediately after the new President was sworn in, he drove Dorothy directly from Washington to a New York hospital in distress stating, "One of the things that brought it about was having one or two drinks and not eating." It resulted in the star panelist missing two *What's My Line?* broadcasts, only to return in secret on the subsequent Sunday night to appear as the mystery guest.

On the morning of her death, the file folder of notes that Dorothy had been flaunting just a few hours earlier was nowhere to be found. In fact, everything she had written about the Kennedy-Oswald-Ruby case went missing. Also gone was her bootleg copy of Ruby's Warren Commission transcript. The townhouse was searched several times, all to no avail. Amidst the paranoia created by the surveillance, the phone taps, and FBI visits, Dorothy reportedly confided in a longtime trusted friend Florence Pritchett, another *New York Journal American* columnist, that she had begun to have concerns that Pataky was more than just a reporter, but she didn't know what government agency or other entity he might be working for.

Whatever documents Dorothy may have shared with Pritchett were also nowhere to be found.

In a strange irony, it was Pritchett who first introduced Dorothy to John Kennedy. The reporter later came to learn that Pritchett had long been one of the President's mistresses. If you can handle another coincidence, Pritchett was married to Earl Smith, the U.S. Ambassador to Cuba. Of course Cuba was where Kennedy's Bay of Pigs fiasco turned into a huge embarrassment for the President, and was the nation run by the Communist Party's Fidel Castro, a long-time target of Kennedy-sanctioned CIA assassination attempts.

Call it parallel fate, or freakish irony, or strange happenstance, but exactly two days after Dorothy's death, Pritchett also died. Conveniently, it meant that all of the reporter's work that might have been shared verbally or in writing could well have been successfully snuffed. After Dorothy's death, her husband, Richard Kollmar, was repeatedly visited by the FBI in their search for any of the reporter's remaining papers. He swore he knew nothing of her work and had none of her notes.

In the orgy of mysterious deaths, Richard Kollmar's came a few years later, also recorded as a suicide. Even 22 years after the Kennedy assassination, Dorothy's son Dickie was surprised to be contacted yet again by the FBI concerning his mother's files. Apparently the feds were still worried about what she uncovered, and still hadn't given up hopes for recovering the reporter's potentially inflammatory notes.

Chapter 24

No, Steve Allen had nothing to say about Dorothy Kilgallen's fate, and I wonder if he was being cautiously closed-mouth on the controversial matter of her demise, or perhaps he shared the same disdain for the columnist as the heir to his *Tonight Show* host gig Jack Paar did. Paar had filled in for Steve and was seated right next to Dorothy on the *What's My Line?* panel. After that night, he and Dorothy feuded mercilessly over everything from her garbled speech to his support of Fidel Castro to her chin—Frank Sinatra had taken to calling Dorothy "the chinless wonder," likening her appearance to a chipmunk in retaliation for writing that he was "hot-tempered, egotistical, extravagant, and moody."

Steve Allen was very capable of turning against his fellow TV personalities and disparaged many of his peers when he commented about other early broadcasters, "Genial gentlemen who were neither comedians, nor actors, nor entertainers of any sort, [who] found ready work as hosts. Almost overnight, folks were thrown before the camera. People who had never distinguished themselves in any way became perceived as celebrities."

What a snobbish slam, even if it was partially true. Steve's fellow New York broadcaster Ed McMahon might well have been one of the personalities he alluded to as being thrown before the cameras without any traditional theatrical talent. Then again, how much Shakespearean training is necessary for Ed to have run around in clown makeup for *The Sealtest Big Top Circus*? His resume shows experience perfect for a lifetime of levity on the tube. It includes touting an amusement park's attractions through the speakers on a traveling sound truck, selling stainless steel cookware door to door, pitching as a barker for a carnival tunnel of love attraction, driving a semi-trailer filled with equipment for the traveling Bingo game he operated, and demonstrating the Morris Metric Vegetable Slicer on the Atlantic City Boardwalk.

Ed McMahon (l) began in television before most living rooms had one, arriving in Philadelphia to work at WCAU-TV in 1949 for $75 a week. There he met his neighbor in the Drexelbrook apartment complex, Dick Clark, another local broadcaster who suggested he audition for a New York gig as sidekick to game show host Johnny Carson (r).

Ed was a class act from the first time we met. I was a kid, and when I thanked him for an autograph, he responded by flipping the appreciation to "Thank YOU!" I was charmed. At our final encounter decades later, Ed's health was slipping. His demeanor, however, was as upbeat as ever when he joked about the twisted roots from which grew the earliest audience participation concepts. He recalled that when country music personality Tennessee Ernie Ford hosted *Whole Hog or None*, contestants could win ham, bacon, or an entire dead pig.

The TV veteran remembered that the co-creator of *I've Got a Secret*, song parodist Allen Sherman, hosted a short-lived gem of a show with even stranger prizes. Ed said that during its run more than one player left with a garbage disposal and a year's worth of garbage. There was 1958's *For Love or Money*, which teased contestants with the choice of keeping a prize or opting instead for an unknown supposedly-random amount of cash of up to $9,999 from "the dancing decimal machine." On the very first episode a woman traded a prize worth $239, only to leave with the machine's miserly endowment of a mere 2¢. Yes, two cents. CBS quickly upped the minimum prize to 25¢.

Ed also reminisced about his series *Bride and Groom* on which a pair of lovers were interviewed, married, and then awarded gifts. He remembered one guest who started arguing with his fiancé after being disappointed to learn that the destination of the honeymoon trip being offered that day was to the less than exotic nearby Princeton, New Jersey. The groom's behavior was so off-putting that his intended bride canceled the on-air wedding. She walked out on her bridegroom, the host, the preacher, and the home audience. Ed had to fill the time and cover for the awkwardness. It was all in a day's work. Oh, Ed added that the would-be groom was still enraged hours later when he was arrested after breaking into his former fiancé's home that night.

In those days before satellites, programs seen live on the mainland aired in Hawaii from kinescope films that were mailed to Honolulu. Ed recalled that during the final weeks of his *Bride and Groom* emcee gig he awarded a Hawaiian honeymoon to another couple so dysfunctional that they almost immediately filed for divorce. The marriage was over and the trip to Hawaii was canceled before the film of their wedding reached the Honolulu affiliate station. Not knowing what had transpired, the station was stymied in arranging an interview, trying to find out where the lovebirds were staying.

A remembrance from producer Norm Blumenthal, showrunner of NBC's mid-morning stalwart *Concentration*, summed up Ed McMahon's character. The network overrode Norm's casting choice of announcer Bob Clayton to be the new host late in the series' run, and installed Ed McMahon shortly after Hugh Downs retired in early 1969. Norm stayed long enough to see the ratings slide and then walked from the show in protest. NBC rescinded their decision and gave control of *Concentration* back to Norm. Bob Clayton then became permanent host, destined to concentrate for another four years.

It fell upon the producer to break the news to Ed that he was being fired after roughly six months of satisfactory service. He remembered dreading the task, but the *Tonight Show* sidekick made that potentially awkward confrontation easy and breezy. In a turn of the tables it was Ed who gave Norm a consolation prize. More meaningful than the parting gift of an electric shaver was the heartfelt note of appreciation that Norm said accompanied it. A class move, indeed.

Ed McMahon. After over 50 years of continuous lucrative work on network television he retired with nothing but the memories.

There can be no mention of Ed McMahon without including an unbelievable reality I was shocked to confirm. As a broadcaster Ed was never out of work in a TV career that began as far back as 1948. From performing as the Sealtest circus clown, to hosting Philadelphia's local nightly *Million Dollar Movie*, to nearly 30 years of providing belly laughs for Johnny Carson's monologues and desk bits, to a dozen years in primetime as host of *Star Search*, Ed earned tens of millions of dollars. He earned millions more as a commercial spokesman endorsing Budweiser Beer and American Family Publishers to name just two long-time benefactors. There was *Who Do You Trust?* and *TV's Bloopers and Practical Jokes*, plus *Missing Links*, *Concentration*, and *Snap Judgment* as well as other long-forgotten TV assignments. Add to that, Ed authored eight books, guested on two dozen TV series, and enjoyed a handful of minor movie roles. All that and more, and unbelievably Ed died broke.

Worse than broke, he was over $1 million in debt with an American Express judgment for about $750,000 in unpaid charges, and $644,000 behind in payments on mortgage loans that totaled $4.8 million. It boggles the mind. Besides earnings so huge that they'd be hard work to squander, Ed had ongoing income. His monthly AFTRA pension checks were among the very largest of all performers, in six figures annually. He also had a military pension as well as a generous monthly Social Security check of several thousand. Then, in 2003 Ed was awarded $7.2 million in a lawsuit following health problems caused by toxic mold in his home. Apparently that all proved insufficient when it came to try to catch up with debts. Undone by divorces and old fashioned poor money management, Ed McMahon was a truly nice guy and generous friend to many who needed one.

Paid far less over his career than Ed for an even richer and more elegant voice was Dick Tufeld. While his name isn't well known outside of industry circles, you do know some of his work. Dick could pack intense energy into a read while still maintaining warmth and resonance. As mentioned earlier, his opening spiel for *The Hollywood Palace* was so vibrant and enthusiastic that it built enough momentum for the show to coast through even the corniest monologue from any of its guest hosts.

As much as Dick was also a popular voice for countless commercial campaigns, TV variety hours, and Irwin Allen sci-fi adventures, he'll always be best remembered for one role. Dick brought life to the *Lost in Space* robot with his "Danger, danger, Will Robinson!" Even if you never watched the show you can hear the line in your head—it's a cultural touchstone for a generation and had become part of the popular lexicon, mimicked by class clowns in schoolrooms across America. In fact, Dick's own daughter used to give the Tufelds' home phone number to her classmates who enjoyed calling and asking to speak to the robot. Dick joyfully indulged them.

That defining role as the Class M-3 Model B-9 General Utility Non-Theorizing Environmental Control Robot only became Dick's as a fluke. He told me that while he was the narrator for Irwin Allen's original *Lost in Space* pilot, another actor had been cast as the voice of the robot. While editing that first episode Irwin decided that he didn't like the characterization they'd recorded. He called Dick to ask if he would audition to replace that unseen actor. Dick told me that when he came into the studio the direction he received was, "I don't want the voice to sound robotic." Irwin explained that the clichéd 1950s B-movie sci-fi mechanical-sounding representation of a robot with the arrhythmic monotone was old and hackneyed. It would be wrong for this robot as the producer envisioned a more refined and sophisticated artificial life form.

Dick recalled that Irwin was on the other side of the glass as he experimented with every conceivable delivery in a long session of trial and error. Many of his attempts to find a suitable robot's voice were keyed from Irwin's concept of sophistication and refinement, and his resistance to anything robotic. So, Dick did a lot of variations of a British butler's voice and pretty much everything else Irwin's description inspired. Finally, after what Dick remembered as feeling close to three hours, it was agreed that apparently he couldn't create a personification that the producer liked for this important character.

As Dick was about to leave, Irwin consoled him by saying, "Well, at least you'll be the narrator." Dick responded, "Let me try one more thing." It seemed fruitless as he had already run through his entire catalogue of non-robotic voices. He went back into the booth, took his place behind the microphone and delivered the interpretation we now have come to know and love. He let loose with the monotone, detached, choppy, mechanical and, yes, totally robotic voice that's now so familiar. "Danger, danger, Will Robinson!" As Dick intoned this most unsophisticated and unrefined robot voice Irwin Allen jumped to his feet and said, "That's it!!! What took you so long?!"

Another of Dick's favorite stories involved his long-running association with Gallo wines. He was their commercial spokesman for many years, but as the founders' children began to take more active roles in the family business they convinced brothers Ernest and Julio that a fresh voice was needed for the changing times. As with every big ad campaign the casting call went out to all of the major voice agents in town. Independent voice casting houses such as Bob Lloyd's The Voicecaster, as well as Kamelson and Kamelson were also submitting for the lucrative gig.

In all, over 1,000 taped auditions were received at the Gallo's ad agency. They were each carefully reviewed in order to find the intangible, undefined quality that would somehow reflect the image that Ernest and Julio's kids and their marketing mavens envisioned for the company. It was the audio version of a wine tasting, searching for the highly subjective balance between body, bite, and bouquet. As with a wine tasting, no doubt after the first dozen samples all of the voices soon seemed to sound alike.

Unknown to the Gallos, among the tapes was an audition by Dick, the present voice they were looking to replace. It was submitted by his agent pretty much on a lark and was labeled with a fabricated name. Amazingly, that voice became one of the front runners for the lucrative job. Perhaps it's not so amazing in that the company had chosen Dick's voice years earlier. After hundreds of commercials his vocal qualities and delivery had a subconscious association with the brand—he had become the voice of Gallo. Little had changed except perhaps the idea of making a change for the sake of change.

The vintners' palates were far more discerning than their ears. They couldn't tell that the voice they had now made a prime candidate was indeed Dick's, again, just under an assumed name. They did however recognize that it wasn't too much different than that of their previous spokesman, and the Gallos then requested that their old announcer submit a new audition for reconsideration. Another tape was sent, and the choice for the plum gig was boiled down to be between Dick and... Dick!

Only Dick himself, his talent agent, and soon the Gallos' ad agency account executive knew that both tapes being compared each featured the voice of the same pitchman. Ernest, Julio, and the family went back and forth, listening and re-listening to the two similar-sounding candidates before finally deciding to give the job to their old spokesman, Dick Tufeld. Dick said he was relieved that he didn't need to open a new checking account in the assumed name.

The sound of a voice, a graphic image, a combination of words, a photograph, a sound, indeed any expression of an idea creates an impression and an emotional response when heard, seen, or experienced. It's all so esoteric that it's next to impossible to predict how a sight, a few notes of music, a face, or a voice will be received by an audience. Even with all of the extensive focus-group testing that manufacturers, ad agencies, TV producers, and network programmers have employed, they're all only making guesses.

The available research methodologies have all proven to be wrong so frequently that the job is almost entirely a right brain pursuit, more about mysticism than logic. The system employed for testing pilot TV episodes with potential viewers hasn't changed much over the decades. It's antiquated and, some say misguided. No wonder among the shows to test poorly were *All In The Family*, *The Mary Tyler Moore Show*, *Cheers* and *Seinfeld*, to name just a few of the mega-hits that defied the research and surprised the prognosticators.

Among those with supposedly golden ears and iron guts are a few of television's most celebrated programmers. As mere mortals their successes are subject to the law of averages and plain old dumb luck. Even the best of these gurus buy far more failures than hits. As one of the best handicappers in the world of daytime programming, Michael Brockman, told *The New York Times*, "I must see 150 to 200 game shows a year. We may invest in 15, and order pilots for four or five. Of those, one will get on the air. And only one out of every 4 that get on the air succeeds."

That dim track record was sufficiently bright for Michael to have been wooed from ABC to NBC to CBS, and then back to ABC. Lorimar, Sony and Mark Goodson Productions also recruited him for his expertise. Yet, when speaking to students anxious to play in the big leagues, he surprises them with the harsh reality of programming a network, "Be ready, because 90 to 95 percent of what you create will fail." Anticipating their question Mike adds, "Why get into this business? Because the other five to 10 percent is so rewarding, it makes it all worthwhile."

Michael devours all the research he can use, but is aware that the raw data doesn't tell the whole story. Personally, I think there have been sufficient miscalculations to warrant reconsidering the whole farce of asking members of the public to press buttons and turn dials to indicate when they liked and when they disliked something on the screen. Someone once told me that program predictors' time spent pouring over printouts of this kind of research is like trying to navigate through New Hampshire with a map of Vermont. There's just enough information to try and guess which roads might lead to where the Nielsen families live.

Of course there are some performers who have always been welcome in living rooms, no research needed. Few as beloved as Betty White

Chapter 25

Don't believe for a moment that America's effusive love affair with Betty White meant that she got to play by special rules. The immutable laws of commerce were applicable at her last sitcom, the successful and funny *Hot in Cleveland*. While visiting the set I learned about the staff's concern over the potential for the cancellation pink slip to be served at any time. While the show drew around three million viewers in season one, by season five it was barely attracting one million. At the post-taping cocktail party more of the inner mechanisms of the business of show business were revealed.

With approximately 100 episodes already produced, *Hot in Cleveland* had become a viable sale into the world of perpetual reruns—cable, the broadcast sub-channel "diginets", streaming, pay-per-view, over-the-top, on-demand, and whatever comes next, perhaps infrared pulses beaming from Mars. That second life is where the profits usually begin for the entity that owns a series. However, with a salable package already produced, investing in another season of *Hot in Cleveland* might not significantly increase the price when licensed into that realm of secondary and supplemental markets. The deficit financing required to cover the cost of manufacturing those additional episodes might create little added value and possibly never be fully recouped. Betty's bargain-basement salary of $75,000 was just one line item in each *Hot in Cleveland* episode's budget of over a million dollars.

What I was told next seemed pretty callous. Let me paraphrase. "With a critical mass of shows already in the can, why move forward with another season and face the unfortunate prospect that our senior star might die mid-production?" Sure, nobody wants to be in the process of cranking shows when the inevitable happens but, wow, that struck me as cold. I got the message. If their very senior citizen, dear Betty White, were to drop dead while working on additional episodes, it would be bad for business.

Already 93, betting incorrectly on Betty's continuing longevity would have wiped out the investment in each of the unproduced episodes. It would result in all manner of non-recoupable pre-production expenses in addition to the scriptwriting, and would end up with the bean counters having to buy-out the above-the-line people who might have pay-or-play contracts. The show would end up even deeper in the mire of debt before any chance to turn a profit in the aftermarket. In the limited context of that discussion, the concern for Betty's continued health was devoid of emotion. As beloved as she was at that show and throughout the industry, this calculation was only about dollars and cents.

The same analyses go on all day, every day among the people in the high-rise corner offices whose job it is to monetize assets. While it's part of every industry, it does seem a bit more unsympathetic in the realm of television where the product at the end of the assembly line makes such an intimate and emotional connection with the consumer. Lots of hearts and careers have been broken for people on the wrong side of this simple reality: the business half of show business always dominates.

At the end of all the closed-door discussions, economic projections can be just as fatal as underperforming ratings. Happily, in the case of *Hot in Cleveland* there was a sixth season. The show wrapped with a total of 128 episodes and, more importantly, with the first lady of TV still making America laugh. Betty continued to work until 2019 in the role of Bitey White as part of an all-star cast contributing voices to the feature film *Toy Story 4*.

Even those who have breathed the rarified air of superstardom are considered little more than cogs in the big machine. That's true for even the most celebrated, and few were ever held in higher esteem in the world of entertainment than Gene Kelly. The dancer-singer-actor of those great MGM musicals was also box office gold. In an evening of juxtaposed stars at a 2016 Malibu Film Society event I heard a curious story that illustrates the point.

That night Billy Crystal screened and chatted about filming his hysterical movie *Mr. Saturday Night* several years earlier. The great story of a comedian who had once been a TV star was finding a well-deserved second life in 2022 as a Broadway musical. A footnote among the memories Billy shared about making the movie was the wonderful surprise of meeting Gene Kelly when the 80-year-old happened to dance onto Billy's set at Culver Studios to say hello. Billy laughed, "I still have no idea what he might have been doing on the lot that day."

At that moment, a well-dressed, statuesque middle-aged woman stood and identified herself as Patricia Ward Kelly, Gene Kelly's widow. What a wild coincidence that she was among the few dozen at that night's screening when her husband's name happened to be mentioned in passing. Ms. Kelly explained that her hubby—47 years her senior—had indeed been on the lot that day years earlier, working for Madonna. The singer had hired Gene to help choreograph and to coach her dancing for a new music video. Patricia recalled her husband remarking that night about the unexpected spare time he had, and how he had dropped by Billy Crystal's set. She clearly remembered Gene's comments about that afternoon as it was the day that Madonna fired him.

That's right, dancing great Gene Kelly was sent walking. He then soft-shoed onto an adjacent sound stage before heading home to tell his wife he had been fired by Madonna. How do you do that? Dismiss Gene Kelly in the middle of a day, in the middle of working on a project. I believe him light years too professional and too savvy to have done anything stupid or self-destructive. I can't imagine he shot off his mouth with some invective, showed up drunk, or vandalized her car—it's ludicrous. Even if dissatisfied with his contribution, common decency mandates better manners. Patricia Kelly didn't share any other details, but if ageism was behind the firing, hell, Gene wasn't even on camera. Get Madonna on the phone. I need to hear her side of this!

Meeting a legendary superstar can be a wonderfully memorable event. For a dancer, a chance to shake hands with Gene would likely be unforgettable. However, to my thinking the biggest stars today are not the folks with the perfect implants, dental or breast. It's the people who toil day in and day out in near anonymity. These are the unsung heroes who, in the realm of television, cook up our video comfort food by creating and producing our favorite dramas, soaps, talk, game, reality, and interview shows. As an adolescent I did reconnaissance on the comings and goings of the people with whom I most wanted to arrange to accidentally cross paths.

These weren't traditional stars, but they were my stars. The network voices. Don Pardo, Fred Foy, Bill Wendell, Wayne Howell, Bill McCord, Jerry Damon, Bill Hanrahan, Fred Facey, Arthur Gary, Mel Brandt, NBC's last on staff Howard Reig, and my favorite from among them, the one who was the most accessible and most encouraging, Johnny Olson. Conversations with these guys proved far more relevant, infinitely more valuable, and light-years more condensed than what five years of college study taught me about broadcasting. No tuition, all it required was showing interest and listening.

At the same time that I was following Johnny O. from show to show in midtown Manhattan, he had prolific counterparts 3,000 miles away, bouncing between Burbank and Hollywood. Charlie O'Donnell, Jay Stewart, Gary Owens, Kenny Williams, Don Morrow and Johnny Gilbert were accessible, and generous with their time. While they all deserve to be celebrated, here's a nod to just one of those greats.

Born before broadcasting, Kenneth Williams Fertig told me that he was a proud native of Baltimore. Some accounts plant his flag elsewhere, Edmonton, Canada perhaps, but the best network broadcasters all seem to be citizens of the listener's hometown. Kenny Williams became one of the inner-circle go-to guys in the small cadre of west coast announcing talent. Blessed with classic baritone broadcasting pipes, Kenny's delivery was filled with equal parts stentorian resonance and joyful personality. That rich timbre first blasted out of speakers in the era of radio drama. Later, it refused to be diminished by early television receivers' tiny speakers. From 1949's *Auction-Aire*, his first outing at TV's dawning days, and through the glory years of daytime game shows his voice was instantly recognizable, until it was silenced in 1984.

Kenny was radio's original "Wildroot Cream Oil Charley" on *The Woody Herman Show*. For another program he opened a spaceman's adventures bellowing, "Buck Rogers in the 25th Century!" In game shows, Kenny boomed his unmistakable "Stop the music" for both Bert Parks and Dennis James, hosts of the show so titled. When Dennis later became the Old Gold cigarette pitchman on Herb Shriner's quiz *Two for the Money*, Kenny was there as the program's announcer. Not unusual for those in that role, his co-workers remember Kenny as an eternal purveyor of positive energy. Kenny was tall and stout, large and loud, and his hair was often tussled. He had the ruddy complexion common among both outdoorsmen and recreational drinkers, and nobody remembers ever seeing Kenny outdoors.

Once Kenny partnered with the prolific producing duo of Merrill Heatter and Bob Quigley for their premiere outing, *Video Village*, he remained a member of their team for the remainder of his career. In fact, it's hard to name any Heatter-Quigley show without Kenny behind the mic as well as performing the audience warm-up. No doubt he's best remembered these days for his 15 years introducing the stars in the little boxes on the producing pair's biggest hit, *The Hollywood Squares*. There, on set in NBC's Studio 3 Kenny talked about his simple joys on the days between tapings when minding the store he and his wife operated. During the 1970s and 1980s the couple indulged their interest in early Americana by opening Williams Antiques in Santa Monica.

Apparently business was good. Once they outgrew the original small shop on Montana Avenue, Kenny expanded to a new and larger location on the beach community's main drag at 1919 Wilshire Boulevard. What Kenny didn't share as openly was the secret behind his saving a fortune on the couple's vacation travel expenses. In addition to globe-trotting fun, the Williams' considered their many exotic expeditions to be the lifeblood of their business. Kenny could convince anyone that searching for and purchasing unique pieces from the far flung corners of civilization was what made the antiques store successful.

With that justification suddenly every trip is an important business expense, bulletproof in any IRS audit. He ultimately explained that at least half of the original motivation for having a retail shop was to substantiate the legitimacy of sizeable travel tax write-offs. Peter Marshall recently confirmed that his sidekick's antique business was a solid moneymaker. It generated a steady cash flow which easily justified Kenny's significant tax deductions without attracting scrutiny. He shrewdly turned the tables—the tax tables—on the IRS.

On the home front, Kenny's youngest daughter, Anne, remembered her father boasting that he played the first person in a radio soap opera to ever commit suicide. It was a claim to fame that disturbed his young son Kenneth as he heard his dad's death on-air and thought it was real. The boy couldn't be consoled until mom called the radio studio where Kenny was put on the line to explain that it was all make believe. Yes, daddy was fine and would be home later. There was similar silliness among their siblings Fran and Liz who, in later years, enjoyed some of the perks that came with dad's career - Liz worked on *Hollywood Squares* for a time.

Kenny and his fellow radio performers enjoyed a charade when the cast went for drinks after a broadcast. The silliness started when people at the bar recognized their voices and were drawn to eavesdrop. The actors would then adlib some outrageous scenario to hear the gasps from the adjacent patrons. In the same way, when out in a restaurant Mr. and Mrs. Williams could be overheard pretending to be cheating spouses subversively plotting the murder of Kenny's supposed wife. It was live radio drama for an audience of one or two, improvising the roles of a couple that were stepping out on their spouses and painstakingly planning a homicide.

Close your eyes and conjure a vision of the photos of Teddy Roosevelt's bigger-than-life presence and personality and you're well on your way to capturing the essence of Kenny Williams. At least one theatre director saw the resemblance and cast him in the memorable role as the rough and ready Teddy, charging up the stairs in a summer production of *Arsenic and Old Lace* in Baltimore's Hilltop House Theater. Kenny brought the same gusto to entertaining studio audiences in pre-show warm-ups with an act rated a solid family-friendly "G."

Peter Marshall recalls Kenny's two most risqué lines: "How many women in the audience today were formally introduced to their husbands? So the rest of you got picked up, huh?" Kenny also used the old chestnut standard of adding an addendum to the stage manager's announcement that informed everyone on set that show time is imminent. Stage Manager: "Only one minute to go." Kenny: "In case anybody has to." Some of these jokes can be carbon-dated to the dawn of broadcasting, if not earlier. The hackneyed material always got laughs because by the time Kenny hurled any of these lines he had already won over the audience. He had broken down their inhibitions and had endeared himself. It's an art form all its own. Once they like you, an audience will do pretty much whatever it takes to please their newest friend. Usually all we want is laughter and applause at all the right places.

Kenny had a few warm-up openers. One was a simple stride into view with a big loud and proud, "I'm Kenny Williams from Baltimore, Maryland! Where are you from?" Immediately everybody is aroused and energized as many guests start vocalizing their hometown pride. From there he was set for the jokes that gently play off of the audience members' specific responses ("San Bernadino? How'd the air look today?"). There are dozens of locations that have earned their own rapid repartee, and there are many more generic lines which can be paired perfectly with any place in the country. Most foreign lands are also covered, but the stereotyping behind the humor adds a bit of danger these days.

Kenny's simplest and silliest line was his admonition for the audience to avoid responding to Peter Marshall's questions intended for the players and celebrities on *Hollywood Squares*, "Don't blurt out the answers. There's no blurting allowed. If you feel the need to blurt, don't blurt here. You can blurt all you like later in the parking lot."

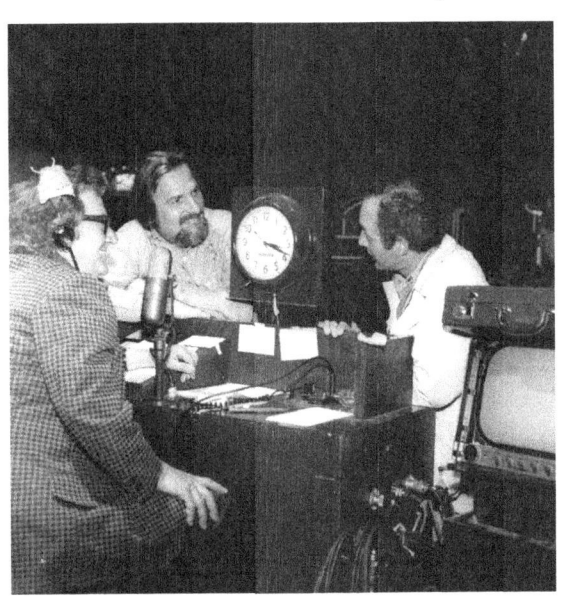

Announcer Kenny Williams at the classic RCA microphone enjoying the on-set camaraderie at NBC's *Baffle* with producer Art Alisi (center) and executive producer Bob Noah (1972).

Kenny had a unique set-up at his NBC shows. Unlike the majority of his peers, he sat through his announcing. The well-known truth is that sitting impedes the diaphragm's free movement and limits lung capacity, but eventually age trumps all of those rules when legs get weary. Kenny favored a big chair and a full-sized workspace. It was a big Early American desk because, after all, he was a big early American. More than anything else it was a big and messy desk with a clock, a table lamp, tissues, water, and his script pages which were often strewn haphazardly. At some earlier point those pages had been organized, hole-punched, and neatly entered into a loose-leaf binder, or at least stacked with a paper clip. It must have been too neat for his tastes.

I once believed that the loyalty between some producers and their go-to announcers, such as Kenny Williams' teaming with Merrill Heatter, was a reflection of personal friendships. I quickly learned that was often not the case. Mark Goodson and one of his most utilized voicers, Gene Wood, were never friends. For that matter, Mark Goodson and Johnny Olson were also simply cordial acquaintances. In fact, the game show impresario was dismissive on a couple of occasions when I brought up Johnny O's name. The complexities of that duo's relationship is a subject more fully explored in the Johnny Olson biography written a few years ago, *Johnny Olson: A Voice in Time*.

Goodson's announcers were not alone. As brilliant as he was and as much as he sought respect, friendship, and approbation, there was a serial streak in Goodson's personality that seemed to limit his drawing close with many of the people in his world. Professionally, he preferred to be referred to as "Mr. Goodson" even by many of the people he interacted with daily for years and years. More telling of his personality was his discouraging any of his employees' attributing glory for success to anyone other than him. As creator of three of Goodson-Todman's biggest hits Bob Stewart said, "Goodson takes credit for inventing oxygen."

In Gene's and Johnny's cases there was the added baggage from Goodson's own shattered career as an announcer. Suffering from an episode of extreme microphone fright left Goodson demoralized and especially sensitive about the success of those who were better suited to the role. During a period in the 1940s when he was successfully announcing several soap operas and earning far more than he thought he ever would, Goodson reported that he woke up in the middle of the night hearing a voice in his head. It said, "You're never going to be able to announce again."

As Goodson told it, he engaged the voice in conversation, responding with, "That's not true." The voice answered, "You watch!" The next day at NBC Goodson said he felt his throat constrict as his mouth became painfully dry. He recalled, "I was reading a commercial when my hands started to perspire and my voice began to tighten." With each show that day and with each day that followed, Goodson became more and more disabled. As he remembered, "Soon I would become nauseous if I walked into a studio."

With no organic illness it seems apparent that, for whatever reason, he created a psychosomatic reality that cost him his livelihood. He began psychotherapy and courageously faced a litany of neuroses and control issues over his many years on couches. As wildly successful as he was through most of his career, and despite his copious hours in several shrinks' offices on both coasts, Mark Goodson conceded that he continued to suffer with self-doubt and bouts of depression.

Self-admittedly, he carried painful and defeating memories of childhood poverty throughout his adult life. "I was very fat and not overwhelmed with self-love," he remembered. "We were very poor… My memory was always of where to eat, who would pay the rent, five-day-old bread, secondhand clothes. I loathed that idea. There was a whole feeling of catastrophe right around the corner." Poignantly, the bounty of good luck that helped to propel his success and brought the ample loot he sought proved insufficient to quell his fears of financial insecurity or fully purge his feelings of inferiority. It was especially evident during his and Bill Todman's first blush of success.

Producers Bill Todman (l) and Mark Goodson (r) take a moment with Johnny Roventini, sponsor Phillip Morris's spokesman "Johnny the bellboy," at a special radio episode of *What's My Line?* Produced for NBC (1952).

The duo already had a trio of thriving series running on CBS—*Winner Take All*, *What's My Line?* and *Beat The Clock*. However, director Frank Heller remembered the quiet moment in the 1950s when Goodson admitted that he felt like a second class citizen when hobnobbing with other CBS producers. In that era of live drama, game shows were clearly less respected by the critics, the network, and the TV community in general. He was intent on rising above that prejudice to prove himself equal to the talents of the showrunners for CBS's prestige scripted productions.

Those esteemed series, including *Suspense* and *Danger*, were being written by celebrated scribes that included Rod Serling, Gore Vidal and Reginald Rose. The cream of the era's rising New York theater actors rotated in and out of these respected authors' dramas which were being directed by esteemed heavyweights such as John Frankenheimer, Sidney Lumet and Yul Brynner.

When *Suspense* was granted a summer hiatus, the sales department was in a bind as they had already sold the time to a sponsor. Suddenly, a comparable replacement program was needed for 1950's eight warm-weather weeks. It was a serendipitous moment for Goodson and Todman. When the call came to CBS's production department with the order for a summer replacement series, they happened to be visiting those very offices on the 14th floor at the network's Madison Avenue headquarters. The pair immediately jumped on the opportunity to mount their first dramatic outing, even though there were only four weeks to prepare everything. Budgets, scripts, casting, rehearsals, wardrobe, set construction, and everything else for two months of weekly shows needed to be generated immediately.

Despite none of the three having any dramatic experience, Heller was instantly invited aboard as a producer for this maiden voyage into the new genre. The team soon feared the task was an impossible mission, but Goodson's pride stood in the way of calling the network for help. Heller remembered the 18-hour days and the indigestion that came with somehow pulling it all together. Under the umbrella title *The Web*, their anthology of stories focused on people snared in a web of confounding situations beyond their control.

Their July debut program, *The Twelfth Juror*, garnered a vote of confidence from the network, having never realized how close to airtime the show had finally come together. The trio's subsequent summer programs gave *The Web* enough momentum to continue as a weekly series for the next four years. It also laid the foundation for Goodson-Todman to add several later series to their output. Among them was the successful *Goodyear Theater* (1957–1960). Don Rickles' comedy-variety outing for ABC in 1968 failed to gain traction despite a sterling roster of guest stars.

The New York-based game show mavens' one and only sitcom was a money-loser that survived for only 15 episodes on NBC in 1961. *One Happy Family* was a full-budget first-class production that filmed 3,000 miles away in Hollywood and seemed to have all the makings for success, except for an audience. Its only claim to fame was casting Dick Sargent as the male lead in his first comedy series, eight years before he broke through as Darrin Stephens on *Bewitched*. There was a crime drama, *Philip Marlowe* (1959-60), but ultimately it was a couple of the team's westerns that added cash and cachet to their young company's coffers, *The Rebel* (1959-61) and *Branded* (1965-67).

Although often proven otherwise, money is generally considered to be the antidote for insecurity. With his partner's astute investment choices eventually Mark Goodson had what's commonly known as "fuck you money." Yet he found it fell short of being either a healing remedy or an inoculation against future problems, large or small. "Money never became to me things I could buy, nor the ability to purchase a boat or 50 watches," the producer explained. "Money to me gave me an overwhelmingly strange sense of security. It is a symbolic sense of achievement and control of the world. There's something I must confess, although it sounds cocky. Environment controlled me; I was helpless in it. I want to control it, have authority, not be at its mercy, have dignity."

As a regular among his company's runthrough and pilot contestants in later years, I was fascinated watching Goodson. Although he was a compact man who stood a ways short of six feet, he appeared bigger-than-life, intriguing and complex with incredible instincts and a razor-sharp mind. The self-made mogul was universally respected for the empire he built, and was known for being a man of his word. By virtue of his refined appearance, studied deportment, and well-rehearsed polished manner, Goodson instantly commanded respect at a first meeting. He had thoroughly disguised all evidence of the overwhelming insecurity and childhood poverty he now rarely acknowledged.

The secondhand clothes were replaced by an exceptional wardrobe of custom-fit bespoke threads. It's true that FedEx was flying his shirts round-trip from Los Angeles to be purified and pressed by his trusted launderer in New York. Whether in a tux, suit, or sweater, formal or casual, the game show king was always dressed impeccably. Wielding a pipe enabled this self-made magnate to punctuate as well as add dramatic pauses in conversation. Slowly drawing on its smoke added a professorial sophistication that seemed to give added import to the comments that followed.

Perpetually tan and fit, Mark Goodson was the undisputed king of 20th century game shows, bringing several classic formats to the small screen that continue to thrive on network television 65 years later.

Goodson's employees were loyal and admiring, but where other production company moguls engendered an atmosphere of informality and familiarity, most of his workers remained at arm's length. That cool distance extended to Goodson's—sorry, Mr. Goodson's—relationships with a number of his hits' hosts. His disagreements over presentation and compensation with both Gene Rayburn and Richard Dawson ranged from nuanced to explicit at various times.

Going back decades, there was one very public moment of on-set dysfunction when Mark Goodson's cover was blown, along with that of another host, a polished public personality whose roots were equally humble. It was the day when the greatest game show producer of all time fought with the first game show host of all time. Mark Goodson vs. Dennis James. They didn't just do battle in some metaphoric sense, they were all but ready to brawl. The disagreement started with Goodson distracting the host by gesturing just a few feet from his face. Goodson was throwing cues, trying to direct Dennis's interview of a contestant. It was perceived as an insult by the man who had conducted the very first and perhaps more of these impromptu player Q-and-A moments than anyone else in the universe. During the next commercial break Dennis put his boss up against a wall and barked, "Don't ever do that to me again when I'm on camera!" Witnesses said that Goodson didn't simply cower, but responded in kind with words, tone, and physicality that suggested the altercation might quickly escalate.

Dennis's Jersey City Italian temper had reared its head before, but this was a side of Goodson that was infinitely more startling. It was perhaps most shocking to the producer himself, as he had worked hard and spent lavishly to sublimate any evidence of his working-class roots. Reverting to fisticuffs would be completely out of character with his dignified public image, refined manners, elegant wardrobe, impeccable grooming, and other affected trappings of genteel society.

Never coming close to anything resembling a brawl, the producer's long partnership with Bob Barker was amiable but never close. One knowing staffer described their relationship as "cool symbiosis," a loveless marriage of convenience from which they each profited handsomely. Whatever friendship could be ascribed to their association was little more than what was necessary to protect and nurture that business partnership. Bob held his boss in the highest regard with respect for his genius intuitive insight into television games, but categorized their relationship as "business, not social." He told me that when he assumed the executive producer role on *The Price is Right* the two regularly spoke by phone concerning their mutual golden goose, the show, but little else.

For those who didn't already know the nature of their pairing, there was one extremely conspicuous opportunity to discern it. Although not widely known at the time, in late 1991 Goodson's health was in decline. The diagnosis was pancreatic cancer. It was the motivation behind the production of a birthday party that rivaled any I'd seen. The 77-year-old was feted with a video retrospective of his half century of success. Planning was extensive for the meticulously-staged event in the Mark Goodson Screening Room at the American Film Institute. Scores of Goodson's employees, friends, business associates, and family members were in attendance. That included celebrities, producers, directors, writers and every emcee anywhere near Los Angeles. Barker's failure to make even a token appearance at his benefactor's career-closing tribute told the tale.

We enjoyed a 90-minute collection of rare clips that chronicled Goodson's career, and some in-person lauding from the hosts and panelists in attendance. Those who were too old, infirm, distant, or otherwise unavailable were there via videotape. They included Arlene Francis, Richard Dawson, Garry Moore, Henry Morgan, Kitty Carlisle, Dennis James, and others. There was nothing from Barker. A couple of others who weren't present sent cards or flowers that were on display. Again, no Barker. It was especially obvious since the affair was held mere walking distance from The World's Greatest M.C.'s home. He abstained from attending the final public tribute to the impresario for whom he worked during the 20 most lucrative years of his half century on television.

Borrowing from Jack Nicholson's line, "You want the truth?" Of course the dichotomy of on-set harmony and off-set rancor was not limited to the Goodson camp, and not at all limited to the realm of game shows. While there was friction between Michael Strahan and Kelly Ripa that reportedly was rooted, in part, in a salary disparity, it was less volatile than an earlier case of despairing pairing. Regis Philbin and Kelly Ripa appeared to be such adoring pals to their loyal morning audience, but Kelly has since hinted about the awkwardness between them. "Regis had a mandate—absolutely no talking off-camera," she told *The New York Times*. "He had almost a superstition about it. You save it for the show. I'd be like, 'Good morning,' and he'd say, 'Save it for the air!'"

I first dismissed Kelly's complaint as merely a misunderstanding about Regis's quirky way to keep the duo's on-air adlib chat fresh. Then, in 2017 Regis himself came clean with Larry King, confirming that while working as a pair, he and Kelly Ripa didn't speak when not on-camera, he claimed not at all. He then admitted that following his retirement they still weren't speaking. Word is that they even did their best to avoid bumping into each other at parties, and it was especially obvious at one particular get-together thrown by *Live!* producer Michael Gelman.

As time passed after his 2011 retirement, Regis could be heard complaining about never being invited to return to the show that he inaugurated back in the

1970s as *A.M. New York*. Adding insult to injury, after a proposed salary cut motivated his resignation Regis was surprised and wounded when not afforded even a cameo for Kelly's 15th anniversary celebration in 2016. He said, "Never once did they ask me to go back." Memory can be selective. Regis did return once, greeted by a seemingly pleased Kelly for a 2015 Halloween special segment.

While Johnny Carson and Ed McMahon appeared to be great buddies, by the last decade of their pairing the duo barely spoke during the 23 hours they were off camera. If not for Ed's daily fleeting courtesy visit with his benefactor before each show, they could go months without social interaction. Ed said that his daily seven or eight minute pop in was more like a performance than a chat between pals. He was sure to end it on a laugh from the boss. According to *Tonight Show* executive producer Peter Lassally, the pair would lunch but once a year and Johnny dreaded the annual indulgence.

At the risk of shattering a beloved illusion, things weren't all sunshine and flowers even in the idyllic TV town of Mayberry, home of *The Andy Griffith Show*. Andy and co-star Don Knotts were both good friends and pros, and each had a loving relationship with little Ronny Howard. Andy was very much a father figure to the young actor, which would make Don the fun uncle. He and Ron had their baseball gloves handy and would sometimes play catch during crew setups.

By most accounts Andy was as down to earth, warm, and countrified as the character he played, devoid of a star's ego, serious about the show's content, and with a sense of humor about his rural ideals. However, like all of us, Andy could be provoked. His restrained resentment was reserved for a Broadway and film veteran who was classically trained and considered herself dreadfully constrained in her role. As Aunt Bea, Frances Bavier felt creatively unfulfilled and unchallenged, locked into her two-dimensional domesticated role. Her frustration was no secret, but Andy was neither sympathetic nor indulgent. He answered the annoyance by being controlling and sarcastic, openly calling her "cranky" and "miserable."

Others reportedly walked on eggshells around Bavier so as not to offend her. A perceived affront could trigger an angry outburst, a period of sulking, or even a few tears. As the only citizen of Mayberry to play her role for the 10 year life of the series and its spinoff, more than any other actor her individuality was lost in her character. Forever to be known as Aunt Bea, the actress explained that it was difficult to be "so identified that you as a person no longer exist."

Some relationships sour more than others, and a few even elevate to long-running blood feuds. For some, harsh feelings mellow with age. Andy Griffith said Francis Bavier eventually apologized for her being "difficult" during their years together. There was no mellowing for one pair of combatants that took their hatred to their graves.

Chapter 26

"She set the Jews back 1,000 years." That was part of a 2014 Jerry Lewis rant about his decades of seething disdain for another New York comic. About the object of his contempt Jerry said, "I always feel bad when somebody passes away," then added, "except if it was Joan Rivers." The timing was prophetic, as a bungled medical procedure a mere three months later preempted his need to follow through with a letter he sent. It reads like a death threat.

Here's the invective Jerry wrote: "Dear Ms. Rivers, we've never met, and I'm looking forward to keeping it that way." After a few other un-pleasantries, Jerry got serious: "If you find it necessary to discuss me, my career, or my kids ever again, I promise you I will get somebody from Chicago to beat your God damned head off."

Of course, the kids Jerry referenced were not his brood of biological children, but the dozens of children with Muscular Dystrophy who appeared on his annual MDA telethons. Over the years the broadcast became his *raison d'être*, and was rumored to provide him with very significant compensation for his efforts. Jerry's hosting of the yearly affair was the bone of contention in this feud.

Jerry Lewis and Joan Rivers, and the flip side of comedy.
(Joan Rivers photo courtesy of djnaquin67)

After appearing on the fundraiser one Labor Day Joan minced no words restating the number-one criticism that others have also levied against Jerry over the years. Joan went public stating, "He was standing there with a child next to him saying, 'This kid is gonna die.'" She described it as blatant exploitation of the children and vowed that she would "never do the telethon again." She continued, "You do not say in front of a little boy who is going to die, 'This child is going to die.' Who are you? You unfunny, lucky, stupid asshole."

Jerry responded with, "Joan attacked me in the press. All she said was, 'Jerry Lewis has to be thankful that he has the telethon, because it helps his career.' And then she went on and was even a little more salty." He knew his note about having Joan's head beaten off crossed a line as that initial loveless love letter included, "You're not allowed to threaten people. So if you go to [the police], show them this letter, they'll arrest me, but I want you to never forget what I said."

Joan didn't show Jerry's letter to the police and said she chose not to file a harassment charge. Just the same, she took the threat seriously. Explaining in a SiriusXM interview, "I don't need my knees broken by Jerry Lewis." The comedienne claimed she even "hired guards," explaining, "My last words are not gonna be 'But I was only kidding!'" In 2016 author Leslie Bennetts quoted Joan on the matter, "'Done.' she said, 'Never talking about him again!'" For two people born only about 15 miles from each other, each gifted with a world-class sense of humor, there was nothing funny about the bad blood between them that was indeed carried to their graves.

In his threatening letter Jerry claimed he'd never met Joan. Hey, in this era of fake news what's one more lie. Actually, two lies. They were obviously together when she appeared on the telethon. In addition, by chance, I happened to be in the audience on another day when they were together. Jerry guested on Joan's 1968 talk program, *That Show*, which taped in a small third-floor studio at NBC, New York. It was a cute little low-budget syndicated outing that I visited frequently because of Joan's showbiz guests. The other attraction was the extraordinary access she afforded audience members every tape day by taking a moment to personally greet each visitor with a quick chat and a handshake, hug, or autograph.

The surprising coincidence was compounded decades later when Joan wrote about that specific day with Jerry on her show. Obviously some of the seeds of their mutual disdain were planted back then, before her telethon appearance. "Jerry Lewis," Joan remembered, "came on our dumb little show like a big king, demanding everything." She claimed he "arrived late, full of being Jerry Lewis [wanting] a bigger dressing room. . . champagne. . . and flowers."

Joan said she was dumbfounded by what she saw during the quick 30-minute program: "Two thirds of the way through the show [Jerry] looked at his watch and said, 'I've got to go' and walked out." A little research indicates that Jerry only guested on *That Show* once, and for what it's worth, I don't remember him leaving before the taping was over. I was there, and I'd certainly have remembered that. Joan's last words on the matter were in an interview with Anderson Cooper. He mentioned Jerry's threatening letter and Joan took no time responding, "Well, when did we last laugh at Jerry Lewis? Look, the French think he's funny. Those idiots."

Comedy can turn to tragedy and backstage can become a battleground when a couple of strong-willed personalities clash, especially under the pressure of a daily deadline. Like the time in October, 2004 when a long simmering hostility came to a boil at David Letterman's show. One of Dave's comedy writers and his cue card man had a memorable physical altercation. Havana-born Tony Mendez had been a classically trained ballet dancer who performed on Broadway before aging past his spry days of pirouetting and gamboling. Mendez then returned to his earlier work in the world of cue cards, having once learned the fine art of feeding lines to top-tier talent from the king of cue cards himself, the beloved Barney McNulty.

Before fully-electronic teleprompters were perfected in the 1980s, Barney was Hollywood's go-to guy, helming an entire industry he built with 14 by 22-inch bright white heavy card stock and Marsh T99 refillable markers. Among many employees over the years, Barney hired Mendez to flip cards for his clients. That roster included all of Bob Hope's specials, *The Lucy Show*, *The Hollywood Palace*, and a steady diet of daily soaps. "Inky" Mendez came to the Letterman show following nine years at *Saturday Night Live*. The other combatant in the showdown was Letterman's comedy scribe Bill Scheft, a Harvard graduate with 15 Emmy nominations for his inventiveness.

The comedy writer had micromanaged the abbreviation of his jokes on the cards once too many times. The next day it started again and Mendez, then age 69 and five-foot seven-inches, lunged at the taller 57-year-old Scheft. They were up against the wall. "He tells me what to do and… I know what I'm doing," Mendez screamed. He later acquiesced, "I should have never put my hands on him, but I never hit him. I just grabbed him and got my face in his face… He didn't say a word. He was cowering, his eyes were real big, he probably peed a little bit on his pants." Mendez's 21 years with Dave ended that day when he was permanently escorted off the premises.

The sadder clash at *The Late Show* involved one of the great network voicers, Bill Wendell, at what turned out to be his career-capping gig. Bill was in radio when invited to join the first generation of TV performers. While some chose to steer clear of radio's poorer-paying unproven little brother, Bill was there at the DuMont Network hosting a talent showcase, *Stage a Number*, when casts and crews were still formulating through trial and error how to best work in the new medium. Almost 50 years later he was still in the game on a daily basis, up until his 1995 retirement at age 71. However, calling it a retirement is to spin the reality of his firing. It was the crowning moment of the long increasingly-contentious relationship he had with Dave, the seeds of which came into full bloom at CBS.

Before the hours in late-night, Bill was one of the peacock's staff announcers providing the voice for countless live and taped broadcasts of all genres over the years. He even hosted occasionally, as was the case with *Tic Tac Dough*, subbing for Jack Barry during the Congressional probe into game show rigging. Among his later assignments was to announce and warm-up the crowd at Dave's original daytime program. The young host took an immediate liking to Bill, admiring both his classic broadcasting sensibilities and his extensive resume. He was impressed that Bill had worked with so many video VIPs, including Bob Hope, Dave Garroway, Jack Paar, Merv Griffin, Garry Moore, Tom Snyder, Billy Crystal, and Jerry Seinfeld.

There was also much to be said for Bill's direct connection to one of Dave's influences, Ernie Kovacs. The DNA of many of Dave's physical bits can be traced directly back to Kovacs' skewed sensibility and magical manipulation of the medium. Director Hal Gurnee happily credits much of the trick photography and special effects that he and Dave collaborated on as being inspired by Kovacs' innovative early shows. For years, Bill Wendell had been Kovacs' trusted on-camera partner, foil, and straight man as they ad-libbed their way together through the spontaneity of live TV. Just as Dave did when he reviewed Kovacs' shows, you can also see Bill featured prominently on some of the surviving Kovacs kinescopes.

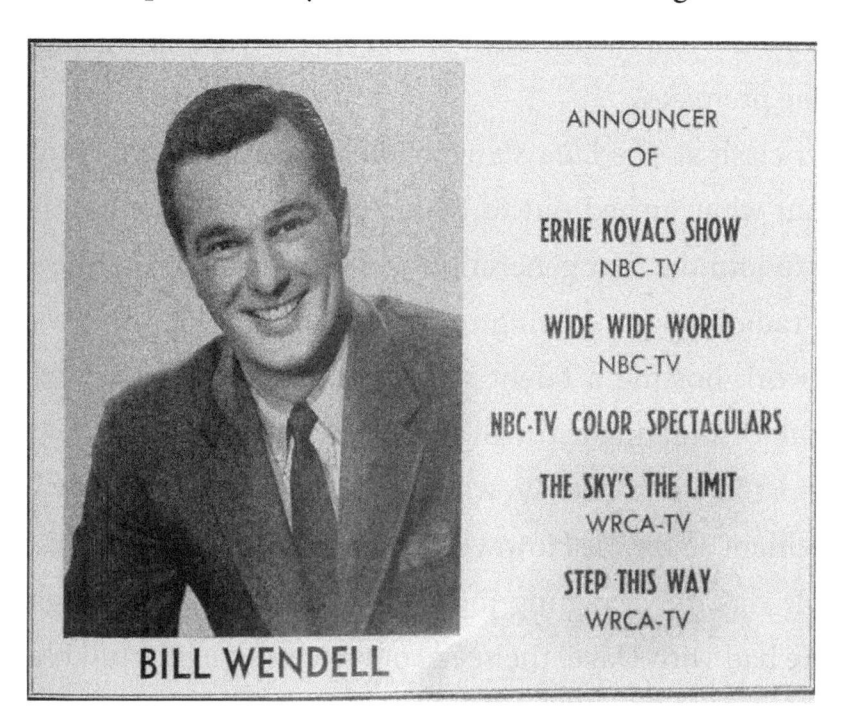

Bill Wendell, with credentials that inspired confidence.

Bill Wendell's daughter, Francette, told *The New York Times* about the wealth of wonderful memories Bill had from his years with Kovacs in video's infancy. "They were always playing practical jokes on each other," she recalled. "One time Ernie was supposed to gulp a big martini, but it was supposed to be filled with water, only it was really filled with vodka. He spit it out and started coughing like crazy on live national television. Dad and his cronies were laughing their heads off."

In addition to the Kovacs connection, Dave is on record saying he was amazed by the way Bill's audience warm-up could generate gale-force applause from an assemblage of barely 250, even long before Dave was a household name and an attraction unto himself. Bill loved the newfound public profile and the higher-wattage reflected light that came with Dave's move from daytime to late night. He took to driving a pink Lincoln Continental with the license plate "WARMUPS."

The Wendell-Letterman pairing was still strong in the aftermath of the late night wars during which Dave Letterman was heartbroken from being passed over when Jay Leno was proclaimed the heir to *The Tonight Show*. It was Carson's producer Peter Lassally who helped Dave regroup, explaining that with Johnny Carson gone *The Tonight Show* no longer existed as it once had. It was time to move on and accept CBS's generous offer to create a new 11:30 p.m. franchise at double his previous salary. Dave extended an invitation for Bill Wendell to join him for the short walk to CBS.

A dozen years into Bill's bond with Dave the camaraderie dissolved. Not that they were ever great friends. When asked by The *Los Angeles Times* to describe his relationship with Dave, Wendell said tersely: "I've never been to his house and he's never been to mine. OK?" He revealed that he and his boss hadn't seen each other or spoken in over eight months. How is it possible to work on the same show every day and, for more than half a year, not so much as exchange a greeting when passing in the halls? Easy. Dave had turned a cold shoulder. Bill was frozen out from the active role he'd enjoyed when the show was at NBC. His time in the Ed Sullivan Theatre was cut to the barest minimum. He was replaced as warm-up, and was relegated to performing the bulk of his announcing at a studio a block away.

Indeed, as part of his being sidelined Bill was banished off-site to record the usual promos and sponsorship IDs, as well as the opens and closes for elements of the show that were being stripped as stand-alone daily radio and internet features. Dave preferred to have *The Late Show* incur the added cost of renting studio time at a facility across Broadway from the theater rather than have the old pro in the building. Bill was severely marginalized and, under his gruff veneer, he was hurt.

The situation devolved to where Bill had nearly zero involvement with the program. He would deliver his top-of-show spiel from offstage, and then wait the longest 60 minutes of his day before he could leave the studio. He was required to hang around for the complete taping on the rare chance that he might need to re-record the opening to accommodate any last minute change in the guest line-up. Bill was then happy to finally head out the door, one time telling me how that theater felt ice cold to him in more ways than one.

The veteran broadcaster considered it all to be a huge indignity, and indeed it was. Bill put on a reasonably happy face on the extremely rare occasions when he came face-to-face with Dave, but cursed him openly, loudly, and quite creatively at the remote recording sessions. Bill never understood how the once vibrant on and off-air relationship had soured. He dismissed it as some idiosyncratic whimsy of the quirky star, and that may not have been far from the truth as Dave later acknowledged he long suffered with "crushing depression" and anxiety. He's since admitted they were the key components of his increasingly dysfunctional relationship with a number of key co-workers. He spoke of being frustrated with many things including the glacially-slow committee approach to creativity. Dave may have been the only talk host who simply stopped going to his own show's production meetings.

Control issues and neuroses extended to to where intricate protocols were instituted to properly stack the studio audience's seating each evening. Mega-fans were positioned in the orchestra section, the younger and more reactive, the closer to the front rows. The least desirable were relegated to the balcony. Although transparent to ticket-holders, the complexity of the rating system rivaled the charting of the D-Day invasion.

The comedian seems to have found some relief from his anxiety in fairly harmless ritualistic and compulsive behaviors. A visit to his dressing room at the Ed Sullivan Theater revealed that he took to stacking Styrofoam cups. He added one to the soaring stacks before each show. Had the practice begun with the very first taping of his 23 seasons, Dave would have amassed towers totaling some 6,000 polystyrene coffee cups. Stranger yet was another practice that began at an unknown date during his CBS years. Well known for wearing pricey Paloma Picasso's Minotaure cologne, David's office had its own very different scent. That one came from the copious amounts of the less expensive Roger Golay 4711 cologne that he generously sprinkled around the room, leaving the office carpeting to begin to dry as he headed down to the stage each night.

Resistant to seeking any treatment, Dave's frustration grew over a period of many months into 2000 when his trusted heart surgeon convinced him to get help. Dave finally put himself in the hands of a psychiatrist and surrendered his long-held refusal to take psychotropic medication. In a 2015 interview with the *Associated Press* he shared that "drugs like Paxil and Lexapro [along with transcendental meditation] changed my life." The proof: "And now I don't punch Sheetrock and scream as much."

Executive producer Robert "Morty" Morton couldn't put a finger on exactly when Bill Wendell was first marked for extinction more than a handful of years before Dave's psychic healing, but admits that the star had wanted his once-valued announcer fired many months before he was finally canned. You'll never believe what Morty said were the crowning moments that sealed Bill's fate. First, there was the problem with the announcer's uncontrolled flatulence. Seriously. Morty reported that Bill would stand at the producer's table that was directly in front of the first row of the audience and let loose with audible and odious farts. He would act as if nothing was amiss as he released a continuing barrage of gas bombs throughout the hour show.

Morty said he, cue card guru Tony Mendez, and a cameraman were all within a few feet of each other and next to Bill at that location. They couldn't help but laugh each time their eyes met, looking up upon hearing the old-timer's discharges only to find him appearing completely unaware of his offensives. His air of obliviousness was either the result of some unexplainable biologic anomaly or an award-worthy performance of nonchalance. There was no pet dog for Bill to blame it on. Morty said there were times when Dave would ask him what triggered the laughter at the producer's table, "Gas leak over there?"

Finally, there was an act of outrageous pettiness that couldn't be ignored. In 2018, Morty told podcaster Mark Malkoff that he once saw Bill leaving the theater carrying a case of the bottled water that the show regularly had delivered for the staff. When confronted, Morty said Bill just kept walking while he mumbled something to the effect of, "Yep, taking some water home." Although he was later asked not to do that, it wasn't long before Morty again saw Bill schlepping a case of water out an exit door. As inconsequential as a few dollars of water was, Morty said he couldn't simply turn a blind eye to the combination of Bill's insubordination and sense of entitlement. With Dave's love and respect for Bill long faded, the host didn't intercede. The old pro was fired for the first and only time in 40 years.

In August of 1995, ready to voice his last Letterman shows, Bill wasn't disguising his vitriol. "It's… strange between us. We used to do skits, [I'd] go over and talk with Letterman, all of that is gone." During his awkward final days Bill claimed that neither Dave nor the network bothered to call. He told The *Los Angeles Times* that not one of the *Late Show* producers was any better, "[They] haven't said a thing to me, either. Frankly, I don't think they care." On Bill's final *Late Show*, Letterman gave Bill an on-camera moment, announcing his departure after decades of service. The expected "Thank you," "We'll miss you" or "It won't be the same without you" were all absent. It was little more than simply, "Bill's been with us a long time, and this is his last show."

There was a telling moment after Bill accepted an invitation from Tom Snyder, who wanted to celebrate his pal's retirement. It came when Bill corrected Tom on-air, explaining that, no, he wasn't retiring but he was unemployed. The last time I spoke to Bill he told me, "I never should have left the network." That network being NBC, where he had been under contract for decades before exiting with Dave. NBC, where he now found his calls unreturned, dashing his hopes of returning.

If Bill had asked his buddy Don Pardo for advice when deciding whether to stay at 30 Rock or exit with Dave, he would have been advised to stay with the network. That was Don's choice in 1963 when he was faced with much the same dilemma—stay with his NBC deal or leave with Bill Cullen and *The Price is Right* when the show moved to ABC. Don stayed, despite Mark Goodson's offer to double his annual salary to $100,000. It was huge money, equivalent to approximately $900,000 in 2022 dollars. Don told me his wife threatened to divorce him if he didn't grab that cash. In retrospect, staying in the peacock's well-feathered nest was the right move.

Bill Wendell's blind-siding dismissal happens in all kinds of businesses. Outside of the entertainment industry it's usually sparked by some offense far worse than a "gas leak." It's just unfortunate when there's no grace, gentility, or courtesy to be found. A gold watch isn't necessary, but a kind word as you're being frozen out would be nice. In the case of Dave and Bill, a little more civility would have helped elevate the entire industry while providing some solace for *The Late Show* staff and others who toil both on and behind the mics and cameras. Younger and hipper, Alan Kalter slid smoothly into Bill's role and immediately became a bigger part of Dave's show. Alan performed regular comedy bits and enjoyed lucrative camera time that far overshadowed the involvement Bill had ever enjoyed.

After the announcer trade-off it appears that Dave Letterman indulged in a bit of revisionist history that further diminished Bill Wendell's cachet. Dave was quoted numerous times over the years paying homage to the innovative broadcaster from whom he drew inspiration, Ernie Kovacs. Bill was rightfully proud of having shared the stage and the TV screen with Kovacs, feeling it strengthened his bond with Dave. Perhaps it's an unexplainable coincidence or maybe it's more evidence of how petty even successful performers can be, but after the love was lost between Dave and Bill, the host disavowed his previous crediting Kovacs' influence.

In an interview with John O'Connor for a March 8, 1987 story in *The New York Times*, Dave cited Kovacs as a source of inspiration. Nine years later, on February 26, 1996, just months after severing the relationship with Bill Wendell, Dave was a guest on Charlie Rose's PBS broadcast. In that conversation Dave corrected Rose's observation that some of Dave's comedy was obviously inspired by Kovacs. Suddenly, that was no longer the case.

So ended Bill Wendell's once illustrious career. Among the last words I heard from the veteran broadcaster was a note of optimism about the prospect for other work, but I think truthfully he was already resigned to a different reality. Soon after we spoke he retired to Florida to try to enjoy whatever time he had remaining. His long battle with prostate cancer was lost in April of 1999 in Boca Raton. Bill was 75. In his last interview with *The New York Times*, Bill reflected, "All in all, it's been a good life. And, as they say, no heavy lifting."

As for Bill's license plates, "WARMUP," there's no clue if they've ever been on anybody else's car. There have been lots of pros who very deservedly could have displayed that moniker with pride.

Chapter 27

Mission Impossible: Find something new and different, but comfortably familiar.

No wonder programmers go in and out of the networks' revolving doors in record time. I've met about a dozen of these past and present hopeful hit-pickers, and this business of handicapping dozens of producers' pitches is not for the faint of heart. Recently ferreting out successful series for NBC was Robert Greenblatt who did likewise at Fox and, later, HBO. He says, "…You can't strategize your way into it. You can't formalize a process that figures out how to check off the boxes so you can just manufacture [a hit]."

Channing Dungey of ABC, Netflix, and now Warner Bros. adds, "When you're actually sitting in this seat, every decision that you make has real creative and financial repercussions. It's much more complicated." It sure is. Just ask Lou Ehrlich. He was the ABC executive who said "No" to Bill Cosby's 1980s record-breaking smash sitcom. When pitched the show a second time by former executives at his own network, Marcy Carsey and Tom Werner, he turned it down a second time. Off Carsey and Werner went to NBC to make history.

The best known of the prognosticators was Fred Silverman who *Time* ordained as "the man with the golden gut." When we last left Fred in these pages, he was two-thirds of his way through his tenures at all three networks. When he was hot he couldn't be beat. Just the same, there was a limit to the magic that even the golden-gutted Fred Silverman could pull from his bag of tricks. After assembling a lineup of smart sitcoms (*M*A*S*H*) and quality dramas (*The Waltons*) at CBS, he then counter-programmed those creations at ABC by targeting younger, bluer-collar males with working-class sitcoms (*Laverne and Shirley*) and buxom blonds in what was called "Jiggle TV" (*Charlie's Angels*). Then, as president at NBC his reputation for successes (*St. Elsewhere* and *Cheers*) was overshadowed by low-rated notorious blunders (*Pink Lady* and *Supertrain*).

Among the series with which he allowed both success and misery to slip through his fingers at CBS was *Sanford and Son*. He made a snap decision to turn it down, only to then find it undefeatable when the sitcom dominated its time period on NBC. Creators Norman Lear and Bud Yorkin said that they couldn't get Fred to even take just a few minutes to look at the new concept they had earmarked for their home-turf network—it couldn't have been easier, as Lear was renting space right there at Television City preparing to shoot the pilot. After his refusal, Fred had no idea that Norman then coaxed NBC's buyers to actually drive onto the CBS lot in order to watch the live presentation intended for him.

Fred confirmed it in the press. "It was one of the stupidest things I did at CBS." He confessed to author Michael Seth Starr, "We had *All in the Family* on the air and Bud and Norman came in with the idea, and it was called *Steptoe and Son*. They failed to mention that Redd Foxx was on it, or that it was going to be a black show. They never said that. And they just described it and I said, 'Well, I don't understand, you are selling us a show we already have. I mean, we have *All in the Family* and this sounds like *Archie and Meathead*.'"

I doubt the pitch was that vague as *Sanford and Son* was groundbreaking, debuting as the first network series with a predominantly black cast since *Amos 'n' Andy* in 1951. Revisionist history is only incontrovertible after everyone else in the story is dead. When Norman Lear celebrated his 99th birthday in July of 2021 he successfully locked his origin story as the definitive version. While Fred missed out on Norman and partner Bud Yorkin's hit, he unwittingly saved himself the grief of dealing with Redd Foxx.

Harder to swallow than his story about the *Sanford and Son* pitch are Fred's grabs for glory in the realm of game shows. It's an area he variably dismissed as being a somewhat baffling corner of the business populated by a "strange breed" of producers, and then gloated that it's a field in which he has engineered great successes. The long relationship between CBS and Goodson-Todman Productions that had faded by the early 1970s was renewed on Fred's watch in 1972, but it was championed by Bud Grant who had just arrived from NBC. Then, shortly after Fred's move to ABC, he almost scotched a really big deal insisting that the format for *Family Feud* was flawed. He advocated against the opportunity for an opposing team to steal points with a correct answer after the other family's strike out.

In reality the steal is the moment of greatest drama, a vital element in the game, and Mark Goodson knew it. The stalemate between these two TV tycoons ultimately came to a head when they sat across a table from each other. Each had a couple of generals from their respective armies present, presumably as a show of force. Michael Brockman and Michael Eisner were there for the network, while former NBC and ABC vice president and now faithful Goodson-Todman executive Jerry Chester sat next to his boss. "The half hour of analysis and negotiation felt like three hours of back and forth," Brockman remembered. "It was like they were arguing about the Bible."

Finally, Mark Goodson took a couple of puffs on his pipe, stood and said, "We're doing it my way." He and his entourage left Fred Silverman to ponder his next move. Wisely, he demurred to the master TV game architect. Who won? They both did, as the show was a success for Fred for the short time he remained at ABC, and even more of a bonanza for Goodson and the subsequent owners of his properties as the show is still running. It's highly rated 45-plus years later, with the opposing team's steal arguably its key climactic moment.

Among Fred's most ludicrous assertions was the boast that he created *The Hollywood Squares*. With a straight face he claimed that coup came on the heels of producer Merrill Heatter presenting him a confusing celebrity game without a single X or O that bore no resemblance to tic-tac-toe. NPR's TV critic Eric Deggans alluded to Fred's overzealous grab for credit from decades ago on the January 30, 2020 edition of *All Things Considered*. Fred first taped a simple runthrough of the format he claimed to have masterminded for CBS using their former top money-making personality Arthur Godfrey as emcee. Burt Parks then flashed his high-gloss double-wide smile on a pilot, but was out of step with the lighthearted party vibe, and Fred rejected the series. If the programming genius is to be believed, these rejections were strange abandonments of one's own baby. It was another thumbs-down when comedian Sandy Baron took his turn milking laughs from the stars.

Kellogg's Frosted Flakes were G-r-r-r-e-a-t for Peter Marshall.
A TV commercial led to the job that changed his life.

After the option with CBS timed out and the other two networks rejected the series, producers Merrill Heatter and Bob Quigley ultimately found a happy home for *The Hollywood Squares* after a second pitch to the peacock. When Bob's wife Shirley saw fresh-faced Peter Marshall pitching Kellogg's cereal on TV commercials in 1966, the young actor was offered hosting duties. Peter told me he arrived for his audition wearing shorts. "I had been playing golf, and I figured there was no way they were going to hire me for this thing," Besides, he intended to turn down the opportunity in order to return to Broadway, but that plan changed the moment he heard that next in line for the gig was one of only two people he held a grudge against, comedian Dan Rowan.

Why the animosity? In short, Peter and his comedy partner at the time, Tommy Noonan, had been incredibly generous in getting Rowan and Dick Martin teamed and established in the business. He remembers, "Dan Rowan was selling used cars and Dick Martin was a bartender at a place here in the Valley and they didn't even know each other." Once the future *Laugh-In* team was partnered, Peter and Tommy literally handed them some of their bookings so they could develop their new act. It was a tremendously generous gift.

When still an unknown pair, Dick and Dan were bombing at a dinner show playing to an empty house in a Miami hotel showroom on the same night that star-making columnist Earl Wilson was expected at the late show. Even a great comedy team looks pathetic playing to a tiny audience, and this team wasn't close to even being good. A drunken stranger at the bar had a hand in the team's success. With the cooperation of the club manager, Dick and Dan had the lounge lizard call his friends from the local car dealership where he worked and packed the house with comped patrons. Wilson saw the crowd and, without bothering to stay for the show, wrote that Rowan and Martin were a sensation.

On the strength of that blurb the nightclub's business boomed and the duo was instantly booked by fellow columnist Ed Sullivan for a spot on his top-rated show. With the credibility from that exposure they were suddenly hot. Many years later, when Dick Martin was still thanking Peter and Tommy for giving them a career, Dan Rowan confirmed the truth behind Peter's grievance. He admitted that he repeatedly failed to make even a single visit to see Tommy Noonan during the eight months that his unselfish benefactor lingered at the Motion Picture Home after brain surgery.

Leading man Peter Marshall proved to be inspired casting, and *The Hollywood Squares*' slow-growing popularity added to the peacock network's pride. Then, after Fred landed at NBC, he canceled *The Hollywood Squares* along with other fan favorites. Indeed, the quick-quipping celebrity version of the 3,000-year-old game from ancient Egypt, tic-tac-toe, was marked for extinction by the guy who claimed to have created it. To first take the wind out of the show's sails, Peter and the stars suffered through so many scheduling shuffles that it seemed Fred was daring the audience to follow the series. As Peter put it, "And then he came over to NBC and he kept changing our time, trying to get us off. And finally he brought David Letterman for an hour and a half. And that's when he canceled it." Indeed, after three time shifts within a 10-month period Fred served the pink-slip in early 1980. "He always hated the show," is how Peter remembers Fred Silverman's attitude towards *Squares*.

Dave Letterman had been on Fred's radar since his *Tonight Show* stand-up debut on November 26th, 1978. After guest-hosting the following year he was seen as a possible replacement for Johnny Carson who, in 1979, gave notice of his intent to leave his cushy throne when his current contract expired. NBC was prepared to give in to pretty much any demands for the opportunity to continue milking their late night cash cow. Before surrendering to Johnny's unprecedented renewal terms the network looked to Letterman as a possible replacement as backup. Finding airtime to groom the young comic necessitated hollowing out a hunk of their daytime game show line-up. That 1980 hack job included cancelling the venerable *Wheel of Fortune* to open part of the 90-minute slot for Letterman's June 23rd debut. The game's cast and crew bid farewell, part of the set was destroyed, and announcer Charlie O'Donnell lined-up his next gig.

In a last minute substitution, *Wheel* was reprieved. Along with *The Hollywood Squares*, both Alex Trebek's version of *High Rollers* and Bill Cullen's *Chain Reaction* got the axe. Game maven Bob Stewart had been an early Letterman booster and signed on as producer. However, finding too many cooks in the kitchen with differing recipes, Bob jumped ship a full month before the newly minted *David Letterman Show* was added to the daytime menu. That could well have been a harbinger of the grief that would follow in attempting to make this new 10 a.m. entry palatable to the masses. One of Fred Silverman's ideas was to model it after Arthur Godfrey's syrupy ancient mid-morning mainstay, complete with a folksy family of regulars. Attempting to hammer the edgy newcomer, Dave, into the squarest of holes, Godfrey's, was the kind of ham-fisted move that provided more ammunition for Fred's growing circle of detractors.

On the other hand, the programmer does deservedly get credit for first catching wind of the small animated creatures from Belgium who live in mushroom-shaped houses. His subordinate, NBC's head of children's programs Micky Dwyer, had a case of the blues early in the development of *The Smurfs*. Micky's network note for Hanna-Barbera's Margaret Loesch was, "You can't tell the Smurfs apart. Make them different colors." It was left-brain thinking about a right-brain endeavor. Please, leave the artistic choices to the artists.

In Fred and Micky's defense, fellow network colleagues through the years have willingly admitted that with the difficulty of handicapping potential hits and considering the magnitude of the wager, once saying "yes" to a program the temptation to corroborate with the creators during development seems impossible to resist. A broadcast network's cost for a typical half-hour comedy pilot has reached $2 million and up, while the price tag on an hour-long drama pilot can easily top $5 million. It's no wonder that over the years a few of the prognosticators who have placed these hefty bets have found their fates to also be at risk.

Fred Silverman was crowned NBC president in June of 1978 with a compensation package estimated to have totaled about three times what he was earning at ABC. With too many fizzled wagers he was fired exactly three years later with time remaining in his $1 million a year contract. Word of Fred's ouster and the naming of new network chief Grant Tinker came while Fred was vacationing in Hawaii, the same place he sweated out his previous transition, from ABC to NBC. After programming all three, Fred ran out of networks and went on to form his own production company where he churned out hits including *Matlock, In the Heat of the Night, Jake and the Fatman,* and *Diagnosis Murder*.

Fred Silverman made friends and he made enemies. Among the latter a few considered him to be eccentric and unpredictable. At a NATPE convention where shows are sold into the syndication marketplace, a producer who had apparently struck out with his network pitches ranted that the famous gatekeeper was a "purebred wacko." Making the rounds of the hospitality suites as the free booze flows, there's no telling what you'll hear.

Non-wacko former NBC executive and present-day super-agent Susan Simons is a positively charming, smart, perceptive and beloved lady with a world of insight into all things television. She's the first to point out the shining example that defies any broad-brushed criticism of the people who have held sway over program schedules, Brandon Tartikoff. The guy was obviously a prince. It's one of the few things on which seemingly everybody in the industry agrees. Over two decades after his death, he was still the subject for a full evening of discussion at a 2018 Television Academy event. Prolific producer Chuck Lorre remembers being in a writers' room where network honcho Brandon was pitching jokes to a receptive group of scribes brainstorming for one of his pet series. That's rarer than a cobra and a mongoose mating.

Brandon was NBC's wunderkind who ultimately took the programming reins from Fred Silverman. When he was crowned the youngest-ever entertainment division president not long after his 30th birthday, Brandon adapted to a life in the dizzying heights of the corporate structure. The Yale graduate had already mastered all of the nitty-gritty fundamentals—demographics, audience flow, research, marketing, and promotion while in local television in New Haven and Chicago, then at ABC, all while in his 20s. He then turned to a most unlikely pro for help in nursing the peacock to health. The old cobra himself, Jim Aubrey, served as his advisor and consultant.

NBC wunderkind Brandon Tartikoff programming Thursday night comedies *Cosby* and *Family Ties* against action hits *Magnum P.I.* and *The Fall Guy*.

Among the things Brandon excelled at and could never have learned from Aubrey were the fine arts of building loyalty and motivating the best work from people. When it came to judging a program's air-worthiness, Brandon was fond of asking whether a particular show could be anybody's passionate favorite. It's how his higher-brow *L.A. Law* could peacefully coexist with fare for the *hoi polloi*, such as *The A-Team*. Each show was clearly capable of being a viewer's favorite, although for very different audience members. "Brandon understood what viewers wanted," said the highly respected TV done-it-all and former president of PBS, Pat Mitchell. She added, "He loved making television because he loved watching television."

That love engendered something extra, showmanship. No, the world of advertising and marketing didn't coin the term "branding" to honor Brandon, but he was a strong proponent. Brandon's branding included putting the memorable stamps "Be There" and "Let's All Be There" on his lineup. It helped bring the peacock from worst to first in the ratings for five years during the 1980s. His power-packed roster of hits included *Hill Street Blues, Law & Order, Family Ties, The Cosby Show, Cheers, The Golden Girls, Miami Vice, St. Elsewhere, Night Court* and *Seinfeld*. Jerry Seinfeld credited Brandon with saving his landmark sitcom from cancellation during its first struggling year. He put a secret personal stamp in 1984's *Punky Brewster* by naming the title character after a girl he had a crush on in school. In a way Brandon became that classmate's best friend when he named Punky Brewster's pet dog Brandon.

Not that everything Brandon touched was destined to win in the ratings race. He was first to laugh at his blunders that included *Manimal, Beverly Hills Buntz, Bay City Blues* and *Berrenger's*. However, nothing could ever come close to Brandon's misstep of assigning the label "news special" to two primetime hours of Geraldo Rivera talking about butchered babies, dismembered corpses, cannibal cults, and sex orgies on *Devil Worship: Exposing Satan's Underground*.

TV's boy wonder was also responsible for bringing Lorne Michaels back to helm *Saturday Night Live* after the captain abandoned his ship in 1980. At a broadcasting convention in Las Vegas around that same year I spotted a couple of friends in a circle of folks chatting. Brandon was in the group, and I joined just in time to hear him espouse a pearl of wisdom from his playbook. I paraphrase, "You can always get a leg up on the competition by creating an environment that will attract the best people to come to you first." The primary criticism lodged against Brandon was that he couldn't be relied upon to return phone calls. His later-day boss, Grant Tinker, took the sting from that condemnation while simultaneously praising his successful track record by noting, "Brandon seemed to intuitively know which calls to return."

Never shy on-stage playing cheerleader at all manner of press events, Brandon took the next step by performing in small roles on several shows. He accomplished it all while fighting a particularly devastating decades-long battle with Hodgkin's lymphoma. There's great inspiration to be taken from Brandon's courage and resolve. At a 1982 affiliates' meeting he sang the praises of NBC's schedule fresh from a strong course of chemotherapy. Only the most senior executives knew he was wearing a wig and had false eyebrows glued to his face to cover for his hair loss.

Brandon gave another valiant performance later that year, hosting a program he loved and championed through its rough seasons, *Saturday Night Live*. His widow, Lily, recalled that Brandon's body was ravaged from nine rounds of chemotherapy the week he fronted the show. She noted, "If you look at the footage of Brandon, he is totally moon-faced. The steroids were still very much in his system… he didn't have a hair on his head."

Obviously I have tremendous respect for Brandon as well as other bright and talented network bigwigs who have earned their stripes. However there's far more fun in joining the legions of Monday morning armchair quarterbacks who make sport of ridiculing these folks' work. They do make an easy target. Like the network genius who felt it imperative that Mary Richards not be a divorcee on the 1970s' *The Mary Tyler Moore Show*. The brainiac was worried that people would be confused from the previous decade when she played Laura Petrie on *The Dick Van Dyke Show*. He was actually concerned that viewers would mistakenly believe that Mary divorced Dick Van Dyke. Hey, if the audience is that stupid they might also believe that, in the years between those two shows, Mary Tyler Moore submitted herself to some sort of top-secret Area 51 medical procedure that changed her from black and white to color.

Diane English, showrunner for the 1980s hit *Murphy Brown*, remembers the development meeting at which CBS programmers asked if Murphy could be re-written. Instead of being a recovering alcoholic they wanted her to simply be someone returning to the workforce after a long spa respite taken to recover from too much stress. Oh yes, and can she be re-imagined as turning 30 instead of 40? That was their direction—take the sharp edge off the character and make her closer in age to the prized viewers' demographic.

That brain trust must have been afraid that nobody aged 18 to 34 could possibly be interested in watching anybody 39 years old. Diane got off easy. In the middle of that clash the Writers Guild went on strike. It meant that not a word in the script could be changed for the foreseeable future, not until after the union and the producers found common ground. She explained that reality to the network: "If they wanted to shoot the pilot, they had to shoot that first draft." They did and, of course, it was a landmark series for its time.

Writing for TV is a challenge because the medium chews up material at a frightening pace. Writers who can be counted on to mill out finished teleplays from their own original stories can make boatloads of cash. For an independent, not on staff, the union minimum paycheck for any of the network hour-long dramas is in the neighborhood of $40,000. Go ahead and spend it, there's another $20,000 coming after the first repeat broadcast. Similarly, the paycheck for selling a sitcom script is no laughing matter. Although each replay generates a decreasing residual payment, anyone lucky enough to have sold even one script a year for any long-running hit series will find the ongoing reruns will add up to an annuity that rivals anything Merrill Lynch can sell you. *M*A*S*H* and *Cheers* scribe Ken Levine is a wise friend—wise enough to never let me broach the question about career compensation. Maybe he's afraid I'd ask for a loan.

Among the all-time top-tier veteran sitcom writers was Leonard Stern. His words came out of the mouths of the casts on *The Phil Silvers Show*, and *The Steve Allen Show*. He earned a producing credit for his contributions to Mel Brooks and Buck Henry's *Get Smart*; he helped create *McMillan and Wife* and the cult classic *I'm Dickens, He's Fenster*. Stern even gave birth to the box game *Mad Libs*, but his most lasting work was writing many of those brilliant scripts for Jackie Gleason's *The Honeymooners*. Of course, Ralph and Alice Kramden with their friends the Nortons made it to TV without any network programmers' meddling, right? Wrong!

Leonard claimed to still have the memos from the fools who tried to improve upon perfection. Those network notes included, "Please consider changing Norton's occupation. You can't expect people to watch a sewer worker while they're having dinner." Then Leonard said he received this note from some CBS claircognizant, "When Ralph says 'You're going to the moon, Alice,' it may be the wrong destination. The moon is generally regarded as romantic. Could Ralph send her to Mars?"

Another suggestion from a pencil pusher was based on a valid concern, but would have required a subplot about Alice Kramden's gender dysphoria: "The license fee for the use of *Happy Birthday* is prohibitively expensive. Could Ralph celebrate Alice's birthday by singing 'For He's a Jolly Good Woman?'" One more ditty from the executives: "On page seven, Ed Norton says 'Va-va-va-voom.' Before we can give clearance, what does it mean in English?"

You'd think the producer who delivered a hit as huge as *Gomer Pyle, USMC* would be immune from this kind of nitpicking, but few escaped the often senseless backseat driving. After Sheldon Leonard proudly presented that series' pilot it was all he could do to keep from exploding in the face of one network know-it-all who said he hated the show's "phony set that looked nothing like a real Marine Corp facility." Leonard calmly explained that the entire pilot was shot at the Marine Corps base in San Diego. If they wanted the set changed the network was free to contact the Secretary of Defense.

Classic among network memos are the ones concerning Louis Cowan at CBS. Cowan was the producer of *The $64,000 Question* and, based upon that show's massive success, he was elevated to the network's presidency. There he reigned, his ass in one of the mightiest thrones in all of broadcasting, breathing much of the same rarified air as CBS's founding father, William Paley. It all came by virtue of his brilliance in manipulating the most notorious of all of the era's quiz shows. Then the whispers about rigging began. As the storm clouds of the massive scandal gathered and subpoenas began to roll in like the ominous rumbling of approaching thunder, Cowan ran for cover.

CBS's president cowered in fear at the thought of testifying, or testi-lying. He suddenly took ill, was hospitalized, and managed to get excused from being sworn in for quizzing by Congress. The battle of the memos about rigging and his good health, bad health, good health and bad health that preceded Cowan's 1959 ouster from the network makes for fun reading. There's no time to peruse them all because the next derriere domiciled in that network president's office was an even greater scoundrel with an even more egregious legacy, James Thomas Aubrey.

Aubrey was a man so reviled that thespian John Houseman famously nicknamed him "The Smiling Cobra" during his first year running the network. It came as the result of the soul-crushing grief Aubrey imposed on both the actor and his friend, former CBS chief Hubbell Robinson. Among other sacred cows' careers Aubrey unceremoniously attempted to crush were those of Jack Benny and Arthur Godfrey, firing them both. It took him just seconds to deflate Garry Moore with a "Not a chance" reaction to weeks of work on a new format.

Aubrey himself often bragged about the time he called in a vice president, allowed him to ramble on for 35 minutes, then abruptly told him he was through. However, those disrespectful dismissals were the least of this reprobate's sins among his breathtaking collection of misdeeds and misdemeanors. It wasn't Aubrey's manner or demeanor, but his ratings and revenue that were being richly rewarded with an exorbitant salary of $124,000, plus a $100,000 bonus, and an option on 65,000 CBS shares worth approximately $3 million.

TV historian and author Wesley Hyatt confirms that CBS held top honors as the number one network overall, each and every year during the 1960s. Some years it was close, but credit goes to Aubrey with an assist from his vice president of programming Mike Dann for 1963's amazing feat of scoring 14 of the season's top 15 shows. That's not to suggest that quality was the only criteria at play when selecting a new series. It seems there were several ways to get a new program added to Jim Aubrey's network schedule. Having a good pilot might be the least important. Aubrey's vice president of programming, Mike Dann, postulated that his one-time boss was far more than simply an oversexed serial womanizer who bedded many of CBS's female stars, much more.

Speaking informally after a Paley Center event Dann suggested that Aubrey was also considered to be on the fringes of organized crime. In one of our conversations he cited examples of The Smiling Cobra's alleged acceptance of sexual favors of all flavors as well as cash for giving the elusive green light to shows from producers who were appropriately "friendly." Details of the double-dealing are coming after a look at the aftermath. Aubrey was fired in 1965 which led to Dann calling the shots in filling the time slots. A diminutive man with a huge heart for CBS's talented stars, Mike Dann had a lot of housekeeping to do once Aubrey was booted. John A. Schneider was next in the president's office. He had the casting couch sterilized while Dann disinfected the schedule.

CBS had the lead in primetime viewership that year. ABC's *Batman* and *Bewitched* placed in the Top 10 while NBC had only one entry, but it was a giant. *Bonanza* was the number one show on all of TV as it had been for a couple of years. With one-quarter of all American households watching the western each week it was an aptly named series—a bonanza indeed for NBC in both ratings and revenue. To challenge the juggernaut's success, in 1967 Dann scheduled *The Smothers Brothers Comedy Hour* in that suicide timeslot. With their closely cropped hair, matching red blazers, skinny neckties, catchy folk songs, and G-rated patter Tom and Dick were fair-haired all-American boys. The brothers had been quickly signed by a fellow network executive after seeing their act at the Flamingo Hotel in Las Vegas. Following their February, 1967 debut the duo quickly became CBS's darlings of Sunday nights. They succeeded in denting the *Bonanza* leadership as quickly as a few short weeks into their run, and started to serve up a more desirable demographic slice of the viewership.

As time went on Tom and Dick Smothers bounded across the generation gap and began to share newfound political and social enlightenment. CBS standards and practices increasingly took their blue pencils to their new stars' topical jokes and satirical commentary that were spun from the issues of the day—the Vietnam War, sex, drugs, and rock and roll. Folk music gave way to memorable appearances by The Who and Buffalo Springfield. The ninth show was the first time CBS barred the broadcast of an entire sketch. It was written by and featured guest star Elaine May satirizing one increasingly controversial aspect of television itself. The censors cut her parody about… censors.

Even with the battle over content escalating, viewership and ad sales were strong. Madison Avenue agencies were locking in avails for their clients for the coming fall, and in March of 1969 the brothers were notified they'd been picked up for a fourth season. It was a season that never came to be as the censorship issues raged to where CBS pulled the plug. The *Smothers Brothers Comedy Hour* originally slotted for April 13th, 1969 was rescheduled for April 6th but remained unaired in the United States. It was in the can but a repeat from November 10th of the previous year was fed to affiliates instead.

Tom had hit the jackpot in antagonizing the network during that unseen hour by inviting comedian David Steinberg back to revisit a bit that incensed the Bible Belt when first presented six months earlier. David played a soft-spoken preacher delivering a sermon that, while a clever and funny parody, had generated an avalanche of complaints for its perceived blasphemy. This reprise of David's preacher character flew in the face of the censors' advance warning about David's booking: "No sermon!" That's when the network canceled the series. They lost a top-rated hour, the brothers lost an outlet for their creativity and advocacy, and audiences lost brilliantly funny and stimulating entertainment.

The show's relevancy was undeniable in the tumultuous closing months of the 1960s, but TV had always chosen to avoid controversy, especially in the form of sharp and poignant satire. The goal had always been to eschew offending anyone, even at the expense of failing to enlighten anyone. Creativity is fine, so long as it stays miles from contentious issues. Religion and politics were always the hot buttons and the brothers pressed them both from the wrong side of the once surmountable but now widening chasm that had grown between kids and their parents. It was defined by the maxim from Berkeley's free speech movement, "Never trust anyone over 30."

The heat was on from no lesser mortal than Lyndon Johnson. The President of the United States dialed the president of the network, William Paley, on more than one Sunday night to complain about the criticism of his administration. The White House called again weeks after Richard Nixon's inauguration with a warning about the new boss's zero tolerance for the lampooning that eventually landed the Smothers on Nixon's famed "Enemies List." There among columnists, Congressmen, and labor union leaders, Tom and Dick were in good company with John Lennon, Jane Fonda, and surprisingly, animation voice artist June Foray.

How could the sweetheart who breathed life into Warner Bros. cartoon characters become an enemy of the President? She'd helped organize a meat boycott in response to Nixon's 1973 anti-inflation price freeze.

Ultimately CBS took advantage of what they cited as Tommy Smothers' late delivery of one week's show as the excuse to end the war and declare victory. Despite their alleged tardiness the Smothers were ultimately vindicated four years later. After successfully demonstrating that they had not violated the terms of their contract, a federal court ruled in favor of the brothers and ordered CBS to pay them $776,300. Tom and Dick's cheerleader who championed them through all the turmoil, Mike Dann, passed away in 2016 at age 94. Near the end of his life the Smothers still considered him their sole truly faithful ally in their long pugnacious battle, singling him out with a glowing introduction at that Paley Center salute to their groundbreaking series. It was perhaps Dann's last moment of professional glory.

While Mike Dann may have made some minor rewrites to history in recounting his career highlights, the stories I've heard clearly support his suspicions about his predecessor, Jim Aubrey. Those confirmations go a far way towards convincing me that all of The Smiling Cobra's felonies and foolishness were true. All of it, and more.

Chapter 28

As Jim Aubrey, that era's poster boy for sexual harassment often put it himself, "If a man can be indicted for liking pretty girls, I'm guilty." Actress Tina Louise was said to be among the many starlets bedded by Aubrey. As the story goes, when Tina became a bit too clingy for his tastes, Aubrey was looking to get her out of his hair by getting her out of town. He supposedly arranged for Tina to be cast as movie star Ginger, replacing actress Kit Smythe who played a secretary in the fifth lead role on the *Gilligan's Island* pilot. In the context of his far greater abuses, it's not hard to believe.

Golden Globe winner as 1958's New Star of the Year, the vivacious Tina Louise was classically trained in acting by the legendary Sandy Meisner, only to be shipwrecked on *Gilligan's Island*.

Unlike most of her Hollywood-based shipmates, Tina was a New York performer cast for the sitcom from her Broadway appearance with Carol Burnett in *Fade Out-Fade In*. In October of 2021 Tina skirted the straightforward question about personal experiences with "hands on" producers and their inappropriate advances by telling the *New York Post*, "I don't think there's any woman walking in this business who hasn't had situations… they should speak out on that." Speaking of her character, Tina added, "Ginger would have led the [#MeToo] pack… I would have liked to play that scene."

The philandering Casanova was the "C" in CBS, and his BS was in ample supply when Aubrey apparently promised the glamorous Tina that this would be a lead role with star billing for a dazzling movie-star character created specifically for her. It was on a series Aubrey hated, and it turned out to be no starring vehicle. Contractually, not one but five lead actors, including Tina who suddenly replaced actress Kit Smythe, were all to share the same lead billing. No matter, for the New York-based Aubrey it was mission accomplished, as *Gilligan's Island* filmed 3,000 miles away at CBS's Radford studio lot in the San Fernando Valley. Being marooned inside Stage 2, adjacent to the four-foot-deep $150,000 lagoon excavated and dredged for the show was as close as the executive could get to having Tina actually stranded on a real remote island.

As with *The Dick Van Dyke Show* and Danny Thomas's sitcom *Make Room for Daddy*, Aubrey actually had no interest in having *Gilligan's Island* on CBS's air. He'd told its creator Sherwood Schwartz that the series would be more to his liking if there were rotating cast members instead of the same characters on every episode. Certainly he couldn't mean there should be a new ship, a new storm and a new wreck each week. How else could new characters be deserted every week?

Sherwood wasn't about to consider anything nearly as silly. All that mattered was Aubrey's rejection of the show and his suggestion to its creator that the best use of the film would be to cut it into a few million guitar picks. In an attempt to make the premise more to his liking, the Smiling Cobra approved another reptilian move. It was within his legal rights, but it was highly disrespectful. As the network owned Sherwood's pilot about the shipwrecked sightseers, Aubrey signed-off on having his sycophant, producer Hunt Stromberg Jr., assign another director to shoot additional footage with the cast, without notifying Sherwood.

In conversation with Sherwood's son, Lloyd Schwartz, during Christmas week in 2021, he referred to what was added as "packing scenes"—several minutes of static and boring exposition tacked on to the top of the sample episode with the S.S. Minnow's future passengers packing for the trip. It introduced the characters and set up some of the premise for how castaways could find themselves in their predicament on the uncharted island. Perhaps Aubrey thought it was necessary, not fully trusting viewers' willing suspension of disbelief to simply accept the premise and go along for the laughs. More cynical observers suggested it was purely a last minute attempt at sabotage, hoping to abort the series before it was born. Aubrey may have hoped that during last looks at the shows earmarked for the new season's air, Sherwood's damned ship of fools would capsize out of contention. For all he cared Willy Gilligan, skipper Jonas Grumby, Professor Roy Hinkley, Thurston and Eunice Howell, Mary Ann Summers, and especially Ginger Grant could all drown in their Studio City lagoon.

When Sherwood learned of the secret desecration of his baby he hired an editor to help him rush through a clandestine re-re-cut of the show's pilot to restore its former glory. Aubrey's new footage was excised with the show's creator confident that the exposition could be sufficiently explained musically at the top of each episode. Trying to cement a timeslot before the network schedule was locked and announced to the press the coming Monday made this a manic race against the clock. On Friday, Sherwood was able to get co-owner United Artists to sign off on his just-completed edit. Then, forgoing the union requirement of having a member of the Teamsters transport the reel of film to the executive offices in New York, he surreptitiously got his re-edited print to CBS's research department overnight, in time for the planned testing on Saturday.

Screened for random members of the public, Sherwood's restored cut of the show about the accidental island inhabitants scored so high that CBS thought something was amiss with their research. They repeated the testing on Sunday only to find a similar result. Although Aubrey had nixed the show once before, the new edit tested so well that he couldn't simply ignore the research. He summoned Sherwood to a meeting just hours before the schedule was to be finalized and publicized. Oh boy, this was going to be one hell of a sit-down, right in the cobra's nest.

Consulting director John Rich was present, as were suits from United Artists and from Phil Silvers' company, as he was another investor. Here's the play-by-play of the scene in Aubrey's executive dining room as reported by Rich: "Two uniformed waiters stood at the coffee urns, but only Mr. Aubrey was served, and his coffee cup was periodically replenished. Nobody else was offered a sip." The philandering boss was, once again, cementing his image as a first-class prick. Rich recalled how the reptile then launched into a tirade: "He hated it—despised the premise, excoriated the writing, and frothed at the mouth about how he would love to keep it off CBS." The audience research results, perhaps along with his desire to keep Tina Louise a continent away, were said to be *Gilligan's* saving grace. However, Aubrey wasn't going to adjourn the meeting until he exacted a pound of flesh from the man who birthed the premise.

Sherwood had already passed out copies of the opening theme song's lyrics to support his claim that there wasn't any need for expositionary footage, but perhaps in great part to humiliate him Aubrey said, "Songs are supposed to be sung, not read. Sing it!" Lloyd Schwartz reported that his dad hesitated until his agent kicked him under the table. What followed would have been funny to an observer, but was skin-crawlingly awkward for most who were in the room. Sherwood sang, unaccompanied, the entire opening theme song that Aubrey detested. While the showrunner crooned his composition *The Ballad of Gilligan's Island*, Aubrey jeered and heckled him.

Then, mercifully, the meeting adjourned with Aubrey's pronouncement, remembered by Sherwood, told to his son Lloyd, and told to me as, "I still hate your fucking show, but I'm putting it on the air." Indeed, *Gilligan's Island* was locked onto the 1964-1965 schedule at the last moment. Once production started, Aubrey became instantly disinterested in hearing anything about the series or Tina Louise's occasional sulking on the set and isolating from the cast at meal breaks. She was 3,000 miles away and that was all that was important. Tina was on a hit show, but her suffering was barely disguised when she told *TV Guide* for their May 8, 1965 issue, "I was ashamed when I saw the first show. . . I wouldn't watch it if I wasn't on it." Sherwood's reaction to her scathing comments included, "I would think she would be delighted. She's an integral part of a major hit. What else does an actress want? I don't know what would make her happy. It seems to me that she's not a very happy person. I don't thoroughly understand her."

Tina eventually accepted being only one of several lead characters in an ensemble, and not the primary subject in a series about the misadventures of a movie star. She gets credit for her entertaining characterization and for enduring her frustrations. As she did in her *TV Guide* interview, Tina reminded the world that she was a classically trained actress when she told blogger Jackson Upperco in 2020, "I was looking forward to getting back to doing work that was more in line with my studies at the Actors Studio."

As to bringing her training to the role, in 2021 the former model and nightclub chanteuse said she created Ginger's backstory as a rising movie star who had been cast to play Cleopatra on Broadway when she boarded the three hour cruise from hell. Describing the scripts as having been "snarky," she explained that she tried to match the eccentricity of the comedy by utilizing the breathy voice that was "part Marilyn [Monroe] and part Lucy [Ball.]"

The actors' original talent contracts' clause specifying that there would be no more than five lead roles made things awkward when the Professor and Mary Ann were subsequently cast. It relegated Russell Johnson and Dawn Wells to be referred to anonymously as "the rest" in the opening theme and to share a double-card credit. It was Bob "Gilligan" Denver who helped secure equity for the sixth and seventh characters in time for the second season. After the series' 98-episode three-season run, Tina refused to participate in any of the handful of follow-up TV movies. Likewise, she distanced herself from any spin-offs, rehashes, reunions, and the subsequent animated series. Although she worked with some regularity after her cruise on the S.S. Minnow, for many years Tina blamed being typecast as Ginger for shipwrecking her career.

Adding to frustrations was the chilled on-again off-again subtle rivalry between sexy Tina and down-to-earth next-door good-looking good-girl co-star Dawn Wells. The public unknowingly exacerbated their dysfunctional real-life pairing with that whole "Ginger or Mary Ann" competition. It may have helped to keep things divisive decades after the show became a cultural touchstone through international rerun syndication. Perhaps Tina felt cheated after coming to believe the myth that Dawn had a special deal. Was she really the only actor with profit participation in all of the off-network sales of the show?

I've heard the story told both ways, I think even from Dawn herself at different times. It would have been an extremely unusual arrangement considering the era and the ensemble nature of the series. In 2018 the question was answered when Dawn shared her estimate that Sherwood Schwartz pocketed a total of some $90 million, while the bulk of the marooned castmates' income, hers included, came from marketing the memories and memorabilia.

Believing the rumored pay inequity may or may not have been another of the various reasons why, as late as a half century after it all began, Dawn said Tina still refused to consider any of the many overtures she'd made for these two surviving *Gilligan* gals to appear together. Tina lives in New York, but the many miles were seemingly nowhere near the emotional distance between them. In her final months Dawn told me how much she would love to thrill fans and make some honest cash playing opposite Tina in a two-girl twist on Neil Simon's *The Odd Couple*. The more she spoke about that idea the more it sounded like a winner to me. At one of our last discussions Dawn told me that Tina's daughter again rebuffed her latest proposal. Frankly, the refusal was a gift, as Dawn was then too far from her prime to tackle the rigors of daily performances of a live stage production.

Sadly, whatever small fortune Dawn might have amassed was all gone by 2018. Suspected mismanagement of her funds decades ago, the stock market crash of 2008, expensive medical complications following a fall, and penance for an innocent error on an old tax return combined to create everyone's worst nightmare. The IRS's high penalties and interest charges, their legendary aggressive collection practices, plus their ability to attach assets and garnish income created havoc in the weeks before Dawn's 80th birthday.

The unpaid tax obligation made it all but impossible to find a residential rehabilitation facility that would accept her for the remaining physical therapy needed following that fall. This dear lady and treasured friend was humbled and embarrassed when she learned that an acquaintance had started a GoFundMe page. Humiliating as it might have been for Dawn to have her predicament publicized, it was heartening to see her many fans jump to help to the tune of $197,000. I was happy that 2020 started with our friend finally settled, healthy, and happy. The joy gave way to sorrow two days before the end of the year when she died, a victim of the Covid-19 coronavirus pandemic.

Even if Jim Aubrey were still alive there's little doubt he would have been absent from those who came to Dawn's aid during her financial bind. As a serial womanizer his interest in females seems to have been entirely selfish. While it didn't fit with the CBS Tiffany network image, Aubrey was far from being unique among TV execs as his was only one of many casting couches. Author David Halberstam labeled him "The hucksters' huckster," David Susskind called him "A monster," and Lucille Ball rarely said his name without prefacing it with "That S.O.B." Where Aubrey distinguished himself as a truly scurrilous reprobate was in the conflicts of interest created by his apparent connections to organized crime.

Here comes the single most amazing story about a man for whom there are many outrageous tales. It's a saga that epitomizes the legends about Mafia favors, the kind that invariably result in the benefactor becoming entwined in a web of obligated reciprocity for life. How does the president of a television network find himself in business with and beholden to organized crime? While this sounds like a creative plotline for a movie, it's fully vetted and documented. Keep your hands and feet inside the car for this true-life roller coaster ride.

The story starts at a party. Aubrey was drunk and got into an argument with a woman. It became physical when he pushed her and she fell, injuring her arm. That's how some heard it. The more damning version of the confrontation comes from excellent sources, respected comedy scribe Larry Gelbart and CBS staffer

Marc Merson, with confirmation by author Stephen Battaglio. It had Aubrey bruising the woman's arm during an episode of rough sex.

For those dialed-in to the New York nightlife scene that would have been no shock as the city's gossip columns were carrying thinly-veiled reports of the TV executive who, as *Life* magazine put it, "pummeled and bruised playmates" during "ungovernable after-hours rages." The playmate for this particular alcohol-infused tryst turned out to be one member of the singing DeMarco Sisters, who happened to be the girlfriend of a highly-placed participant in La Costra Nostra. After Aubrey refused to apologize and then slandered the woman by unkindly and unwisely shooting off his mouth, a hit was placed on his life. Yes, he was marked for death. The plot thickens.

An actor named Keefe Brasselle intervened on Aubrey's behalf, ostensibly saving his life. Brasselle was a song and dance man with a couple of fresh acting credits in underperforming movies. He was a member of the DeMarco family by marriage, but the muscle needed to call off the hit came not through the sisters but Brasselle's own reputed and little-disputed status as mob connected. That was not particularly unusual for nightclub performers of that era, as a majority of the venues were owned or operated by members of organized crime. Brasselle is alleged to have fronted for the mob, serving as the face and the owner-of-record of one of their New Jersey nightclubs. After the place burned to the ground in 1961 under what was termed as suspicious circumstances—fire officials found six empty cans of gasoline at the scene—the entertainer was subsequently given other assignments from time to time.

On the surface, Brasselle's willingness to mediate between the mob and Aubrey was a kind thing to do, but kindness was not the motivation for getting the hit called off. As is the case with all favors extended by those who are connected, there was indebtedness. You know, the kind of pending obligation to which a wise man should never say "No." However, Brasselle had an especially outrageous request in exchange for his good deed. He asked for coveted primetime slots on the CBS network schedule for not one or two, but for three television series. They were all to be bought sight unseen, without any scripts, pitches, or pilots. It was a spectacularly audacious proposition, but Aubrey complied. Hell, it's only television, a stupid box with wires and lights as Ed Murrow called it. I can hear it now: "Can you really clear me with 'da boyz', Keefe? Well then, sure, hell, whatever you want!"

Anybody paying attention might have recognized Brasselle's name from three years earlier, when Aubrey gave the actor's company at the time a very generous $430,000 in exchange for a pilot in which he was both the star and the producer. *Beachfront* was such a turkey that it was rumored Aubrey himself never bothered to screen it. With this new three-series commitment Brasselle was back in business in a big way, and he delivered *The Baileys of Balboa*, *The Cara Williams Show* and *The Reporter*—two sitcoms and one drama respectively. If they had been hits, everybody would have been all smiles. Brasselle would have been lauded as a visionary, and Aubrey a genius. However, all three were bombs. Huge bombs that sucked much of the life out of the network's 1964-1965 primetime lineup.

More bombs than even Hiroshima and Nagasaki. The infamous trio of CBS series shepherded to air in 1964 by Jim Aubrey didn't look or sound terrible, until America tuned out.
In the comedy *The Baileys of Balboa* Paul Ford (background) and Sterling Holloway play the captain of the Island Princess and the commodore of a high-class yacht club who make waves.

The Cara Williams Show, a comedy about a honeymooning couple trying to conceal their marriage from their boss. Familiar faces Frank Aletter, Paul Reed, and Jack Sheldon rounded out the cast.

Harry Guardino starred as *The Reporter*, a hard-driving newspaperman with a knack for getting the tough stories, teamed with a boss who tries to keep him out of trouble. George O'Hanlon, better known as the voice of George Jetson provided comic relief. Jack Lord, Jessica Walter, and Frank Gifford were guests in the season's second episode.

After the trio of Keefe Brasselle's series hit the air, CBS's overall rating dropped 11 percent for the season. It meant advertisers benefited from lower rates and the addition of free commercials known in the industry as make-goods. The network's shareholders demanded an explanation for the resulting financial hit, and the FCC wanted to hear all about related allegations. In 1964 the CBS board of directors started an investigation that unearthed much of the Brasselle backroom bargain and other malfeasance.

They learned that Aubrey lived in an apartment paid for in part by a production company, with use of a car and driver courtesy of another program supplier. Aubrey rarely used his CBS-provided chauffeured limo preferring to maintain the confidentiality of his comings and goings. As pal Brasselle said, "He didn't want them to know what he was doing." The network filed a lawsuit against Aubrey and Brasselle for the very odious sweetheart deal, and Aubrey was unceremoniously ousted from the presidency. It was likely the first time a cobra bit itself in the ass.

This snake didn't slither away in shame to spend the rest of its life under some rock. Exiting with $1.5 million in CBS stock options and severance, Aubrey was subsequently hired at Columbia and, later, MGM. At the latter he was the executive responsible for executing studio owner Kirk Kerkorian's idea to liquidate the once proud MGM lion's assets. Real estate, props, costumes, everything that wasn't nailed down, and a few things that were all went to the auctioneer to unload, pairs of *The Wizard of Oz* ruby slippers and all.

Chapter 29

Jim Aubrey spent an afternoon as a guest speaker at a 1970s UCLA TV class taught by William Dozier, the 20th Century-Fox executive behind ABC's *Batman* and other hits. Only with the naivety of youth would someone unwittingly dare to ask the obvious but indelicate question. After Aubrey's lecture an especially brazen inquiry came from one of the students, posed directly to the former CBS president. Dozier remembered, "In the question-and-answer period he was asked, 'What prompted you to put on the air three new series in the same season without making a pilot of any?'" Dozier remembers gasping for air as Aubrey hesitated. After a moment came the reply, "Arrogance, I guess."

Quite the enigmatic man himself, Keefe Brasselle's name also pops up in various contexts, including a few almost as sinister as his hijacking hours of CBS prime time. As talent he'd guested on a number of 1950s dramas and a few sitcoms from *The Ford Television Theater* to *The Phil Silvers Show*. When he still had friends at CBS he got himself booked as an impressionist on one Sunday night's *Ed Sullivan Show*, and then bookmarked Garry Moore's timeslot with his own summer replacement variety series. Ann B. Davis, best known for her portrayal of housekeeper Alice on *The Brady Bunch* was a regular on that Brasselle summer show. She remembered it with trepidation.

In a 2004 interview Davis described "small groups of strange people," soft-spoken, well-tailored guests she referred to as "scary," who came and went from the set. Pressed on the point, Davis said that she never wanted to go through an experience like that again, as Brasselle's visiting mob members made the sound stage very uncomfortable. She did her best to stay uninvolved. "Whatever I learned, I forgot just as quickly as I could," she said.

The mystery man, Keefe Brasselle. Actor, singer, comedian, author, television producer, film director, impressionist, or mob wiseguy? Apparently all of the above. (1954)

Even odder is a tale recounted by Johnny Carson's longtime friend and attorney, Henry "Bombastic" Bushkin. In his biography of his boss, Bushkin claims that during Johnny's first couple of years on *The Tonight Show*, during the time that Keefe Brasselle's three bombs were polluting the competing network's air, Johnny got himself in trouble by making a few on-air jokes about Brasselle. According to Bushkin, Johnny claimed to have been taken by surprise one night during a late dinner by a man named Walter Stevens. Uninvited, Stevens took a seat at his table.

Johnny described the interloping dining partner as a burly man who told the late night host that he had been hired by some friends of Keefe Brasselle. He said they had tracked down the loudmouth funnyman to make it clear that the Brasselle jokes would stop. Bushkin says that, according to Johnny, Stevens then hauled-off and delivered a series of strong punches to the host's abdomen, painfully pounding away at Johnny until other diners separated the two. As Stevens was being ejected from the restaurant Johnny yelled after him, "What the fuck, I'll drop it. Nobody gives a shit about Keefe Brasselle."

Others with objections to being fodder for Johnny's joking found a softer touch was all that was needed to opt-out of his monologues. After a few comments about Ronald Reagan's hair being prematurely orange, Nancy Reagan spoke up. She asked Johnny to stop, and he did. Apparently politeness packs the power of a pugilist-for-hire when it comes from the right person. It couldn't have hurt that Johnny's producer, Fred De Cordova, had remained friends with the orange-haired ham ever since he directed Reagan in the very un-presidential film *Bedtime for Bonzo*.

Jim Aubrey and Keefe Brasselle may have poked their middle fingers deep into CBS's eye, but that was only one of the former network president's legacy of lesser indiscretions. The respected Sheldon Leonard was also among the many frustrated by Aubrey. Leonard came to television as an actor and graduated to join the ranks of the tube's most successful producer-packagers. His greatest hits included *The Andy Griffith Show* along with its successful spin-offs, as well as the pioneering *I Spy*. He claimed that Jim Aubrey gave him grief about no fewer than four of his hit series that were all top-rated.

In his autobiography Leonard summed up the executive's complaints: "*Andy Griffith* and *Gomer Pyle*, too shit-kicking; Danny Thomas's and Dick Van Dyke's, too show biz." In a conversation we had decades later, Carl Reiner confirmed Leonard's claim that swords were crossed over the beloved *Dick Van Dyke Show*. Carl remembered that Aubrey only reluctantly added the sitcom about the TV comedy writer and his family after asking Leonard to change Rob Petrie's occupation to real estate agent. Without that concession he'd threatened to keep the show off the CBS schedule. Aubrey did eventually birth the series in the fall of 1961, only to mark it for death during the subsequent months.

Indeed, it's been written that *The Dick Van Dyke Show* was nowhere to be found on early drafts of the fall 1962 schedule. A formal cancelation was said to be pending as the final episode of the debut season was in production. Sheldon Leonard took advantage of that window of opportunity to try to change what appeared to be the inevitable fate of a series he believed needed more time and better exposure to grow its audience. Leonard resented the Tuesday night

8:00 p.m. timeslot. Although reruns of *Gunsmoke* were a fair lead-in, Leonard called it "lousy" because his adult sitcom was running as early as 7:00 p.m. in the Midwest.

Next came a plan daring enough to be the plot of another Desilu show, *Mission, Impossible*. Leonard learned that the first season's sponsor of *The Dick Van Dyke Show* intended to withdraw its support, but reasoned that Aubrey couldn't deny a second season if he brought the series to him fully sold to that or another national advertiser. He figured it would be harder for his adversary to defend turning away the ready cash, so he flew to the company's Cincinnati headquarters with that sponsor's ad agency rep. The cancelling first-season benefactor was no less of a mega-advertiser than the company also behind many of the network's daytime soaps, Proctor and Gamble.

A gamble it was, as Leonard made his impassioned pitch laced with dramatic showmanship. He was successful in making the sale, and happy at the prospect of getting the program past his nemesis and onto the schedule. However, upon returning to L.A. he learned the soap shop's commitment wasn't 99-and-44/100-percent pure. In the few quick hours since his visit they'd rolled back their pledge from full to only half-sponsorship. With incredible moxie Leonard immediately boarded another plane for an overnight red-eye. This time his destination was into the belly of the advertising beast, Madison Avenue. With his very first pitch of the morning he locked Kent cigarettes. In an unprecedentedly heroic resuscitation that suggests nothing is impossible, *The Dick Van Dyke Show* survived.

Jim Aubrey had his many detractors, but he also had friends where it counted most; CBS's bean counters loved him. Fred Friendly, news icon Edward R. Murrow's producer, charted the corporation's profits. He noted that Aubrey's province was the single largest contributor to the bottom line. When he earned his VP stripes in 1959, CBS was celebrating a $25,267,000 profit. The numbers dropped over the next two years but, between 1961 and 1964, Aubrey's years as president, Friendly's math showed profits had doubled, reaching a high of $49,656,000. Then came the crash. Aubrey ultimately couldn't survive the following year's losses, especially after an investigation verified it came from relinquishing a generous slice of primetime for the infamous low-rated trio of series. Aubrey was out.

There have been others among the sometimes-strange breed of TV hopeful hit-pickers to equally puzzle the industry with bizarre casting and scheduling pronouncements. The legacy of another network executive is extraordinary in its own completely different way. Newsweek described NBC's daytime dynamo Lin Bolen as, "Stick-thin and ever on the move, the single Ms. Bolen sometimes comes across like a Cosmopolitan Girl on uppers," correctly assessing the executive as "a persona that her less successful colleagues find hard to swallow"

The one-time nemesis of aging daytime hosts is believed by many to have been immortalized as inspiration for the take-no-prisoners character portrayed by Faye Dunaway in the movie *Network*. That's not a compliment. Others deny that characterization and sing her praises, swearing that the acuity of her incisive mind and her straight-shooting honesty were matched by the kindness and generosity of her spirit. Just the same, she got laughs claiming that she was owed royalties for being the inspiration for Faye Dunaway's fictional character, UBS programming chief Diana Christensen, acknowledging for *The Washington Post* in 1978, "I certainly was a very prominent network executive at the time he created that character."

While disagreeing about her manner, pretty much everyone agrees that Bolen changed television by deconstructing years of traditional thinking and bringing a new zeitgeist to daytime. She extended soaps like *Days of Our Lives* and *Another World* from 30 minutes to an hour, allowing for more complex plots, a gamble that paid off. And she jazzed up the game show landscape with good-looking hosts and livelier game play, a look that came to be called "the Bolen style." "When I came to the network," she said, "a game show was celebrities sitting behind desks pushing buzzers. I felt the shows needed more fantasy and excitement."

Although the audience was still predominantly female, Bolen knew this was a new generation of young women that was eschewing established roles. Even those who weren't in the workforce were reading feminist authors, becoming politically active, and awakening to sexual freedoms. During the earlier era, when the new generation's mothers and grandmothers dutifully washed and dried the family laundry they never read magazine articles suggesting they lean against the washing machine during the spin cycle for sensual arousal. The times had changed.

Quite charmingly, network TV's first female vice president of daytime explained by telephone her passion for innovation. She spread development money among a few young creators with encouragement to work on original concepts that would be relevant to a youthful audience. NBC was in third place and needed to reinvent its daytime. Advocating for taking chances with fresh ideas, Bolen ruffled some of the peacock's grayest feathers. As she explained, "I took a lot of heat because I was a woman in a man's world."

Innovation included introducing a team of young emcees for her game shows. In one printed interview she referred to them as her "studs." Alan Thicke recommended his curly-coiffed, mustachioed young pal, fellow Canadian Alex Trebek. She saw his tape, talked to him by phone, and flew him to New York. The three spent a weekend at the midtown Hilton developing the first-time game show host's talents before casting her new discovery as *The Wizard of Odds*. The break onto U.S. network TV came so effortlessly that Alex wasn't convinced it couldn't disappear just as easily. He took accumulated vacation time from his work at the Canadian Broadcasting Corporation and slept on Thicke's couch until the NBC show proved sufficiently successful to earn a renewal.

Geoff Edwards was indeed studly *sans* necktie in his flashy leisure suits. Meanwhile, Tom Kennedy was fitted for a safari jacket, Peter Marshall's hair appeared restyled and Jim MacKrell admitted to feeling silly in his custom-designed loud plaid bell-bottomed pants and matching Nehru jacket.

Entertainer and former lead singer for The Four Preps, Bruce Belland, produced one of the shows Bolen bought and was on-staff at NBC during her reign. He remembers that by the time the mid-1970s came around it was deemed that television's very first game show host had become decidedly unstudly during the intervening 25 years. As the face of her network's *Name That Tune*, Dennis James needed freshening—some youth-enasia, to coin a word. Bruce said that Bolen had NBC pay for Dennis James' facelift, a thought the James family at first blush found to be ludicrous. Nearly as ludicrous, Dennis himself found Bolen's request that he wear artificial mutton-chop sideburns while sporting a new wardrobe of plaid sport jackets.

Where *The New York Times* explained, "She pushed through the changes with brash confidence," Bruce summed up his boss's leadership style as "Two-fisted. . . Do it my way or I'll nail your balls to the wall!" Rightly or wrongly, Bolen is charged with the demise of a couple of beloved television shows, *Concentration* and the original *Jeopardy!* among them. She's also taken the heat for the undoing of several popular personalities. Bolen remembered bringing model and actress Susan Stafford onto *Wheel of Fortune* in 1975 for the job of revealing puzzle letters because the electronics devised for that function hadn't been perfected in time for the first taping. As to the hostess's 1982 departure, I can neither confirm nor deny what Bruce told interviewer Stuart Shostak about Bolen firing Susan.

He claimed it was in order to quash water-cooler gossip about the letter-turner's suspected romantic liaisons with an executive associated with the series. It seems perhaps more credible knowing that Susan was attracted to a series of other media moguls, as well. Mega-wealthy radio tycoon Gordon McLendon and NBC's fast-rising superstar executive Dick Ebersol were her husbands before she formed a longtime live-in relationship with another broadcast heavyweight, game show kingpin Dan Enright.

As for being let go because of a workplace affair, with some re-castings stories get spun to such an extent that the truth is often hard to discern. Susan herself simply stated in her autobiography, "I mean, for seven years I stood there and turned letters. I had to ask myself if that was any way for a grown woman to live her life." Certainly not for what she was being paid. It was no secret that Merv Griffin's perceived miserliness was a frustration. It was around this time that Susan began studying psychology and was becoming deeply involved in religious and charitable pursuits. That calling included work with the healing ministry of Christian evangelist Ruth Carter Stapleton, sister of former President Jimmy Carter. Other contributions Susan made in humanitarian service have been extensive and have earned her great honors.

Any explanation for her transition rings far more credible than Roseanne Barr's more recent account regarding her disappearance from the 2018 reboot of her eponymous sitcom *Roseanne* aka *The Connors*. The network dropped the stand-up-turned-actress following her outrageously racist comments. She had tweeted that an African-American aide to President Obama was the product of The Muslim Brotherhood and *Planet of the Apes.* Yikes! Backpedaling, the comedienne blamed the racial rant on her sleeping medication, Ambien. That's right, the pills made her do it. Whoever wrote the response for the drug manufacturer deserves a bigger laugh than anything Roseanne ever said. Ambien's patent holder issued this statement, "While all pharmaceutical treatments have side effects, racism is not a known side effect of any Sanofi medication." Now that's comedy.

As to Lin Bolen, Merv himself remembered her in his memoir as a "hard-driving" and "difficult" woman, with whom he had many "bitter fights." Still, he noted, "I developed a grudging respect for her talent and determination." In dissention from her detractors, NBC's legendary daytime programmer has an impressive roster of loyalists who celebrate their relationships with her every time her name is mentioned. They were heartbroken when Lin passed in 2018.

Respected emcee Jim MacKrell credits Ms. Bolen as being the talented executive, charming lady, and dear friend who contributed greatly to his career. He explained how she offered him opportunities both in and outside of TV, and how she opened her L.A. home for him to stay during a return visit years later. Of course his story is true and his opinion highly respected, but I was doubtful at first because his friendship with the executive seemed to run contrary to what had become legend and lore. Then I spent the day with Tom Kennedy. In discussing his career and relationships I came to realize Lin Bolen was perhaps not so much an enigma as simply someone who didn't feign affection or kiss many asses. She just wasn't shy about letting folks know how she felt about them.

Like Jim MacKrell, Tom was effusive with his praise for Bolen's expertise and even more outspoken about his enjoyment of her company. Tom was also appreciative of her contribution to his career. Bolen loved Tom's work so much and found him so versatile that for a period he was given a shot at every new game show that premiered after another's cancellation. That's why Tom said "Goodbye" on at least a couple of Friday finales, only to be in the same time period saying "Welcome" on yet another series' debut the following Monday. Having Tom as an ace up her sleeve was so important to Bolen that she broke with precedent by placing him under a pay-or-play exclusive contract. It assured a weekly paycheck to keep him in the stable, unable to be lured away by an outside offer.

The creator-producer-writer who has challenged thousands of contestants with his many fun formats, perplexing puzzles, and punishing puns, Mark Maxwell-Smith once watched with quiet amusement as Ms. Bolen tried to stage a pilot in a way that audience members wouldn't be able to see opposing teams' choices of numbers and then potentially influence game play. Her suggestion for roping-off audience seats to remain vacant escalated to include one section, then another, then another to where it appeared there'd be no audience at all. As unworkable and frustrating as that exercise was, at least everybody remained calm.

There were other situations in which people who were close enough ended up on the receiving end of Ms. Bolen's less tactful treatment. Even one of her hand-picked young open-collared host-studs, Geoff Edwards, explained how his relationship with her started well only to sour later. Another gaudy plaid sport jacketed stud, Art James, had similar mixed feelings. He and Geoff likely never had the opportunity to compare notes as the closest they got in 1975 was to pass each other weekly at 30,000 feet. Art was flying from New York to L.A. for tape days of Bolen's *Blank Check* as Geoff commuted from L.A. to New York for *Jackpot*.

Johnny Carson (l) with tennis buddy Geoff Edwards (r). Geoff was a respected actor and broadcaster who brought his talents to an assortment of hit sitcoms, variety and talk shows before coming to game shows where he's best remembered for *Jackpot* and *Treasure Hunt*. Photo courtesy of Geoff Edwards.

Geoff was highly intelligent, quick-witted and one of the most forthright, friendliest, and funniest guys ever to be on camera or behind a microphone. Over our years of friendship I came to know that he wouldn't have spoken negatively about anyone unless he felt it was well deserved. He opened up with his tale of woe about the network chief, giving me a personal earful not suitable for print.

He also had a few choice comments sufficiently subdued for publication that he shared with author Adam Nedeff: "She killed *Jackpot*! *Jackpot* as a show was doing great. It was fun and we had great ratings. *The Young and the Restless* came on and beat us in the ratings. Lin said 'OK' and got a focus group. And the focus group said, 'We don't like riddles.' So she changed it, and that was the end of the show… I remember talking to [Producer Bob Stewart] about it up there, and saying, 'We're finished.' The whole fun of the show disappeared." Indeed, *Jackpot* was soon on the scrapheap of NBC's canceled formats.

I once got a huge laugh invoking Ms. Bolen's name while introducing Geoff Edwards at one of several Game Show Congress events, functions attended by TV insiders and knowledgeable fans. I explained that over the years of Geoff's fantastic career in both news and entertainment broadcasting his work brought him face-to-face with three, that's no fewer than three, brutal cold-blooded murderers. I enumerated that, in fact Geoff had been just a few feet away from Presidential assassin Lee Harvey Oswald in November of 1963 when he was shot in the basement of the Dallas police station. Of course, at that moment Geoff was equally close to Oswald's killer, Jack Ruby. Plus, I noted that "during another dangerous moment in his career Geoff had been face-to-face with a third heartless murderer… Lin Bolen!" (insert rimshot). Geoff fell off his chair.

In addition to being a masterful ad-libber, Geoff was among the pros valued by producers and beloved by crew members by virtue of his being a strong proponent of the unwritten first commandment: Get the show done on or ahead of schedule. The accountants appreciated how adhering to this credo contributed to keeping production within budget. Everybody else celebrated the opportunity it created to go home, go play, or go drink. When a tape day of as many as seven episodes is quick and simple, it's a joy worth celebrating. On the flip side there are a few performers who might be thought of as, well, seemingly reluctant to leave the dream factory. Here comes the surprising story of one malingerer you know well.

Chapter 30

Home can't compare. The conditioned air, the flattering lighting, the endless free food, and the attractive designer touches from a show's art director make a TV studio a utopian terrarium for some, I suppose.

With the job of keeping audiences entertained through their entire stay, thankfully I was unscathed by one of the turn of the century's worst offenders of the on-set malingerers. That burden fell to my friend and occasional rival for gigs, fellow voicer Burton Richardson. Poor Burton never complains but, on occasion, he was forced to perform the never-ending warm-up from hell at *Family Feud* during the years that Louie Anderson hosted. As time-conscious as broadcasters like Bob Barker, Geoff Edwards, and Maury Povich were, there were tape days when Louie seemed to be just the opposite. Comedians and actors who are primarily stage performers and have limited experience working in live or live-to-tape television, or in radio, seem sometimes to come from an entirely different world.

During the later years of his fronting that evergreen series, Louie seemed content to let the minutes tick away while he indulged in any number of distractions and pursued other baser instincts. In fairness, despite production delays almost everyone who worked with Louie enjoyed their time with him. He was always kind and friendly with me, and I'd seen him be extremely gracious, even willing to stand for repeated selfie-snappings alongside fans. Within the production community he was universally appreciated as a compassionate, caring, and generous guy who some say would open his heart and his wallet for anyone in need, anytime. As an example of his generosity, one Thanksgiving Louie bought frozen turkeys for everyone on the *Family Feud* staff and crew explaining that, as a child he was never really sure if his family would be celebrating with all the traditions of the holiday.

With that kind of generosity of spirit and kindness, Louie forged deep and loyal relationships that stood the test of time. For example, when Rodney Dangerfield was in a coma for over a month following heart surgery, Louie was at his bedside almost daily. He held Rodney's hand while he spoke and joked, tirelessly trying to reach or perhaps even wake his friend from unconsciousness, not knowing whether or not he was even being heard.

When they talk about the cliché of sadness behind comedy, and the difficult lives that have produced some of the great comic minds, Louie was one of the most illustrative examples. He was born in Saint Paul, Minnesota in 1953, the second youngest of 11 children that survived a total of 16 births. Louie made no secret of the sadness and despair in his childhood, created by a mother whom he described as passive-aggressive. As he joked for the *Associated Press* in 2015, "Rolling eyes were big in our family." Louie's father was a brilliant musician and inventor whose alcoholism brought out a fiercely abusive cruel patriarch. Louie conjectured that his father's rage was rooted in his being put up for adoption by his family as a child, finding himself working as a farmhand for an unloving family.

But as abrasive years produce the most beautiful pearls, Louie's hard times yielded both a gifted comedian and a caring, considerate friend to so many. Those who knew Louie knew well the gentleness that was in his heart and the compassion that was in his soul. As to the wit through which he distilled the human experience, Louie was on the radar as an up-and-coming comedian when still in his 20s. In 1981 he accepted the first-place trophy from the Midwest Comedy Competition presented by the event's host Henny Youngman, who instantly hired Louie to write for him.

Johnny Carson's bookers made their boss's eyes light up when Louie made his national television debut on the *Tonight Show* in 1984. He won over the audience with his opening line that played off of their first impression, his weight: "I can't stay long. I'm in between meals." In an unusual move, after his exit Johnny called Louie back to the stage for a second bow. The comic revealed that Johnny then surprised him yet again while he was basking in the afterglow of his outstanding reception from the audience. Louie remembered, "He came by my dressing room on the way to his, stuck his head in and said, 'Great shot, Louie.'"

As had been the case for countless others, Johnny's stage was ground zero from which careers skyrocketed. Appearances on Jay Leno's, David Letterman's, and Craig Ferguson's shows, on "Comic Relief," and on his own Showtime and HBO specials followed, which brought Louie the credibility that opened a wealth of additional opportunities.

As career success doesn't always correlate with personal fulfillment, Louie's elation was obscured by bouts of profound sadness. In describing his professional setbacks for *The Wall Street Journal* he compared his life to being at an amusement park. "Sometimes it's like the big Matterhorn roller coaster and sometimes it's the little boat in the water." Louie described a period of intense depression during which one night on the road, in a dressing room before a performance, he had a gun to his head. He said he remembered hearing that depending upon the placement of a pistol in a suicide attempt, death was not assured. As such, he took careful aim but then realized the mess a bullet to the head would leave. He told me that he wrapped a towel around his head to try to minimize the horrific splattering, eventually giving up on the suicide attempt, not wanting the scene he would leave to be anyone's last memory of him.

When he took the *Family Feud* gig Louie was more of a sad soul than most comedians. He was suffering a painful physical malady and was especially troubled as he was the victim of a blackmailer. Louie said that he was so low then that he contemplated suicide. While he was enough of a pro to appear as though he was enjoying all of the laughter with contestants, one of those bouts with abject depression fell during his tenure fronting *Family Feud*.

Even though you may love and care for someone, they can still frustrate you. In fact, the more you care about someone the more they can be a source of aggravation. Louie did indeed try the patience of some co-workers with his between-the-episodes diversions and seeming reticence to take the stage. Those delays were made all too easy by an especially unusual accommodation I'd never before seen that was designed to keep Louie's painful walking to a minimum. A king-sized custom-constructed dressing room was built in NBC's Studio 11. It wasn't down the hall from the studio like most talent retreats, and it wasn't simply off to a corner inside the studio, it was actually on the set.

There, stage right, barely millimeters out of camera range. Seriously, it couldn't have been closer to Louie's tape-marked sweet spot at center stage if it had been scientifically engineered by NASA to provide the absolute minimum distance for Louie to walk, yet elude the various cameras angles. The room was encased in unfinished plywood, and the interior was also far from lush. The simple furniture and kitchen amenities were comfortable enough that, on some days, Louie had to be coaxed and cajoled by the stage manager, usually Bill "Bones" Vosburgh, to get out on set. I'm sorry to report that Louie did much, single-handedly, to reinforce the false stereotype that all fat people are lazy.

Sometimes watching TV, most often eating, sometimes napping, at times simply vegged-out alone and, reportedly on occasion, in the intimate company of a young friend, Louie presented a challenge for *Feud* to remain anywhere close to its daily multi-show taping schedule. Keeping the audience entertained for so many hours was a challenge to Burton's warm-up skills and stamina. In fact, little known, that year Burton had the first of several surgeries to repair damage to his vocal chords caused by overuse and strain.

A cat may have nine lives, and Louie seemed to have nearly as many. As disheartened as he felt at times, and as terminal as his career may have seemed when CBS cancelled his 1996 sitcom *The Louie Show* after just six episodes, and when he agreed to don a bathing suit for a high-dive into a swimming pool for the now-forgotten ABC-TV reality show *Splash*, I'm happy to have since seen him enjoy yet another welcome peak. Louie's major triumph from a few years ago was a whopper. Falling in with Zach Galifianakis and Louis C.K. for their comedy series *Baskets* on FX, Louie won a 2016 Emmy for playing Christine Baskets, a Costco-loving suburban widow living in Bakersfield.

Yes, it was a gender-bending role, and she—I mean he—was terrific. Just that quickly, the tide had turned from sad to glad. Louie seemed very happy during the last years of his life. He was all smiles and generous with his time at a 2018 event as he charmingly trolled for Emmy votes from TV Academy members. With the success of *Baskets,* Louie enjoyed the spiritual nourishment and the exhilaration from being celebrated by his community of fellow performers. That likely held true even if some of them were the same people who weren't there for him when he was hurting. *Baskets* wrapped its successful four-season run in 2019. Proving the axiom "when you're hot, you're hot," Louie quickly moved onto a five-episode arc of HBO Max's *Search Party,* and a reprise of his role as Maurice in Eddie Murphy's *Coming 2 America.*

Louie came to be cast in Eddie Murphy's original 1988 *Coming to America* after spying Eddie and his entourage across the room at the famed Beverly Hills hip see-and-be-seen restaurant, The Ivy. Louie explained in 2017 that, on a whim, he whipped out his credit card and paid for the group's meal with the instruction that Eddie's waiter not know the tab was covered. He recalled directing the maître d, "Don't tell him 'til after I leave. I'm not doing it to be a big shot. I'm doing it because I'm from the Midwest and that's how we would do [it]." Louie said that the next morning Murphy called saying, "Nobody ever bought me anything," and returned the surprise by telling Louie he wanted to cast the big-hearted comic in his film. Louie recounted, "That's life, isn't it? It was the best $660 I ever spent."

Eddie and co-star Arsenio Hall put their own spin on Louie's casting. "I love Louie, but I think we were forced to put Louie in it," Arsenio joked with Jimmy Kimmel in 2021. "We were forced to put in a white person." Eddie added that it was a studio requirement, "'There has to be a white person in the movie.' I was like, 'What?' So who was the funniest white guy around? We knew Louie was cool, so that's how Louie got in the movie."

More recently, Louie appeared on *Young Sheldon,* had a recurring role in the dark comedy *Search Party,* brought more laughs to *Funny You Should Ask,* and had joined the cast of the hit BET series, *Twenties.* Sadly, that's where the string of recent triumphs ended. Louie entered a Las Vegas hospital in January of 2022 after being diagnosed with diffuse large B-cell lymphoma, a type of non-Hodgkin's lymphoma. He passed quietly on the morning of January 21st.

Lovable Louie Anderson on the set of *Family Feud*. Louie rode into Hollywood on the mid-1980s wave of stand-ups with an act that skewered dysfunctional family life. Standup made Louie a household name and created his earliest opportunities to be cast in hip movies (*Ferris Bueller's Day Off*), TV dramatic roles (*Touched by an Angel*), and to create his Emmy-winning *Life With Louie*.

Among the triumphs and challenges, Louie went through a life crisis at the hands of a blackmailer named Richard J. Gordon. According to police reports, Louie had approached 24-year-old Gordon at a Southern California casino back in 1993 and propositioned him. Gordon claimed Louie asked his new friend to go home with him, strip, and let Louie touch him. Gordon said Anderson then changed his mind, deciding he just wanted to see him disrobe. Gordon refused both requests. Not a word was spoken about the supposed proposition until four years later. Gordon had then traveled to Las Vegas where Louie was appearing at Bally's and handed over an envelope addressed to the comedian with a note inside.

Press reports stated that the envelope contained a demand for hush money, and included a warning that Louie's failure to buy Gordon's silence would be career suicide. Gordon threatened that "stars are falling left and right, [and] now that you are working with kids it makes it even worse." Indeed Louie had a lot to lose, both his fronting of *Family Feud*, and Fox's animated kids show *Life with*

Louie that he'd created and for which he'd won two daytime Emmys for producing, writing, and starring in. Court records disclose that in 1997 and 1998 Louie paid Gordon most of the $100,000 hush money demanded. Ah, but just like in the movies, blackmailers always return for more easy cash. Gordon upped his demand in 2000, asking for an additional $250,000. That's when Louie brought his lawyer into the picture, and the lawyer brought the feds.

The final chapter played out like an action movie. A date was set to make the quarter-million-dollar payoff at a Santa Monica Boulevard restaurant. The comedian didn't want to make the drop, so an undercover FBI agent posing as Louie's assistant followed Gordon's instructions and handed over a quarter-million dollar check. As two other agents were moving in to make the arrest, Gordon bolted into a waiting pickup truck. His pal and accomplice, Matthew David Auten, punched the gas. They led the feds on a chase through West L.A.'s busy streets at speeds reported to be as high as 80 miles per hour. News accounts reported that, while fleeing, Gordon tossed two loaded pistols out the window of the speeding pick-up. After his capture Gordon pleaded guilty to a blackmail charge. He was sentenced to 21 months in federal prison and ordered to pay $4,000 in restitution to Louie. After his release Gordon faced an additional three years of probation.

Comedy is no laughing matter. Twenty years later another comedian was being similarly extorted for an illicit payday in exchange for silence in a Las Vegas sex scandal. This time it was comedian Kevin Hart and the alleged blackmailer was his friend Jonathan Todd "Action" Jackson. Far more damning than a simple allegation, this time the evidence was on videotape featuring Hart engaged in sexual activity with a woman. What the comedian referred to as "a bad error in judgment" took place while his wife, Eniko Parrish, was eight months pregnant.

It was an entirely different scandal that more fully challenged stand-up and actor Kevin Hart's career. After being announced as the host of the 2019 Academy Awards, public criticism led to his stepping down from the high-visibility gig. At issue were homophobic tweets made almost a decade earlier. He explained, "… thinking that things you say will come back and bite you on the ass…[means]… I can't be the comic today that I was when I got into this." As any story about the

Oscars generates ink, Hart's name and indiscretion were dragged through the dirt and his image, his "brand" if you like, took a hit. Fame can feel like living life under a microscope. Yet, for all but the most abominable outlandish behaviors it seems that, with time, audiences forgive and forget. The industry's decision makers are then willing to quickly follow suit as soon as they smell the potential for profits.

Louie Anderson's public image was temporarily tweaked by news of the blackmail affair, but it didn't shorten his run on *Family Feud*. It was a combination of lackluster ratings and a contractual pay bump coming due that caused Louie's name to join the pantheon of the show's other ex-hosts. Credit the strength of the format and the casting of engaging families for its surviving a half-dozen emcee re-castings, including four in just over a decade.

Despite suffering twists and turns on its way to being birthed, this long-running spinoff from the *Match Game '73* bonus round was quickly feted as Outstanding Game Show a year after its debut. It was then unusually resilient waiting to regain its 1977 crown. Not until 2019's reboot was it again recognized with that honor. Accepting the award was the executive producer who had started 40 years earlier as a young production staffer on the original version, Gaby Johnston.

The perennial family game did indeed have a long circuitous route before finally flickering on home screens. In fact, it wasn't originally conceived as a game for families, ABC wasn't its intended buyer, and Richard Dawson wasn't on the radar as a possible host. Previous contenders included William Shatner during the months the show was first being developed for CBS. Sure, the *Star Trek* actor was well known and had appeared as a celebrity player on game shows, but there was a strategic political motive for the choice. Shatner was married to actress Marcy Lafferty. How could the network's executive Perry Lafferty possibly give thumbs-down to a show hosted by his daughter's husband?

Ultimately it was Richard Dawson who inaugurated *Feud* on ABC after the godfather of game shows, Mark Goodson, was reminded that Dawson's contract to continue as a *Match Game* panelist required that he be considered as a possible host for the company's next pilot. The network's Mike Brockman recalls that Goodson had low expectations for Dawson's office runthrough. However, Mike said he remembered having seen an earlier pilot in which Dawson was wonderfully personable with contestants. That proved to be the case as Goodson watched the prospective host run the show with office staffers.

Dawson was again outstanding on the subsequent pilot and brought that same charm to a total of over 3,000 highly-rated episodes on both network and syndicated runs. By 1985, with *Wheel of Fortune* and *Jeopardy!* stealing viewers, Viacom stepped on the brakes, withdrawing *Feud* just before that year's NATPE syndication marketplace opened for business. ABC then did likewise with their daytime run and both aired the last of their new episodes that spring.

Just three years later, Goodson-Todman cut a deal with CBS to revive the juggernaut on Independence Day. Producer Howard Felsher had been banned from the studio in the latter years at ABC over issues of on-set dysfunction, but he was back in action in 1988 casting for a new emcee. On a call to the 1970s football sensation-turned-actor and pop-culture phenomenon "Broadway Joe" Namath, a breakfast date was set for the Beverly Hills Hotel. When the quarterback asked, "Can I bring my wife?" it should have been the first hint that convincing Deborah Mays was going to be the bigger challenge. Felsher told author Mark Kriegel that although she was 21 years Joe's junior, "She had great influence over him... every time he made a comment, he looked to her for approbation." "It could do him a lot of harm if it fails," she warned.

Ultimately Joe was brought into Mark Goodson's runthrough studio at 6430 Sunset Boulevard, where the building almost vibrated with the sample contestants' adulation. "Just charming," remembered Felsher. "He brought such a feeling of innocence to it." Everybody everywhere had the same reaction to Broadway Joe. He was spectacularly charismatic and the sweetheart deal cut with Mark Goodson reflected that popularity. Even a last minute request for a $25,000 signing bonus didn't deter the game show guru.

The money "didn't mean that much," Felsher recalled. "But my boss got cold feet." Had word leaked about Joe's alcoholism? Did Howard Felsher scotch the deal over concerns Joe was too big a star for him to control? We'll never know, but that kind of power struggle had been the producer's big issue with Richard Dawson, and was again years later when Ray Combs' starshine occasionally eclipsed the game. When fully riled, Felsher's rage could rival the stink from the time a skunk got under the *Family Feud* set's steps. ABC's senior video engineer Chuck Pharis remembers, "It took days to get the smell out of stage 54."

After being catapulted from obscurity by an outstanding standup appearance on the *Tonight Show* two years earlier, Ray Combs was hired in 1988. His tenure as *Family Feud* facilitator included CBS's daytime revival that ran until 1993, as well as six seasons in syndication that ended the following year. Dawson returned for a seventh and final season before the show was rested in 1995. Louie Anderson's three-year syndicated run started in 1999. It brought the series into its fourth decade, and into the new millennium. Louie's loss was Richard Karn's gain. Richard was followed as emcee by John O'Hurley in 2006, during whose watch there was a network *Celebrity Family Feud* attempted in the summer of 2008 with Al Roker on NBC.

O'Hurley kept the gameplay within the realm of a solid family-friendly G-rating at a time when Fremantle hired a consulting producer whose mission it was to add a little PG-13 spice to the recipe. That producer told me that he found O'Hurley resistant to the changes—changes that clearly foretold the future direction of the show's content. That hesitance was not necessarily the sole reason there was yet another change in emcees. Louie Anderson shed some insight into the unusual parade of hosts for a single series back when he predicted during his third year that it would be his last. He explained that his contract called for a significant pay increase should he be renewed for a fourth season. "They won't want to pay it. I'll be gone," he predicted. That kind of escalating clause is not at all unusual, with the specifics of each performer's deal part of the negotiation ritual.

I was working at NBC the week in 2002 when Richard Karn was being interviewed for an EPK, an electronic press kit to be used to promote the new *Feud* emcee. On a break, Richard came over to say hello and get a moment of relief by dropping the facade of self-assurance he had been projecting. We'd only met once before, yet he confided in me with his admission that he considered this transition from sitcoms into a new and more demanding realm to be a big leap of faith. Beyond the challenge of working without a net—unscripted, live-to-tape, with no retakes—

he found the idea of producing as many as six half-hour episodes of a show on the same day to be the most daunting dare of his career. On *Home Improvement* it had been pretty much the reverse, closer to six days to produce one 30-minute program.

Success had come quickly for Richard as he scored his sitcom role alongside Tim Allen within just a couple of years of moving to L.A. While he lucked into the role intended for Stephen Tobolowsky, I never asked Richard if there was any truth to the story that he was cast with the help of an agent he met while attending traffic school for running a stop sign. I suggested that his early success was proof he obviously had greater talent and appeal than most, and hinted that the game show gods might well smile upon anyone from the world of primetime who approached their new trial with his kind of respect and trepidation. Although firmly rooted in truth, I was afraid I'd ladled on a smidge more well-meaning encouraging bullshit than he might buy. Instead, it appeared to be just the kind of support Richard needed as he left to face the camera again. He did indeed rise to the challenge and handled the job splendidly.

Introducing a new host can be a strategic move to prolong the life of a show after a season of uninspired ratings. That's especially true in syndication where affiliates unsure about renewing after a poor-performing cycle can be encouraged to continue to carry a series that's "on the bubble" by making potentially positive changes. Hiring Karn, still fresh from a hit comedy and one of viewers' favorite sitcom supporting players, could well have served as that kind of confidence builder.

Early in his helming of his father's game show dynasty Jonathan Goodson confirmed for me that, indeed, finding a new name with which to entice affiliates had been the strategy behind dismissing Ray Combs in 1994. Reluctant stations renewed with the news of a new host, especially when the new host was Richard Dawson, the old host, the original host whom audiences had come to love. A homecoming by Dawson brought the expectation that the show's presentation would be refreshed with some of its former glory returned. It would also provide a highly promotable event for the local affiliates on-board for the new season. While switching out Ray Combs for Richard Dawson may have temporarily breathed a modicum of new life into the aging 18-year-old series, Ray's firing was one in a sequence of events that literally sucked the life out of a good man. It was one affront of several that contributed to the heartbreaking crash and burn of that great talent. There's much to be said about that tragedy later in these pages.

Dawson's return proved a viable Hail-Mary play that bought the franchise one more season, but he couldn't live up to the grandiose expectations placed on his return. Richard was still charming, funny, entertaining, the contestants' best friend, and thoroughly proficient in the role he created. His fans still loved him, but none of us are the same person at 62 that we were nearly two decades earlier. The wattage of dear Richard's starshine had clearly decreased.

It was Steve Harvey who ultimately returned the perennial to ratings dominance when he replaced John O'Hurley in 2010. The Nielsen bells rang throughout the game show universe as he captained the S.S. *Feud* through its sail past the perennial leader *Wheel of Fortune* into the number one berth in first run syndication. Fremantle boasted the slow and steady climb, year over year, from a 1.4 in the 2009-2010 season, through a 2.4, 3.0, 4.6, 5.0, 6.2, and 6.6, to its new high of 6.8 in 2017. Steve Harvey turned out to be the unlikely savior, invigorating the tired format and more than tripling its viewership. Beyond being a host who could carry that syndicated series for the foreseeable future, Steve also managed to reignite the show back onto the network where it had started four decades earlier. This time a celebrity version of *Feud* out-performed expectations during summer runs on ABC. With the striking PG-13 edginess in its questions, the network found the old favorite suddenly scoring as many weeks' top-rated show.

Steve Harvey is one of the great media success stories of the early 21st century, shepherding no fewer than a half-dozen TV projects. His appeal can't be underestimated, as he's been among the most prolific personalities on the tube in this generation. He's also the only entertainer in recent memory to star on three of the big four broadcast networks almost simultaneously. That popularity fueled the indefatigable dynamo's master plan that he shared with *The Hollywood Reporter* in 2018: "I'm gonna have the biggest television production company in Hollywood. I'm gonna be producing more hits than any production company in the industry." The following year he made investments in media entities including

Anthem Sports and Entertainment. Meanwhile, incongruently, Steve apparently lent his name to a mega-retailer who, late in 2021, had him was hawking "Join Sam's Club for under $20 and get FREE chicken + cupcakes."

Although painfully embarrassing at the time, Steve can now joke about his fluke from 2015 when he momentarily and mistakenly crowned runner-up Miss Colombia as the new Miss Universe. The confused host then instantly stripped the South American of the title and congratulated the actual winner, Miss Philippines. What happened? Steve says that at rehearsal, stand-ins for the three finalists were on stage and he read only two names, the second runner-up and Miss Universe. It was then obvious who the first runner-up was. During the live broadcast there were three names on the card instead of two. It clearly identified the proper winning order, but Steve claims his concentration was thrown by the crutch so many emcees now rely on, an IFB.

Technology advanced around the turn of the millennium to where a wireless IFB (interrupted foldback) can be manufactured to be so tiny that it can be worn invisibly in their ear canal. It allows on-camera talent to surreptitiously hear the program audio mix, including the voices of other performers that might otherwise not be clearly audible from elsewhere on the set or from a remote location. That feed can be dimmed or completely interrupted by a director or producer to pass information or instructions. Steve remembers, "The dude in my ear, said, 'Read the next name on the card!'" It was all a ball of confusion.

In addition to pageants and special, Steve was the face of *Little Big Shots* and its spinoff *Forever Young* on NBC. Fox's *Showtime at the Apollo* was his favorite. He also fronted two shows for ABC, *Celebrity Family Feud* and *Funderdome*. Finally, there were his daily hour talk-variety show and a syndicated daily radio program. He seemed to be so admired and favored by his talk show's distributor, NBCUniversal, that if the studio had an employee bowling league it's likely Steve would have handed out the trophies.

Then the 2017 headline: "Steve Harvey ends his NBCUniversal syndicated talk show" was followed by "Steve Harvey starts an NBCUniversal syndicated talk show." The translation: after five seasons the ratings-challenged *Steve Harvey* ended production in May of that year. More than 100 Chicago-based staffers for NBCUniversal and Endemol Shine North America were cut loose. A new Steve Harvey show simply titled *Steve* debuted that September from Los Angeles.

Why end one talk show for another? Like most baffling questions in the entertainment industry this one can also be answered with one word, "money." The star found himself in the shifting tides of a sea change in how Hollywood works. Content is now king, and ownership the new Holy Grail. Talent agencies were once forbidden from having a direct financial interest in programs. Yet, suddenly Steve's agent at William Morris/Endeavor offered him the chance to partner with their new production arm, IMG. It meant eliminating NBCUniversal's ownership stake in the show that was earned in exchange for clearance on its major market stations, and it meant parting ways with production company Endemol Shine. Endemol was reportedly taking an estimated 25% to 30% of the program's earnings.

The talent agency guaranteed Steve a larger share, lower overhead costs, more creative control, and a big salary boost. "Hollywood is a game," the host explained. "You've got an agent, a manager and a lawyer, and all those people get a percentage. That's a lot of people eating off the pie. If I combine the manager and the production company and I get a larger share of the show ownership, that's a better business move for me." When you put it that way, sure. Of course, NBCUniversal took an entirely different view of the affair. The conglomerate was incensed that the talent agency would brazenly make a move that, at best, they viewed as unethical and quasi-legal. Because being in bed with a hit show means money even without an ownership slice, NBCUniversal agreed to distribute the new *Steve* and cleared it on their major market stations. However, they reportedly were not happy. Could that be why the studio yanked *Little Big Shots* off Steve's plate, serving it instead to Melissa McCarthy?

After two seasons the NBCUniversal stations announced they were dropping *Steve*, the host's enriching daily L.A.-based talk show, giving the airtime to Kelly Clarkson with whom there was greater potential for profits. With clearances cratered, the series ended midway through 2019. After a six month hiatus, Endeavor stuck a deal with the internet platform Facebook Watch, where *Steve on Watch* premiered on January 6, 2020. Two years later, 2022 started with Steve Harvey on ABC in an unusual twist on the court show genre. At this rate he's gonna put Ryan Seacrest to shame.

Variety called his big talk show transition "a casualty of animosity," stating NBCUniversal executives were furious at losing their stake in Harvey's show after the move to IMG, even though the peacock studio remained the distributor. Steve's comment summed it up with, "This ain't the black man's game, this ain't the white man's game, it's the money game." How much money you ask? Let's not get too far ahead of the story. Not until the new paint job is dry on Universal's Stage 1 that had previously been adorned with Steve's likeness.

Indefatigable Steve Harvey says he isn't driven towards success,
but instead is running from poverty.

When I last spoke to Steve he was one month into a new life as a vegan. Still on a honeymoon with the change in his diet, he publicly volunteered that he almost immediately saw such an improvement in his overall health that he was able to drop his use of the anti-inflammatory medication Celebrex. He revised his master plan: "I'm gonna own a huge organic food business. I'm going to help people reshape the way they eat. A doctor told me, 'Steve, what you eat in your 40s we will diagnose in your 50s. What we diagnose in your 50s, we will treat you for in your 60s. Whatever we're treating you for in your 60s, we will bury you for in your 70s.' It changed the way I ate."

More than his diet was in flux. I didn't ask about the pending book from convicted drug lord Jim Townsend that allegedly implicates Steve's wife in a string of felonies. Before exchanging vows with Steve in 2007, Marjorie Elaine Harvey was Mrs. Jim Townsend, the same Jim Townsend who was given a life prison sentence courtesy of the FBI and DEA. After being busted during a thwarted attempt to buy 40 kilos of so-called happy dust, he earned the dubious distinction of being dubbed a cocaine kingpin. He served 26 years of the life sentence before a Presidential pardon. Like a ticking time bomb Townsend is now free, making it easier than ever for him to publish his long-threatened book.

There was no mention of that mess. Fact is, since his engagement to Marjorie over 15 years ago Steve has spoken openly about having found the love of his life now that the couple reunited after a fling in the 1980s. With this marriage he's proving that the third time can indeed be a charm. Love and stardom have both completely changed Steve's life, mostly but not all for the better.

Chapter 31

When Steve Harvey signed for his daily talker, he was warned that it would be hard work to prep and then fill that many hours every week. His response: "Excuse me? I worked at Ford Motor Company putting eight spark plugs in 1,400 engines a day. That's hard work. Now I talk, and I wear suits. People put make-up on me, polish my shoes, trim my mustache, shave me. Someone fucking puts my belt in my belt loops! A dude ties my shoes. That shit's crazy. This isn't real life."

At the time we first spoke, the pampered host boasted that he was watched by an average of 12 million viewers every day, all year long. Those kinds of tallies surpassed most of his contemporaries and harkened back to the days when fewer than a handful of channels were available in most cities. It resulted in the ubiquitous visibility of early TV personalities such as Art Linkletter. Unlike Linkletter, Regis, Oprah, Donahue, Dick Clark, Hugh Downs, Ryan Seacrest and others among television's most-watched, Steve Harvey said his endless adrenalin has been fueled by fear. Yes, fear. He told the *L.A. Times*, "I've been homeless before. I'm running from that—full-gait running from that ever happening to me again. That memory is vivid. There's not a day that goes by that I don't recognize that."

On each of my visits to his sets Steve was enthusiastically giving his best to both the cameras and to the live crowd, taping multiple shows a day, day after day. He was obviously fully invested in delivering maximum laughs at *Celebrity Family Feud* as he offered second takes and alternate reactive jokes while he clowned, kidded, cajoled, and teased with each pair of families for well over an hour. In addition to recording the program's line cut (the usual switching between cameras), there were ten more recorders simultaneously capturing isolated video feeds from every meaningful angle. With that, 40 different tracks of audio were saving the isolated sound from each of a dozen on-stage microphones as well as the audience reactions, the music, and the all-important pings, dings, tweeps, blings, buzzers and other sound effects. It gave the show's editors an abundance of options for creating an outstanding 44 minutes for each network hour. Likewise, the syndicated half-hours were similarly overshot.

Between the blasts of energy the host recharges silently with a cigar, sitting in a chair that bears his name, placed a few dozen feet outside of the soundstage. During one of those between-episode smoke breaks I learned how much of Steve's happiness comes from having moved on from the world of standup comedy where he first found fame. He lamented, "They keep moving the line of political correctness. It keeps getting closer and closer to where you can't open your mouth negatively. Throw away freedom of speech. That's out the window now."

He has a point. Why fight the same battle that has convinced Jerry Seinfeld and others that this era of political correctness is not conducive to touring as a stand-up? The word among Jerry, Chris Rock, Dave Chappelle, Kevin Hart and other comedians who can afford to pick and choose their gigs is to especially avoid bookings on college campuses where they report there's little appetite for making fun of people.

Instead of a mind-blurring series of flights and hotel rooms while traveling across the fruited plains, Steve prefers generating laughs in a comfortable and controlled space. He's at home breathing recycled cool studio air in vast dark sealed chambers where any hint of stray light is no match for the acres of black duvetyn fabric. His soundstage becomes his pulpit as he appears to be borrowing from a motivational speaker's playbook, offering life advice to the audience with a fervor bordering on a church sermon. During a stopdown at a recent taping he answered a question about fame with rare incisive clarity. It was obvious he'd thought a great deal about how it has changed his life.

Steve gave the surprised crowd a slice of the same kind of candid reality you're finding in these pages. He explained how the trade-off for wealth was so disruptive to his life that he might consider a different path if faced with the choice again. Steve explained, "I can't go to the beach, I can't go to the movies, I can't take my family to a restaurant, I can't take my grandkids to Disneyland… I have a great home, but I can't leave it."

The hushed visitors seemed stunned by Steve's no-punches-pulled honesty about an aspect of celebrity they never considered. They listened attentively as he continued, "And the cameras in everybody's cell phone make it impossible to do anything. Somebody's always videotaping, and the tabloids can't wait to get a picture of something they can twist into a scandal… I can't go anywhere and I can't do anything, and all I have is the money." After a silent pause, with the timing of a skilled jester he then smiled widely and got his laugh with, "And I guess I wouldn't change any of it!"

Let me answer that question that was in the minds of each audience member that day, and likely now yours as well: "How much money?" In 2021 Forbes pegged Steve's net worth at $160 million. His annual compensation was estimated by both *Forbes* and *The Hollywood Reporter* in 2017 as $42.5 million. It bumped to $45 million in 2019. Almost certainly the single largest component of that total had been his eponymous daily talker, before he was switched out by NBCUniversal for freshman gabber Kelly Clarkson.

Another studio contributed to the 2022 and 2023 bottom lines as Disney has renewed Steve's unusual weekly hour-long court show just mentioned. With it, ABC created a new genre, calling their experiment a courtroom comedy. The joker played judge and jury as he mediated, preached, and satirized all manner of conflicts, with the show paying participants' penalties and awards.

Despite the fame that keeps the host at home when not in the studio, there is one public place Steve can go, and often. Guys like him, in their 60s, find themselves mysteriously gravitating to the men's room more frequently than ever seemed necessary. During one tape date for ABC's *Celebrity Family Feud,* Steve and I found ourselves satisfying the same call of nature in the same small facility just off the set in Television City's Studio 36. With his head no doubt swimming with details of the multiple episodes taping that day and likely unexcited about the prospect of having another non-essential conversation, I merely nodded my acknowledgement. With his hands full at the moment he simply returned the gesture.

In that compact men's room I had accurately estimated the size of Steve's desire for small talk: none. It wasn't too much later that he told *Entertainment Tonight,*

"I've always had a policy where, you know, you can come and talk to me—so many people are great around here, but some of them just started taking advantage of it. Look, man, I'm in my makeup chair, they walk in the room. I'm having lunch, they walk in, they don't knock," he continued. "I'm in the hallway, I'm getting ambushed by people with friends that come to the show and having me sign this and do this. I just said, 'Wait a minute.'"

Apparently that aspect of fame had bugged Steve for years, as the overwrought host finally dropped the facade to say, "I just didn't want to be in this prison anymore where I had to be in this little room, scared to go out and take a breath of fresh air without somebody approaching me, so I wrote the letter." Ah, the letter. The staff at his talk show was shocked by a proclamation circulated in 2017. Steve himself later admitted it was too heavy-handed:

"There will be no meetings in my dressing room. No stopping by or popping in. NO ONE. Do not come to my dressing room unless invited. Do not open my dressing room door. IF YOU OPEN MY DOOR, EXPECT TO BE REMOVED. My security team will stop everyone from standing at my door who have (sic) the intent to see or speak to me. I want all the ambushing to stop now…"

The capital letters are directly from Steve's memo. It goes on,

"I have been taken advantage of by my lenient policy in the past. This ends now. NO MORE. Do not approach me while I'm in the makeup chair unless I ask to speak with you directly. Either knock or use the doorbell… Do not wait in any hallway to speak to me. I hate being ambushed. Please make an appointment. I promise you I will not entertain you in the hallway, and do not attempt to walk with me. If you're reading this, yes, I mean you…"

Unthinking staffers and sometimes even experienced crew members can't resist the temptation to introduce their visiting guests, who then try to engage a performer without any apparent objective other than to tell friends they met someone who's famous. The meaningless chatter necessary to avoid earning a reputation for being a jerk requires at the very least a courteous acknowledgement, a smile, and a modicum of small talk laced with a sprinkling of charm. Well, those are the same commodities that talent gets paid big bucks to effuse, on cue, hour after hour.

In his letter no doubt Steve dared to say what many have felt, despite risking blowback for having offended the very people on whom he relies to keep his mega-million dollar brand well polished. However well-intentioned Steve Harvey's rules of engagement might have been, would he circulate that memo again? He's already answered with an emphatic "No." I guess it takes a big man to promptly back-peddle and apologize, as he did.

A big man, indeed. Steve is extra-large, tall and hefty. His appearance is enhanced by incredibly fine bespoke tailoring. His custom-constructed suits and custom-sewn shirts are of elegant and sturdy high-thread-count cloth. Every time I've seen Steve he was accessorized to maximum capacity with cufflinks, suspenders, pocket square, rings, and every gentlemanly accoutrement. Clothes don't make the man, but they play a great supporting role for Steve. His tailor and stylist deserve Emmys.

Preaching to his congregation. *Family Feud* studio audiences get more than a game show, Steve Harvey offers life advice along with the laughs. Photo from the author's collection.

Looking back in 2021 Steve seemed undaunted about the talk show he lost in 2019, having made the experience the springboard for a new studio audience sermon:

"You can come to work one day and they just say the show is canceled… I produce so much content, I got radio, I write books, I write movies, I do TV shows… I do a Facebook Watch show. I do so many, so when they come and cancel something I don't really give a damn because I've got eight more jobs… The job you have is not going to last forever… start living your life with the preparation for change. No matter how much you're doing, you could be doing more… If your ass wants to hit it and be rich, you got to stop bullshitting. You got to start getting your hustle and grind on… I've always prepared myself for what this business is, and for the first time I actually thought about retiring."

Retirement, or at least a temporary withdrawal from the daily visibility. It was an obvious choice for Ellen DeGeneres after being credited for creating enough animosity to dim her starshine and devalue her brand. After employees and even a few celebrity guests went public about backstage strife, her workplace was declared toxic in 2020. More than a million people reached for the remote as Nielsen pegged the drop from 2.6 million to 1.5 million viewers. Ellen's Instagram presence had drawn 12 sponsored posts from eight different brands, but in November of that year half of the sponsorships were gone. Suddenly there were only six sponsored posts from only two different advertisers. With the multi-million dollar gravy train having jumped the rails and her contrite on-air apology registering as insincere with some staffers, Ellen gave notice that she was ending the show just short of its 20th season. Her NBC series *Ellen's Game of Games* was pink-slipped in early 2022 after four seasons.

Upon returning for season 19, she told Savannah Guthrie at *Today*, on the network whose owned stations carry *Ellen*, "I really did think about not coming back… it was devastating. I am a kind person. I am a person who likes to make people happy." That was indeed the case at the Daytime Emmy awards ceremony the year she was first feted—she charmed the place. However, as early as 2018 *The New York Times* was asking the comedy star about anonymous tabloid reports of internal strife.

Of the continuing complaints from employees and guests at her stage and offices on the Warner Bros. lot Ellen said in May of 2021, "If I was a fan of somebody and even if I loved them, I would think there must be some truth to it, because it's not stopping." Ellen understood the bottom line when she noted, "It is my name on the show, so clearly it affects me and I have to be the one to stand up and say, 'This can't be tolerated.' But I do wish somebody would have come to me and said, 'Hey, something's going on that you should know about.'" Absolutely, but although I've never been within 500 feet of her show, for a couple of years I knew something was going on, so it's hard to think it could have been much of a secret.

So, Steve Harvey is perhaps slowly transitioning between indefatigable and retirement, and Ellen is stepping down from her high-profile talkfest and game show. There's another talent we've seen less of in recent years. Even when he was on the tube daily, he occasionally appeared reluctant to take the stage. Ben Stein was known around town for having delayed the scheduled start times of his *Win Ben Stein's Money* tapings while he attended to personal needs. No, the President didn't call for emergency advice on some economic crisis, and he didn't need to be hooked up to a dialysis machine or anything nearly as significant. Ben just needed to walk his dogs. So, I'm told that all productivity ceased for the indeterminate lengths of time needed for his German shorthaired pointer and his Weimaraner to finish processing the previous night's dinners.

On a March morning in 2005 Ben arrived at CBS Studio 36, on time, to be the glue between the elements on five one-hour episodes of *Game Show Moments Gone Bananas* for Fremantle. Ben hosted while I supplied the voice of his co-host, "Mr. Game Show." The character began life as a plastic toy with an exceedingly plastic voice and patronizing personality. Hiring me for the role was obviously perfect casting. On the thinly disguised set of the company's *American Idol* we

Ben Stein. Attorney, author, actor, comedian, political commentator, presidential speechwriter, and game show host. *Win Ben Stein's Money* (1997). Photo courtesy of Fred Wostbrock.

engaged a live audience in recycled *Beat the Clock* stunts, showed clips of outrageous game show moments from the past half century, and I described a litany of parting gifts.

The day started encouragingly. Ben was punctual and *sans* pets. I checked. I assumed that meant taping wouldn't stretch to become a long dog day afternoon. Unfortunately, Ben's arrival was the last thing that occurred on schedule. The distraction that day was not a dog, but a frog. The frog in Ben's throat from a cold or flu had all but silenced his voice. Already sounding like hell upon arrival, I wondered how anyone expected to tape five hours of program content with this guy.

In England there's a job at recording studios called tea boy. Singer Rick Astley was a tea boy before he ever stepped before a microphone. I don't know if a tea boy's responsibilities actually include brewing tea, but Ben brought a tea girl with him to CBS that day. This Brit's job was, indeed, to brew tea as well as to medicate Ben with all manner of remedies, potions, and herbal cures during the tightly-timed breaks between episodes.

Orson Welles said that Paul Masson sold no wine before its time, but I didn't know similar critical timing is required for tea to be brewed and steeped to its peak of curative powers. There was no rushing this young lady's brewing rituals. Despite his best efforts, producer Andy Felsher couldn't charm Ben, the tea girl, the tea gods, or any of the powers at play when it came to hurrying the complexities of custom concocting Ben's healing elixirs. It was a day of delays during which an audience of a couple of hundred tourists got to know me very well. I ran through most of my warm-up material killing time. Actually there was so much time killing that it was more like cold-blooded murder in the first degree.

Finally, after taping the five shows with Ben's voice becoming increasingly weak and raspy, he went home that night unable to speak. He faced a more pressing problem than his raw throat, he had to decide which home. At my most recent count Ben owned at least 12. These weren't rental properties with tenants. At any moment about half of them were loaded with his clothes, toiletries and personal effects, awaiting his arrival. There was a home in Beverly Hills and another in Malibu. The closest would have been either of the two condominiums in West Hollywood, each valued at around $1 million. He originally had only one in that development, but bought the adjacent condo unit when the ringing phone next door bothered him. He explained, "I don't like noisy neighbors."

Those were just the four retreats he might have chosen for their location near the studio. If up for a ride, Ben also had both a big house as well as a condo in Palm Springs—Rancho Mirage, actually. There were also two different apartments in Washington D.C. For summer getaways Ben preferred his three-bedroom lakeside spread in Sandpoint, Idaho. It's a condo, actually four condos, in a resort property. You see, to avoid any possible disturbance he bought the home next door and the two condos below them. There's nothing worse than having your summer ruined by stray sound or, as Ben said, "any vibration."

Ben Stein was unique in coming to TV from the world of politics, but he did do some acting along the way. Remember "Beuller? Beuller? Beuller? Beuller?"

Not to say that lawyers and Presidential speechwriters necessarily make any better television personalities than actors. In the case of *Win Ben Stein's Money* he proved himself to be a great adlibber. Unlike career broadcasters, many actors are lost without a script or at least a predictable sequence of events. The problem is that engaging game show competitions are rarely without unexpected twists and turns. It's a vital ingredient in creating the drama every producer hopes for. As such, a host's patter has to be spontaneous and capricious to appear authentic. As television production itself is always unpredictable, whoever is fronting a show must be able to think on their feet and roll with whatever happens. It's an entirely different skill set than acting.

Despite being primarily an actor, Bert Convy was among the personalities who had that ability. It gave him a second career on the tube after singing and dancing on Broadway in *Fiddler on the Roof* and *Cabaret*, as well as acting in films (including Roger Corman's cult classic *A Bucket of Blood*), and a slew of guest roles on TV classics. He's even immortalized vocalizing with two UCLA pals as The Cheers on that wonderfully insipid Jerry Lieber and Mike Stoller 1950s hit *Black Denim Trousers and Motorcycle Boots*. With its high-earworm potential, I'm not anxious to hear the tune again, but declaring Bert a singer on the basis of that record alone would be a stretch. He earned his credibility as a crooner on stage and in clubs.

Around 1977 Bert was the opening act for a comedian I wanted to see in Las Vegas. They were playing a smaller room with a raised, narrow thrust stage that projected into the audience. It was an awkward set-up, as the crowd was seated at those tiny round tables slammed right up against and surrounding the projecting stage. It was a promoter's wet dream to maximize ticket sales as the audience was packed in, some behind the performer with a view of his ass. Others were eye-level with his crotch and so close that they were resting their elbows on the stage.

As the band started to play, Bert established himself as an experienced showman, making his enthusiastic entrance crooning "I can see clearly now…." He was all smiles with perfect teeth and cute dimples as he walked to the lip of the thrust stage, carefully dressing his microphone cable so as not to get it wrapped around a patron's throat. He dropped the excess at his feet, as he sang "I can see all obstacles in my way…" And BAM!

There was one obstacle he didn't see. Bert took a couple of steps, tripped on the coil of cable and fell. Hard. He was down, and obviously in pain. The musicians immediately stopped playing. The room fell silent and frozen for a few beats before Bert started to slowly lift his upper body. It took an uncomfortable few seconds before he began to get back on his feet. He wasn't seriously injured. Not physically, but I could feel his immense embarrassment. Bert surely tried to find a joke to cut the tension, but was speechless until he finally simply said, "Let's do that over again, OK?" The band started from the top and Bert was now singing to an ice cold room. By the end of the second song much of the tension had dissipated, and soon after he had the audience back. Thankfully he remained vertical for the rest of the show. I know I wasn't the only one whose skin was crawling, empathizing with Bert through the awkward moments.

Note to self: Always have a self-deprecating saver—some stock line, locked, loaded, and ready for the out-of-control moments. To Bert's credit, with a bruised body and injured ego he went on with the show. I can't begin to think how embarrassed and uneasy he must have felt until he finally re-engaged with the crowd. I chose not to make good on the invitation to visit his dressing room after the show. What the hell do you say? "Loved the stunt work, got some somersaults planned for the late show?"

Have sympathy for Bert. Even a man who was overtly wronged by him and filed a breach of contract lawsuit against him instantly found more than enough compassion to immediately drop the legal action in 1990. That was when Bert was diagnosed with the brain tumor that took his life the following year. That man with the legal action was Peter Marshall. The "master of *The Hollywood Squares*" has long been beloved as one of the most upright, true gentlemen to inhabit the industry. It earned him a wide circle of admiring friends and fans. Peter had been signed to host a show Bert Convy was co-producing with Burt Reynolds called *3rd Degree*. When Bert suddenly felt his own career taking an unexpected downward turn, he ignored his commitment to Peter and grabbed that gig for himself. It was indeed a straightforward breach of contract, but Peter dropped the lawsuit. Bert was gone just months later, after having spread a lot of love in his all-too-short 57 years.

Peter was seemingly able to do it all, singing and dancing from nightclubs to Broadway and beyond. In that regard, his and Bert Convy's careers were not all that dissimilar. Where they differed was in the world of comedy. Before most of us came to know him as a solo act, Peter had already enjoyed a dozen years of laughs paired with comedian Tommy Noonan. The team was successful on television, in nightclubs, and on film. They worked together for as long as the magic lasted, simultaneously laying the foundation for their subsequent individual careers.

Comedy teammates Tommy Noonan and Peter Marshall played the nightclub circuit starting in the 1940s. Tommy moved on to films before passing away at age 46 in 1968, the same year that the team's friends and protégés Dan Rowan and Dick Martin debuted on NBC's *Laugh-In*.

Besides a warm manner and even warmer heart, Peter Marshall has an amazing depth and breadth of talent that fueled his career successes that started when he first stepped on a stage in the 1940s. In that sense, Peter was already a survivor before he cheated death in 2021. His 95th birthday celebration on March 30th was a Zoomed affair attended by Loni Anderson, Sandy Duncan, Ruta Lee, Karen Valentine, Rich Little and other longtime friends. We toasted the milestone and watched some wonderful rare clips from Peter's 80 years in show business. Although he put on a happy face, it was clear he had still not fully recovered from the severe bout with the worldwide Covid-19 coronavirus that nearly claimed him as another one of over one million U.S. victims.

Peter had recently been released after a couple of weeks of hospitalization during which he was sadly deteriorating under the care of an overburdened doctor and overwhelmed staff. As his wife of 32 years, lovely Laurie Stewart Marshall, said, "It was clear the diagnosis was grim." Peter reflected, "From the time I went to the hospital, I worried I wouldn't make it because of how many people seemed to be dying from it, and given my age, I knew I was at high risk." He explained, "I knew I was dying in the hospital. Every time I spoke to my wife, I wondered if it was the last time we'd speak."

The family decided to bring Peter home to live out his final days surrounded by loved ones, and Laurie was advised to make final arrangements. Instead, she enlisted a doctor and a patient advocate who fought for Peter, coordinating every aspect of the necessary home care. His den was transformed into what Laurie described as an intensive care unit. She remembers, "with the aid of around-the-clock nurses and surrounded by his family, [the doctor] turned a fatal diagnosis into a miraculous recovery." As Peter said at his 95th birthday celebration, "Sure didn't think I'd be here for this one."

Chapter 32

After successes on Broadway, in nightclubs, casino showrooms, motion pictures, dinner theater and television, Peter Marshall added radio personality to his resume when he began a gig playing the big band era music he'd always loved.

It brought Peter dangerously close to a corner of show business where the worst behavior by its most talented has long been tolerated. In return, these low-rent performers have had to endure bouncing checks, labor-law violations, and pre-OSHA outrageous working conditions. No, not the circus. Some would say this is an even lower tier in the entertainment hierarchy. Radio. During the middle of the 20th century radio was where contests were routinely rigged, half-baked promotions regularly went awry, and carnal conquests were consummated behind equipment racks during the three minutes or so that each record allowed. Remember the turkey drop episode from *WKRP in Cincinnati*? It was based on a true event.

Hugh Wilson, the creator of the mythical WKRP, ran a regional ad agency that often took him to Atlanta's top-rated WQXI, known then as "Quixie in Dixie." It was that station's general manager, Jerry Blum, who inspired the bumbling Arthur Carlson character. Years earlier Blum had been at Dallas's powerhouse KBOX. It was in Big D that he was responsible for the well-meaning fabled Thanksgiving promotion. Blum dropped turkeys off a flatbed truck in a shopping center parking lot. His son Gary Blum said, "The public went nuts fighting over the turkeys and it was a mess." He laughed, adding that his dad never did anything like that again.

New England radio giant Tom Shovan swore that he was witness to an even worse ill-fated Thanksgiving stunt in which a small panel truck had been loaded with live turkeys direct from the farm. The van arrived to meet the radio station's fans who were waiting in the center of town for the promised free turkeys. Frozen turkeys, they thought. They were shocked at the sight of live birds when the morning personality swung open the rear doors. The turkeys must have been equally shocked as they and the loyal listeners all froze in place until the DJ started banging on the side of the truck. The birds then leaped out of the van into the crowd and mayhem ensued. Squawking and screaming, the crowd ran for cover as the birds scattered.

Over the years the 1260 AM frequency in Boston has beamed a variety of formats through Beantown, including religion, Radio Disney, conservative talk, and easy-listening music. In 1959, during the time the station carried the call letters WEZE, a DJ was fired for driving the news van all the way from Boston Common to New York City. The guy wasn't covering some breaking story, it was a pot run. It was barely a successful pot run as only the stupidest dealers were willing to sell dope to someone in a van emblazoned with call letters and the word "NEWS!"

Timing is everything. With the remote equipment MIA in NYC, the station wasn't able to cover a prison riot that suddenly erupted back in the Boston suburb, Walpole. That DJ who commandeered the news van and was fired upon his return was none other than George Carlin. Carlin graduated from DJ to standup legend and, later, from pot to LSD. As much as I admired his brilliance, I never followed his counsel, "More people should do acid."

Historical or contemporary, many of TV's greatest talents came from radio. Jack Benny to Johnny Carson, to Dick Clark and Walter Cronkite, all had adventures in radio that they recalled with smiles. Jimmy Kimmel, Rachel Maddow, Carson Daly, Ryan Seacrest and countless contemporaries also took that well-traveled path. Pat Sajak and Alex Trebek both toiled in radio after first finding their earliest work in the hospitality business. Pat was a desk clerk at Chicago's prestigious Palmer House. Alex's first job was as a bellhop at the Nickel Range Hotel in Sudbury, Ontario where his father was a pastry chef. Each spent later years spinning entertainment from nothing more than their creativity with words and armfuls of phonograph records.

Similarly, Monty Hall conjured exciting mental images with his radio play-by-play of sporting events. Where Monty took to television and game shows immediately, and rose through hosting to produce a string of hits, Pat Sajak was cool to the idea of fronting a TV game. Michael Brockman was the NBC executive who, along with Merv Griffin and many others, found Pat's impromptu comedy in his nightly local KNBC-TV weather forecasts brighter than the California sunshine. He remembers approaching Pat in 1980 with the thought of his hosting the pilot for Goodson-Todman's *Puzzlers*. Michael remembers, "I went to the newsroom and, after introducing myself to him, asked if he had any interest in hosting game shows. He said 'No.'" Pat explained that he didn't want to be typecast as just another smiling lame-brain smarmy game show emcee.

Michael is wise enough to know that the most productive part of a conversation is usually the time spent listening. He recalls then asking Pat, "So what do you want to do when you grow up?" Pat had an immediate answer. Mike remembers, "He said he wanted to 'do Carson'. I reminded him about Johnny's start as a game show host and that got him to re-think his original answer." Later, it was seeing that *Puzzlers* pilot that brought Merv Griffin to consider Pat as more than simply the witty weathercaster at channel 4 who had repeatedly tickled Merv's funny-bone. He cast Pat as Chuck Woolery's replacement on *Wheel of Fortune*.

When it came to the network signing off on the new emcee, Fred Silverman nixed the choice. He second-guessed Merv's decision, being cautious to protect the massive daytime hit that was generating the significant income stream from which they each dipped their beaks. Fred, with his so-called "golden gut," dismissed Pat as just a "local act" not capable of steering the big *Wheel*. Merv would have been resistant to anyone doubting his supreme mastery in such matters even if he wasn't confident about his choice, as to do so would be considered an affront to his preeminence. Both he and Fred dug in so deeply in their positions that there was no way for either to back down and acquiesce without losing face.

Merv then slammed on the brakes, cancelling all *Wheel* tapings. There'd be no new episodes without his choice of Pat Sajak as the new host. For all he cared the network could play reruns until they came to their senses. Hell, he owned the successful show and likely figured he could easily sell it to ABC or CBS if it came to that. Merv felt he held all the cards, or at least enough of them to doubt the network would cancel the moneymaking hit. Time was ticking down in the staring match. The battle of the network egos was about to become a Combat Zone Wrestling death-cage event when, suddenly, Silverman was fired.

Within days, Pat Sajak sold his first vowel. It was the start of what turned out to be a host's longest association with a single game show in all of television. So unsure was he at the start however, that Pat didn't quit his local weather gig for another 13 weeks, just in case. He did eventually get a shot behind a talk show desk at CBS, recalling at the time how he used to crawl out of bed as a kid to indulge his pre-teen fascination with Jack Paar's wit and artistry.

Another former weatherman, David Letterman, had a huge fan who patterned his career after Dave's, following his idol's path into radio. That fan was Jimmy Kimmel. He recalled, "I always thought I would be an artist, but I started watching late night television while I was drawing. I read in a *Playboy* article that Dave Letterman said he started in radio. I thought that was a great idea." Getting into the business wasn't as tough as staying in it. Jimmy remembers, "I'd been fired from my first radio job and was living with my parents."

Mom and pop Kimmel were then no doubt thrilled to have their son try his luck behind another microphone as it at least got him back out of the house. Jimmy's second job began the nomadic gig-to-gig itinerant existence of most who toiled in the trenches of local radio. From college DJ work at Arizona State University's KASC, and the University of Nevada at Las Vegas' KUNV, Jimmy climbed through stations in Seattle, Tampa, Palm Springs, and Tucson before coming to Los Angeles. He then landed at KROQ in 1994, where he spent five years as "Jimmy the Sports Guy."

He remembers developing his on-air persona at KUNV: "The first thing I ever did in show business was a college radio show… I would look in the telephone book and I would find people who seemed like interesting characters and then I would goof on them, but they would not know that I was goofing on them because, first of all, I was a kid, and secondly, they were excited to be on the radio… I'm able to lightly make fun of people in a way that doesn't upset them."

Early on Jimmy struck up a relationship with his hero, something most say is not an easy thing to do. He says Dave Letterman was always kind to him, before, during, and after they were competing for viewers. Upon Dave's retirement Jimmy got a very unusual package from his pal. He remembers, "It was a huge box of ties, yeah, all his ties. I don't remember exactly what the note said. But he said, 'Maybe you can use these,' something to that effect. And I did wear one of his ties on the show. They are long ties, by the way—they're hard for me. I really have to tuck them in." Wearing Dave's ties is nowhere close to the extent of Jimmy's sartorial salute to his idol. He confessed, "On my first show I was wearing a *Late Night with David Letterman* T-shirt under my clothes."

Think of all the insanity Jimmy would have missed had he not first done battle in radio, the showbiz ghetto. He says those dues-paying years helped to hone a lightning-fast mind, the coin of the realm for any comic. Jimmy established a strong foothold and is now the senior member among the current 11:30 p.m. crop of hosts. The hospitality in his green room is a hint to the show's success. It's the best in the west, with a bartender dispensing guests' requests from a fully-stocked backstage tavern. The spread is second only to the nightly bacchanal that once took place one floor down at the old Metromedia Square, beneath the stage of the Fox network's Joan Rivers late night affair.

I worked for Jimmy's ABC show a couple of times, providing voices for pre-taped comedy bits. While he makes it all look easy, the old Masonic Hall that the network bought and refurbished for his launch buzzes all afternoon, building to a crescendo just before tape rolls. Each of a posse of producers is multi-tasking, sticking their heads in and out of the writing rooms and editing bays in a daily frenzy of pre-production. After all, the insatiable TV beast must be fed anew each day and, as the saying goes, you're only as good as your last show. I respect the hell out of these folks and am convinced they'll all be dead or in a rubber room by age 40 as a result of working under that pressure.

Mr. Ed McKay's gig was nowhere nearly as stressful. Perhaps it was the hypnotic effect of the far less grueling job of watching records rotating on turntables that led him to snap in midlife. Ed was another disc jockey, usually heard out in the boonies of Riverside County. He was also briefly a competitor for jobs. He fell off the radar as a game show announcer a long time ago, perhaps done in by his own eccentricities. I'm still scratching my head in wonderment following the strangest of our encounters. It started at the time of my first go-round as a potential member of *The Price is Right* extended family.

Since my 2003-2004 stint as the announcer on CBS's venerable game show, I've received a bounty of reflected goodwill that Bob Barker and Drew Carey engendered in the hearts of the landmark program's fans. From filling-in on the TV classic, to performing in the live stage show, to voicing some of the *Price* video games, related opportunities still continue to come knocking nearly 20 years later. However, all of this fun almost started a decade earlier than it actually did. In 1994 I was among the announcers under serious consideration for a new nighttime syndicated version of the show.

Of course nobody had a clue that this highly-anticipated series would only earn an extremely short run. Barker demurred from hosting, so announcer Rod Roddy did likewise. Daytime showrunner Roger Dobkowitz sat in on a few meetings during which elements of the new and radically different presentation were discussed before divorcing himself from the series. Producers Phil Rossi and Kathy Greco from the daytime team joined with one of the architects of the format, Jay Wolpert, to produce. Soap star Doug Davidson beat out local L.A. weatherman Mark Kriski for hosting duties after their two pilot episodes were compared and tested. Despite launching with a team of pros, it appeared the desire to differentiate this new incarnation from the show America already knew and loved was its downfall. Perhaps it was the dark set and altered games that were off-putting, or maybe the O.J. Simpson trial coverage adversely affected viewership as was claimed, but to my knowledge at four months this production won the distinction of being the shortest-running of the multitude of *The Price is Right* presentations in dozens of countries around the world over the course of half a century.

Here's the blow-by-blow of the Ed McKay madness. The casting notice for the announcer position on this syndicated adaptation was released to the talent agencies that specialized in representing voice clients. I got a call to record at my agents' studio, the tape was sent to the Goodson offices, and I received the happy news from the agency's Don Pitts and Fred Wostbrock that I was under definite consideration. From the first words of direction at the top of the audition page it was clear this was right up my alley, so much so that I saved the script:

> SHOW OPENING (<u>very</u> enthusiastic; you are almost <u>shouting</u> to be heard over the loud audience applause and music)

Then came the copy for the prizes with these directions:

> Car: with energy and enthusiasm, but don't oversell; range: stress the prize, then a <u>fun</u>, somewhat conversational description.

I remembered stories of people who took advantage of the opportunity at this kind of moment to gain an edge with some creative extra. Sometimes an added effort can score with producers, even if it does little more than simply reinforce how passionate you are about their show. It couldn't be some classless stunt or an inducement that could be perceived as anything akin to a bribe. I'd heard stories of that kind of incentive working for some people and some companies in the past, but I never considered anything like that. After all, this was the respected and respectful Mark Goodson Productions.

To get a jump on the competition I ponied-up cash to rent the facilities at Interlock Studios. It was a terrific production complex where I was voicing promos for *The Chuck Woolery Show* at the time. I brought some pages from old scripts that Johnny Olson had given me, as well as copies of several of the *Price* music cues. Don and Fred came over to help direct me, and we came away from the session with tracks that showcased how well I could match the show's style and energy. I think it helped to get my foot further in the door. There's no way to ever know why, but I was still in the race and ready to clear the next hurdle which was an office run-through at the Goodson headquarters on Wilshire Boulevard.

I read more prize copy and yelled a bunch of "Come on downs!" I was then called to read again on yet another day, this time to sync with the video from a random episode. My audio was stripped into the second audio track on the tape so I could be heard in the context of the show. The same was done with some of the other finalists. Who were the others? I heard that the usual Goodson veterans were in the running, Gene Wood, Bob Hilton, Rich Jeffries, and Burton Richardson. There were also some guys new to the company, like myself and possibly Ed McKay.

I say possibly because I don't know what to believe. Ed was the only person who mentioned his name to me in relation to the soon-to-be-birthed spinoff. He was not a well-known game show voice, but he did have a credit or two as well as the necessary pipes for a power-packed delivery. Ed and I unexpectedly ran into each other one day during the week that the Goodson brain trust was to make their casting decision. We were both buzzing with anticipation and had repeatedly been checking our pagers. Yes, this was when cell phones were impractical, nearly the size of a toaster. That's when Ed told me, "Hey Randy, forget the *Price* gig. I just got it! I was at CBS yesterday. I tested in the studio on Rod's mic, and the producers approved me for the gig. We did it just before they taped a daytime episode, they had me at the podium. I did the opening and some prizes, and they told me I got the gig. Sorry, buddy." I was crushed and miserably depressed for a week, until I learned that not a word of that was true!

Ed didn't have an audition at CBS and, oh yes, as we all know, he didn't get the job. Burton did. I had to wait another decade to join the show's family. Damned if I can figure out what the hell Ed was thinking. You can't bluff your way into a gig, certainly not by screwing with the mind of another of the contenders. Second only to politics, it seems there's more creative liberty taken with the truth in this business than anywhere else. When last heard of, Ed was working at 870 AM, L.A.'s Christian teaching and talk station. There's hope that his mental health has improved since all this went down. Luckily for Ed, radio stations no longer have turntables incessantly rotating, slowly inducing insanity.

Psychology and broadcasting formed an unlikely alliance at the end of television's first decade when Dr. Joyce Brothers began her ascent to becoming the mother of all mass-media shrinks. Brothers was a winner with her very first television appearance. It wasn't as a psychologist, but as a quiz show contestant. Right at the height of the era's rigging she outsmarted "the fix" on *The $64,000 Question*.

With her choice of the category of boxing for her questions, Dr. Brothers' winnings climbed higher and higher, week after week, despite the sponsor's hope to trip her up and get her comparatively dour demeanor and sour face off their screen.

As the manufacturer of cosmetics, Revlon's Martin Revson was image conscious and felt that the good doctor's personality, looks, and clothing were all wrong. Revson wanted her off the show, so producer Mert Koplin hit her with a big left-handed jab at the $16,000 mark by upping the challenge beyond questions about fighters, matches, title bouts, and record holders. The sucker punch: "What man refereed the comeback attempt of an ex-champ against Jack Johnson at Reno, Nevada." Dr. Brothers easily named Tex Rickert and her continuing series of knockouts had Revlon down for the count.

Dr. Joyce Brothers won the top prize answering host Hal March's *$64,000 Question*. She shrewdly parlayed those winnings into millions as a ubiquitous media personality.

With her strategic selection of a subject that has limited depth, and one that her husband was familiar with, combined with her agile memory, ferocious determination, and a little luck, Dr. Brothers not only became the first woman to break the bank on *The $64,000 Question*, she doubled that prize with a return on the spinoff *The $64,000 Challenge*. Indeed, luck was on her side when she chose reference materials to cram for her quizzing as the book she studied most, "Ring Facts," was written by the author of her questions, Nat Fleischer. Brothers is said to have memorized the entire almanac of boxing history, but could have had a little extra help. Producers had reason to believe that Dr. Brothers' husband may have been friendly with Fleischer, but turned a blind eye to that suspicion. After all, how would it look if the show decided to take back any of their winners' hard earned prize money?

Brothers' greatest achievement however had nothing to do with her seemingly total recall. It was turning those championship nights on quiz shows into a five-decade-plus career in TV, radio, movies, newspapers, and publishing. The petite Ph.D didn't waste time counting her winnings; while hot she quickly landed a gig as a commentator on the local New York program *Sports Showcase*. You and I know that a sports show doesn't need a psychologist, but the good doctor never let those sorts of trivialities get in the way of her plan for media domination.

As a masterful self-promoter Dr. Joyce Brothers grabbed a photo op with the four most famous people on Earth on February 9, 1964, The Beatles, in the lobby of the Plaza Hotel. It was the same day 73 million people watched the group's American debut on *The Ed Sullivan Show*.

Brothers doggedly built her reputation with the goal of achieving the status of preeminent go-to authority for all matters related to psychology. It worked. Then, with her willingness to cooperate with producers' requests for light self-parody, she enjoyed an unprecedented reign as an omnipresent entertainment personality in America's living rooms for a period of over 30 years. Dr. Brothers ran the guest-star gamut from *The Jack Benny Program* to *Happy Days*, *Taxi*, *Entourage*, *The Simpsons* and even *Baywatch*. None of that good fortune came as an accident, coincidence, or surprising serendipity. The good doctor brought the same resolve and drive to building her brand that she'd applied to memorizing the history of boxing.

Perhaps eclipsing Dr. Brothers as today's best-known broadcast counselor is Dr. Laura Schlessinger. Dr. Laura wasn't ever a doctor of any psychology-related field of study, she is a doctor of physiology. Spelling counts. Sounding similar doesn't count. Physiology is not psychology, but why let insignificant trifles inhibit your aspirations? Only years later did Laura get credentialed by the state of California as what was then called an MFCC, a marriage, family and child counselor. Although far from a doctorate, it helped to legitimize her once-entertaining advice-giving when her local act eventually went network.

My first introduction to Dr. Laura was long before she became a nationally-known and controversial figure. In building her early broadcasting career, Laura was jumping from one L.A. and Orange County radio station to another. That was after blazing a very unusual path into the business. Laura had been a frequent caller to the originator of titillating talk radio, KABC's *Feminine Forum* host Bill Ballance. In 1975 Bill gave her some airtime and Laura contributed a little weekly feature to his program. Laura expanded that opportunity, ingratiating herself into Bill's world.

It's always strange, even a bit creepy when an audience member first crosses over into a performer's personal life, and this listener crossed over to become more than a full-fledged groupie. That's not a stretch, as there was no shortage of hanky-panky in their relationship. Many years later as Laura came to be viewed by many as increasingly intolerant and reactionary, Bill said he found himself being unwittingly dragged out of a quiet retirement and into the controversy. To return the favor, in 1998 at age 80 with his health beginning to decline, Bill sold nude photos of Laura from their years together back in the 1970s. At first Laura denied their authenticity, but then relented to the unmistakable truth of her youthful liaisons. Yes, nude and fully revealing photos with not an inch of her body left to the imagination. There's no beating around the bush, hair styles were very different back then. But I digress.

Laura and I had several mutual acquaintances, mostly from having both worked at L.A.'s KMPC. It led to our both being guests at the same Halloween costume party in Beverly Hills one year in the mid-1980s. Laura's penchant for offering unsolicited analysis started immediately upon my arrival. Noting that I was outfitted as a doctor for the Eve of All Hallows with blue scrubs, stethoscope, latex gloves, and assorted medical props, Laura told me that the choice of a costume reveals an unconscious desire to possess the attributes, powers, and benefits from the public perception most associated with the disguise. She insisted that my dressing as a doctor spoke volumes about my longing for respect and authority.

In my opinion, respect and authority were more Laura's issues than mine. I explained that the only reason for dressing in medical drag was that I had easy access to all of the accoutrements. I was honest when I said that there was no deeper force at play than simple laziness in not putting more creativity into an outfit. Laura insisted that the subconscious mind is mysterious and powerful, influencing what we believe to be our free will whether or not we know it. The good doctor was unrelenting in her insistence that my choice of costume spoke volumes from the secret world of my deepest yearnings.

I almost bit right through my tongue trying to keep from pointing out that Laura herself had chosen to dress… are you ready… as Wonder Woman! Honest. She was wearing a rented Wonder Woman costume. Did she not realize the irony? I can't speak to Laura's Wonder Woman identity issues. I have no credential that qualifies me to offer an opinion. As for me, I know that I masqueraded as a doctor for only that one night.

No conversation about Dr. Laura can be considered complete without a mention of the incredible story of this relationship expert's relationship with her own mother. By most accounts Yolanda Schlessinger was a cheerful lady who once supported her daughter's career by helping with appointments and answering phone calls. Lord only knows how the pair ended up estranged to the extent that

Yolanda died at her home in 2002, with Laura clueless of her fate for who knows how many weeks.

Apparently the two hadn't spoken for a long, long time, estimated to perhaps have been as long as 20 years. Reportedly, Laura finally learned of her mother's death when the police notified her that Yolanda's body was found naked, decomposed, and partially consumed by flesh-eating bugs and larvae. After contacting the Beverly Hills detectives who were on the case, authors Barbara Schroeder and Clark Fogg recounted that Laura's immediate response to the initial notification by the police was, "What do you want me to do?"

So, I guess if Yolanda had been a stereotypical Jewish mother she'd be forgiven her cliché complaint, "You never call, you never write. . . ." Neighbors had contacted the police with suspicions that something might be wrong at the home of the lady down the hall. The coroner's report says it all, stating that the victim was found with "Dried-out skin blistering and slippage, skin leathering, mummification of distal extremities. Prominent maggot activity of different stages." Based on her condition, it was estimated that Yolanda's body had been rotting for approximately two months. Before all of that decomposition the cause of death was a heart attack.

Of course the report doesn't say why Yolanda Schlessinger's death went unnoticed by family, despite living just a few miles from where her daughter worked. For that, we can only recount what *The Times* of London quoted Dr. Laura having said about her dear old mom: "When it was clear that my career was taking off, I needed her to learn typing. She said, 'If I'm going to take any class, it'll be ceramics.' I said, 'Well, you can take that too, but I really need you to take a typing class,' and she packed her bags and refused to talk to me ever again." I'm no expert on anything, but it's probably easier to find a typist than it is to find a new mother.

How does the story end? Laura has been living a grand lifestyle, enjoying world-class views from her luxurious 9,000 square-foot estate overlooking the Pacific Ocean. In 2021, at age 74, Laura listed the compound for sale at nearly $23 million. If that all sounds like it adds up to a happy ending consider the fact that, once divorced then widowed, assumedly she's been all alone in that 10 bedroom mansion with nobody but herself in any of the beds.

Chapter 33

Like Laura, Jay Wolpert is a fellow former New Yorker. He'd proven his smarts as a Tournament of Champions winner on the original version of *Jeopardy!* Soon after he proved himself a worthy gamemeister working for Dan Enright, then Chuck Barris before being added to the brain trust at Goodson-Todman. There, as previously mentioned, he was a major architect in building CBS's record-breaking hit, *The Price is Right*. Some of the games Jay created for the 1972 reboot were still being played a half-century later.

Jay left that show's producing chair for the autonomy of developing his own original ideas that wouldn't become someone else's hit. Legally, by virtue of being a salaried employee of Goodson-Todman, Jay's ideas were the property of the boss. Your job may work that way as well, with the fruits of your labor legally classified as "works for hire." That was among the reasons that mastermind Bob Stewart left the same well-feathered Goodson-Todman nest years earlier.

By 1979 Jay had earned his stripes as an independent creator and showrunner with *Whew!* landing a coveted slot on CBS's daytime lineup. He then sold his video game-inspired *Hit Man* in 1982, which NBC debuted the following January. He found a new face to front that show. It belonged to Peter Tomarken, who had been penning magazine articles before working in public relations. He'd also floated through the worlds of advertising, publishing, TV commercial production, and acting. The latter included a fair number of film and television bit parts, and a meatier role on a two-hour *Rockford Files*.

Peter remembered, "I never had any interest in hosting game shows. My agent was the one who planted the idea in my head. It's hard not to get interested in great pay for two months of work." He was acutely aware that despite the number of pilots that get produced very few series actually make it to air. More to the point, he knew that even fewer hosts have lasting careers. He's widely quoted as saying, "I've hosted my fair share of duds. Hosting is not for the faint of heart… you're at a high risk of sudden unemployment at any time. You have to have loads of confidence and the ability to never get too comfortable." Jay sharpened Peter's skills through a couple of pilots. The one that NBC bought, *Hit* Man, launched his new career. Jay seemed to intuitively know how to work with Peter. It was a task that some employers found infinitely more challenging.

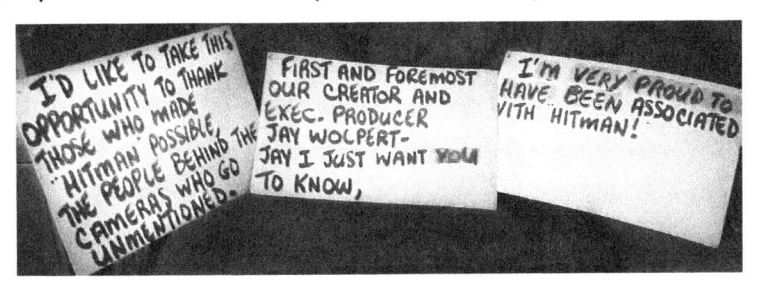

Jay Wolpert's *Hit Man* wrapped in only 13 weeks after establishing Peter Tomarken's credibility as a network host. Although he read his appreciative farewell message from these cue cards, the sentiments were heartfelt (1983). From the author's collection.

I was the last *Hit Man* champion and, after its 13-week run, lightning struck again later that same year for Peter when the newly minted emcee was plucked by producer Bill Carruthers to front CBS's *Press Your Luck*. It was a freshened version of his *Second Chance* which had been cancelled prematurely to make room on ABC's daytime lineup to honor a previous commitment for a Goodson-Todman show. Fans emphatically agree that Peter was perfectly cast as the warden of the format's newly added animated Whammys.

Announcer Rod Roddy performing his audience warm-up while the lighting crew works overhead in CBS's Television City Studio 33 before one of the weekend tapings of Peter Tomarken's *Press Your Luck* (1984). From the author's collection.

No reference to *Press Your Luck* can be complete without mention of the ice cream truck driver who spent countless hours alongside his VCR, eyes glued to his TV screen, analyzing the gameplay for some weakness that could be exploited to his advantage. Michael Larson was studying with sufficient intensity that he discovered a finite number of repeating patterns in the ever-changing display of highlighted slides denoting different cash and prizes on the game board. He realized there was nothing arbitrary or capricious about the seemingly random rotation that illuminated the various awards for a split second during which a player could pound on the big red plunger in front of him to stop the action. Armed with that revelation Larson exploited the limitation that producers knew all along existed but never thought was vulnerable to being corrupted.

Programming the electronics for true randomization was considered an unnecessary added expense when producing the not-for-broadcast *Press Your Luck* pilot. Continuing to switch from among five different patterns was considered to be more than adequate. Then, when the show was picked up for air, neither the network nor the production company had budgeted the sizable dollars necessary in 1983 for an upgrade to true randomization. As to the hidden vulnerability, production staffer Byl Carruthers remembers raising the question when the key personnel from his father's company and the network were all sitting around the conference table: "What if somebody buys one of those new VCRs with fame-by-frame advance and studies the board?" Ron Schwab, then an in-house CBS electronics wizard, broke the momentary silence with, "Let's just hope the show becomes that popular."

When Larson ended his marathon streak at $110,237 he stepped offstage soaked in sweat and emotionally rattled. It was then and there that he came clean, telling Byl and contestant coordinator Bobby Edwards the truth behind his and his friend's amazing adventure. That's right, he was not acting alone in this gambit. In the rear of the audience that day sat the pal who put up the money to buy the VCR and paid for the trip to Hollywood after hearing Larson passionately promise he could break the bank. The champ explained that during his winning streak he had periodically been looking over his shoulder, having pledged to honor a signal from his benefactor to stop. Apparently after accounting for expenses, their splitting $100,000 was considered a sufficient windfall. Pushing too much further would indeed have been pressing their luck.

Coincidentally, a year earlier, at a break in taping during my three-day championship run as a contestant on the show, a friend in the audience had tried to explain a pattern he noticed during episodes 9 and 10. Any small hope to exploit it proved far too complex when I returned to tape episode 11. Kudos to Larson for breaking the code, or perhaps congratulations aren't warranted. You see, he had most of his $50,000 cut converted to one-dollar bills, hoping to have bills with serial numbers that would help him win a contest in one of his several get-rich-quick schemes. The $50,000 in cash was stashed at his home where it was soon stolen. Then, after a litany of other questionable pursuits, Larson ended up wanted by the police before being found dead in 1999 before his 50th birthday.

I was also following prize money, not following Peter when making the rounds as a contestant. Pure luck crowned me a champion on both of the first two network series he fronted. For three years Peter also avoided the Whammy before CBS retired those diabolic harbingers of bad luck. Try as he did, Peter was never able to again enjoy the level of success he did on *Press Your Luck*.

Fresh from the successful run of over 700 episodes of *Press Your Luck*, Peter Tomarken enjoyed happy times with his brethren on the set of *Crosswits'* special game show hosts week. (l-r) Jim Peck, Tom Kennedy, David Sparks, Bob Goen, and Peter (1987). From the author's collection.

Over time, Peter's and my paths crossed more and more frequently, no longer as host and contestant. It included sitting in commercial audition waiting rooms, at the Culver City studio at GSN, and at industry events. We struck up conversations and became friendly. Although we weren't particularly close, I considered Peter a kindred spirit, a fellow traveler navigating for increased presence in our small corner of the business. That's why some of the strange behavior attributed to him is a bit painful to stir up. He wasn't always everybody's friend or favorite co-worker.

While still hot from *Press Your Luck* Peter had several fresh opportunities with which he hoped to reprise his earlier triumphs. In 1986 he hosted the pilot for NBC's *Wordplay*. Although the Syd Vinnedge and Rob Fiedler-Peter Berlin co-production was picked up based on Peter's pilot hosting, he was abruptly dropped from the show after he tested poorly with focus groups. At one point Peter reflected on that experience saying he was being stifled in his personality-driven presentation, feeling like he was being stuffed into what he called a "Pat Sajak-like mold." He attributed his poor showing with the focus groups to be the result of being asked to adopt a style unnatural for him. Those measured thoughts came after he had a chance to reflect on being replaced on *Wordplay*. I was told his very first words were "Who gives a fuck?"

I spent a few days as a stand-in for the *Wordplay* celebrity comics as replacement host Tom Kennedy meticulously went step by step through the format. With only a few days before the series began taping, Tom spent hour after hour running through all of the potential twists and turns that could arise during the game. He later explained that in order to give any show the charm and wit he'd been hired for over the years, officiating over the gameplay needed to be completely second nature. As he had for over a dozen other formats, Tom assimilated all he needed to know and appeared to steer the game effortlessly through its 39 weeks.

Peter rebounded from being replaced on that show of daffy definitions, happy to have been hired by an even more-respected showrunner for a breakthrough new concept. Going solo after his partnership with Bob Quigley, successful producer Merrill Heatter suffered a few hiccups in his string of hits. *Bargain Hunters* has been considered the most challenging, in part because it sought to break new ground, attempting to wed elements of a game show to those of the mid-1980s rage of mass merchandising, home shopping. With viewers having the opportunity to buy the on-screen prizes, the series was sold with the tempting allure of being a potential gold mine for all involved.

ABC bit the bait. Peter had not hosted the pilot, but was chosen to front *Bargain Hunters* for its 1987 debut. Respected television executive Erni DiMassa remembers helping to shepherd the show to air leaving soon after taping started on his way to produce *The New Hollywood Squares*. Erni ticked off a few of the impediments to *Bargain Hunters'* success, among them limited promotion as well as engineering glitches. Most insurmountable was that *Bargain Hunters* was scheduled in a slot marked for death, opposite *The Price is Right*.

At quick glance the show even resembled its rival, as the stage was filled with three large doors, side-by-side. It was much the same layout that Monty Hall complained *The Price is Right* had appropriated from his even earlier *Let's Make a Deal*. With *Bargain Hunters'* contestants guessing prices in their search for bargains, nobody missed the obvious resemblance to the competition. In fact, to distinguish between the programs ABC didn't allow producers to use the words "price" or "prize." Instead, Peter asked the players s to estimate the "value" of "items."

Merrill Heatter's was among the first of several attempts over a few decades that proved any marriage between TV home shopping and game play appear doomed to divorce. Merrill's long-time producer Art Alisi told me that their *Bargain Hunters* was served its pink slip after only five weeks; however, ABC's director of daytime programming, Wally Weltman, insisted that Merrill produce the contracted 13 weeks of shows. To say that Wally wasn't a fan would be a significant understatement. From the batch of 65 he chose those episodes he hated the least. It appears he could only find about 45 worthy of airing before yanking the under-performing series from the schedule. One of the show's former staffers sincerely believes Wally physically destroyed all of the 20 unaired tapes.

With *Bargain Hunters* branded an abysmal failure mid-run, the experience further fueled Peter's growing discontent. Here he was, taping the remaining shows of an embarrassing lame duck for which he partially blamed himself. On several occasions Peter walked off the set during commercial breaks. Art Alisi confirmed that production did indeed grind to a halt while the host bitched and cursed during retreats to his dressing room, assumedly to exorcise his demons. Sometimes that took thousands of dollars' worth of idle time. Eyewitness accounts of Peter's dramatic meltdowns became apocryphal stories that reverberated throughout the ABC Prospect lot, making it all the way to the engineering shop where members of the network's tech staff at the time still remember the gossiping.

Then there was the final tape day when, just before the last episode's end game, Peter was said to be like a short-circuited pinball machine that suddenly lit up TILT. When the stage manager announced that they were coming back from a commercial break to play the bonus round, Peter said something remembered to be, "Fuck you. You can play it without me!" He reportedly then kicked the set a few times while walking off, leaving the live audience aghast.

I was told that as the minutes ticked away without Peter, the stage manager was sent to knock on his dressing room door. No response. Staffers began searching for Peter in the bathrooms, the commissary, and beyond, all to no avail. The story has been blown out of proportion in some tellings to include Peter having gone to his car and driven off the lot on his way home, leaving the bewildered crew and the audience still waiting in the studio. Art was there and didn't recall things flying that far out of control, but it has become accepted fact that Peter never did return to the set and the episode was never finished.

Art Alisi was a sweetheart of a guy who had befriended hundreds of performers during his long reign producing celebrity-based shows including *Hollywood Squares*. He rarely had a harsh word about any of them, but was outspoken about not having a single good memory from working with Peter. The grimace on his face while discussing the experience some 30 years after the fact told the story. His most vivid recollections were about the ongoing grief of trying to create television with what he recalled as an "angry, sullen, and temperamental emcee." The ill will was echoed at the network. With its yanking *Bargain Hunters* prematurely after only nine weeks, ABC swore off the game show business. It would be three years before they mounted another.

Peter had hosted projects that earned swift cancellations before this one. He'd also experienced the emotional speed bumps of tough taping days. To date, none were known to have so thoroughly usurped his underlying professionalism. The derisive escapade he staged on the final tape day was a mind-blowingly poor choice of ways to cope with frustration, and it foretold even more difficulty that still lay ahead for poor Peter. Oh yes. Sadly, it got worse.

Most performers struggle at times in their efforts to find greater success in a fiercely competitive industry. Some, it seems are simultaneously trying to escape some personal psychic pain. The dazzling 5,000 watts of carefully-focused incandescence bouncing off their porcelain-veneered smiles blind the public from these folks' true existences. Part of the wonderful magic of television is its ability to disguise truth and electronically paint lifelike alternate realities. Behind their smiles, some people are working through secret heartbreaking circumstances far more tragic than any soap opera subplot. Those who can keep it together under stress are the true troupers.

During his final months on the job, Alex Trebek's superhuman perseverance was an inspiration to every member of the *Jeopardy!* staff and crew, as well as millions of viewers. He never failed to soldier through the five-episode tape days while suffering the agony of his advancing pancreatic cancer as well as the ravages of repeated rounds of chemotherapy. I was on set on the final tape day for the 2019-2020 season when word was whispered that Alex was literally lying on the floor of his dressing room in tears, writhing in pain between episodes. When it was suggested the show wrap for the day, he was adamant in his refusal.

Alex finished that afternoon's shows and continued to tape his beloved series up until 10 days before his death. You may not have noticed the wig he wore to replace the hair he surrendered to chemotherapy, but you can hear his voice weak and his diction occasionally a bit sloppy in some episodes. Alex said he looked forward to the opportunities to be working as each provided welcome distractions from the physical and psychic pain of knowing his remaining days were quickly slipping away. Viewers saw none of that melancholy.

Other performers behind host podiums, in front of weather maps, seated on talk show sets, or acting on soaps, dramas and comedies have stumbled and fallen, unable to maintain their balance while battling no greater challenges than the simple frustrations that we all deal with. With his good health, a loving family, and a steady income, those in Peter Tomarken's inner orbit say the signs of his internal conflict were well camouflaged during his most successful days at *Press Your Luck*.

While Byl Carruthers remembers, "Peter was the model of professionalism," one well-placed network executive told me he personally experienced escalating verbal affronts from the host soon after the series wrapped. The offenses were sufficient to render the accompanying litany of hollow apologies worthless, never coming close to erasing the sting. He added that Peter's many proclamations of having finally overcome his frustrations never rang true.

All these years later I was finally able to confirm a rumor that lingered for years that more than supports that indignation. It concerns the *Press Your Luck* production company paying a stiff penalty to CBS for canceled tape dates. The staff and crew were on set that particular Saturday, but Peter had gone M.I.A. He simply failed to show up for either of the two scheduled days. Nobody is sure exactly where he was, but showrunner Bill Carruthers characterized his absence in at least two conversations at the time with variations of a terse "… coked out of his mind in an elevator in Las Vegas with two broads."

There seemed to be a Dr. Jekyll—Mr. Hyde aspect to Peter's personality. The times I spent with him away from cameras he was calm, pleasant, witty, charming, and great company; he loved to laugh. Out of respect, of course I never asked Peter about the source of the consuming rage that I began to hear of but hadn't seen. Over lunch sometime around 1984 Peter did share with two co-workers that he had been seeing a psychiatrist for help with unresolved grief from his childhood. Peter explained that his father had committed suicide and left him a personal note, the contents of which he didn't share but were apparently distressing. In that same conversation he then revealed the odd coincidence that the psychiatrist treating him also committed suicide, also leaving him a personal note.

Peter's demons didn't completely derail his career. He sufficiently overcame a tarnished reputation in 1988 to produce and host a single season of the syndicated game *Wipeout* for Paramount. Peter was also tapped for pilots over the years, including one each for the prestigious Goodson-Todman and Merv Griffin organizations, *TKO* and *Monopoly*, respectively. Perhaps he was fated to work off some of his accumulated bad karma in being chosen to wrangle the dysfunction at some of the *Monopoly* runthroughs leading up to the show's pilot for a planned 1990 series rollout. I watched an unforgettable presentation early in its development. As Peter made his entrance a tuxedoed little person began a march around an oversized Monopoly game board. From its opening seconds it seemed this staging of the real estate-based classic was instantly marked either for fantastic success or doomed to abysmal failure. Is it cute or exploitative to have a professional actor, unique by virtue of proportionate dwarfism, hopping, skipping, and jumping with each roll of the dice? All gussied up like a doll, wearing bowtie and tails, the actor strutted with an oversized top hat and cane. Even though I might be among the last to succumb to political correctness, this portrayal of the box game's mascot, Rich Uncle Pennybags, struck even me as the height of poor taste.

It must have stung at the time, but in retrospect it's clear that Peter was lucky that the pilot he hosted never make it to air. I'm told it became the laughing stock of that syndication buying season, as well as an embarrassment to both Merv and King World, its distributor. Disputes resulted in Peter being replaced by pilot contestant Mike Reilly for the 12 re-tooled episodes that ended up on ABC, thankfully without the anonymous pirouetting Pennybags. More unsold pilots came and went as Peter's cachet cooled, including *Rodeo Drive*, *Duel in the Daytime*, *Two Heads Are Better Than One*, *Winds of Fortune*, *Live Wire*, and *Show Me the World*.

After an involuntary hiatus, at first Peter was happy to get a steady check and be in a spotlight again in the mid-1990s when he began hosting GSN's live game breaks. *Decades* was a series of live interstitial segments with viewer phone-in quizzes that aired during, between, and around the channel's schedule of mostly off-network reruns. Despite working beneath both his skill and pay level it was smooth sailing, for a while. Perhaps dissatisfied by the lack of other opportunities or resentful of the critiques and direction he was getting from GSN's program department, Peter's attitude became increasingly negative and his behavior increasingly problematic. He was earning a reputation as a hothead with the inability to sublimate his hair-trigger temper.

While I'd like to dismiss the whole saga of Peter's rage as gross exaggeration or a series of misunderstandings, there were too many crew, staff, and even audience members who eye-witnessed his turmoil to allow me to whitewash this sad reality. Those who worked long enough or close enough with Peter saw flashes of the internal conflict that occasionally drove him to self-destructive outbursts. The litany of events that appalled his co-workers included unprovoked angry rages, items thrown against the walls, kicked and punched set pieces, and screaming fits. An unambiguous account from a staffer at *Decades* included his surprise upon seeing his emcee throw a chair across the stage. It joins the stories from others who witnessed similar angry eruptions in that tiny Culver City studio. GSN producer Pat Alder summed it up saying, "Peter could range from darling to angry in a New York minute." One of GSN's executives recounted the times Peter's wife was called at home so she could come to the studio to talk Peter down from his manic flare-ups.

It was shocking because those incidents were in such contrast to the delightful guy we had all first come to like and admire. With these revelations into Peter's volatile nature there was little surprise when we began to hear of growing disharmony on the home front with he, his wife, and their daughter struggling with their relationships. Professionally, it wasn't too much longer before karma caught up with Peter and the business gave him the cold shoulder. He took to waiting tables in a Beverly Hills restaurant in order to make ends meet during a period in which he started again receiving professional help. Out of the game, Peter later began a new career in real estate. He studied and passed the licensing test and was also dabbling as a mortgage broker. To me, it seemed whatever anger that had once been simmering just beneath the surface had faded into quiet kindness and humility. When I next saw him in agent Fred Wostbrock's office, I was amazed by what appeared to have been a profound transformation. Peter seemed in great spirits, lighthearted and laughing.

Early in 2000 Peter's phone rang again with the opportunity to return to the screen. Sadly, it became a painful one. *Paranoia* was a live coast-to-coast, highly-promoted big-money event for the Fox Family Channel. Among the problems with both gameplay and production were issues with the cutting-edge technology. They included a computer-generated virtual set and live participation by contestants playing via satellite, over the phone, and through the show's website.

It was the year 2000, but this technological jump into the next millennium was premature and created some awkward live moments for Peter to tap-dance around. He came through it reasonably unscathed, covering for the glitches as well as anyone could be expected to. Sadly, when the troubled big-budget production was yanked after just 10 airings, Peter's anger resurfaced. Apparently much of the hard-won personal growth and emotional health he had gained began to unwind.

Then Peter suddenly had an opportunity to regain his lost glory. There are too few second chances in life, but this one had the potential to instantly rehabilitate his image and revive his career. In 2002 the aging host was asked to front a pilot for the revival of the show that had made him famous 20 years earlier, *Press Your Luck*. Peter appeared to be at the top of his game fronting one of two tests of GSN's *Whammy: The All New Press Your Luck*. The format was the same on both pilots but the hosts were different. Two emcees were in competition and focus group research would help make the selection from between Peter and Todd Newton. After viewing, the opinion of the assembled civilians was loud and clear. Those who were hoping to spin the data in support of Peter didn't stand a chance. Todd Newton was the clear choice.

Sadly, Peter didn't take the news well. Who would? He was again challenged with a long climb up from dejection. As he was approaching his 60th birthday, perhaps Peter was slowly resigning himself to the reality that his two-decade run was over. In my presence he appeared to be calmly accepting his involuntary retirement. Others who knew Peter vehemently disagree with that observation. The change I believe I saw led to his beginning to take an active role in charitable pursuits. That included piloting for Angel Flight West, a non-profit organization that provided free air transportation for medical patients.

I last saw Peter at the 2003 memorial service for Bill Carruthers, the creator and producer of *Press Your Luck*, Peter's big hit. The evening was more a celebration of Bill's life and outstanding career than any somber memorial. The event was held at CBS Television City and the red-jacketed pages escorted each guest as if we were royalty being led to an affair of state. We were delivered to the world's most famous game show facility, Bill's former home, Studio 33. There was a video tribute that took us all the way back to Bill's start, directing stars of an earlier era including Soupy Sales and Ernie Kovacs. A few dozen friends and co-workers from the L.A. game show production community were there in celebratory mode, sharing memories over cocktails and a fully catered meal served on the stage. Peter and I sat within whispering distance at adjacent tables and our joking along with others' was irreverent but far from inappropriate. My friend was in great spirits, upbeat and lighthearted, laughing with the kind of gusto that can't be faked. The weight of personal baggage that had burdened Peter in years past once again seemed to have been lightened.

That observation was borne out months later when a last minute call for Peter to host a runthrough of 2004's *Balderdash* was met by a very cooperative and enthusiastic "Yes!" One of that show's producers recently explained to me how this wasn't simply one of many runthroughs for polishing the gameplay. It was also an opportunity for Peter to win another hosting gig. After all, an emcee hadn't yet been cast and the network's executives were among those observing. Peter's wit was a perfect match for the light-hearted game, and his execution of a format which was explained to him just an hour or two earlier was flawless.

We'll never know if he had finally exorcised his demons and was capable of rehabilitating his reputation with *Balderdash* because the visitors from the conservative PAX web of stations gave a thumbs-down. They felt that Peter had a sharper, harsher edge than the white-bread personality they envisioned for their more prim and proper viewers. It was offered to the softer Pat Bullard, a great choice, but after a deal couldn't be reached the even softer Elayne Boosler was signed.

It was a shock to learn two years later, in March of 2006, that engine failure caused a small plane to crash in full sight of tourists and locals visiting the Santa Monica Pier. It turned out that Peter was piloting. He and his wife were killed just after takeoff from Santa Monica airport when their four-seater plunged into the Pacific. They were on a volunteer run to pick up a cancer patient in San Diego for transport to UCLA Medical Center. The transformed, calmer, charity-minded Peter deserved far more than his 63 years.

Although there have been many thousands in the air without incident, Peter and his wife met their demise in a Beechcraft Bonanza. It's the same single-engine aircraft in which Buddy Holly, J.P. "Big Bopper" Richardson, and Richie Valens were flying on the day the music died. That tragic crash in a snowstorm was attributed to a combination of bad weather and pilot error, not equipment failure as it was in Peter's case.

I'm told that, in retirement, we get to view events from previous years with fresh perspective and context. If Peter knew earlier all that he came to learn by the end of his six-plus decades, no doubt many of those years would have been very different. I suppose that's true for all of us.

Chapter 34

There's a difficult story to share that I'm often asked about. I've put off telling the tale through all of these pages simply because it's one of TV's saddest. It's the story of Ray Combs, a good and generous man, a gifted comedian, and a beloved practicing Mormon whose troubles consumed his soul. A near-fatal car wreck, addiction to pain killers, huge financial woes, family turmoil, and being fired from a network TV show in order to accommodate his predecessor's return were just some of the rocky roads that intersected to drive Ray to the brink, and beyond.

Ray Combs sold furniture in Hamilton, Ohio, but with his sense of humor, gift of gab, warmth, and empathy Ray's life quickly changed after arriving in Hollywood.

Audiences loved Ray Combs, and to watch him work was akin to watching an artist so skilled that he made his craft seem deceptively simple. Whether hosting a game show or tickling an audience's funny bone in preparation for a sitcom taping, Ray was a truly masterful showman. Johnny Carson turbocharged Ray's career with a late-night stand-up booking after first overhearing the roars of laughter from Ray's warm-up act. Once the crowd's reaction couldn't be contained within the adjacent walls at a taping of *Amen*, Johnny had to see who that comedian was. It took only a moment before making the mental note to tell his talent coordinators, "book him."

Ray's 1986 debut stand-up routine on *The Tonight Show* was unique even from Johnny's introduction, singling him out as, "a little bit different kind of a comedian… [warm-ups are] a tough job. And he's the best at it." The six minutes that followed were a graduate course in how to charm an audience. Sensing the unique emotional connection he'd made with the crowd through his act, at the last minute Ray decided to close with something other than the strong laugh line he'd prepared. Instead, he chose to offer a bit of the kind of relatable humanity he brought to all his work: "My entire life I'd always had a dream that someday I'd be able to walk out on this show and make people laugh, and tonight made that dream come true. Thank you and good night."

Six years after his 1982 move to Los Angeles Ray was suddenly on the radar as having star potential, and was soon scouted to host no fewer than four game shows. He had the choice to front a reboot of Carson's 1950's *Who Do You Trust*, the new *Win, Lose or Draw* from Burt Reynolds and Bert Convy, *Scruples* for Columbia and NBC's Brandon Tartikoff, as well as a *Family Feud* revival. That last offer came from Mark Goodson Productions with an $800,000 annual payday and options for an additional six years at escalating compensation. His choice proved to be a perfect pairing of emcee and format and, starting on Independence Day of 1988, Ray enjoyed a great run with Feud—five years on CBS and six years in syndication from which he reportedly grossed $8 million total.

Ray told Cincinnati public radio reporter John Kiesewetter, "I've prepared my whole life for what is going to happen. It's my dream and I'm living it … It's amazing you can make this kind of money without throwing a football or risking breaking a leg. It's great to have the money to do whatever you want to do with your family for just being yourself and having fun." His world couldn't have been any brighter.

Then, Ray Combs' life fell apart.

It doesn't get much better than making a million dollars a year starring on network television, working a few days a month, backed by the best support staff and crew in the business, giving away money to wide-smiling, playful, upbeat families. Photo courtesy of Fred Wostbrock.

Ray's and my paths crossed dozens of times, but never like the night of November 8, 1995. It was unforgettable because my friend was a drastically changed man, struggling to do the work that had once appeared to be effortless. I was filling in for announcer Gene Wood as we taped a special Ice Capades episode as the season finale of *Family Challenge*, a Woody Fraser production that Ray hosted for The Family Channel.

Before that evening I hadn't seen Ray since July of the previous year. That's when this talented comedian and broadcaster was in a devastating automobile accident on the Ventura Freeway in Burbank. Coincidentally, it was very near to where we were now taping this show, on an ice rink at Universal Studios. Ray's 1991 Jaguar was totaled in a three-car mishap. Surprisingly, pre-1993 models of this high-priced luxury automobile were not equipped with airbags. As a result, poor Ray's head smashed into the steering wheel and became lodged between the wheel and the dashboard with his neck twisted and spinal cord injured. He was unconscious and had stopped breathing.

Miraculously, CPR administered at the scene was able to bring Ray back to life; however, it soon became apparent that Ray couldn't move. He reported having no feeling in his arms or legs. Rushed to Burbank's St. Joseph's Hospital, tests revealed a shattered disc with nerve damage. It was an unthinkable horror to imagine the spry, super-energized 35-year-old would be facing the rest of his life as a quadriplegic. Feeling slowly began to return to his arms. Peripheral nerves are capable of regenerating and eventually sensation spread; soon the outlook for Ray's recovery improved. Wearing a cervical collar and in great pain, the comedian indulged a request by NBC's *Tonight Show* for a quick cameo from his hospital bed which was just a couple of blocks from the show's studio. Always a trouper, Ray mustered the energy, smile, and wit for a quick volley of jokes with Jay Leno. It was clear that Leno, the show's staff, and its viewers had no idea of the extent of Ray's severely compromised condition.

It took three months to graduate from a wheelchair to walking tentatively with a cane. Once ambulatory there were still many months of healing before Ray could eventually advance to where there was no visible indication of the hell he had been through. It was ostensibly a complete recovery of sensation and range of motion, but the extent of his suffering with residual pain was undetected by audience members when he returned to stand-up and warm-up gigs. Ray hid much of his pain even from family and friends, minimizing the occasional agony that he couldn't disguise. The pain lessened but never went away, requiring he remain on pain medication indefinitely.

Ray continued to have some difficulty with his fingers and hands, yet here he was 16 months after the accident whirling around the frozen rink on ice skates, hosting two families through wacky physical stunts. It was a truly astounding return from clinical death. Sadly, even before his car was smashed, Ray's life had already begun to crash. The gifted mirth-maker had been enjoying a linear climb to ever-escalating new heights. His fame, prestige, and salaries all rocketed as he rose from club comic to network personality. The quickly changing trajectory of that career may have been the darkest cloud to gather in what became the perfect storm that ultimately consumed him.

After Mark Goodson's death, Ray was unceremoniously fired from *Family Feud* in early 1994 by Jonathan Goodson who had hopes of saving the series' future from sagging ratings with a return by the original host, Richard Dawson. It was a Hail-Mary play, but arguably a sound business decision even if it only temporarily forestalled the cancelation of a show that had been hemorrhaging viewers and was being dropped by stations. The business half of show business always trumps all other considerations and, despite his talent and loyalty, Ray had to go. He was devastated. As the show's director, Marc Breslow recounted, "Losing *Family Feud* was a huge blow because it became his world."

I don't know how you can ease the impact of being dumped as the host of a high-profile legacy series, but if it was possible I'm sure Jonathan tried. The second-generation TV mogul is a complex guy, but during the years in his employ I always found him to be gifted with a superbly sharp mind, empathy, and an abundance of heart. Many years later Jonathan confided in me that firing Ray was a very hard thing to do. He's since come to understand the full impact of that action, but at the time there was no way of knowing the depth of the host's hidden despair.

That professional setback exacerbated Ray's money troubles, caused in great part by his unprofitable investment in comedy clubs. In 1990 he lost the Caddy Combs Comedy Club after a legal battle with his partner, Charles Schneider, over its ownership, operation, and alleged thievery. Amid their feuding, Schneider had Ray arrested for criminal trespassing after a performance at the club he partially owned. He was released with no charges filed, although a picture of Ray being led away in handcuffs made one of the supermarket tabloids. He then filed a $20 million defamation suit after Schneider told the *National Enquirer* that Ray "engineered his own arrest as a publicity stunt—and he even tipped off the TV cameras to be there."

The next year Ray opened the elegant 500-seat Cincinnati Comedy Connection, only to shutter it early in 1995 after over three years of it sapping more than its fair share of his income. After losing *Family Feud* Ray still had a home in Los Angeles, two homes near Cincinnati in Hamilton, and a Jaguar in each city. He bought investment property in Hamilton, and he contributed time and money fundraising for Hamilton High School's new stadium. By tapping cash that would otherwise be used to pay mortgages, he eventually lost the Ohio homes in foreclosure. In L.A. he was behind in paying down his $467,675 mortgage debt.

Ray was not a saint. A man with his charm and prestige attracts all kinds of people, women among them. As his eldest son Ray Combs Jr. explained, there were "women my father dated while as a married Mormon with six kids... [including] a former Penthouse pet and a Cincinnati Bengals cheerleader." When long-simmering Combs family disharmony began to boil over, Ray and his wife Debbie filed for divorce in 1996.

There were two years without a steady paycheck before poor Ray took a major step down in prestige as well as a 75% cut in salary. He joined Ryan Seacrest, Gene Wood and me for the Family Channel's dual series *Wild Animal Games* and *Family Challenge*. It was quite a comedown for Ray to now be hosting an ersatz knock-off of Nickelodeon's *Double Dare*. Publicly, he wore his game face telling Cincinnati's WVXU, "To fight my way back, and come back to do this show—I don't call it a miracle, but I do see things differently. Every day, I feel a little bit better." It was admirable, but any remaining illusion I may have had that Ray was capable of rising above these setbacks to return to a network show—or at least to live a calm and comfortable life—evaporated on the second floor of the Glendale Studios complex in late 1995.

I was assigned a dressing room a few doors down from Ray's during the months our two series were being produced in adjacent studios. On the days when we were both on the Glendale Studios lot, I could hear angst and anguish drifting down the hall. While the words were muffled and mostly indistinguishable, the tone of his phone and in-person conversations was unmistakable. I knew that there was a good amount of showmanship behind Ray's all-smiling on-set persona, but I was surprised and saddened to learn of the magnitude of that act. On some days between taping episodes it seemed to be all frustration, anger, and exasperation.

Unknown at the time, the *Family Challenge* Ice Capades episode that we worked together turned out to be Ray's last appearance as the emcee of any show. His departure that evening wasn't as noteworthy as his late arrival. Ray was still not on the set at Universal nearly an hour after his call time, and about a half hour after taping was scheduled to begin. My keeping that audience warm on a cold night, sitting inches from the ice, required all the BTUs of charm I could muster. As soon as Ray arrived, he came to apologize for the delay and joined me in goosing the audience's energy. He was fantastic with people, truly gifted. Even in an obviously compromised condition Ray was nothing less than a force of nature with that crowd. He seemed firmly in the here and now, quick-witted, sharp and charismatic, but up close I could see a strange vacancy in his eyes.

With his pupils dilated, there were moments when his gaze suggested that he was miles away. Yet, solidly balanced on ice skates, Ray kept the stunt show wildly kinetic. Unlike the totally in-control host that we knew Ray to be, his work was sloppy, requiring a few retakes. He was a bit off his game and seemed to be slowly deteriorating as the taping progressed. He need only make it through this night to wrap the season. Ray's dedication was undeniable and he was giving all he had, but he'd lost his edge and his usually rapier-sharp mind was addled, assumedly from pain killers. Surely after the necessary editing he'd appear uncompromised to the home audience, but it was sadly clear that Ray's gift was diminished.

Some months after *Family Challenge* and *Wild Animal Games* went on hiatus I saw Ray again at the last place I'd have expected. We had both temporarily moved into the legendary Oakwood Garden Apartments adjacent to Toluca Lake. Ray was separated from his family, while I was waiting for my home to be rebuilt after the devastating 1994 Northridge earthquake. Oakwood Apartments, now known as Avalon. You may have heard of the place. During his years helming *The Tonight Show*, Jay Leno often taped comedy bits there, utilizing some of the dozens of acting hopefuls who were always among the transient residents.

Ray and I were surprised to discover each other soaking in one of the hot tubs at the massive complex late one night. At first he seemed as bubbly as the whirlpool spa, but financial challenges, family conflict, and a stalled career were among the frustrations that he casually tallied between jokes. Despite the conversation's gloomy subtext Ray was great company. He always was. A staffer with whom I'd worked on *Family Challenge* back then only recently explained that our nights at the spa were at about the time that the decision was made to replace Ray for that show's second season. If Ray had already been told, ouch! Just imagine the career heartbreak of first being fired from a network and syndication hit, *Family Feud*, and then, months later unceremoniously dumped from a lower-rent cable series.

As I remember it, our last of several nights in the bubbles together was during the Memorial Day weekend, 1996. Ray was booked that holiday Monday on *Home and Family*. It was a production populated by many of his friends, as it was also produced by *Family Challenge* showrunner Woody Fraser for the same Family Channel. No gig could have been easier for Ray as *Home and Family* was shot literally across the street from Oakwood, at Universal. It would be low stress as Ray would simply be demonstrating some of the games played on *Family Challenge*. Even with all that was weighing on his soul, I was told that he was a charming guest. Still, some of his friends on the set must have seen that he was struggling. It was only a few days later that Oakwood security told me that Ray had been taken off the premises by ambulance.

Too soon came the news of my friend's demise. It was unbelievable. Those last few days of his life must have felt like a nightmare for Ray, swept up in a whirlwind of self-destruction. Ray Jr. helped me in reconstructing the timeline of his father's last days. Indeed, Ray had been taken from Oakwood to nearby St. Joseph's Hospital on May 31st after his wife Debbie called police to the scene from the family home in Glendale. She reported that Ray had just told her in a phone conversation that he was committing suicide and had taken an overdose of valium. That proved not to be true, as he was examined and soon released from the emergency room.

Had he been considering suicide? Ray turned on the charm and convinced the doctors and police that Debbie's call was nothing more than a case of "marital discord," and that they should all consider the trip to the hospital a "courtesy ride." Ray walked out of the same emergency room that, months earlier, had admitted him following his auto accident. It was where the first of his prescriptions for pain killers was written.

The next day, Saturday, June 1st, Ray had the house to himself when he visited the family home on Sonora Avenue in nearby Glendale, reportedly to get more of his medication. His quiet Kenneth Village residential neighborhood is charming, but dense with post-World War II-era homes. When Ray began to trash his five-bedroom house, it's believed one neighbor who heard the strange noises called 9-1-1. Police reports indicate they were also called by a friend Ray had visited earlier that day, with the friend reporting that Ray left "in a rage," threatening to "hurt his wife."

When the cops arrived, Ray met them at the front door with blood on his scalp and face. He told the officers that he had hit his head accidentally in the bathroom. In reality, he had been banging his skull against the walls. Soon after the cops arrived, Ray's wife Debbie pulled up. She explained to the police that Ray had just been released from St Joseph's following a suicide attempt. With that information and considering his present condition, Ray was taken to the nearest psychiatric facility and placed on the California legally-mandated 72-hour hold. It was standard procedure under section 5150 of California's Welfare and Institutions Code.

Just 14 hours after being admitted at Glendale Adventist Hospital, Ray ended his struggle at 4:10 a.m. on June 2nd, 1996, Debbie's 40th birthday. Despite doctors' orders for him to be under close observation, Ray was able to end his misery unseen. He knotted bed linens around his neck tightly enough to put pressure on his Adam's apple, and secured the other end to a clothes rod. Then, leaning forward with knees bent, he used his own body weight to induce unconsciousness and death by cutting off oxygen to the brain.

This isn't a quick or easy way to die, and most such attempts fail because of the length of time necessary to continue to prevail in overcoming the body's natural tendency to fight for life. Ray was found asphyxiated with his body dangling from the clothes rod in a narrow wardrobe not large enough for an adult to fit inside. Upon being discovered, a tracheotomy was performed to bypass his crushed windpipe, but it failed to help induce breathing. Too many precious minutes had passed. Ray's body was still warm when the coroner arrived.

Ray Combs Jr. asserts that his father apparently charmed the staff, masking the severity of his condition. He was gregarious and telling jokes, signing autographs while scoffing at the idea that he was suicidal. As a result, inexplicably, Ray was allowed to keep his clothes, shoes, and shoelaces. The aides assigned to closely monitor his movement and condition while in isolation failed to comply with hospital protocols and doctors' orders, going so far as giving Ray unfettered access to a phone along with a modicum of privacy. Ray Jr. says it's a matter of record that the orderly responsible for observing his father casually told the charge nurse "Mr. Combs is sleeping in his closet."

The horrendous breach of even the most rudimentary measures for a patient on suicide watch resulted in the family filing a lawsuit for gross negligence. The hospital delayed the proceedings for years before ultimately settling the case with a lowball award of $1 million. After attorney fees, each of Ray's six children finally received $100,000. Ray Jr. calls it "blood money" that several of his brothers and sisters used to fuel their drug and alcohol addictions. Of course no money could ever hope to approach Ray's value or worth as a father, husband, or friend. Nor could it ever compensate for the millions of lost laughs.

At the time of the family's loss I shared words of solace with Ray Jr. who was, and still is, devastated by this tragedy. Although only 17 years old at the time, he took on the responsibility for making funeral arrangements, and caring for his five younger siblings. In retrospect, he believes that his dear father had been suffering for quite some time with severe depression. He explained that during those final days his father succumbed to recurrent, severe major depressive episodes which were complicated by acute psychosis and paranoia that exacerbated his suicidal ideation.

Ray Jr.'s search for meaning led him to earning a master's degree in clinical social work. To gain insight into the life of the father he loved so deeply, he also spent a few years getting his own share of laughs—the life force that had once energized his dad. Ray Jr. sampled the world of a stand-up comedian. As he explained it, "I want to know about my father from the perspective of his friends and in some cases his rivals... a fuller picture of the man that he was—imperfect, flawed, charismatic, compassionate, driven and well-loved."

As the Combs family mourned, so did his industry friends who had lost a fantastically talented, friendly, and generous professional. Ray was only 40 years old. Although over the years Ray's gross earnings approached $10 million, his outstanding debts were crushing. He'd been resolute and unyielding to the realities of business in trying to make a success of his investments in those hometown comedy clubs. He'd been extremely generous in helping his brothers and sisters as well as extended family members in need, some of whom struggled with addictions and chronic unemployment.

Ray had been munificent and trusting with friends, especially fellow comics; a soft touch, as it's been called. He awarded $2,500 to Bob Zany, a pal on the comedy circuit to whom he, years before, promised a reward if he'd lose 100 pounds. Another time, without provocation, Ray bought new custom-tailored suits for a couple of fellow comics the morning after they worked at his club, feeling the two needed to up their games. Even strangers were treated to Ray's generosity. He liked to entertain friends with a bit of *al fresco* improv. He'd walk up to a homeless person and, for a switch, ask them for change. He'd say, "I need to use the payphone," and they nearly always gave Ray some change. Ray would say thanks and then reciprocate by giving them all the cash in his pockets, sometimes hundreds of dollars. As Ray Jr. explained, "The money came fast and easy and left the same way. It was only important to him in how it allowed him to do things for people without a second thought."

With him gone and without his income, Ray's widow Debra soon lost the heavily-mortgaged family home to foreclosure. It was only then that she learned just how deep in the financial mire the Combs clan truly was. She told Cincinnati reporter John Kiesewetter they were $500,000 in debt adding, "I don't have anything." The community of L.A.'s comedians raised money to help, but it was another generous gift that caught Debra by complete surprise. An early champion of his career, Johnny Carson immediately sent $25,000 from his personal checking account with a note that read, "I understand you are having some problems. I hope this will ease the burden." It did indeed, as Ray Jr. said it was that gift that paid for his dad's funeral.

Only after Johnny Carson's death did it become known that the painfully shy late night host had been quick to reach out with a helping hand to others, in and out of the business. Debra and the Combs kids were just one family among many beneficiaries of Johnny's quiet generosity. He had been sending unsolicited checks to people in distress for many years. Dante Charles Stradella was the Danny who owned the New York institution Danny's Hideaway. When the restaurateur's own legendary generosity took a critical toll on his personal finances, that well-known mayor of midtown nightlife was surprised to receive a $100,000 check from Johnny.

By the end of Fred De Cordova's reign as executive producer of *The Tonight Show*, the film and television veteran held little more than the title. Friction in his relationship with Johnny had passed the breaking point and Fred was permanently banned from the set. Just the same, upon his 2001 death Johnny rose above the estrangement to send Fred's widow this heartfelt note with a check for $100,000:

"Dear Janet, I am sorry for the loss of Freddie. I will always remember the great moments we shared. I know he would understand my not attending his funeral services, and I hope you will also. It is not out of any disrespect for him. I admired him greatly. I know Fred was not a great money manager, and you are no doubt encountering unexpected financial demands. Please look on the enclosed as a bonus for almost 25 years as Tonight Show producer. Right now I have this strange feeling that Fred is telling Saint Peter how to do his job better. Love, Johnny"

In a town where relationships are often not as they seem, Ray Combs was a straight-shooter. He truly liked people, he was intuitively compassionate, and he had a rare, rich gift that could brightly light even the darkest room. I still remember hearing the contrasting highs and lows of his triggering wild laughter from his audience, juxtaposed by the stressful and frustrating conversations leaking through his second floor dressing room walls. Like most others, until the news of his suicide I had no idea of the full depth of Ray's despair.

One of the times fellow announcer Gene Wood and I were in complete agreement was when he said of Ray, "He was one of the rare people who totally cared about what he was doing." Indeed, he gave every ounce of himself to every performance. Gene added, "He was full of life." In a reflective moment more than a dozen years later, Jonathan Goodson candidly told me that he still felt he had a drop of Ray's blood on his hands as a result of the dismissal from *Family Feud*. Simply put, Ray was a good egg who cracked in a bubbling cauldron of bad situations.

INDEX

Accardo, Anthony 169
Adams, Cindy 117
Affleck, Ben 75
Alba, Jessica 176
Alder, Pat 436
Alisi, Art 431-432
Allen, Fred 7
Allen, Irwin 314-315
Allen, Lane 151
Allen, Steve 6-7, 35. 46, 54, 81, 107, 212, 214-215, 217, 296, 299-301, 310
Allen, Tim 394
Allyson, June 265
Alpert, Marv 1
Amedure, Scott 24
Anastasia, Albert 168
Anderson, Ernie 107
Anderson, Gillian 130
Anderson, Loni 412
Anderson, Louie 384-391, 393
Andrews, Julie 297
Ansari, Aziz 76
Arden, Eve 172
Arledge, Roone 303
Arnaz, Desi 134-135, 160-164, 169-173
Arnaz, Desi, Jr. 104, 172
Arnaz, Lucie 172
Arthur, Bea 152-157
Arthur, Carol 52, 92
Asner, Ed 54, 99-100, 111-112
Astaire, Fred 106

Astin, John 104, 263
Astin, Sean 104
Astley, Rick 407
Aubrey, James 243, 248-249, 252, 353, 358-377
Austin, John C, 230
Austin, Ray 62
Auten, Matthew David 390
Bach, Bob 306
Bacon, James 212
Bacon, Kevin 38
Baio, Scott 75
Balance, Bill 423
Ball, Lucille 134-135, 160-161, 171, 194, 281, 366, 368
Ballantine, Carl 110-111, 112
Ballard, Eve 172
Bankhead, Tallulah 153, 248
Baranski, Christine 5
Barbeau, Adrienne 2
Barker, Bob 1, 16, 19, 69-70, 77-78, 80, 83-85, 119-128, 332-333, 384, 418
Barker, Dick 151
Barker, Tillie 85
Barnum, P.T. 11
Baron, Sandy 348
Barr, Roseanne 6, 380
Barrett, Charlie 183, 201
Barrett, Rona 173
Barris, Chuck 52, 91-98, 426
Barry, Jack 131, 339

Barrymore, John 20
Basie, Count 142
Batali, Mario 75
Battaglio, Stephen 370
Bauman, John 39
Bavier, Francis 334-335
Bean, Orson 166
Beatty, Roger 108
Beavers, Louise 66
Begelman, David 243
Bel Geddes, Barbara 256
Belafonte, Harry 248
Bell, W. Kamau 72
Belland, Bruce 378-379
Belli, Melvin 304-305
Bennett, Tony 54
Benny, Jack 54, 60, 119-120, 194, 242 358, 414
Bergeron, Tom 120, 126-127
Bergman, Ted 144
Berle, Milton 1, 8, 134-135, 261, 296
Berlin, Peter 430
Bernstein, Shirley 101
Bernstein, Leonard 101
Billingsley, Sherman 117
Bilson, Bruce 275
Bioff, Willie 164-165
Birkitt, Stephanie 133
Bishop, Joey 166
Blair, Selma 130
Blanc, Mel 113-114
Blanc, Noel 114
Bloodworth-Thomason, Linda 8
Blum, Gary 413
Blum, Jerry 413
Blumenthal, Norm 312-313

Boden, Bob 84
Bogart, Humphrey 54
Bolen, Lin 12, 15, 196, 377-383
Bolger, Ray 65
Boll, Harlan 156
Bompensiero, Frank 170
Bonaduce, Danny 257, 261
Bono, Sonny 296
Boone, Pat 208
Boosler, Elayne 439
Borelli, Bill 167
Borgnine, Ernest 105-107, 110, 112-113, 114-115
Bosak, Liz Fertig 324
Bottone, Bruce 14
Brady, Wayne 46
Brando, Marlon 114
Brandt, Mel 322
Brasselle, Keefe 369-375
Braxton, Earl J. 87
Breen, Neil 158
Brenner, David 130-131
Breslow, Marc 86, 444
Brockman, Michael 317, 348, 391-392, 415
Brokaw, Tom 75
Bromfield, John 135
Brooks, Albert 110, 134
Brooks, Mel 51, 135, 262-263, 268
Brothers, Dr. Joyce 420-423
Brown, Joe B. 304
Brown, Les 186
Browne, George 164-165
Bruce, Lenny 214
Bruno, Angelo 168
Brynner, Yul 328

Bufalino, Russell 168
Bulifant, Joyce 272
Bullard, Pat 438
Burke, David 303
Burke, Delta 8
Burnett, Carol 108, 109, 120, 294, 363
Burns, Edd 14
Burns, George 54, 135, 208, 252
Bushkin, Henry 201, 374
Butler, Brett 6
Caesar, Sid 2, 8
Cagan, Claudia 42, 44-45
Cagney, Jimmy 46
Cambridge, Godfrey 214
Cameron, Sue 200
Cannon, Dyan 189
Cantor, Eddie 134
Capone Albert Francis 170-171
Capone, Al 164, 169, 289
Capone, Mae 169-170
Carey, Drew 418
Carlin, George 143, 239, 414
Carlisle, Kitty 333
Carlson, Arthur 413
Carnegie, Dale 43
Carrey, Jim 218
Carroll, Pat 66
Carruthers, Bill 193, 427, 434, 438
Carruthers, Byl 428, 434
Carson, Alexis 181, 190
Carson, Christopher 189-190
Carson, Cory 189
Carson, Joanne 186, 200
Carson, Johnny 2, 9, 10, 13, 20, 38, 43, 44, 73, 78, 87-88, 138, 146, 177-190, 193-195, 197-203, 206-207, 217, 218-219, 222, 252, 264, 270, 282, 293, 313, 334, 341, 350-351, 374-375, 385-386, 414, 415, 440-441, 450-451
Carson, Ricky 189
Carson, Ruth 188
Carter, Jimmy 193
Carter, Nick 75
Cartright, Angela 67
Cassidy, David 256, 259-261
Cassidy, Jack 260-261
Cassidy, Patrick 260-261, 264
Cassidy, Ryan 260
Cassidy, Shaun 260
Castro, Fidel 302, 309, 310
Cavett, Dick 20, 176, 178, 212
Cerf, Bennett 305
Chaplin, Charlie 209
Chappelle, Dave 218, 401
Chase, Chevy 202
Chase, Sylvia 303
Chasman, David 202
Cher 296
Chester, Jerry 348
Christal, Green 189-190
Chubbuck, Christine 11
Chung, Connie 234
Churchill, Winston 128
CK, Louis 75, 387
Clark, Dick 400, 414
Clark, Petula 248
Clarkson, Kelly 397, 402
Clayton, Bob 312
Cochran, Phil 151
Hughes, Howard 151
Cohen, Andy 180
Cohn, Harry 298

Coleman, Townsend 195
Collarusso, Charlie 21
Collins, Gary 45, 46-48, 51-53, 57
Collins, Joan 129
Combs, Debbie 445, 447-448, 450-451
Combs, Ray 393, 394-395, 440-452
Combs, Ray Jr. 445, 447-451
Como, Perry 208
Connery, Sean 54
Conreid, Hans 66
Conte, Richard 114
Convy, Bert 83, 409-411, 441
Conway, Tim 106-110, 112, 113
Cooper, Anderson 338
Copperfield, David 75
Coppola, Francis Ford 114, 168
Corman, Roger 409
Cosby, Bill 72-76, 242, 346
Cosell, Howard 3, 265
Cowan, Louis 357
Cowsill, Barbara 257-258
Cowsill, Barry 258
Cowsill, Bob 258
Cowsill, Susan 257
Cowsill, William 257-258
Cramer, Doug 273
Crawford, Cindy 294
Crawford, Joan 288
Cronkite, Walter 73, 234, 414
Crosby, Bing 54, 161, 296-297
Cruise. Tom 176, 294
Cryer, John 5
Crystal, Billy 29, 178, 277, 320-321, 339
Cugat, Xavier 288
Cullen, Bill 37, 344, 351
Culp, Robert 75, 242

Curtis, Tony 60
Cybil Shepherd 2, 6
Cyrus, Miley 2
Daly, Carson 414
Damon, Jerry 322
Dana, Bill 35, 80
Dangerfield, Rodney 385
Dann, Mike 191, 239-240, 242, 243, 245, 247, 358-359, 361
Dark, Danny 194
Davidson, Doug 126, 418
Davidson, John 46
Davis, Ann B. 273
Davis, Bette 176
Davis, Frenchie 1
Davis, Sammy 55
Dawson, Richard 17, 19, 83, 122, 321, 333, 391-393, 394-395, 444
Dean, James 302
Dean, Paula 2
DeBartolo, Dick 31, 44
DeCordova, Fred 2, 73, 188, 202, 375, 451
DeCordova, Janet 451
Degans, Eric 348
Degeneris, Ellen 157-159, 175-176, 405-406
DeLuise, Dom 51-54, 92
DeMarco Sisters 369
Demarest, William 161
Denver, John 366
Dick, Andy 76
Dickenson, Angie 189, 252
Diller, Barry 201-204
Diller, Phyllis 198
Dillon, Rita 262

DiMassa, Erni 431
Disney, Walt 59, 71
Dobkowitz, Roger 84, 126, 127, 418
Donahue, Phil 400
Dotrice, Karen 59
Douglas, Kirk 60, 194
Douglas, Michael 75
Douglas, Mike 20
Downs, Hugh 38, 282, 285, 303, 400
Dozier, William 373
Dreesen, Tom 218
Dru, Joanne 112
Dubrow, Burt 31, 36
Duchovney, David 130
Duke, Patty 100-105
Dunaway, Faye 377
Duncan, Sandy 137, 412
Dungey, Channing 346
Durante, Jimmy 288
Dussault, Nancy 285
Dwyer, Micky 351
Dyer, Wayne 43
Eastwood, Clint 294
Ebersol, Dick 379
Eden, Barbara 255
Edward, John 294
Edwards, Bobby 428
Edwards, Geoff 122, 378, 381-383, 384
Edwards, Vince 161
Egan, Bill 301-306
Ehrlich, Lou 346
Carsey, Marcy 346
Einstein, Bob 134, 144, 242
Einstein, Harry 134-135
Eisenhower, Dwight 59
Eisner, Michael 348

Ellington, Duke 215
Elliot, "Mama" Cass 2
Ellison, Larry 295
English, Diane 355-356
Enright, Dan 96. 379, 426
Estrada, Eric 63-65
Eubanks, Bob 25, 91-93, 98, 120-121, 176
Evanier, Mark 146, 289
Facey, Fred 322
Fairchild, Morgan 180
Falk, Peter 111
Fallon, Jimmy 206
Farnsworth, Philo 6
Farr, Jamie 210
Fearn-Banks, Kathleen 143
Feldman, Elliot 31
Felsher, Andy 408
Felsher, Howard 392-393
Ferguson, Craig 78, 286
Ferkle, Robert 232
Fernandez, Abel 162
Fertig, Ken 324
Fidler, Jimmy 302
Fiedler, Rob 430
Field, Sally 180
Fields, Freddie 243
Fields, W.C. 49
Fillion, Nathan 130
Finch, Dee 32-34
Fine, Sylvia 239, 242
Fisher, Eddie 60
Fleischer, Nat 422
Flesh, Ed 14
Flynn, Joe 106
Fogg, Clark 425

Fonda, Henry 54
Fonda, Jane 360
Foray, June 360-361
Ford, Dan 73
Ford, Tennessee Ernie 311
Forrest, Arthur 176-177
Forsythe, John 129
Foxx, Jamie 137
Foxx, Redd 1, 137-146, 347
Foy, Fred 322
Fraley, Oscar 164
Francis, Arlene 306, 333
Franco, James 75
Frankenheimer, John 328
Fraser, Woody 442, 447
Fratianno, Jimmy 169, 170
Frawley, William 2, 129, 161
Freeman, Morgan 75
Friedman, Budd 218
Friedman, Steve 8
Friendly, Fred 376
Frost, David 46
Funt, Allen 3, 198
Gable, Clark 288
Gabor, Zsa Zsa 60
Galifianakis, Zach 387
Gallin, Sandy 201, 272
Gallo, Ernest and Julio 315-316
Gandolfini, James 1
Ganzel, Teresa 181-182, 292-293
Garland, Judy 60, 78, 243- 288
Garlin, Jeff 76
Garner, James 113
Garret, Alvin 3
Gibbs, Joe 3
Snyder, "Jimmy the Greek" 3

Garrett, Brad 158
Garrison, Greg 52, 207
Garroway, Dave 4, 282-286
Gary, Arthur 322
Gary-Cox, Patty 89
Gelbart, Larry 242, 368
Gelman, Michael 333
Giancana, Sam 166, 167, 168, 169
Gibson, Charlie 26
Gibson, Mel 54
Gilbert, Johnny 322
Gillette, Penn 129
Gleason, Jackie 8, 154, 208
Godfrey, Arthur 2, 6, 78, 348, 351, 358
Goldberg, Whoopie 157
Gomez, Selma 237
Goodson, Jonathan 120-121, 394, 443-444, 452
Goodson, Mark 2, 27, 29-31, 36, 96, 152, 192, 326-333, 344, 348, 443
Mark Goodson Productions 419, 420, 441
Goodson-Todman 29, 30, 80, 82, 125, 152, 299, 301, 304, 307, 326, 328-329, 347, 392, 415, 426, 427, 435
Gordon, Kater 76
Gordon, Richard J. 389-390
Grandinetti, Michael 10
Grant, Bud 196
Gray, George 63
Greco, Kathy 418
Green, Cee Lo 2
Green, Shecky 166
Green, Tanena Love 189-190
Greenberg, Ron 131
Greenblatt, Robert 346

Griffin, Kathy 158
Griffin, Merv 13-14, 46, 81, 281, 339, 379, 380, 415, 435
Griffith, Andy 172, 201, 334-335
Guilbert, Ann 63
Gumbel, Bryant 8
Gurnee, Hal 340
Guthrie, Savannah 159, 405
Hackman, Gene 278
Hagen, Jean 67-68
Hagman, Larry 255
Halberstam, David 368
Halderman, Joe 132-133
Hale, Lee 207
Hall, Arsenio 220, 388
Hall, Monty 41, 49, 414, 431
Hallstrom, Holly 85-86
Hamer, John 67
Hamer, Rusty 66-69
Hamilton, George 126
Hammett, Dashiell 160
Hammett, David 22
Hanks, Tom 202
Hanrahan, Bill 322
Harrington Jr., Pat 66
Harris, Susan 153-154
Hart, Kevin 390-391, 401
Hartman, David 26, 285
Harvey, Marjorie Elaine 399
Harvey, Steve 99, 175, 395-406
Hawn, Goldie 215-216
Heatter, Merrill 323, 326, 348-349, 430-431
Hecht, Joel 31
Heflin, Van 162, 288
Heller, Frank 328-329

Henderson, Elizabeth 269
Henderson, Florence 4, 258, 268-277, 279-284, 286-287
Henner, Marilu 46
Hepburn, Katherine 176-177
Heston, Charlton 54
Hilton, Bob 420
Hilton, Paris 237
Ho, Don 192
Hoffman, Dustin 44, 75
Holly, Buddy 439
Hoover, J, Edgar 171
Hope, Bob 60, 194, 212, 252, 338, 339
Hopper, Hedda 302
Horowitz, David 9
Houdini, Harry 129
Houseman, John 358
Howard, Ron 334
Howell, Wayne 322
Hunter, Bill 301
Hunter, Jeffrey 278
Hunter, Rielle 294
Hyatt, Wesley 358
Ingels, Marty 136, 260-265, 268, 294
Israel, Lee 307
Jacknis, Anne 324
Jackson, Sherry 67
Jackson, Todd "Action" 390
James, Art 381
James, Brad 182
James, Dennis 37, 182-183, 323, 331-332, 333, 379
James, Tommy 168
Jarvis, Al 147
Jeffries, Rich 420
Jenner, Kendall 237

Jewison, Norman 246
John, Elton 54
Johnson, Jack 421
Johnson, Lyndon 360
Johnson, Russell 366
Johnson, Van 162-163, 288
Johnston, Gaby 391
Jolson, Al 134
Jones, Jenny 24-25
Jones, Shirley 122, 256, 258-261, 265, 268, 271-272, 294
Kalter, Alan 345
Kanter, Hal 49, 174
Kappas, George 269
Karn, Richard 393- Kasem, Casey 195
Katic, Stana 130
Kaye, Danny 239-243
Kean, Betty 8
Kean, Jane 7-8
Keillor, Garrison 75
Keller, Helen 101, 240
Kelly, Gene 320-321
Kelly, Patricia Ward 321
Kelly, R 75
Kennedy, Edward 303
Kennedy, Ethel 303
Kennedy, Jacqueline 249-250
Kennedy, John 56, 165, 191, 249-250, 301-309
Kennedy, Mick 292
Kennedy, Robert 163, 303
Kennedy, Tom 83, 84, 378, 380-381, 430
Kent, Robert 165
Kerkorian, Kirk 372
Khan Genghis 295
Khrushchev, Nikita 59

Kiesewetter, John 441, 450
Kilborn, Craig 78
Kilgallen, Dickie 309
Kilgallen, Dorothy 8, 300-309, 310
Kilgallen, Elinor 302
Kilgallen, James L. 302
Kilgallen, Kerry 306
Kimmel, Jimmy 217, 388, 414, 416-417
King, Alan 198
King, Larry 333
Kinison, Sam 218
Kirchenbauer, Bill 143
Klein, Robert 267, 269
Klugman, Jack 115-118
Knotts, Don 54, 265, 296, 334
Koethe, Jim 301
Kollmar, Richard 309
Koplin, Mert 421
Korman, Christopher 218
Korman, Harvey 108-109, 218, 241
Kovacs, Ernie 340-341, 345, 438
Kragen, Ken 220
Kriegel, Mark 392
Kriski, Mark 418
Kroft, Sid and Marty 298
Kushnick, Helen 183, 219-220
La Rochefoucauld, Francois 295
Lafferty, Perry 240, 242. 391
Lange, Jim 98
Langella, Frank 76
LaRosa, Julius 2
Larson, Mel 112
Larson, Michael 428-429
Lassally, Peter 78, 80, 187, 334, 341
Lasser, Louise 1
Lastfogel, Abe 65

Lauer, Matt 75
Lawford, Peter 294, 303
Lawrence, Richard 122
Lawrence, Vicki 46, 109
Lear, Norman 8, 137-138, 142, 144, 156, 174, 347
Lee, Ruta 412
Leeds, Thelma 135
Leigh, Janet 60
Lennon, John 360
Leno, Jay 183-184, 200, 206, 216-227, 341, 386, 443, 446
Leno, Mavis 222, 227
Leonard, Jackie 178
Leonard, Sheldon 61-62, 65, 74-75, 357, 375-376
Lescoulie, Jack 284
Lessy, Ben 66
Letterman, David 8, 78, 131-133, 217, 220, 268, 269, 338-345, 350-351, 386, 416-417
Levine, Ken 356
Levy, Morris 168
Lewis, Jerry 178, 262-263, 297, 336-338
Lewis, Joe E. 7, 167
Liberace 294
Lieber, Eric 20-24
Lieber, Jerry 409
Linkletter, Art 134-135, 254, 400
Linkletter, Diane 2
Little, Cleavon 138
Little, Malcolm (Malcolm X) 141
Little, Rich 177, 187-188, 411
Livingston, Stanley 161
Lockerman, Gloria 248
Loeb, Phillip 2

Loesch, Margaret 351
Lombard, Carole 117
Lookinland, Mike 275
Lopez, Jennifer 176
Lopez, Mario 126
Lord, Jack 163
Lord, Marjorie 67
Lorre, Chuck 5-6, 352
Lott, Doyle 248
Louise, Tina 362-367
Ludden, Allen 120, 131, 134, 148-151, 269
Luft, Sid 243
Lumet, Sidney 328
Lunden, Joan 26
Lynde, Paul 115
Mackie, Bob 78, 245
MacKrell, Jim 19-20, 137, 196, 378, 380-381
MacLaine, Shirley 54-62, 65, 74
MacLeod, Gavin 110-112
Maddow, Rachael 414
Madonna 320
Maher, Bill 2
Maier, Kurt 306
Majors, Farah Fawcett 265
Malkoff, Mark 343
Mandel, Howie 218
Marceau, Marcel 156
Marcello, Carlos 306-307
March, Fredric 240
Macy, Bill 2
Marie, Rose 107, 287-290
Marshall, Garry 118, 172
Marshall, Laurie Stewart 412
Marshall, Peter 15, 19, 20, 30

Marshall, Peter 2, 112, 137, 167, 323, 324, 348-350, 410-412
Martin, Dean 52, 55, 60, 207-208, 270
Martin, Dean and Jerry Lewis 8, 68
Martin, Dick 349-350
Martin, Steve 202, 219, 242
Martin, Tony 135
Martindale, Wink 46, 65
Martino, Al 167-168
Martino, Allison 167
Marx, Groucho 178, 212
Mason, Jackie 6
Massey, Raymond 50-51
Masterson, Danny 76
Maugham, Somerset 295
Maxwell-Smith, Mark 381
May, Elaine 359
Mays, Deborah 392
McCann, Chuck 110
McCarthy, Melissa 5, 397
McClanahan, Rue 153
McCord, Bill 322
McCormick, Maureen 280
McGowan, Rose 129
McGuire, Phyllis 168
McGurn, Jack 167
McKay, Ed 417-420
McKibben, Chuck 114
McLendon, Gordon 379
McMahon, Ed 20, 185, 310-314, 334
McNulty, Barney 338
Meadows, Jane 115
Melnick, Dan 202
Melton, Sid 66
Mendez, Tony 338-339, 343
Meriwether, Lee 282, 286, 290

Merman, Ethel 116-118, 135
Merrick, David 295
Merson, Mark 370
Messing, Debra 129
Michaels, Lorne 354
Michele, Lea 130
Midler, Bette 75
Milano, Alyssa 129
Miller, Jeffrey 189
Miller, Miss Lillian 80-81
Minelli, Liza 245
Mitchell, Pat 353
Mobley, Mary Ann 48
Molin, Bud 173
Monroe, Marilyn 303, 366
Monroe, Marilyn 60
Moonves, Les 76, 78, 256
Moore, Garry 299, 333, 339, 358, 373
Moore, Mary Tyler 2, 111, 355
Morgan, Henry 333
Morrison, Van 168
Morrow, Don 322
Morton, Howard 290-292
Morton, Robert 343-344
Muggs, J. Fred 285-286
Muir, Roger 91
Mulgrew, Kate 129
Mullally, Megan 129
Murdock, Rupert 203-204
Murphey, Eddie 145, 388
Murray, Ross 109
Murrow, Ed 6, 370, 376
Music, Lorenzo 141
Namath, Joe 392
Narz, Jack 46, 82
Neary, R. Patrick 31

Nedeff, Adam, 382
Nelson, Jimmy 8
Ness, Eliot 160-162, 164, 169-170
Nesterhoff, Kliph 167, 265
Neustein, Joe 31
Newhart, Bob 52, 267
Newton, Todd 126, 437
Newton, Wayne 9
Nichols, Nichelle 248-249
Nicholson, Bobby 91
Nicholson, Jack 333
Nimoy, Leonard 273
Nitti, Frank 164-165
Nixon, Richard 360-361
Noonan, Tommy 349, 411
Noth, Chris 75-76
Novak, Kim 60
O'Brien, Conan 220
O'Connor, Carroll 8, 144
O'Connor, John 345
O'Donnell, Charlie 322, 351
O'Donnell, Rosie 126-127
O'Hurley, John 126, 393. 395
O'Reilly, Bill 75
O'Sullivan, Maureen 282
Obama, Barack 380
Olivier, Laurence 114, 241
Olson, Johnny 43, 44, 77-78, 80, 84-85, 322, 326, 419
Osbourne, Sharon 130
Oswald, Lee Harvey 304, 381
Owens, Gary 322
Paar, Jack 2, 6, 8, 81, 148, 151, 178, 282, 310, 339, 416
Paley, Bill 191, 250, 357, 360
Palmer, Betsy 282

Pardo, Don 43, 322, 344
Parker, Penney 67
Parker, Sachi 60-61
Parks, Bert 323, 348
Parrish, Eniko 390
Parsons, Louella 302
Pastore, John 171
Pataky, Ron 307-308
Pearson, Drew 302
Peaslee, John 122
Peckinpah, Sam 115
Perry, Luke 176
Perry, Tyler 41
Pesci, Joe 168
Peterson, Paul 67, 100
Pflug, Joanne 13
Pharis, Chuck 393
Philbin, Regis 38,333-334, 400
Pick, Saul 298
Pierce, Jack 291
Pillott, Judd 122
Pinsky, Dr. Drew 36
Pitts, Don 65, 418-419
Piven, Jeremy 76
Pollack, Sydney 267, 269
Ponti, Carlo 114
Porter, Darwin 294
Povich, Maury 233-234, 384
Precht, Bob 258
Presley, Elvis 6-7, 145
Price, Dave 126
Prince, Danforth 294
Pritchett, Florence 308-309
Provost, Jon 161
Pryor, Richard 137, 142-143, 217
Puck, Wolfgang 186

Quigley, Bob 323, 349, 430
Quigley, Shirley 349
Quinn, Anthony 114
Quinn, Bobby 43, 188
Rafkin, Alan 143
Raft, George 288
Randolph, Amanda 66
Raphael, Sally Jesse 36
Rayburn, Gene 27-40, 284, 321
Rayburn, Helen 38. 40
Rayburn, Lynne 38, 39-40
Reagan, Nancy 375
Reagan, Ronald 375
Reed, Donna 254-256
Reed, Robert 274-278
Reese, Della 140
Reeves, George 2
Regil, Marco Antonio 126
Reig, Howard 322
Reilly, Charles Nelson 27, 38, 52
Reilly, Mike 435
Reiner, Carl 38, 172. 202, 375
Reiner, Rob 172-173, 242
Reubens, Paul "Pee Wee Herman" 3
Revson, Martin 421
Reynolds, Burt 53-54, 410, 441
Ricca, Paul 169
Rich, John 68-69, 143, 273, 365
Richards, Michael (actor) 2
Richards, Michael (producer) 126
Richardson, Burton 384, 387, 420
Richardson, J.P. 439
Richmond, Bill 262
Rickert, Tex 421
Rickles, Don 115, 252, 299, 329
Ripa, Kelly 333-334

Rivera, Geraldo 75, 303, 354
Rivera, Naya 130
Rivers, Joan 44, 156-157, 178, 197-207, 219, 220, 336-338, 417
Rivers, Melissa 205
Robbins, Tony 43
Roberto, JD 126
Kriski, Mark 126
Roberts, Julia 157
Robertson, Cliff 163
Robinson, Edward G. 60, 114
Robinson, Hubbell 358
Rock, Chris 137, 208, 267, 268, 401
Roddy, Rod 77-78, 84-85, 230, 418, 420
Rodgers, Jimmy 168
Rodriguez, Paul 218
Rogan, Joe 218
Rogers, Ginger 60
Roker, Al 393
Romano, Ray 5
Romero, Caesar 288
Rooney, Andy 3-4,
Rooney, Mickey 247
Roosevelt, Franklin 210
Roosevelt, Teddy 324
Rose, Charlie 75, 345
Rose, Lacey 235
Rose, Reginald 328
Roselli, Johnny 164-165, 170
Rosen, Al 98-99
Rosen, Milt 279
Rosenberg, Edgar 201-205
Rosenthal, Phil 5, 254
Ross, Diana 297
Ross, John and Ethel 103-104
Rossi, Phillip Wayne 418

Rowan, Dan 349-350
Ruben, Aaron 143
Rubino, Vinny 97
Ruby, Jack 301, 304-308, 381
Ruhe, Jeff 303
RuPaul 273
Russell, Nipsey 52
Ryan, Jeri 129
Saget, Bob 218
Sahl, Mort 214
Sajak, Pat 19, 120, 414-416, 430
Saks, Matthew 155
Sales, Soupy 438
Salisbury, Fran 324
Sanders, Helen 186
Sandrich, Jay 154
Sargeant, Dick 329
Sarnoff, David 286
Savage, Fred 76
Schaeffer, Rebecca 237-238
Scheft, Bill 339
Schell, Ronnie 214-216
Schenck, Joseph 165
Schlatter, George 110, 243, 246
Schlessinger, Dr. Laura 423-426
Schlessinger, Yolanda, 424-425
Schmitz, Jonathan 24
Schneider, Charles 444
Schneider, John 359
Schroeder, Barbara 425
Schuck, John 290
Schulman, Nev 75
Schwab, Ron 428
Schwartz, Al 213
Schwartz, David 94
Schwartz, Lloyd 212, 275, 279, 364-365
Schwartz, Sherwood 212-213, 272-277, 279, 280, 363-366, 367
Schwarzenegger, Arnold 222
Scorsese, Martin 168
Scott, George C. 114
Scott, Melody Thomas 48
Scully, Vin 120
Maher, Bill 120
Carroll, Diane 120
Seacrest, Ryan 75. 398, 400, 414, 445
Seagal, Steven 75
Seal 75
Segelstein, Irwin 179
Seinfeld, Jerry 339, 354, 401
Selleck, Tom 89
Serling, Rod 328
Shafer, Ross 29, 223-224
Shatner, William 54, 248-249, 273, 391
Shawn, Adam 137
Shawn, Dick 135-137
Sheen, Charlie 2, 6, 130
Sheindlin, Judy 45
Sheldon, Sidney 103-104
Sheppard, Sam 302
Sherman, Allen 311
Sherman, Bobby 31
Sherman, Richard 59
Shore, Dinah 208, 225-226
Shore, Mitzy 217, 225
Short, Columbus 2
Shostak, Stuart 288, 379
Shovan, Tom 413
Shriner, Herb 323
Shriner, Wil 46
Siegel, Benjamin (Bugsy) 288-289
Silver, Roy 199

Silverman, Fred 191-197, 284-285, 346-352, 353, 415-416
Silverman, Sarah 218
Silvers, Phil 365
Simmons, Russell 75
Simon, Neil 202, 367
Simons, Susan 352
Simpson, O.J. 418
Sinatra, Frank 6, 54, 55, 60, 62, 166, 167, 168, 171, 310
Sinclaire, Marc 306
Sirhan, Sirhan 163-164
Skelton, Lothian 208
Skelton, Red 8, 120, 178, 208-214
Skutch, Ira 28, 36
Smiley, Tavis 75
Smith, Buffalo Bob 34
Smith, Earl 309
Smith, Joe 168
Smith, Will 267-268
Smothers, Dick 209-210, 242, 359, 360, 361
Smothers, Tom 242, 359, 360, 361
Smythe, Kit 362-363
Snyder, Tom 78, 130, 138, 339, 344
Somers, Suzanne 180-181
Spacey, Kevin 76
Spade, David 218
Spelling, Aaron 290
Spelling, Cardinal 171
Spelling, Tori 176
Springer, Jerry 11, 36
Stack, Robert 160-164, 169, 170-171, 174
Stafford, Susan 17, 379-380
Stanley, Don 10
Stanwyck, Barbara 288
Starr, Malcolm Seth 141, 347
Stein, Ben 46, 406-409
Steinberg, David 360
Steines, Mark 126
Stern, Howard 39, 206, 220
Stern, Leonard 263, 356-357
Stevens, Walter 374
Stewart, Bob 30, 131-132, 151, 326, 351, 382, 426
Stewart, Jay 49, 322
Stewart, Jimmy 254
Stewart, John 78
Stewart. Kristin 238
Stoller, Mike 409
Stone, Katherine 306
Stradella, Dante Charles 451
Strahan, Michael 333
Streisand, Barbra 176
Stritch, Elaine 154
Stronberg, Jr., Hunt 364
Struthers, Sally 174
Sullivan, Ed 6, 198, 258, 302, 350
Summers, Marc 48, 122-128
Sunga, George 246, 251
Susann, Jacqueline 117
Susskind, David 368
Taft, William Howard 106
Talman, William 71
Tambor, Jeffrey 76
Tankersley, William 209
Tarloff, Frank 62
Tartikoff, Brandon 201, 352-355, 441
Tartikoff, Lily 355
Tauber, Jake 31
Taylor, Elizabeth 60, 63, 294
Taylor, Renee 63

Taylor, Robert 288
Tebet, Dave 252-253
Tell, Michael 104
Thicke, Alan 194-195, 378
Thomas, Danny 65-69, 114, 135, 363, 375
Thomason, Harry 8
Thompson, Alana "Honey Boo Boo" 1
Thompson, Lea 158
Three Stooges 298
Tinker, Grant 352, 354
Tobolowsky, Stephen 394
Todman, Bill 27, 327
Tom, David 11
Tomarken, Peter 426-439
Torme, Mel 245, 252
Tortorici, Anthony 73
Toscanini, Arturo 32
Townsend Jim 399
Travolta, John 54
Trebek, Alex 17, 46, 281, 286, 351, 378, 414, 433
Tritt, Travis 220
Truman, Harry 165
Tufeld, Dick 297, 314-316
Turner, Lana 228, 288
Tuttle, Lurene 211
Un, Kim Jong 122
Blair, Frank 284
Underwood, Sheryl 130
Upperco, Jackson 366
Vale, Jerry 273
Valens, Richie 439
Valentine, Karen 412
Vallee, Rudy 211
Van Dyke, Dick 37-38, 109, 355, 375

Van Patten, Joyce 241
Van Sant, Gus 290
Vance, Vivian 2, 129, 161
Vanoff, Nick 35, 296-298
Vidal, Gore 295, 328
Vierra, Meredith 152
Vinnedge, Sid 126, 430
Vosburgh, Bill "Bones" 387
Walberg, Mark L. 126
Walker, Jay 218
Walker, Jimmy 218
Wallace, Mike 184
Walliser, Blair 49-51
Walters, Barbara 4, 138, 151, 282, 283-284, 303
Walters, Lou 151
Warner, Jack 5
Warren, Earl 305
Washington, Dinah 142
Wayne, Carol 2
Wayne, Frank 27, 86
Wayne, John 54, 100
Weaver, Pat 35, 283
Webb, Jack 165
Weiner, Matthew 76
Weinstein, Harvey 76
Welch, Denny 12
Welles, Orson 198, 265, 408
Wellman, Barrie 155
Wells, Dawn 237, 366-368
Weltman, Wally 431
Wendell, Bill 322, 339-345
Wendell, Francette 340
Werner, Tom 346
Westin, Av 303
Westwick, Ed 76

White, Betty 39, 41, 147-157, 281, 319-320
White, Jesse 66
White, Vanna 19, 87
Wickes. Mary 66
Wilcox, Larry 63-65
Wilkerson, Billy 164
Williams, Andy 208, 296
Williams, Barry 280
Williams, Esther 211-212
Williams, Kenneth 324
Williams, Kenny 322
Williams, Mason 242
Williams, Robin 217
Williams, Tony 268
Willis, Bruce 2, 54
Wilson, Carnie 96
Wilson, Desmond 142-144
Wilson, Drue-Ann 73
Wilson, Earl 7, 302, 350
Wilson, Flip 143
Wilson, Hugh 413
Winchell, Paul 8
Winchell, Walter 6.160, 302
Winfrey, Oprah 8, 234-235, 400
Winkler, Henry 62
Winters, Jonathan 13, 5
Winters, Shelley 60
Wolpert, Jay 418, 426-427
Wood, C.V. 112
Wood, Gene 22, 80-84, 326, 420, 442, 445, 451-452
Woolery, Chuck 13-25, 46, 415
Wostbrock, Fred 29-30, 418-419, 436
Wynn, Ed 135
Yearwood, Tricia 220
Yorkin, Bud 137-138, 144, 347
Young, Loretta 117-118
Youngman, Henny 385
Zanders, Roosevelt 308
Zany, Bob 450
Zigler, Zig 43
Ziskin, Ron 42, 44
Zorina, Vera 58
Zworkin, Vladimir 6

Printed by BoD™in Norderstedt, Germany

9 781629 339313